LABOUR MARKET AND SOCIAL PROTECTION REFORMS IN INTERNATIO

Noel

The International Social Security Association (ISSA) was founded in 1927. It is a non-profit international organization bringing together institutions and administrative bodies from countries all over the world dealing with all forms of compulsory social protection. The objective of the ISSA is to cooperate at the international level, in the promotion and development of social security throughout the world, primarily by improving techniques and administration in order to advance people's social and economic conditions on the basis of social justice.

Labour Market and Social Protection Reforms in International Perspective

Parallel or converging tracks?

Edited by
HEDVA SARFATI and GIULIANO BONOLI
International Social Security Association

Ashgate

Published by
Ashgate Publishing Limited
Gower House
Croft Road
Aldershot
Hampshire GU11 3HR
England

Ashgate Publishing Company
131 Main Street
Burlington, VT 05401–5600 USA

Ashgate website: htttp://www.ashgate.com

British Library Cataloguing in Publication Data
Labour market and social protection reforms in
international perspective : parallel or converging tracks?
1.Manpower policy – Cross-cultural studies 2.Social
security – Cross-cultural studies 3.Social policy –
Cross-cultural studies
I.Sarfati, Hedva, 1937– II.Bonoli, Giuliano
III.International Social Security Association
331.1'2'042

Library of Congress Control Number: 2001097266

ISBN 0 7546 1926 5 (Hbk)
0 7546 1927 3 (Pbk)

Printed and bound in Great Britain by MPG Books, Ltd. Bodmin, Cornwall.

Contents

List of Figures

List of Tables

List of Contributors

Jørgen Goul Andersen
Political scientist, Professor of Political Sociology, Director of Centre for Comparative Welfare State Studies (CCWS), Aalborg University, Denmark. Working Group Coordinator and Management Committee member of COST A13 'Changing Labour Markets, Welfare Policies and Citizenship'. Member of the Board of the Danish Democracy and Power Study, and director of the Danish Election Programme.

Peter Auer
Economist and political scientist, former director of the European Employment Observatory, presently Head of the Labour Market Policy Team, Employment Strategy Department, International Labour Office (ILO), Geneva, Switzerland. Current research area (together with Sandrine Cazes): the transformations in the labour market and the role of labour market policies; transitional labour markets; employment strategies.

Lucio Baccaro
Political scientist, currently Senior Research Officer at the International Institute for Labour Studies, Geneva, Switzerland, Assistant Professor (on leave) of Labor and Human Resource Policy at Case Western Reserve University, Cleveland, USA.

Prue Bagley
Researcher, Graduate School of Management, La Trobe University, Melbourne, Australia.

Jean-Michel Belorgey
Member of the Council of State (Conseil d'Etat), France – the French Supreme Administrative Court and the top consultative body to the government on the formulation of laws. Chairman of the expert consultative group on 'social minimum income, income from activity and precarity' of the French General Planning Commission.

Giuliano Bonoli
Lecturer (Maître Assistant), Department of Social Work and Social Policy, University of Fribourg, Switzerland. Has undertaken comparative research on welfare reforms in several European countries, with a special focus on pensions and on the politics of change.

Anne de Bruin
Associate Professor of Economics, Department of Commerce, Massey University at Auckland, New Zealand.

Sandrine Cazes
Labour Economist, Labour Market Policy Team, ILO, Geneva, Switzerland.

Peter Cressey
Senior Lecturer in Sociology, Department of Social and Policy Sciences University of Bath, UK.

Gerry J.B. Dietvorst
Professor, fiscal aspects of pensions, Faculty of Law, Tilburg University, and advisor at Interpolis insurance company, The Netherlands.

Peter B. Doeringer
Professor of Economics, specializing in issues of labour and industry, Department of Economics, Boston University, US and Research Director of the Commonwealth of Massachusetts Blue Ribbon Commission on Older Workers (1998–2000).

Jacques Freyssinet
Director of the Social and Economic Research Institute (IRES) and Professor of Economics, University Paris – I, France.

Jay Ginn
Co-director of the Centre for Research on Ageing and Gender and researcher on gender and pensions in the Sociology Department, University of Surrey, England.

Raymond Harbridge
Professor of Management and Head of School at the Graduate School of Management, La Trobe University, Melbourne, Australia.

Jan Bendix Jensen
Research Fellow, Centre for Comparative Welfare State Studies (CCWS), Aalborg University, Denmark.

Maria Jepsen
Economist, senior researcher at the European Trade Union Institute (ETUI), Brussels; member and occasional lecturer at the Department of Applied Economics (DULBEA), Brussels Free University, Belgium. Research areas: social security and gender issues.

Hugues de Jouvenel
Director General of the International Futuribles Group, Paris, France; Director and Editor-in-Chief of the review *Futuribles*. His most recent co-authored publication is an essay on the future of the retirement systems in France by 2040 (*Un essai de prospective sur les retraites en France à l'horizon 2040*, October 2001, distributed by Futuribles).

Henri Lourdelle
Social Protection Expert, Advisor to the European Trade Union Confederation, Brussels, Belgium.

Per Kongshøj Madsen
Associate Professor in Economic Policy, Institute of Political Science, University of Copenhagen, Denmark. His main research interests are comparative labour market policy and European employment policy. Since 1997 he has been Danish correspondent to EU's Employment Observatory.

Danièle Meulders
Economics Professor, Head of the Labour Economics Research Team, Department of Applied Economics (DULBEA), Brussels Free University, Belgium.

Jane Millar
Professor of Social Policy, Director of the Centre for the Analysis of Social Policy, University of Bath, UK.

Alain Parant
Demographer, National Institute of Demographic Studies (INED), Paris, France; Scientific Adviser to International Futuribles Group. His most recent co-authored publication is an essay on the future of the retirement systems in France by 2040 (*Un essai de prospective sur les retraites en France à l'horizon 2040*, October 2001, distributed by Futuribles).

Frans Pennings
Associate Professor in labour law and social security law at Tilburg University, The Netherlands. He wrote a number of publications in these two areas, particularly on unemployment law, disability law and European social security law. He wrote his PhD on a comparative study of employment and unemployment schemes, *Benefits of Doubt* (1990). He is one of the editors of the *European Journal of Social Security.*

Robert Salais
Director of the research laboratory 'Institutions and Historical Dynamics of the Economy' (IDHE), National Council for Scientific Research (CNRS – Ecole Normale Supérieure de Cachan), France.

Hedva Sarfati
ISSA consultant and director of ISSA project on the interactions between labour market and social protection reforms; political scientist; Analyst of comparative employment, social protection and labour relations policies; former Director of the Industrial Relations and Labour Administration Department, ILO, Geneva, Switzerland.

Roland Sigg
Head of Research, International Social Security Association (ISSA), Geneva, Switzerland; Lecturer in Comparative Social Policy, University of Geneva.

Adrian Sinfield
Professor Emeritus of Social Policy, University of Edinburgh, Scotland, where he has taught since 1979. Co-founder of the Unemployment Unit in 1981 and Chair for its first 10 years. Publications include: *The Long-term Unemployed* (1968), *What Unemployment Means* (1981), *The Workless State* (co-edited 1981) and many articles on unemployment and social security.

Andrew Sum
Professor of Economics and Director, Center for Labour Market Studies, Northeastern University US.

David G. Terkla
Professor, Department of Economics University of Massachusetts, Boston, US.

Pascal Ughetto
Researcher, Economic and Social Research Institute (IRES), France.

Pat Walsh
Professor of Industrial Relations and Human Resource Management and Head of School of Business and Public Management at Victoria University of Wellington, New Zealand.

Foreword
Both Welfare and Work

A few years ago the phrase 'from welfare to work' first began to be heard in the political debate, signalling a fundamental shift in priorities in our welfare societies. When we looked, however, beyond the political slogans, we found that the reform process was indeed more sophisticated. It was not an either/or strategy, but a reform process aimed at both work and welfare. A good social protection system is as important as ever, and I think that it is time for politicians to use the phrase 'both welfare and work' to send the right message bout the intentions behind the reform process.

There are two basic questions running through this debate: How to make social protection systems more employment friendly? And how to increase employment to strengthen the financial basis for social protection, not least of all the pension systems? Changes in both the economy and in demography have lent urgency to the debate and the reform process. Labour markets have already changed beyond recognition since the golden age of the industrial economies. As regards demographic trends, we are still at the beginning of a period of rapid ageing of the workforce and of the population as a whole. Making employment systems and social protection systems mutually supportive is, thus, one of the greatest challenges for the policy-makers and politicians of our time.

I myself have been involved in employment and social protection reform in my home country, Sweden, as well as in the European Union. I have now had the privilege of following the final stages of the preparation of this book and to have a foretaste of the rich material presented in its 17 chapters. My view is that the book will be a great aid to myself and all my colleagues involved in employment and social policy, helping us to catch up with a debate and a reform process that has now begun to gain significant momentum. It is without question a reform process that requires fare more knowledge and reflection to get things right. A wealth of highly pertinent information, ideas and experience are gathered in this book.

The International Social Security Association has every reason to be proud of this initiative and of having found the right people to contribute to the success of the project.

Professor Allan Larsson
Former Director General
European Commission – Directorate General
Employment and Social Affairs
Former Finance Minister, Sweden

Preface

The present volume had its inception some time ago when it became apparent to close observers of national social security programmes that there was a growing intellectual gulf between social security experts, on the one hand, and their colleagues involved in formulating and implementing labour protection policies on the other. This divide subsequently became even more marked as social security programmes undertook increasingly significant reforms while many of the OECD countries struggled to reduce unemployment and encourage their labour forces to become more flexible. Questions were raised on both sides about the ways the different sets of public policy interacted and influenced outcomes, either negatively or positively.

As a long-standing international organization with nearly 75 years' experience working with social security bodies around the world, the International Social Security Association (ISSA) is well placed to encourage a more active dialogue between social security experts and their counterparts dealing with labour market issues. This objective would not seem at first glance to present any particular problem, but experience demonstrates that the execution of such a plan is indeed quite daunting. Experts tend to be very busy serving their own professional interests. Moreover, finding competent and interested specialists who are ready to interact with unfamiliar adepts of other disciplines is in fact more difficult in reality than in theory. And, at the end of the day, a project of this nature requires above all the commitment of one or two individuals who are willing to overcome these constraints, to conceptualize and to convince others to collaborate, and finally to see the process of consultation through to an end by drawing out the most important lessons and conclusions formulated by the various national experts.

The ISSA was very fortunate to be able to count on Hedva Sarfati to spearhead this project from its inception to completion. Ms Sarfati was formerly Director of the Industrial Relations and Labour Administration Department, at the International Labour Office and thus eminently qualified to bridge the gap between the worlds of labour market policy and social security policy. She has been ably assisted by Giuliano Bonoli, Lecturer (Maître Assistant), Department of Social Work and Social

Policy at the University of Fribourg (Switzerland), who served as her co-editor. In spite of many obstacles, Ms. Sarfati's enthusiasm for this undertaking never failed, with the result that we are proud to assert that this volume constitutes a truly ground-breaking work, of use to anyone interested in the complex interplay between social protection policies and labour market policies. The recent wave of concern expressed in most OECD countries about the allegedly devastating effects of globalization on the welfare of workers clearly demonstrates that we need to know far more about what is, in fact, the reality as opposed to unsubstantiated polemics.

I prefer to leave it to the editors to acknowledge the many persons who have made a significant contribution to the success of this project, but I do wish to thank in particular Reiner Hoffmann, Director of the European Trade Union Institute (ETUI), for sponsoring an expert meeting at its Brussels headquarters which permitted authors and other experts to meet and to agree upon their respective roles in producing this publication.

The primary mission of the ISSA is of course to serve its nearly 400 member organizations around the world through its programme of technical activities (research, training, technical exchanges, data collection and analysis, etc.). However, it is increasingly recognized that the ISSA mission must also include outreach efforts to encourage more balanced, objective and interdisciplinary exchanges among specialists whose work and interests intersect with social security. This project on the interaction of social security and labour market policies is a leading example of such outreach efforts. With the same purpose in mind, the Association has also launched a worldwide consultation, known as the *ISSA Initiative,* which will span a period of three to four years and in similar fashion bring together a broad spectrum of experts from different disciplines to focus on the social mission and goals of social security policies. It is anticipated that the *Initiative* will build upon the solid work which has been assembled by the editors, Hedva Sarfati and Giuliano Bonoli, to further the worldwide debate on what form and level of social security protection societies will aspire to and be able to provide to their citizens in the twenty-first century.

Dalmer Hoskins
ISSA Secretary General
Geneva
July 2001

Acknowledgements

Like many collaborative efforts, the ISSA-LMSP project benefited from the advice, help and assistance of several colleagues. First, we would like to thank Lucy apRoberts (ISSA), Jay Ginn (University of Surrey), England, Einar Overbye (Norwegian Social Research (NOVA), Oslo), Werner Segenberger (ILO), and Adrian Sinfield (University of Edinburgh, Scotland), who read parts of the manuscript and provided thoughtful comments. We wish to reiterate our thanks to Reiner Hoffmann, Director of the European Trade Union Institute (ETUI) for hosting and generously sponsoring the project's round table of authors in Brussels in November 2001. We should also thank Martin Hutsebaut (ETUI) for chairing part of the project's round table. Roland Sigg (ISSA) deserves a special mention for providing helpful comments on selected chapters as well as actively participating in the organization of the Brussels round table. Our thanks go also to Anna Christensen (University of Lund, Sweden) for commenting on the project framework and taking an active part in the project's steering committee. She was part of the original group of authors but fell ill and regretfully passed away in March 2001. And last, but not least, we are grateful to Jessica Owens (Economics graduate, Boston University, Mass., US) for helping to collect some of the project's statistical data, and for providing administrative support for the Brussels round table.

Hedva Sarfati
Giuliano Bonoli
Geneva and Fribourg
July 2001

Introduction
Tight Constraints, New Demands and Enduring Needs: Addressing the Labour Market versus Social Protection Challenge

Hedva Sarfati and Giuliano Bonoli

The last two decades have witnessed the unfolding of major changes and developments in labour markets and social protection systems. The highly structured labour markets that were predominant during the first three postwar decades, which were characterized by full-time, stable and full (male) employment, now seem a thing of the past. Today's labour markets continue to produce predominantly full-time stable jobs and welfare for a majority of citizens, but they also generate substantial long-term unemployment, job insecurity, low pay, poverty and social exclusion. At the same time, economic and social trends, such as economic globalization, the ageing of the population and changes in family structures, are making it difficult for governments to deal with these problems in the traditional way. The social protection institutions that we have inherited were effective in the postwar socioeconomic context, but seem less adequate to address today's problems and challenges. They tend to be costly and focus their efforts on core (male) workers, while often overlooking emerging needs and aspirations. The combination of these diverse factors has called into question the sustainability and adequacy of postwar social protection systems and explains why they have been the subject of unprecedented debate and reform initiatives over the past two decades.

The ISSA study on which this volume is based grew out of concern regarding these problems, and particularly the capacity of modern social protection systems and labour markets to adapt to new social and economic conditions. The project was articulated around a number of questions, of which the most important are:

1 What is the impact of current labour market changes on the effectiveness of social protection systems, that is on their capacity to provide security and help to those who need it?
2 What is the impact of current social protection reform on labour markets, that is on work incentives, employment rates and the living conditions of the various social groups?
3 What are the conditions for successful social protection and labour market policy reforms?

In general terms, these questions address the issue of institutional adaptation to changing socioeconomic circumstances. The context in which labour markets and social protection systems operate has, in practice, changed dramatically since the postwar years.

First, the development towards a post-industrial economy, characterized by the employment of the vast majority of the population in the services sector, has important implications for the functioning of labour markets and social protection systems (see Sarfati, Chapter 1, and Ughetto, Feature No. 3). Employment in services is very different from the type of industrial employment that was dominant during the postwar period. It is, for example, difficult to achieve productivity increases in many services, in view of the importance of human contact and service quality. In such areas as education, child care, health care and personal services, work cannot easily be performed more rapidly or more efficiently without a substantial loss of quality, and hence of value.[1] This is, of course, less true in industrial occupations. Productivity increases achieved through the mechanization, standardization and streamlining of production result in rising real wages for all workers.

These developments affect the relationship between the labour market and social protection in two ways. In the first place, the reduced scope for productivity increases means that the extent of the growth-financed expansion of welfare states seen during the first three postwar decades is unlikely to reoccur in the near future. In the postwar period, it was possible for welfare states to expand painlessly: productivity-led economic growth generated rising tax revenues, which could be used by governments to build new social programmes. In contrast, current social protection reforms are being adopted in a less favourable context, in which part of welfare expansion needs to be financed by increases in taxation, or by reductions in other areas of government spending (Pierson, 1998).[2] Second, employment in services tends to be associated with broad wage inequality. Productivity increases are particularly difficult to achieve at the bottom end of the earnings scale, in such areas as personal services, catering and cleaning. Wages in such occupations increasingly lag behind those in occupations where productivity gains are possible, generating the social problem of the *working poor*, a phenomenon that has come to the fore over the past decade and requires social intervention (see Sarfati, Chapter 1).

The *second* important trend is the acceleration of economic internationalization, or globalization, which is resulting in the ever closer integration of financial and product markets worldwide. The process is a consequence of several events and developments. These include the various multilateral trade liberalization agreements concluded by the General Agreement on Tariffs and Trade (GATT) and the World Trade Organization (WTO); the emergence of new zones of low cost industrial production, especially in East Asia and Eastern Europe (see Lourdelle, Chapter 8); and the gradual removal of national barriers to capital movements (see, for example, Ohmae, 1991; Cerny, 1995; Strange, 1996; Scharpf, 2000; for a literature review, see Rhodes, 1996).

In the early 2000s, governments need to take into account this higher degree of economic integration and the associated higher mobility of capital and production. The increased credibility of threats by employers and investors to transfer capital or production abroad may limit the room for manoeuvre available to governments in designing their social protection systems and labour markets. Since the late 1970s, European governments have learned to their cost that policies which reduce the capacity of private companies to generate high levels of post-tax profits are likely to result in unaffordable losses of investment (Scharpf and Schmidt, 2000). This development affects various aspects of the labour market/social protection nexus, including the capacity to regulate employment and to raise the tax revenues that are needed to finance welfare states.

The *third* important trend, which is irreversible in the medium term at least, is the ageing of the population. In OECD countries, the proportion of the population aged 65 and over is expected to increase throughout the next three decades, from the current 15 to 17 per cent to around 25 per cent in most countries. Migration may moderate the demographic ageing process (see Jouvenel and Parant, Chapter 5), but a recent study by the United Nations Population Division shows that the scale of migration required to maintain current intergenerational balances is enormous (United Nations, 2000). The ageing of the population will have a substantial impact on pension expenditure, although it should be noted that the sustainability of pensions also depends on employment rates, which may increase over the next few decades (see Sigg, Feature No. 7). The impact of the ageing of the population will also be felt in terms of higher expenditure on health care, and particularly long-term care.

These three trends will most probably continue to affect the relationship between the labour market and social protection for the foreseeable future, contributing to a socioeconomic and political context aptly characterized as an era of *permanent austerity* (Pierson, 1998). This situation limits the room for manoeuvre of governments which are aiming to modernize and adapt their social protection systems and labour markets. The constraints placed on the capacity to raise taxes due to globalization, a projected lower rate of productivity increase than in the past and envisaged rises in expenditure on age-related social programmes mean that the growth-financed expansion of social protection systems that took place between 1945 and 1970 is unlikely to reoccur in the medium term.

These trends impose a number of serious constraints on policy-makers in the twin areas of labour market and social protection policy. Moreover, they are contributing to the emergence of new needs and aspirations among citizens in Western democracies. In addition to their traditional functions, social protection systems are now also expected to facilitate and encourage access to the labour market, inter alia, by: providing incentive structures that are favourable to employment; offering lifelong education and training opportunities, particularly to unemployed or disadvantaged workers, women returning to the labour market and older workers; making it easier for parents to reconcile employment and family life; and developing social protection schemes that take into account non-linear employment tracks. Some of these new demands are being taken up by current social protection reforms, which increasingly tend to emphasize the activation and employment promotion dimensions of social policy. The key image associated with social protection is its conversion from a 'safety net into a springboard' (World Bank, 2001).

This shift in the objectives of social protection is generally regarded as a positive development, since it demonstrates institutional adaptation to changing economic and social circumstances. However, it should not be forgotten that the needs and aspirations underlying the construction of postwar welfare states have not disappeared. Facilitating access to employment may be an appropriate strategy to improve the opportunities of many disadvantaged people, but not all of them. Due to their circumstances, it may be difficult, or even impossible, for some disadvantaged persons, such as younger and older workers, workers with family responsibilities and, in particular, the disabled, to gain entry to the labour market. For them, springboards may be of little use, and may even be dangerous if there is no adequate safety net below.

Tight economic constraints, new demands and enduring needs are the factors that are framing the current process of the restructuring of labour markets and social protection systems. The challenge for policy-makers is to respond to the new demands within the constraints imposed by exogenous factors, and without overlooking traditional, but nonetheless valid and enduring needs. The fundamental questions that have to be asked in this respect are *if this is possible* and, if so, *how*?

This volume mainly addresses the second question, namely the issue of *how?* In the past, studies on the labour market and social protection have tended to focus on the *if* question, often on the basis of ideologically charged interpretations. In this respect, two opposing theses are often defended: that postwar levels of economic security are not compatible with the current international economic context, or with social and demographic structures, and that welfare states therefore need to be dismantled; or that decisions concerning social protection are essentially political acts, and that the preservation of postwar welfare states is essentially a matter of political will.

An attempt is made in this volume to go beyond this sometimes sterile debate by focusing on actual cases of the restructuring of labour markets and social protection systems, and by assessing their outcomes. The general conclusion is that there is no necessary incompatibility between high levels of social protection and economic performance. Economic constraints clearly have to be taken into account in the reform of labour markets and social protection systems. Nevertheless, there remains a very broad range of political options relating to the kind of society in which people wish to work and live, which will be reflected in the social welfare reform model that is chosen.

Together, the studies in this volume tend to show that the best results in terms of reconciling new aspirations, enduring needs and economic constraints are generally achieved through complex, carefully balanced policy mixes, which are often the result of consultation and negotiation with the social partners. Successful adaptation, perhaps more than in the past, requires the coordination of several areas of government policy and labour market mechanisms. The objectives of social protection must be supported by appropriate mixes of macroeconomic, fiscal and labour market policies. Effective institutions of social partnership are evidently essential for the successful coordination of these different realms of the political economy.

If this volume succeeds in making even a modest contribution to raising awareness among policy-makers, opinion formers and practitioners of the need and benefits of a more coordinated approach to labour market and social protection reform, it will already have achieved its main purpose. If, in addition, it suggests areas and ways in which synergies can be developed between the two areas, it will have amply fulfilled the aspirations of its authors.

* * *

The volume's structure follows a causal chain. It starts in Part I by reviewing the main trends relating to labour markets and endeavours to identify the impact of these trends on the relationship between labour markets and social protection. In Part II, a number of national responses to these trends are described and evaluated. Finally, Part III outlines some possible scenarios for the adaptation of labour markets and social protection, and hints at what labour market-social protection arrangements will look like over the next decade. The concluding chapter attempts to pull together all these strands by identifying instances of successful adaptation, as well as the new problems to which they may be giving rise. Throughout the volume, a series of feature articles provide information on specific points which could not have been treated in sufficient depth in the individual chapters, but which contribute to developing a more comprehensive picture of the contextual issues involved in the debate and their broader policy ramifications.

The geographic scope of the volume consists of selected high-income OECD countries. This choice was made for a number of reasons. These countries have similar levels of economic development. They have been facing similar problems and challenges over the past three decades, which they have addressed with differing policy options and outcomes. Moreover, the data required to answer the questions raised above are easily available in these countries. An additional criterion in country selection was the extent of policy innovation seen over the past few years. For this reason, Central and Eastern European countries have also been included, in view of their status as veritable social protection laboratories in the 1990s.

Notes

1 It has been argued that substantial productivity gains will be possible in the services sector as a result of the new technologies that emerged in the late 1990s (Internet). However, such developments are likely to apply to only some sub-sectors of the service economy, such as the retail trade, banking and some business services. This could exacerbate the broad inequalities that already characterize employment in services.

2 For details of the bibliographical references cited in this Introduction, see the bibliography to Chapter 17, 'Conclusions: the Policy Implications of a Changing Labour Market – Social Protection Relationship'.

PART I

THE INTERACTION BETWEEN SOCIAL PROTECTION REFORM AND LABOUR MARKET SHIFTS: KEY ISSUES

Chapter One

Labour Market and Social Protection Policies: Linkages and Interactions

Hedva Sarfati

Introduction

The linkages and interactions between labour markets and social protection systems are extremely important factors in the successful functioning and overall well-being of modern societies. Together, labour markets and social protection systems determine the distribution of resources within a society and the types of incentives available to individuals in their economic choices, as well as affecting social developments, such as the economic emancipation of women, the increase in life expectancy and fluctuations in the birth rate. The proper management of the relationship between the labour market and social protection is an extremely important challenge. The price of failure can be very high in terms of unemployment, poverty and social exclusion.

Both the labour market and social protection systems have changed dramatically over the past three decades, and their coordination and interaction has not always been optimal. In some cases, social protection systems have been accused of being the cause of labour market problems, such as unemployment and outsider-insider divisions. Moreover, they sometimes seem to lose sight of their original purpose through focusing on individuals who are not the most disadvantaged. Conversely, labour market changes have created problems for the viability of social protection systems: in many countries, low employment rates have reduced the capacity of society to finance generous social protection schemes, while unemployment and precarious low-paid jobs have placed financial pressure on social programmes, thereby aggravating the financial difficulties of welfare states.

What is more, the environment in which the labour market and social protection systems interact has also undergone substantial change over the past few decades. The most important of these contextual changes include:

- the globalization of the world economy, with social contributions increasingly being seen as a threat to competitiveness;
- the prevalence since the mid-1980s of neo-liberal approaches among national and international policy-makers, which call for a reduction in the role of the state in such areas as social protection;
- the advent of European Economic and Monetary Union, with its drastic demands to cut public deficits and debts, of which social expenditure is an important component, representing between one quarter and one-third of GDP in most countries.

These trends have placed additional pressure on labour markets and social protection systems, and need to be taken into account in any analysis of the manner in which they have developed. This chapter focuses on developments that are key to the relationship between the labour market and social protection systems. It describes and discusses eight principal labour market and social trends that have an impact on the functioning of social protection systems in terms of their financial viability, effectiveness or the continued relevance of their objectives.

1 High and Persistent Unemployment Levels, with Regional Variations

Unemployment in the European Union has almost trebled over the past three decades, rising from 4 per cent in the early 1970s to 11 per cent in 1994, and remaining at 8.1 per cent of the labour force in November 2000, despite the recent economic recovery. However, some countries have fared better then others in attaining almost full employment (Denmark, Ireland, Luxembourg, Netherlands, Portugal, Sweden and the United Kingdom), while others have registered major improvements (France and Spain) (Eurostat, 2001).

A similar pattern has been observed in Australia, New Zealand and Canada, where unemployment peaked at over 10 per cent in the early 1990s and declined to around 7 per cent by 1999. However, during the same period, Japan has seen only a slight increase in its unemployment rate from 2 to 3 per cent, but rising to 4.8 per cent by the end of 2000, just below its post-war record of 4.9 per cent. In contrast to this trend, the United States experienced a decline in unemployment from a peak of 9.5 per cent in 1983 to 4.0 per cent by November 2000. This outstanding performance may be on the wane, depending on the depth and duration of the economic slowdown which started at the end of 2000. While some massive lay-offs have been announced in various sectors, the United States labour market was still tight in Spring 2001.

In this context, it is also interesting to examine how unemployment rates have varied within countries. These regional variations have been assessed recently by both the European Commission and the OECD (European Commission, 2000, pp. 61–76; OECD, 2000, pp. 31–79). Regional disparities in unemployment rates are associated with inequalities in earnings and activity rates and are persistent over time, particularly over the past two decades. They are therefore of particular concern in terms of macroeconomic policy and labour market and welfare policies.

Regional disparities in unemployment have changed during the various phases of the business cycle, widening slightly in the European Union in the late 1980s, narrowing in the early 1990s during the recession, and widening again during the post-1994 recovery. However, the narrowing of regional disparities during the early 1990s, where it occurred, was mainly due to large-scale job losses in regions with relatively high employment rates (Germany, France, Sweden and United Kingdom, which were all relatively hard hit by the recession), rather than improvements in unemployment in the less well-performing regions. The narrowing of cross-regional disparities due to a fall in unemployment was observed only in the Netherlands. Moreover, although all the regions of Spain have gained jobs since the 1994 recovery, unemployment disparities have widened.

Regional differences in unemployment are particularly wide in Belgium, Germany, Italy and Spain, as well as in Australia, United Kingdom and United States, while they are relatively narrow in Austria, Finland and Sweden. At the regional level, especially in Greece, Italy and Spain, low employment rates often coincide with high unemployment and inactivity rates. The converse applies in the better performing regions in the same countries, such as in parts of Northern Italy, which boast almost full employment.

The persistence of regional disparities over time implies structural problems that are relatively resistant to political intervention. For example, between 1980 and 1998, there was little change in the ranking of regions by employment performance. The better performing regions were predominantly located in the United Kingdom, followed by Sweden, Denmark, Finland and central Portugal. The regions with the lowest employment rates were mainly located in Southern Italy, Eastern Germany and South and East Spain. However, the regional divide was also persistent in Belgium, France (North and South) and Portugal (North and South), although Portugal has a low unemployment rate (4.1 per cent in 2000) and a very high activity rate in the centre.

While variations in employment growth between countries reflect variations in the growth of output, this correlation does not apply systematically across countries. Indeed, in 1998, the best performers in terms of employment also had the highest increase in GDP per capita, while in some countries GDP growth has not been matched by an increase in employment. This becomes even clearer when looking at regional disparities within countries. It is interesting to note in this respect that in most countries there is little correlation between levels of GDP per capita and employment levels. This should serve as a warning to policy-makers, since it shows that while regions which have benefited from European Union structural funds (which aim to reduce regional disparities in economic performance in the poorest regions) have indeed narrowed disparities in GDP per capita, they have not managed to reduce employment imbalances.

Labour mobility (internal migration) is one of the means of overcoming regional imbalances in unemployment, and seems to have been effective in equalizing regional employment rates in Australia, Canada, Japan, New Zealand, United Kingdom and United States, and to a lesser extent in Germany and Italy and in the rest of the European Union. The same outcome can also be produced by commuting, which is limited to some dynamic transfrontier zones (for example, between France, Germany and Switzerland, or Luxembourg), and which increased between 1992 and 1998. On the whole, however, migration within and between countries across the OECD region has declined significantly over the past three decades. The European Commission estimates that less than 0.4 per cent of the workforce in the European Union moves to another country to work each year, compared with 2.4 per cent in the case of the United States. This probably reflects a variety of factors, including an improved standard of living and higher incomes in poorer regions (as a result, among other factors, of European Union regional policy), the increase in dual wage families and ... the rise in unemployment.

Labour mobility also depends on educational level, the cost of changing housing when moving from a poor to a wealthier area, the availability of social services and community networks and the portability of social protection rights (unemployment benefit and pensions in particular).

Teleworking could provide an alternative to such mobility through the development and extended use of information technologies and telecommunications infrastructure. But, despite the broad speculation about its potential for rapid job growth in both Europe and the United States, it has so far fallen short of expectations.

The combination of regional disadvantages in terms of high unemployment, low activity rates and low labour mobility means that a significant proportion of the population has to depend on social transfers for income support. Moreover, the categories concerned are unable to contribute to the funding of social safety nets and, in particular, to old-age pensions.

As the duration of unemployment has risen over the past decade, unemployment compensation systems, which were designed for temporary periods of joblessness, have come under increasing strain. Long-term unemployment (12 months or more) in the European Union, as in most OECD countries, constitutes a high proportion of total unemployment, reaching 43.5 per cent in 1994, or nearly twice its share in 1980. The proportion of long-term unemployment trebled between 1980 and 1994 in the United States (from 4 per cent to 12 per cent) and in Canada (4 per cent to 15 per cent), but grew at slower pace in Australia (from 19 per cent to 36 per cent). These trends are illustrated below in Tables 1.1 and 1.2. It should be recalled, however, that the duration of periods of unemployment in the United States is fairly short in comparison to Europe. Moreover, although there is a noticeable shift towards longer periods of unemployment, the incidence of periods of unemployment of over 26 weeks has been halved since the early 1990s (Katz and Krueger, 1999).

The recent economic upturn in the European Union resulted in a significant improvement in employment in 1999, particularly for young people aged between 15 and 24, even though their unemployment rate

Table 1.1 Standardized unemployment rates as percentage of total labour force

	1975	1980	1985	1990	1994	1999
EU[1]	4.1	5.9	10.5	8.1	11.1	9.2
Australia	4.5	6.1	8.3	7.0	9.7	7.2
Canada	6.9	7.5	10.6	8.1	10.4	7.6
Japan	1.9	2.0	2.6	2.1	2.9	4.7
New Zealand	0.3	2.2	4.2	7.8	8.2	6.8
Norway	2.3	1.7	2.7	5.3	5.5	3.3
Switzerland[2]	0.4	0.2	0.9	0.5	3.8	3.5
US	8.5	7.2	7.2	5.6	6.1	4.2

Notes: 1) EU 15 except for 1975 where Luxembourg data not available; 2) for year 1990 registered unemployed only.

Sources: *Labour Force Statistics 1974–1994*, OECD (1996), Part III, tables, pp. 521–83 and OECD *Statistical Compendium* on CD-ROM – Rheinberg, DSI, Data Service and Information 2000–01.

Table 1.2 Incidence of long term unemployment (12 months and over) as a percentage of total unemployment

	1980	1985	1990	1994	1999
Australia	19.8	30.9	21.6	36.3	29.4
Canada	3.8	10.3	7.2	15.2	11.6
EU	24.5	45.5	45.1	48.1	47.5
Japan	16.5	13.1	19.1	17.5	22.4
Norway	–	10.0	20.2	28	6.8
New Zealand	–	–	20.9	32.3	20.8
Switzerland	–	–	16.4	28.9	39.8
US	4.3	9.5	5.5	12.2	6.8

Sources: 1980–97 *Key Indicators of the Labour Market* (KILM), ILO, Geneva, 1999. Date for 1990 and 1999 from the OECD *Employment Outlook 2000*, Statistical Annex p. 220. Data for 1994 from OECD *Employment Outlook 1998*, Statistical Annex p. 208.

has remained double the European Union average. By November 2000, some 14 million people were unemployed, half of whom were in long-term unemployment, which constitutes a serious social problem in view of its close association with poverty and social exclusion. While unemployment compensation represents only 8 per cent of total social expenditure (2.5 per cent of GDP), the real costs of unemployment include the taxes and social contributions which are foregone, the substantial increase in disability benefits, early retirement pensions, housing benefit and the various measures adopted to address social exclusion, all of which are designed to compensate for the lack of employment opportunities, especially for men over the age of 50.

2 Low Employment Rates in the Larger European Union Countries Coincide with Slow Expansion of the Services Sector

Many European Union countries are characterized by a low employment rate. Indeed, in the European Union as a whole, the employment rate fell from 64.1 per cent in the 1970s to 61 per cent in 1995. Only by 1999 had the employment rate risen sufficiently to exceed the 1990 level, due to four years of job growth. Low employment rates affect prime age women, youth and male workers aged over 50 in particular. Low employment to population ratios are prevalent in ascending order in Italy, Spain, Greece, Belgium, France, Ireland, Germany and Finland. In the United States, by contrast, where the employment rate was similar to the European level in 1970, it has now risen to 75 per cent. Of course, the European Union average masks major regional differences, particularly in the high-performing smaller European countries and the United Kingdom, where labour force participation is between 70 and 80 per cent (see Table 1.3).

The difference in employment rates, particularly between the United States and the major European Union economies, can almost entirely be explained by the higher employment in the services in the United States, where the services sector accounted for 90 per cent of net job growth. The European Commission estimates that employment in services accounts for 54.5 per cent of the working age population in the United States, compared with 40 per cent in the European Union (European Commission, 2000, pp. 77–94). If Europe had the same level of employment in the services sector as the United States, there would be some 30 million additional jobs in the European Union (Larsson, 1999), or more than double the total number that are currently unemployed.

Table 1.3 Employment to population ratio

	1980	1985	1990	1995	1999
Australia	65.0	63.4	67.9	67.5	68.2
Canada	66.0	65.8	70.3	67.6	70.1
Denmark	–	73.9	75.4	73.9	76.5
Finland	70.7	72.3	74.1	61.0	66.0
France	64.1	59.5	59.9	59.0	59.8
Germany	65.2	61.6	64.1	64.7	64.9
Ireland	–	50.1	52.1	53.8	62.3
Italy	53.9	51.9	52.6	51.2	52.9
Japan	66.8	66.9	68.6	69.2	68.9
Netherlands	54.5	50.6	60.8	64.2	70.9
New Zealand	–	–	67.3	70.0	70.0
Norway	72.2	75.0	73.1	73.5	78.0
Spain	52.2	45.5	51.1	47.4	53.8
Sweden	79.9	80.3	83.1	72.2	72.9
Switzerland	–	–	–	78.1	79.7
UK	–	66.6	72.4	69.3	71.7
US	67.2	69.0	72.2	72.5	73.9
EU 15	63.0	60.0	63.0	61.0	65.0

Notes

1 – = data not available.
2 EU 15 except for 1980 which exclude Austria, Belgium, Denmark, Greece, Ireland, UK; 1985 and 1990 except for Austria, Switzerland.

Sources: Data from the OECD *Labour Force Statistics 1979–1999* (2000) Part I. Data for 1990, 1995, 1999 from the OECD *Employment Outlook 2000*, p. 203.

2.1 The Role of the Services Sector

The job creation potential of the services sector has been demonstrated by the fact that virtually all net employment growth in OECD countries in recent years has been due to the rise in employment in services. This potential varies among countries and subsectors. For example, the smaller European countries and Australia, Canada, New Zealand and

United States lead the way, with approximately a 70 per cent share of total employment in services in 1998, while the rate is just over 60 per cent in Austria, Germany, Ireland, Italy and Spain, and between 50 and 60 per cent in Portugal. As a result of this surge in employment in services, the sector as a whole now employs twice as many workers as industry and agriculture combined throughout the OECD region.

But why are employment rates so closely related to the size of the services sector? This question raises the issue of employment intensity, which may even differ between countries with similar employment structures. The OECD has found that the correlation between intensity of employment in the service sector and total employment is largely due to variations in the share of the various components of the services sector in the economy. For example, in 1996, the United States generated 25 per cent more jobs per inhabitant than Europe. The difference is even more dramatic in two service subsectors, namely distributive services and hotels and catering, where job intensity was respectively 60 per cent and 130 per cent higher in the United States than in Europe (Du Grantrut, 1998). High employment intensity is also a characteristic of the retail sector in Japan in comparison, for example, with France (Gadrey, 1999).

What is the growth potential of the various services subsectors and what triggers or slows the process of job growth? Some elements of a response may be found in an examination of the development of four major service subsectors over the past two decades, namely producer services, social services, distributive services and personal services (OECD, 2000, pp.79–125).

Of the four subsectors, distributive and social services represent the largest shares of total employment in all OECD countries, each accounting for about one-third of employment in services.

However, the most dynamic subsector in most OECD countries is producer services, which consist of business and professional services, financial and insurance services and real estate. It was the smallest subsector in the early 1960s, but has grown at about twice the rate of the services sector as a whole. Business and professional services provide over half of the jobs in producer services, offering high-skilled high-wage jobs and a competitive advantage for countries which are developing the knowledge economy.

Social services, which consist of public administration, health, education and miscellaneous social and community services, have constituted another strong growth subsector since the 1980s in both Europe and the United States, but their share of service jobs has declined since the mid-1990s with government efforts to contain public expenditure on health, education and social protection. This subsector is a major employer of both high and low-skilled women.

Within the distributive services, the largest share of jobs (over half) is in the retail trade, which offers a large number of low-paid and precarious jobs, particularly for women. The other components of this subsector include the wholesale trade, transport services and communications, with the first two having a larger share of employment than the latter. Transport and communications, which are capital intensive, offer better conditions of employment than the retail trade.

The fourth subsector of personal services includes hotels and catering, recreation and cultural services, domestic services and other personal services. Half of the jobs in this subsector are in hotels and catering and about one-fifth are in domestic services. This subsector is a major source of employment for low-skilled and low-paid workers, particularly women.

With regard to the determinants of cross-national differences in employment growth in services the OECD points to: the importance of lagging productivity growth; the rise in incomes and exogenous shifts in demand for services, notably the continued growth in women's labour participation rates; the expansion of the welfare state and the related social services; and cultural and institutional factors (see also Ughetto, Feature No. 3). While slow productivity seems to have been a major feature in the growth rates of some service subsectors, this does not preclude growing demand for high quality services from innovative and expanding business sectors (whether in manufacturing or services). There is a positive correlation between the higher employment share of social and producer services with rising income, higher participation rates of women and a larger welfare state. In contrast, a lower employment share in these sectors and in distribution is associated with stricter employment protection legislation and with a higher tax wedge, which also reduces demand for personal services. Figure 1.1 shows how the distribution of employment among the major three sectors of the economy has evolved over time in the European Union and the United States.

Figure 1.1 Employment by sector

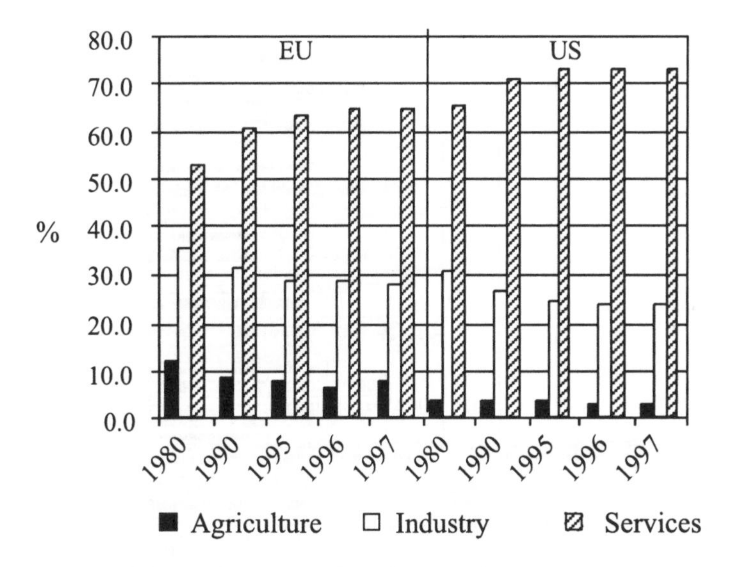

Source: *Key Indicators of the Labour Market* (KILM), CD-ROM, ILO, Geneva, 1999.

3 Significant Increases in the Employment and Labour Market Participation Rates of Women

The third change in labour markets, namely the significant rise in the labour market participation rates of women, is one of the most prominent features of post-war economic development in the OECD region. In the European Union, apart from Scandinavia where the rates were already very high in the 1970s, fewer than 40 per cent of women between the ages of 25 and 54 were at work or looking for a job in 1970. By 1999, this figure had increased to 60 per cent. The most dramatic increases between 1973 and 1999 occurred in three countries where, starting from low level, women's employment rates doubled. These countries are Ireland, where women's employment rose from 32.8 to 54.3 per cent, Netherlands (28.6 to 64.4 per cent) and Spain (32.5 to 49.9 per cent). Large rises also occurred in Austria (47.7 to 62.7 per cent), Belgium (39.9 to 56.0 per cent), France (47.9 to 61.3 per cent), Germany (49.7 to 62.3 per cent) and Portugal (30.5 to 62.8 per cent), as shown in Figure 1.2 below (OECD, 1995 and 2000).

Figure 1.2 Women's labour force participation rate

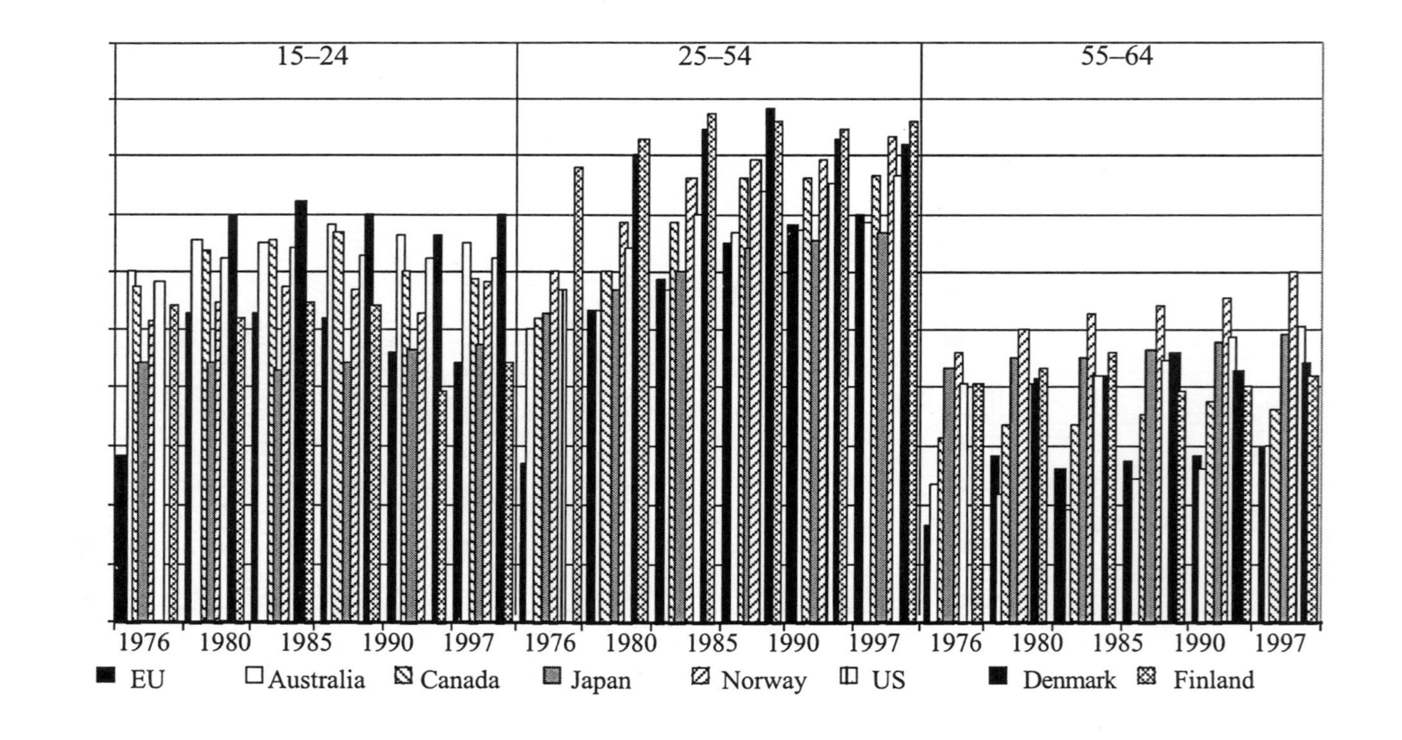

Source: KILM, op. cit.; *Labour Force Statistics 1974–1994*, op. cit.

In the European Union, the employment rate of women has grown four times faster than the rate for men since 1994, reducing the gender gap to 20 per cent (from 26 per cent in 1990). By 1999, women's employment in Europe was still 14.5 per cent below the level in the United States (53.1 compared with 67.6 per cent), despite the improvement over 1998 (when the gap stood at 17 per cent). The magnitude of the gap becomes clear when it is considered that if the women's employment rate in the European Union matched the level in the United States, there would be over 20 million more women in paid work in the European Union. The recent narrowing of the gender gap in employment rates in the European Union partly reflects the fall in male participation rates, particularly among the over 1990s, and the longer periods spent by young persons in education. Conversely, the recent rise in women's participation rates is particularly evident among women aged over 50 (European Commission, 1999, pp. 7–16 and 17–23).

During the 1990s, the employment rate of men in the European Union fell from 74.7 to 72.0 per cent, while the rate for women rose from 48.7 to 53.1 per cent. Australia and Canada have also seen their employment rates for men decrease by around 2 per cent, while the employment rates of women increased by 2.8 per cent in Australia and 2 per cent in Canada over the same period. Although the United States and Japan have experienced a very minor decline in male employment rates (0.2 and 0.3 per cent, respectively), they have seen a growth in women's employment rates of about 3.6 and 0.9 per cent, respectively (OECD, 2000).

Although women were the main beneficiaries of job creation in the European Union in 1997 (62 per cent of net job creation), their unemployment rate was still 2.8 per cent higher than that of men and remained almost at the same level in spite of the global decline in women's unemployment by 1.5 per cent between 1997 and 1999. In contrast, in Australia, Canada, Japan, New Zealand and the United States, men's unemployment rates were still slightly higher or approximately equal to the rates of women in 1998 and 1999. Table 1.4 shows how the unemployment rates of men and women evolved between 1990 and 1999 in the OECD region.

As already noted above, the gap between the employment rates of women in the European Union and the United States has been closing rapidly, from about 18.1 per cent in 1993 to 11.4 per cent in 1999. But the gap is still significant and may be attributed to the slower development

Table 1.4 Unemployment rates by gender

	1990	1995	1996	1997	1998	1999
Australia						
male	6.9	8.6	9	8.7	8.4	7.5
female	7.2	7.6	8	8.1	7.3	7.2
Canada						
male	8.3	9.9	10.1	9.4	8.7	7.9
female	8.1	9.1	9.3	8.9	8	7.3
Japan						
male	2.1	3.1	3.5	3.5	4.3	5
female	2.3	3.4	3.6	3.6	4.2	4.7
New Zealand						
male	8.3	6.3	6.2	6.7	7.7	7.1
female	7.3	6.4	6.1	6.7	7.4	6.6
Norway						
male	5.8	8.2	4.8	3.9	3.2	3.4
female	4.9	4.7	4.9	4.1	3.3	3
Switzerland						
male	1.2	2.9	3.4	4.4	3.2	2.7
female	2.6	4	4.2	4	4.3	3.6
US						
male	5.7	5.6	5.4	4.9	4.5	4.1
female	5.6	5.7	5.5	5.1	4.7	4.4
EU						
male	6.7	9.5	9.8	9.6	8.7	8.2
female	10.8	12.4	12.5	12.4	11.8	10.9

Source: OECD *Employment Outlook 2000*, Statistical Annex pp. 204–5.

of services in the European Union, where the services sector provides just over 40 per cent of women's jobs, compared with 58 per cent in the United States.

The importance of the service sector development for the employment of women can be seen from the following: of the European countries, Denmark and Sweden have high women's employment rates (71 per cent and 68 per cent) and a high presence of women in the services sector, at around 59 per cent. In contrast, the general employment rates of women are low in Italy and Spain (below 36 per cent), with fewer than 27 per cent of women being employed in the services sector (European Commission, 2000). Table 1.5 shows how the share of employment in services evolved in general and by gender in OECD countries between 1990 and 1997.

Table 1.5 Gender composition of service employment
Percentage of service employment of total employment

	Both		Male		Female	
	1990	**1997**	**1990**	**1997**	**1990**	**1997**
Australia	68.8	72.7	58.8	63.0	83.0	85.4
Austria	54.9	62.9	44.3	52.1	70.3	78.1
Canada	71.1	73.0	63.5	62.6	87.9	85.6
Denmark	66.6	69.7	54.8	58.4	80.6	83.4
Finland	60.5	65.7	46.1	52.1	76.2	81.0
France	64.8	–	54.8	–	78.4	–
Germany	56.4	62.8	47.1	50.9	70.4	78.7
Ireland	56.7	60.6	45.9	48.6	77.1	79.2
Italy	58.8	–	53.6	–	68.4	–
Japan	58.2	61.1	54.5	55.4	63.6	69.3
Netherlands	68.6	71.8	59.0	62.1	84.4	85.3
New Zealand	64.4	67.2	54.3	56.0	77.5	81.1
Norway	69.1	71.8	56.3	58.7	84.7	87.3
Spain	54.8	61.7	46.5	51.6	72.5	80.2
Sweden	67.2	71.2	51.7	57.2	84.1	86.5
Switzerland	59.9	68.6	49.8	59.3	76.6	81.5
US	70.7	73.1	59.9	62.6	83.8	85.4
UK	64.8	71.0	52.5	59.3	76.2	84.7

– = Data not available.

Source: KILM, op. cit.

It should also be noted that Southern European countries, such as Greece and Portugal, in the same way as Japan, have experienced an especially rapid growth in the employment of women in services (starting from a very low level). The rise in women's employment is also linked to the growth of jobs in specific subsectors, such as social services and personal services, where the proportion of women employed is more than double that of men (OECD, 2000).

However, the potential for further rises in the employment rates of women may be limited in the European Union by a number of factors in addition to the slower rate of development of the services sector, including: the lack of incentives in the social protection systems for participation in the labour market; inadequate child-care facilities; and the unattractive types of jobs and wages that are available to women, and particularly those who return to work after child-rearing. The burden of unpaid labour in the household continues to fall disproportionately on women. The ILO estimates that the average hours of unpaid work by women are about twice those of men in the industrialized countries, about four times more in Italy and Spain and about eight times more in Japan (ILO, 2000). Levels of education and skills also play a role. On the one hand, a lack of qualifications limits employment rates. For example, in 1996, almost two-thirds of prime-aged women who were not in the labour force had no educational qualifications beyond basic schooling, compared to 35 per cent of those who were in employment. On the other hand, many women are overqualified and work in jobs that are below their level of educational attainment. Moreover, when they do reach higher occupational echelons, wage inequality is even more evident than in lower qualified jobs. This absence of fair remuneration for similar skills levels is likely to be a disincentive to job entry (European Commission, 1998b, p. 18; 2000, pp. 11–14).

4 Changes in Family Composition

The increased demands made on social protection systems are also a results of the major changes that have occurred in family composition. Divorce rates and the numbers of births to unmarried women in the industrialized countries were six times higher in 1990 than in 1960, although these trends were much smaller in Southern Europe and Japan (ILO, 2000). Throughout the OECD, there has been a significant increase in single-parent and single-person households, often associated with the poverty trap and the risk of exclusion (Oxley et al., 2000), as shown in Table 1.6 and Figure 1.3 below. Average household size in the European Union declined by 5 per cent between 1986 and 1996. Over

Table 1.6 Average household size

	1981/1982	1997
EU	2.8	2.5
Belgium	2.7	2.5
Denmark	2.4	2.2
Germany	2.5	2.2
Greece	3.1	2.6
Spain	3.6	3.1
France	2.7	2.4
Ireland	3.6	3.0
Italy	3.0	2.7
Luxembourg	2.8	2.6
Netherlands	2.8	2.3
Austria	2.7	2.5
Portugal	3.3	2.9
Finland	2.6	2.1
Sweden	2.3	2.3
UK	2.7	2.4
Norway	2.7	2.2
Switzerland	2.5	2.3

Source: *Living Conditions in Europe* – statistical pocketbook, 1999 edition, European Commission, Eurostat.

the same period, single-person households increased from 20 to 25 per cent of all households in the North of the European Union. In 1996, single working-age adult households represented over one-third of total households in Canada, Finland and the United States, in sharp contrast with the situation in Southern Europe and Ireland, where two-adult households represented the vast majority (80 per cent). In the same year, some 8 per cent of single-adult households, the majority of whom were non-employed women with children, were dependent on social transfers. The corresponding proportion was over 12 per cent in Austria, Belgium and the United Kingdom (OECD, 1998).

The significance of these trends stems from the correlation between the risk of non-employment and the number of adults in a household. Non-employment is highest among single-adult households. For

Figure 1.3 Composition of households in 1995

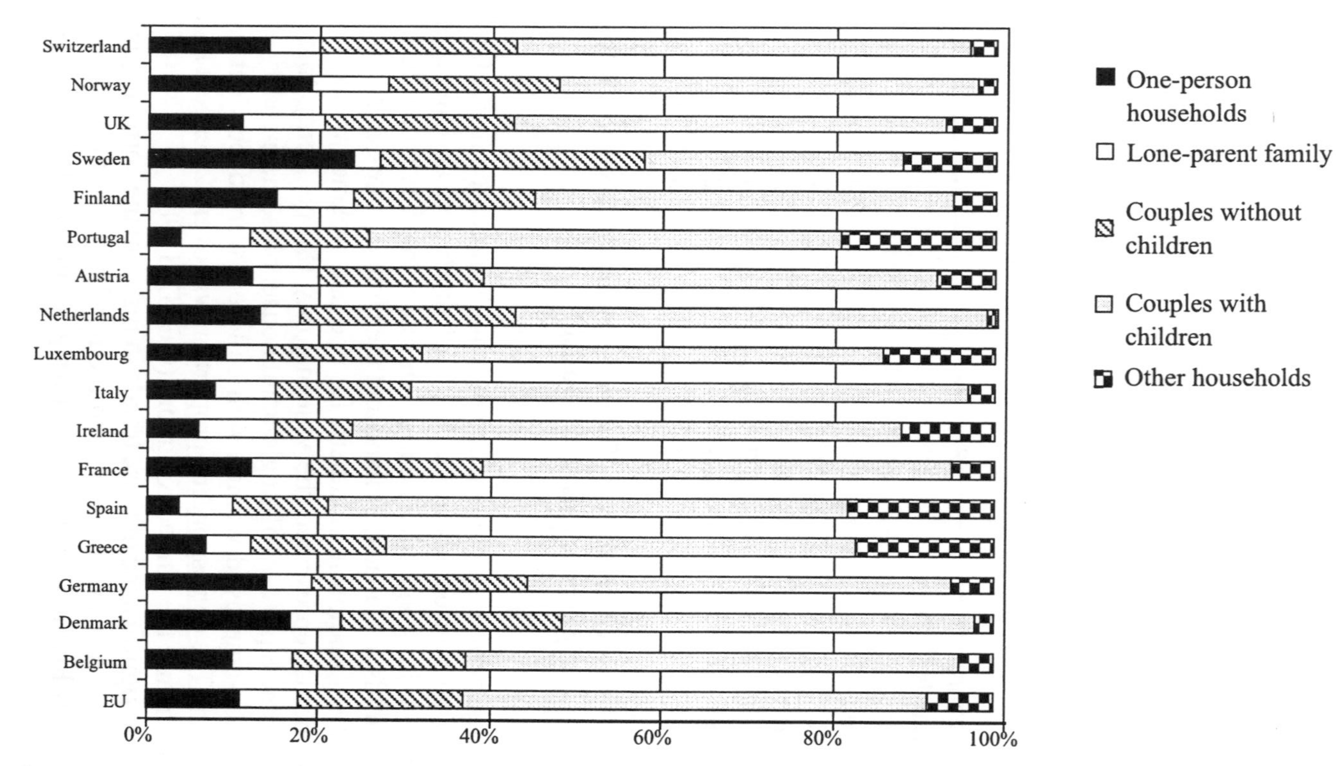

Source: Living Conditions in Europe, op. cit.

instance, in 1996, half of the single-adult households with children were non-employed in Australia, Belgium, Ireland, Netherlands and United Kingdom. The risk of non-employment in single-adult households has increased over the past ten years in most industrialized countries, with the exception of Ireland, Netherlands and United States.

This constitutes a serious threat for the future generation, particularly since about one-fifth of unemployed young people live in workless households and tend to experience high drop-out rates from school, poor job entry and retention rates, and high exposure to criminality and drug addiction. Moreover, there is a widening division in European societies between workless households and those where all the adults are in gainful employment.

It is also important to note the manner in which the economic recovery of the past few years has changed the situation of workless households. In the United Kingdom, for instance, the latest available data shows a significant decline of about 10 per cent in the numbers of workless households, from a peak of 3,444,000 (representing 18.9 per cent of all households) in 1996, to 3,066,000 (16.4 per cent of households) by 2000. At the same time, there was a much bigger decline (of about 20 per cent) in the number of children in such households, from 2,398,000 in 1994 to 1,907,000 in 2000 (Cooper-Green and Gigante, 2001).

5 The Diversification of Forms of Employment

Changes in family composition, the increased participation of women in the labour force and the search for greater flexibility by firms and workers has resulted in the fifth change in the labour market, which consists of the diversification of forms of employment, with increases in part-time and temporary work and in self-employment. Standard full-time employment is arguably still the predominant form of employment in the OECD region (OECD, 1996 and 1999); Supiot, 1999; and Auer and Cazes, Feature No. 1).

While atypical jobs account for a low proportion of total employment, part-time and temporary jobs have nonetheless substantially increased throughout the European Union, self-employment has tended to decline. In 1998, part-time jobs on average represented 17.4 per cent of jobs in the European Union (but 38.8 per cent in the Netherlands and over or about 40 per cent in the United Kingdom and Sweden) and a very high proportion of women's employment. The number of part-time workers with temporary contracts is also disproportionately high. Temporary work and self-employment each account for around 13 per cent of total employment across the European Union (European Commission, 2000). In the United States, temporary employment, although at a low level, has doubled from 1.1 to 2.2 per cent of total employment since 1989. Moreover, temporary jobs accounted for 8.2 per cent of employment growth in the late 1990s (Katz and Krueger, 2001).

The relative predominance of standard forms of employment has been acknowledged by the Trades Union Congress in a recent report, which contests the widely held idea of the end of standard employment in the United Kingdom and the view that the labour market has changed radically over the past 20 years with the growth of flexible forms of employment. While short-term turnover is frequent and there have been substantial changes in work organization and practices, these have coincided with an underlying stability in the structure of employment. Indeed, since 1984, the share of permanent jobs has fallen by only around 1 per cent, while seven out of ten new jobs created have been permanent (TUC, 2000).

Other evidence from the United Kingdom shows that stable employment increased faster than the rise in total employment between 1992 and 1999 (1.7 and 1.6 million jobs, respectively). The number of people working with the same employer for 10 years or more rose from 7.4 to 9 million, increasing from 28.6 to 33.0 per cent of the workforce. The 1992 figure was much lower than the average job tenure rate of 37.9 per cent in the rest of the European Union and somewhat lower than the rate in the United States (30 per cent). The disproportionate growth in long tenure employment in the United Kingdom was much more evident for women, with the total female workforce expanding by 813,000, while long-term employment increased by 1,067,000 over the same period, raising the long tenure rate of women from 21.2 to 28.5 per cent (Doogan, 2001).

However, a different view has been expressed by *The Economist* (2000), which noted a rise in atypical jobs from 22 per cent in 1991 to 27 per cent in 1998 and forecast their likely increase to 40 per cent by 2007.

Turning to Japan and the United States, Houseman and Osawa acknowledge that full-time regular jobs predominate, with 76.5 per cent and 78.5 per cent of total employment respectively. However, they identify a significant increase in nonstandard jobs in Japan. While the share of part-time employment was similar in both countries (below 20 per cent), it increased considerably in Japan between 1982 and 1997, from 11 per cent to 18.8 per cent of paid employment. Part-time employment accounted for 45 per cent of net job growth in Japan between 1982 and 1997 and for 77 per cent since 1992. The incidence of temporary work is relatively low in both countries, but it is almost three times higher in Japan (close to 12 per cent of jobs). Moreover, while only 9 per cent of part-time workers are temporary in the United States, 41 per cent are temporary in Japan, with this figure rising to 66 per cent if students and other non-regular employees are taken into account (Houseman and Osawa, 2000).

A brief overview of the three main forms of atypical jobs is provided below.

5.1 Part-time Work

Close to 80 per cent of the net jobs created in the European Union since 1994 have been part-time (3.3 out of 4.3 million), around two-thirds of which are occupied by women (who also took 52 per cent of the additional full-time jobs!). In 1998, approximately one-third of women workers worked part-time, compared with 6 per cent of men. The proportion of women employed in part-time jobs was 68 per cent in the Netherlands, 45 per cent in the United Kingdom and 40 per cent in Sweden. In Australia, Canada, Japan and New Zealand, over 30 per cent of women workers are in part-time jobs. Only the United States has a lower rate at around 20 per cent (European Commission, 2000; OECD, 2000). Figure 1.4 shows how women's part-time employment evolved as a proportion of women's employment in selected OECD countries and the European Union between 1973 and 1998.

Many part-time workers only work for short hours, and sometimes for fewer than ten hours a week, and are therefore excluded from social insurance coverage (OECD, 1999). Fitoussi and Passet note that the number of part-time workers on such shorter schedules amounts to 10 per cent of total employment in the Netherlands and around 6 per cent in Australia, Canada, Denmark, Norway, Switzerland and United Kingdom. The figure is 4 per cent in Finland, Germany and United States. In view of the significance of these figures, Fitoussi and Passet prefer to apply

Figure 1.4 Women's part-time employment

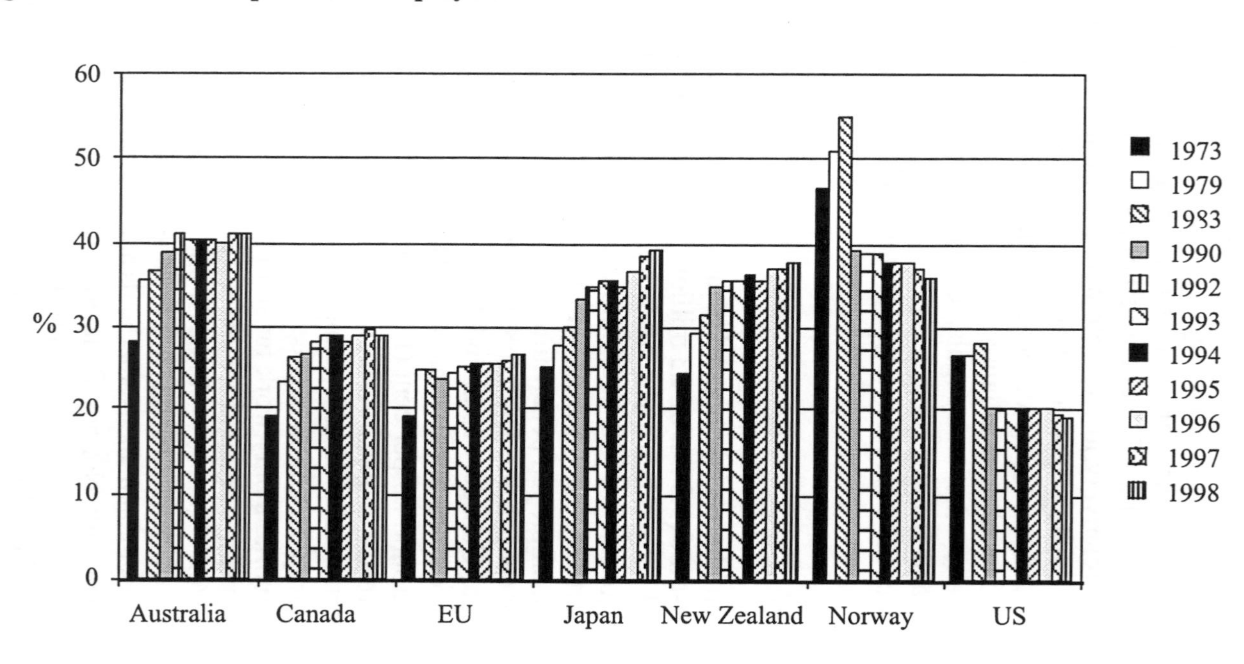

Source: Data for 1973, 1979, 1983, 1993 and 1994 from OECD *Employment Outlook 1995*, p. 210; for 1995 from OECD *Employment Outlook 1996*, p. 192; for 1990, 1996 and 1998 from OECD *Employment Outlook 2000*, p. 218.

the concept of underemployment to such fragmented jobs, which are in many cases the result of a lack of choice and mask the real unmet demand for employment (Fitoussi and Passet, 2000, pp. 64–6).

On the other hand, part-time jobs are not necessarily unstable in many countries. In the United Kingdom, new evidence suggests that a significant element of the growth of long-term employment (remaining with the same employer for 10 years or more) is explained by the growth in long-term part-time jobs. Indeed, between 1992 and 1999, about one-third of the additional 1.66 million long-term job gains were part-time (Doogan, 2001). In many European countries, the proportion of women part-timers working for the same employer for 10 years or more was greater than among women working full-time. Part-time work would therefore appear, at least in some cases, to be a more stable form of employment for women than full-time work.

5.2 Temporary Employment

Temporary employment in the European Union has increased since the beginning of the recession in the early 1990s and in 1998, for example, represented 40 per cent of job growth (see Figure 1.5 below). However, it concerned only 12 per cent of men and 13.5 per cent of women. Moreover, in 1998, for the first time since the beginning of the recovery, the number of people working with permanent contracts exceeded those with temporary contracts. Nevertheless, in countries such as Finland, Portugal and Spain over 18 per cent of women workers are on short-term contracts, while the figure ranges between 10 and 15 per cent in France, Germany, Greece, Netherlands and Sweden. Male rates of temporary employment, although lower than the rates of women, tend to vary between countries. Spain has the highest at 32.1 per cent, while France, Germany, Greece and United Kingdom range between 12 and 13 per cent and the rate in Austria, Belgium, Denmark and Luxembourg is lower than 9.3 per cent (European Commission, 2000, pp. 39–40).

Workers in temporary (fixed-term) employment tend to have certain common characteristics. For example, in Spain and Italy, temporary workers are younger, have lower levels of educational attainment and are concentrated in elementary occupations and in more volatile sectors (Cebrián et al., 2000). In Denmark, temporary employment is dominated by students, who are not interested in permanent jobs, or by workers who will soon leave the labour market (Hoffmann and Walwei, 2000).

Figure 1.5 Percentage of employed persons in the European Union with fixed-term contracts

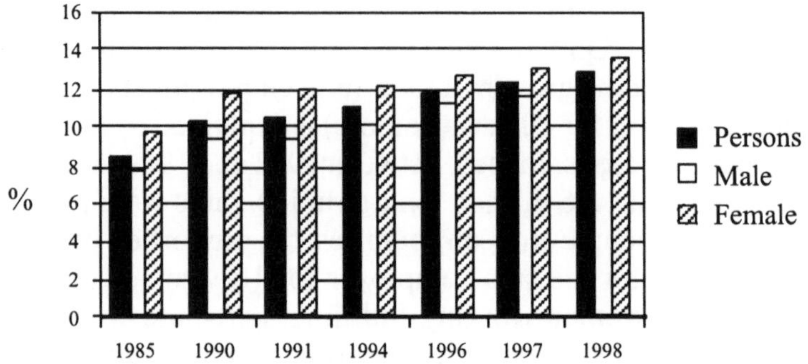

Source: European Commission, *Employment in Europe 1999* (2000).

5.3 Combinations of Atypical Jobs

Part-time workers, and particularly men, are more likely to have temporary contracts. Only 10 per cent of men working full-time had temporary jobs, compared with one-third of men employed part-time in most of the European Union. The proportion is over 60 per cent in Greece and Ireland, and 50 per cent in Portugal and Spain. For women, the difference is much smaller, with around 15 per cent of women part-time workers on temporary contracts compared with 13 per cent of women full-time workers (European Commission, 2000, pp. 25–48). Moreover, as already noted, part-time work is more stable for women than full-time employment in many European Union countries (Doogan, 2001).

5.4 Self-employment

A recent analysis of trends in self-employment in the OECD region (OECD, 2000, pp. 55–188) shows that between 1979 and 1997 non-agricultural self-employment increased from 9.8 to 11.9 per cent (unweighted average). Self-employment in industry and services accounts for about 15 per cent of the workforce. However, the self-employment rate varies between countries with no evident common link to their industrial structure: it is about 20 per cent or more in Greece, Italy, Portugal and Spain; close to 17 per cent in New Zealand; around 10 per cent in Belgium, Finland, Germany, Japan, Netherlands, Sweden and United Kingdom; and below 10 per cent in Austria, Denmark, Norway, Sweden and United States. Over the past 25 years, the self-employment rate has remained relatively stable, with small increases in a number of OECD countries and a small decline in others. The recent fall of 3.5 per cent in the overall self-employment rate in the European Union is mainly attributable to a marked decline in agricultural employment, a sector in which more than half of the workforce is self-employed.

Growth in non-agricultural self-employment has been concentrated in the fastest growing sectors (business and community services), particularly among higher-skilled occupational groups. Moreover, in several countries the phenomenon has become more common of growing numbers of self-employed workers servicing a single company. The combination of these trends may well reflect the increased outsourcing of services by firms (particularly in legal, accounting, computer and related business services), possibly as a means of reducing labour costs linked to training, equipment, taxation and social contributions. This has led some governments to consider them to be false self-employed workers. The German government, for example, has introduced special regulations to define genuine self-employment workers and quasi-dependent self-employed persons for the purposes of social contributions, while in Italy a number of special arrangements have been developed to ensure their coverage by collective bargaining and social protection (Sarfati, 1999).

Self-employment is also concentrated in the wholesale and retail sectors (franchising), repairs and hotels and catering. Job growth in these sectors, together with financial intermediation, real estate, property rental, business services and community, social and personal services has been higher than average. The OECD notes, however, that self-employment is rarely used to absorb the unemployed. Indeed, it has found a strong link between self-employment and wage employment, with most self-employed people previously being wage-earners. When they leave self-employment, it is either to return to wage-earning jobs or to quit the labour force (rather than becoming unemployed).

The diversity of national definitions makes it difficult to form an overview of the phenomenon of atypical forms of employment and its implications for living standards, the establishment of a regular link with gainful employment, the reduction of exclusion and the maintenance of the capacity to contribute to and benefit from social security coverage. The worldwide development of atypical jobs reflects the demand for greater labour market flexibility and means that part of the cost of social protection is eventually shifted to the individual worker or the taxpayer (through social assistance) (Sarfati, 1999).

6 Changes in Occupational Structures and Job Profiles

Over the past three decades, major changes have occurred in occupational structures and job profiles in OECD economies. These are mainly a result of three principal developments.

6.1 Shifts in the Structure of Economies towards Services

Shifts in the structure of economies towards services involve the creation of a large number of low-paid low-skilled jobs, often in the form of part-time and temporary or intermittent jobs, alongside highly skilled and highly paid jobs (the latter are often in short supply). While job growth between 1989 and 1996 in the United States included both well-paid and low-paid occupations, twice as many well-paid jobs were created. In Europe, the shift of employment towards non-manual occupations, and particularly those with a high skills content, has been common to fast growth sectors in most countries. These high-skilled non-manual jobs account for 45 per cent of all the persons employed in these sectors, including health and social work (one-third of job growth), business services (20 per cent), hotels and catering (15 per cent) and culture and entertainment (6 per cent). Only in Portugal has job growth been mainly in skilled manual occupations. The decline in manual jobs in Europe has largely been a result of large-scale job losses (both skilled and unskilled) in shrinking sectors, such as public administration, banking, textiles and clothing, iron and steel and agriculture (European Commission, 2000, pp. 95–108).

6.2 The Rapid Diffusion of Information Technologies

The advent of information technologies results in new organizational structures, is marked by high labour turnover and requires highly-skilled staff. The pace of the introduction and diffusion of information and communication technologies (ICT) determines the performance and competitiveness of companies, enhancing productivity in the industrial sector and, more recently, in parts of the services sector. This has been particularly manifest in the United States, where the heavy investments made in ICT over the past two decades have destroyed manufacturing jobs, but have also created a large number of new jobs in the services sector as a whole and in the so-called new economy. ICT industries, which represent some 8 per cent of GDP in the United States (compared with 2 per cent in France), have accounted for half of the growth of the economy, investment, productivity, job creation and market capitalization. These industries, which now employ some 10 million people, generated 1.7 million jobs in the 1990s and are expected to create as many again by 2001 (Reuters, 2000), with another 10 million being created in related services. This has led the European Commission to pin its hopes on solving Europe's job problems through the e-economy and cyber-education. However, the recent significant drop in the value of shares in technology companies, and particularly those related to computers, telecommunications and the Internet, may dampen these high expectations.

6.3 The Growing Importance of Small and Medium-sized Enterprises

The growth of the share of small and medium-sized enterprises (SMEs) in the economy in the OECD region is a major source of job creation, although their life-span may be short and their financial capacity to pay social contributions regularly may be limited.

Table 1.7 below shows that there is a large flow into and out of employment in SMEs. This is especially true for smaller establishments with fewer than 19 employees, which experience many more start-ups and closures than larger establishments. These smaller companies represent half or more of total employment in SMEs. Their employees are particularly vulnerable in the event of business failure in terms of the continuity of their pensions, disability and unemployment entitlements. Moreover, any voluntary forms of social protection (individual pension funds and supplementary health protection) are either too expensive or constitute too much of an administrative burden for SMEs in most countries.

These changes in occupational structures and job profiles are liable to adversely affect the viability of existing social protection systems,

Table 1.7 Distribution of gross job flows and employment by establishment size

Establishment size	Openings	Expansions	Gross flows Job gains	Closures	Contractions	Job losses	Employment (last year)
Canada 1983–91							
Total	100.0	100.0	100.0	100.0	100.0	100.0	100.0
1–19 employees	53.6	41	43.7	48	32	36.1	27.2
20–99	23	22.4	22.5	21.5	23.7	23.1	22.3
100.0–499	13.7	15.3	15	15.6	17.3	16.9	15.9
500+	9.7	21.3	18.8	14.9	27	23.9	34.6
Denmark 1983–89							
Total	100.0	100.0	100.0	100.0	100.0	100.0	100.0
1–19 employees	55.8	56	55.9	59.5	41.7	48.1	39.8
20–99	22.6	26.5	25	21.5	30.3	27.2	31.8
100.0+	21.6	17.5	19.1	19	28	24.7	28.4
Finland 1987–92							
Total	100.0	100.0	100.0	100.0	100.0	100.0	100.0
1–19 employees	54.9	51.5	52.7	46	35.5	38.4	34
20–99	25.2	24.4	24.7	29.5	25.8	26.9	29.3
100.0–499	16.1	18	17.3	19.4	25.6	23.9	25.5
500+	3.8	6.1	5.3	5.1	13.1	10.8	11.2

Table 1.7 cont'd

France 1987–92							
Total	100.0	100.0	100.0	100.0	100.0	100.0	100.0
1–19 employees	54.8			53.4			35.7
20–99	24.1			25.6			29.7
100.0–499	15			15			22.5
500+	6.1			6			12.1
Italy 1984–92							
Total	100.0	100.0	100.0	100.0	100.0	100.0	100.0
1–19 employees	71.2	63	65.7	63.9	52.3	56.2	39.2
20–99	15.5	18.4	17.5	17.6	21.1	20	22.2
100.0–499	7.2	10	9	9.1	12.1	11	15.6
500+	6.1	8.6	7.8	9.4	14.5	12.8	23
New Zealand 1987–92							
Total	100.0	100.0	100.0	100.0	100.0	100.0	100.0
1–19 employees	53.7	57.3	55.6	53.2	33.4	41.8	45.2
20–99	225.1	27.2	26.2	28.7	31.6	30.4	30.9
100.0–499	16.3	11.6	13.8	12.7	22.8	18.5	18.3
500+	4.9	3 .9	4.4	5.4	12.2	9.3	5.6

Table 1.7 cont'd

Sweden 1985–91							
Total	100.0	100.0	100.0	100.0	100.0	100.0	100.0
1–19 employees	54.1	56.1	55.2	52.8	35.2	41.8	35.2
20–99	20.4	24.9	22.9	21.4	28.9	26.1	28.3
100.0–499	14.2	13.8	14	13.5	22.4	19.1	22.5
500+	11.2	5.2	7.9	12.3	13.5	13	14
UK 1987–91							
Total	100.0	100.0	100.0	100.0	100.0	100.0	100.0
1–19 employees	84	37.4	50	63.6	21.1	45.6	30.5
20–99	11	18.6	16.6	19.1	15.5	17.6	16.7
100.0–499	4.2	15.1	12.2	10.3	16.4	12.9	12.9
500+	0.8	28.9	21.2	7	47	23.9	39.9
US 1984–88 (manufacturing)							
Total	100.0	100.0	100.0	100.0	100.0	100.0	100.0
1–19 employees	14.5	5	6.7	20.1	6	9.6	3.6
20–99	43.5	24.9	28.2	37.7	23.5	27.2	19
100.0–499	30.7	38.6	37.2	30.9	36.7	35.2	37.3
500+	11.2	31.4	27.8	11.4	33.8	28	40.1

Source: OECD *Employment Outlook 1994*, p. 126.

which were created in the context of a completely different set of parameters (full-time lifelong employment of male workers in large manufacturing establishments).

7 Working Life Shrinks at both Ends of the Spectrum

The employment crisis in Europe over the past 25 years has also resulted in a shrinkage of the labour force as a result of delayed entry into the labour market upstream, and increasingly early withdrawal downstream.

7.1 Upstream: Young People

Some, 25 per cent of all unemployed persons in the European Union are currently under the age of 25. At the same time, a growing proportion of young people are remaining in education and training for longer periods and are delaying their entry into the labour force. The participation rate of young persons aged between 15 and 24 fell by 10 per cent during the 1990s, from 55 per cent in 1990 to 45 per cent in 1998. With the economic recovery in 1999, there was a slight rise to 47.2 per cent, a level which is close to the figure in Japan (47.8 per cent), but still very much lower than in Australia, Canada, Norway, Switzerland and United States. The participation rates of young persons were very low (below 38 per cent) in Belgium, France, Italy and Luxembourg in 1999.

The unemployment rate for this age group is twice as high as that of prime age workers (25–54) in seven OECD countries, as indicated in Table 1.8. In some European countries, their unemployment rate exceeds 20 per cent (Belgium, Finland, France, Italy and Spain).

Many young people who are unemployed or not in the labour force for other reasons are excluded from unemployment insurance coverage. The fact that they make no contributions to social protection schemes also aggravates the problem of the growing dependency ratio. There is therefore a need to prepare youth better for entry into the labour market and to secure their earning capacity by improving their employability. Technical and vocational training in Austria, Denmark, Germany, Netherlands, Norway and Switzerland have given good results in this area. (Although the press reported in early 2001 that the German educational system was criticized by the OECD because of the shortcomings of lifelong training programmes and universities in reducing unemployment: *Financial Times*, 7 March 2001.)

7.2 Downstream: Older Workers

At the other end of the spectrum, there is a parallel trend of earlier labour market withdrawal in the European Union. The numbers of men aged 55–64 leaving the labour force increased from 43 per cent in 1986 to 50 per cent in 1996. The proportion of men aged 60–64 who are outside the labour force rose sharply to 70 per cent, even though they are still below the pensionable age. In contrast, as noted earlier, many women in their 50s have been entering or remaining in the labour force, with significantly higher participation and employment rates than in the 1970s in most European Union countries, even where these rates are low. Between 60 and 65 per cent of women between the ages of 55 and 64 are in the labour force in Norway, Sweden and Switzerland, and between 48.4 and 51.5 per cent in Japan, Denmark, New Zealand and United States. Only France, Finland and Spain have seen a decline in women's employment and participation rates for this age group.

Over a quarter of the labour force aged over 50 are unemployed. The situation of older workers reflects inadequate job opportunities, slow economic growth, the reluctance of employers to keep or recruit older workers and the preference of both trade unions and individuals to opt for an early exit from work with disability benefits or early retirement pensions. This trend increases the dependency ratio and adds to the pressure on pension schemes as the population ages, which is the last change in the labour market examined in this chapter.

Table 1.8 clearly shows these trends over the past two decades at both ends of the labour force spectrum and the differences between the labour force participation and activity rates of men and women.

8 The Population Ages as Life Expectancy Increases

The shrinking of the labour force described above, combined with the ageing of the population and the major rise in life expectancy beyond retirement over the past two decades has given rise to concern about the sustainability of existing pension systems, due to rising dependency ratios. This concern is exacerbated by the considerable growth of single-

Table 1.8 Labour force participation rates, employment to population ratios and unemployment rates for males and females aged 15 to 24 and 55 to 64

	Male								Female							
	1979		1983		1994		1999		1979		1983		1994		1999	
Country	*15–24*	*55–64*	*15–24*	*55–64*	*15–24*	*55–64*	*15–24*	*55–64*	*15–24*	*55–64*	*15–24*	*55–64*	*15–24*	*55–64*	*15–24*	*55–64*
Australia																
Labour force participation	75.3	69.5	74.1	62	70.7	60.7	72.6	61	61.9	20.3	64.1	20.5	65.9	26.5	68.6	32.6
Employment/population ratio	67	67.4	59.7	59.6	58.9	54.4	62	57	53.5	19.8	53.8	19.9	55.6	25.2	59.6	31.3
Unemployment	11	3.1	19.5	3.8	16.7	10.5	14.5	6.5	13.6	2.3	16.1	2.9	15.7	4.9	13.2	3.9
Austria																
Labour force participation	–	–	–	–	62.6	39.7	62.6	43.9	–	–	–	–	56.2	18	54.2	18.3
Employment/population ratio	–	–	–	–	59.7	38	59.2	41.6	–	–	–	–	53.2	17.5	50.7	17.6
Unemployment	–	–	–	–	4.7	4.1	5.5	5.3	–	–	–	–	5.4	2.8	6.4	3.4
Belgium																
Labour force participation	–	–	46	50.6	37.3	34.5	35.5	36.8	–	–	41.8	12.3	33	13.2	30.1	16.1
Employment/population ratio	–	–	37.1	47.7	29.7	33	27.5	35.1	–	–	29.7	11.8	25.3	12.4	23.4	14.8
Unemployment	–	–	19.3	5.8	20.5	4.5	22.7	4.5	–	–	28.9	4.1	23.4	5.9	22.4	8.1
Canada																
Labour force participation	71.7	76.3	69.8	72.4	65.2	60.3	65.3	60.7	61.7	33.9	63.6	33.6	60.6	37.4	61.7	39.4
Employment/population ratio	62.3	72.9	54.3	66.4	53.2	54.6	55.4	56.9	54	32.3	52.9	30.9	51.9	34.3	53.9	37.3
Unemployment	13.1	4.5	22.2	8.2	18.5	9.5	15.3	6.3	12.6	4.9	16.8	7.8	14.3	8.4	12.6	5.3
Denmark																
Labour force participation	–	–	68.3	67.2	72.1	63.8	76.7	61.9	–	–	62.2	41.7	65.9	43.1	70.1	50.6
Employment/population ratio	–	–	55.9	63.1	64.8	59.8	69.5	59.9	–	–	49.9	39.1	59.1	40.2	62.8	47.8
Unemployment	–	–	18.1	6.2	10.2	6.3	9.5	3.2	–	–	19.7	6.3	10.2	6.7	10.5	5.6

Table 1.8 cont'd

Finland																
Labour force participation	63.9	56.3	61	54.1	49.2	45.3	49.7	45.4	52.8	41.3	53	47.4	39.8	40.8	49.1	42.4
Employment/population ratio	56.8	54.3	54.7	51.4	33.7	34.3	39.3	40.1	47.2	39	47.3	44.1	27.8	31.7	38.2	38.4
Unemployment	11.1	3.6	10.3	5.1	31.4	24.3	21	10.9	10.5	5.5	10.8	7.0	30.1	22.2	22.2	9.4
France																
Labour force participation	52.5	69.9	50.3	53.6	33.5	42.1	32.1	42.6	44.2	39	41	32.7	27.8	30.1	24.6	32.5
Employment/population ratio	47.6	67.0	42.8	50.4	25.4	39.1	24.3	38.9	36	37	30.5	30.4	19	28.1	17.3	29.6
Unemployment	9.3	4.1	15.0	6.0	24.2	7.3	24.2	8.7	18.6	5.1	25.5	6.9	31.6	6.7	29.7	8.7
Germany																
Labour force participation	62.7	66.9	61	63.1	59	53.3	55.7	55.1	57.2	28.4	54.8	26.3	53.3	28.4	46.3	34.3
Employment/population ratio	60.9	63.2	54.6	57.4	54.1	47.6	50.7	48	54.2	26.8	48.4	24	48.9	24.5	42.8	28.9
Unemployment	2.9	5.5	10.4	9.0	8.3	10.7	9.1	12.8	5.2	5.9	11.7	8.6	8.2	13.4	7.7	15.5
Ireland																
Labour force participation	68.9	77.9	64.2	78.0	49.3	65.2	54.4	64.4	54.2	20.1	52.8	20.2	43.3	20.9	46.8	26.9
Employment/population ratio	62.0	72.8	49.5	69.2	36.9	59.6	49.7	61.7	49.8	19.3	44.1	18.9	34.4	19.2	42.9	25.7
Unemployment	10.0	6.5	22.9	11.2	25.1	8.5	8.6	4.2	8.1	4.4	16.6	6.4	20.5	8.1	8.3	4.3
Italy																
Labour force participation	48.7	37.6	48.9	36.8	42.3	31.4	42.4	42.8	39.9	10.5	40.3	10.5	34.6	8.3	33.8	15.9
Employment/population ratio	38.3	36.8	36.4	36.1	30.0	30.7	30.3	40.8	27.7	9.7	25.6	9.9	21.9	8.2	20.8	15.0
Unemployment	21.3	2.0	25.5	1.9	29.1	2.2	28.6	4.6	30.7	7.4	36.5	6.0	36.5	2.1	38.3	5.6
Japan																
Labour force participation	43.9	85.2	43.9	84.7	48.0	85	47.7	85.2	44.3	45.4	44.4	46.1	47.1	48.1	46.7	49.8
Employment/population ratio	42.3	81.5	41.9	80.5	45.4	81.2	42.8	79.5	42.9	44.8	42.5	45.1	44.6	47.2	42.9	48.2
Unemployment	3.6	4.4	4.6	5.0	5.6	4.5	10.3	6.7	3.2	1.2	4.5	2.1	5.3	1.9	8.2	3.3

Table 1.8 cont'd

Netherlands																
Labour force participation	49.2	65.3	52.3	54.2	62.6	41.8	67.4	49.8	46.3	14.4	50.6	14.4	60.7	18.5	68.0	22.8
Employment/population ratio	45.6	63.2	38.4	46.1	55.8	40.7	62.9	48.8	42.2	14	38.9	13.2	55	17.5	62.5	21.9
Unemployment	7.3	3.3	26.6	14.9	10.9	2.7	6.6	2.1	8.9	2.7	23.1	8.2	9.4	5.2	8.2	3.9
Norway																
Labour force participation	53.9	82.0	66.9	80.3	57.8	71.5	66.7	74.5	52	49.2	56.5	53.1	53.0	55.4	61.0	61.5
Employment/population ratio	50.8	81.1	62.1	78.9	51.3	69.1	60.2	73.6	49.1	49.2	51.8	52.6	48.0	54.3	55.2	61.1
Unemployment	5.7	1.0	7.2	1.7	11.2	3.4	9.6	1.3	5.6	0.0	8.3	0.8	9.4	1.9	9.5	0.8
New Zealand																
Labour force participation	–	–	–	–	69.8	62.9	66.9	71.6	–	–	–	–	62.2	36.7	59.6	48.4
Employment/population ratio	–	–	–	–	58.9	59.5	57.2	67.7	–	–	–	–	53.2	35.4	52	46.3
Unemployment	–	–	–	–	15.6	5.5	14.6	5.5	–	–	–	–	14.4	3.5	12.8	4.2
Spain																
Labour force participation	70.8	77.6	68.3	71.5	54.7	56.1	52.7	57.8	49.4	21.9	46.1	20.3	43.1	19.3	41.8	21.5
Employment/population ratio	58.3	73.8	45.2	65.2	34.3	48.6	41.3	52.4	38.5	21.6	25.9	19.7	21.5	17.4	26.2	19.
Unemployment	17.7	5.0	33.7	8.8	37.4	13.3	21.7	9.4	22	1.1	43.7	2.9	50.1	9.8	37.3	11.2
Sweden																
Labour force participation	71.8	79.2	65.7	77.0	49.4	69.9	52.6	72.3	69.7	54.5	65.1	59.7	49.9	62.5	49.5	64.9
Employment/population ratio	68.4	77.8	60.6	73.9	40	64.5	44.8	67.1	66.0	53.3	59.7	57.4	42.8	59.4	42.8	61.0
Unemployment	4.7	1.8	7.8	4.0	19.0	7.8	14.8	7.3	5.3	2.2	8.3	3.8	14.3	5.0	13.6	5.9
Switzerland																
Labour force participation	–	–	–	–	62.7	82.1	67.9	80.9	–	–	–	–	64.7	58.8	69.3	64.0
Employment/population ratio	–	–	–	–	59.3	78.2	65.1	78.9	–	–	–	–	61.0	56.9	65.4	62.2
Unemployment	–	–	–	–	5.4	4.7	5.6	2.5	–	–	–	–	5.8	3.3	5.7	2.8

Table 1.8 cont'd

UK																
Labour force participation	–	–	69.9	71.5	75.1	64.1	73.3	63.5	–	–	–	–	65.1	40.7	65.1	41.1
Employment/population ratio	–	–	54.2	64.3	60.8	56.6	63	59.4	–	–	–	–	56.9	38.5	58.5	39.8
Unemployment	–	–	22.4	10.1	19.1	11.6	14.1	6.4	–	–	–	–	12.6	5.4	10.2	3.2
US																
Labour force participation	75.0	72.8	72.5	69.4	70.3	65.5	68.0	67.9	62.5	41.7	61.9	41.5	62.5	48.9	62.9	51.5
Employment/population ratio	66.5	70.8	59.2	65.2	61.0	62.6	61.0	66.1	54.8	40.4	52.2	39.4	55.3	47.0	57.0	50.1
Unemployment	11.4	2.7	18.4	6.1	13.2	4.4	10.3	2.7	12.2	3.2	15.8	5.0	11.6	3.9	9.5	2.6

Source: 1979, 1983 1994: OECD *Employment Outlook 1996*, p. 188; 1999: OECD *Employment Outlook 2000*, p. 211.

person households, which tends to reduce the support available within families, and the late entry of young people into the labour market. The combination of all these factors with declining fertility rates is reducing the size of the working population, who provide the resources needed to pay retirement pensions.

The latest scenario described by the United Nations Population Division shows that the population aged 60 or over in the more developed countries currently constitutes around 20 per cent of the population, a proportion which is likely to rise to 33 per cent by 2050. The older population has already exceeded the population of children aged 0–14 (19 compared with 18 per cent). The proportion of older persons is likely to be double that of children by 2050 (33 compared with 16 per cent). In Europe, the proportion of children is projected to decline from 17 to 14 per cent of the total population between 2000 and 2050, while the proportion of older persons is expected to increase from 20 per cent in 1998 to 37 per cent in 2050, increasing the ratio of the number of older persons per child from 2 to 2.6. This trend will be more marked in Germany, Greece, Italy and Japan, where there are currently at least 1.5 persons aged 60 or over for every child, with this figure rising to 4.0 in Italy and Spain by 2050. At the same time, the older population itself is ageing in the developed countries, with the oldest old (80+) constituting the fastest growing segment of the older population and representing 3.2 per cent of the total population in Northern America and 3 per cent in Europe. The oldest old currently make up 11 per cent of the 60+ age group, a proportion which is expected to reach 19 per cent by 2050 (United Nations, 2001).

In the European Union, the rate of population growth has declined since 1960 and is expected to become negative, as has already been the case in Germany since 1972 and in Italy since 1993. For the first time in recent history, the renewal of the labour force will slow down, with fewer entrants than potential exits (Calot and Chesnais, 1997).

Dependency ratios in the European Union have increased dramatically, as the numbers of people aged over 65 have grown from 18.5 per cent of the population of working age in 1970 to 23 per cent in 1995, and are expected to rise to 27 per cent in 2010 and 32 per cent in 2020. The number of people of working age for every person aged over 65 has been halved since 1950, reaching four in 2000 and probably falling to just over three by 2020. The problem is further compounded by the decline in the number of people available for work and the rise in unemployment.

Table 1.9, compiled by the ILO on the basis of data from the United Nations Population Division (*World population prospects: The 1998 revision*), gives a good idea of the magnitude and the pace of the growth of the dependency ratio in OECD countries between 1980 and 2050.

Table 1.9 Old-age dependency ratios (%) (population older than 64 to population at age 15–64)

	1980	2000	2010	2030	2050
Australia	14.7	18.0	19.8	32.2	37.5
Austria	24.0	21.5	24.0	40.3	53.6
Belgium	21.9	25.2	26.0	42.6	48.3
Canada	13.8	18.7	20.7	37.3	40.1
Denmark	22.3	22.7	25.8	38.4	40.3
Finland	17.7	22.2	25.4	43.5	44.0
France	21.9	24.4	25.3	38.7	44.2
Germany	23.7	24.0	29.6	43.3	48.7
Greece	20.5	26.7	30.3	42.3	64.5
Ireland	18.3	16.8	18.2	28.3	39.9
Italy	20.4	26.9	31.4	49.1	65.7
Luxembourg	20.0	21.2	23.4	37.1	45.2
Netherlands	17.4	20.2	23.0	43.0	49.1
New Zealand	15.7	17.7	18.9	30.4	34.3
Portugal	16.4	23.2	25.2	35.9	56.3
Spain	17.0	24.9	27.0	42.3	72.0
Sweden	25.4	27.1	29.7	43.4	46.5
UK	23.5	24.6	25.9	38.3	42.2
US	16.9	19.0	19.5	33.6	35.5

Source: *World Labour Report 2000: Income security and social protection in a changing world*, ILO, Geneva, 2000, Statistical Annex, Table 1, pp. 251–5.

There are diverse assessments of the impact of rising dependency ratios. Some are alarming, predicting that the old-age dependency ratio will double between 2000 and 2050. Others are more reassuring, based on the assumption of increased employment rates, an expansion in the active population, sustained productivity and economic growth and pay levels (Jouvenel and Parant, Chapter 5; Sigg, Feature No. 7; European

Commission Economic Policy Committee, 2000). However, it is clear that demographic changes (ageing, fertility rates) and labour market behaviour will have major implications for pension and health systems, public budgets and the funds available for investment, and hence for economic growth and social policies.

9 Questioning Prescribed Remedies

Economic theory has failed to find empirical evidence for a number of assumptions on which the labour market and social protection responses to slow growth rates and high unemployment have been based over the past three decades. The main remedies have been designed to combat labour market rigidities, particularly through the deregulation of labour and social protection legislation and the decentralization of collective bargaining (OECD, 1986). With over a decade's hindsight, the remedies do not seem to have produced a cure. On the other hand, positive economic, employment and social outcomes have been achieved through very different political approaches, leading to the conclusion that there is no one-size-fit-all solution (Sarfati, 1999).

In some quarters, for example, high minimum wages have been considered the main reason for high and persistent unemployment in Europe. The same reasoning has been applied to wage dispersion and inequality, which was thought to promote economic growth. However, by the late 1990s, there seemed to be growing awareness that the previously assumed positive correlation between low-paid jobs and labour market outcomes, and particularly employment growth, was far from established (OECD, 1996a and 1998):

> Different institutional settings, with regard to wage bargaining, legal minimum wages and the generosity of unemployment and other related benefits, appear to account for some of the wide variation across countries in the overall incidence of low pay. However, there is little solid evidence to suggest that countries where low-paid work is less prevalent have achieved this at the cost of higher unemployment rates and lower employment rates for the more vulnerable groups in the labour market, such as youth and women (OECD, 1996a, p. 76).

One of the problems with low pay is that it tends to be concentrated among women and young workers, who are twice to two-and-a-half times more exposed to low-paid jobs than full-time workers in general. This proportion is even higher for part-time workers and people in other forms of atypical jobs, many of whom are women and young persons. Low-paid jobs are also concentrated in the segments of the services sector which have been the most important source of job creation over the past decade, namely the wholesale and retail trades, hotels and catering and personal services, where many women and young workers are employed (OECD, 1996a).

This gives rise to several major policy concerns. Attempts to reduce unemployment at the expense of equality or social cohesion run counter to the fundamental principles that underpin democracy. Moreover, they may not ensure the best possible outcomes in terms of employment and social protection. Growing earnings inequality over the past two decades in the United States and the United Kingdom, although leading to better employment performance, particularly in the former, have resulted in low productivity in both (productivity started to rise only towards the end of the 1990s in the United States), an increase in the working poor in the United States and a rise in the proportion of non-earning households in the United Kingdom.

If this were the remedy to European unemployment, the implication would be that countries with greater inequality would have lower unemployment rates, while those with high wages would suffer more widespread joblessness. Yet, this is inconsistent with the facts. Unemployment rates are lower in the richer countries of Europe with better equality records, where wages are higher and social welfare systems are stronger, such as Austria, Denmark, Norway and Switzerland. By contrast, unemployment is highest in the lower-income countries with weaker social welfare systems, such as Greece, Italy and Spain. When comparing European job performance with the situation in the United States, it should be recalled that by the mid-1990s about one-third of the European population lived in countries where unemployment was lower than in the United States. Moreover, Ireland, Netherlands, Portugal and United Kingdom have now practically reached full employment, although with relatively low participation rates, while other countries, and particularly France and Spain, have managed to reduce their unemployment rates significantly in the wake of economic growth.

Growing inequality of earnings also runs counter to an efficient and competitive economy. Not only do low pay and income inequality coincide with low productivity, but they also risk acting as disincentives to enterprise investment in innovation and investment by employers and individuals in training and skills upgrading (Wilkinson, 1994). Yet these investments are indispensable for staff commitment, better work organization, improved management practices, increased product quality and the rapid introduction and diffusion of technological change, all of which are prerequisites for competitiveness and economic performance. In this respect, it is interesting to note that by 1996 the OECD was acknowledging that managerial resistance to innovative practices, the segmentation of the workforce and the frequent use of atypical employment contracts were detrimental to productivity growth and business performance (OECD, 1996b).

Other explanations commonly advanced for the high unemployment rates in Europe are the shift in demand towards higher skills, particularly due to the advent of new technologies, and job displacement to lower-wage countries. However, this argument is not fully borne out, as unemployment in Europe affects both skilled and unskilled workers. The same applies to the argument that the market can solve skills mismatches by allowing relative wages to vary according to the demand for skilled labour, or in other words, through greater wage dispersion. In practice, unemployment is just as high for unskilled workers in countries where wage dispersion has increased (particularly in Australia, Canada and United States), as in those where wage gaps have not widened (especially in Europe) (ILO, 1996, pp. 52–3). To quote the OECD once again:

> One explanation for the large differences across countries in the overall incidence of low pay could be that the skill distribution of workers is much wider in countries with a higher incidence of low-paid employment. However, at best, this can only be a partial explanation because the differences between countries in the incidence of low pay for workers in similar occupations or with similar educational qualifications are as large as, if not larger than, differences in the overall incidence. For example, under 10 per cent of workers in France with upper secondary education have low-paid jobs compared with over 32 per cent of workers in the US (OECD, 1996a, p. 71).

However, the skills gap is undoubtedly an important factor in labour market policy. Indeed, almost all new net job creation in the European Union between 1994–96 consisted of jobs with a relatively high skill content, while the only significant expansion in less-skilled jobs was in sales and service, where the bulk of the new jobs (two-thirds) have been taken by women (European Commission, 1998b, p.18).

Such findings have led Esping-Andersen to conclude that 'unemployment levels are principally influenced by macro-economic policy and by women's employment. The less women work, and the more restrictive macro-economic policy is, the more unemployment' (Esping-Andersen, 2000, p.107).

10 Concluding Remarks

This chapter started by focusing on the nature of linkages and interactivities between the labour market and social protection systems. Clearly, the two areas are closely inter-related. Developments in one affect the other, usually with the social protection system reacting to offset the adverse effects of changes in the labour market.

A proper understanding of the complexity of these inter-relations is important in the development of appropriate policy mixes to address problems that are identified and to achieve the desired objectives. However, the identification of the real problems gives rise to difficulties in view of the inadequacy of economic theory to provide explanations of the causal relationships and outcomes that are capable of achieving a broad level of political and ideological acceptance. It is evident in this respect that any policy that aims to reduce unemployment, increase participation rates and guarantee the viability of social protection schemes needs to look closely at a broad range of inter-related issues. However, a number of general developments are liable to be diversely interpreted. They include such factors as:

- the phase of the business cycle;
- the level of exposure of the economy to global competition;
- the relative dynamism of the economy, demonstrated, for example by the pace and frequency of business creation, entrepreneurship, the level of investment in research and development, and the progress achieved in innovation and the diffusion of new technologies; and

- the status of economic restructuring, as evidenced by the magnitude of the transition to services and high value-added activities, but also the extent of de-industrialization.

Moreover, labour market developments, including the changes in labour supply outlined above, are in turn often a result of changes in the demographic situation, reflecting among other factors the post-war baby-boom, early withdrawals from the labour market due to early retirement incentives, the increase in life expectancy as a result of better and more comprehensive health systems, and the shrinkage of labour supply as a result of the decline in fertility rates. They may also reflect changes in culture, behaviour, access to education and levels of remuneration, all of which are contributory factors in the significant rise in women's participation rates, with the coincident growth of single-parent or single-person households. Lastly, they are also influenced by the quality of human resources (*human capital*), as well as the incidence of low pay and the extent of income dispersion.

These factors have important implications for standards of living, the capacity to contribute to social protection and the extent to which people depend on the state for income support, irrespective of whether they are in the labour force with inadequate or unstable earnings or whether they have withdrawn from the labour market. Both situations have important implications for productivity, economic performance and growth, and consequently for the sustainability of social protection systems.

Interactions between labour markets and social protection systems are complex and involve a wide range of considerations, institutions and attitudes that transcend the immediate area in which action is taken to address a specific problem. Some measures adopted in isolation may therefore have unexpected or adverse effects, while similar measures in different political and social or industrial relations contexts may have completely different outcomes.

So what are the conclusions of this review of labour market trends and economic arguments?

First, that some of the labour market shifts described above can be reversed and are indeed actually changing under the pressure of needs and incentives. These include women returning to work after having children, people entering the labour market at an earlier age or remaining to a later age, and changes in the current three-tiered structure of education, work and retirement.

Secondly, active labour market policies are endeavouring to improve the supply, employability and availability of labour. However, they are not addressing the demand for labour, or job creation by firms, except in the form of the promotion of low-skilled precarious jobs through subsidies for employers' social contributions. This approach, while it may temporarily and marginally contribute to reducing unemployment, is insufficient to solve the problem of the hard-core unemployed.

Thirdly, the changes described above depend on existing attitudes, lifestyles and forms of social and economic organization, which also have to be adapted. This could be achieved, for example, through the development of career paths, allowing the combination of paid and unpaid activities, facilitating job re-entry or two-way mobility between full-time and part-time jobs. As argued in greater detail by many of the authors in this volume, adaptation could include measures to promote flexible approaches to retirement, including the combination of work and retirement benefit, subject to the guarantee of a sufficient level of income and the continuation of full social coverage. Changes are also proposed in the areas of taxation, benefits and labour legislation.

While welfare systems can be reformed to respond to new needs, such changes may offer different solutions to the social welfare equation and may imply major efforts of adjustment from all the actors involved, all too often (but not necessarily) at the expense of social solidarity (see, inter alia, Andersen, Chapter 2; and Madsen, Chapter 9). The development of reforms which are equitable and acceptable for both labour market *insiders* and *outsiders* requires an open-minded public debate and social dialogue on policy options, the role of the social actors and the role of the state. A debate which transcends ideology has proven to be successful to varying degrees in a number of European countries, and particularly in the Nordic countries, Austria, Ireland, Italy, Netherlands and Spain (see Lourdelle, Chapter 15; Baccaro, Feature No. 8; and Auer, 2000).

References

Auer, P. (2000), *Employment Revival in Europe: Labour market success in Austria, Denmark, Ireland and the Netherlands*, ILO, Geneva.

Calot, G. and Chesnais, J.C. (1997), *Le Vieillissement Démographique dans l'Union Européenne à l'Horizon 2050: Une étude d'impact*, Travaux et

Recherches de Prospective (6), Futuribles, LIPS, DATAR, Commissariat général du Plan, Paris.
Cebrían, I., Moreno, G., Samek, M., Semenza, R. and Toharia, L. (2000), *Atypical Work in Italy and Spain: The quest for flexibility at the margin in two supposedly rigid labour markets*, paper presented at the Conference on Nonstandard Work Arrangements in Japan, Europe and the United States (25–26 August 2000), W.E. Upjohn Institute.
Cooper-Green, E.-J. and Gigante, A. (2001), 'LFS Household Data: Spring 2000 analyses', *Labour Market Trends* (January), Office for National Statistics, London.
Doogan, K. (2001), 'Insecurity and Long-term Employment', *Work, Employment and Society*, Vol. 15, No. 3, pp. 1–23.
Du Granrut, Ch. (1988), 'Etats-Unis: l'emploi à l'horizon 2006', *Futuribles*, 233, pp. 31–45.
Economic Policy Committee (2000), *Progress Report to the Ecofin Council on the Impact of Ageing Populations on Public Pensions Systems*, European Commission, Brussels (EPC/ECFIN/581/00-EN-Rev.1).
Esping-Andersen, G. and Regini, M. (eds) (2000), *Why Deregulate Labour Markets?*, Oxford University Press, Oxford.
European Commission (1998a), *Social Protection in Europe 1997*, Luxembourg.
— (1998b), *Employment in Europe 1997*, Luxembourg.
— (1999), *Employment in Europe 1998*, Luxembourg.
— (2000), *Employment in Europe 1999*, Luxembourg.
Eurostat (2001), *News Release*, 1, 3 January.
Fitoussi, J.-P. and Passet, O. (2000), 'Réformes Structurelles et Politiques Macroéconomiques: Les enseignements des "modèles" de pays', in Fitoussi, J.-P., Passet, O. and Freyssinet, J. (eds), *Réduction du Chômage: Les réussites en Europe*, La Documentation Française, Paris.
Gadrey, J., Jany-Catrice, F. and Ribault, T. (1999), *France, Japon, Etats-Unis: L'emploi en détail*, Essai de socio-économie comparative, Presses Universitaires de France, Paris.
Hoffmann, E. and Walwei, U. (2000), *The Change in Work Arrangements Denmark and Germany: Erosion or renaissance of standards?*, paper presented at the Conference on Nonstandard Work Arrangements in Japan, Europe and the United States, (25–26 August 2000), W.E. Upjohn Institute.
Housemann, S. and Osawa, M. (2000), *The Growth of Nonstandard Employment in Japan and the United States: A comparison of causes and consequences*, paper presented at the Conference on Nonstandard Work

Arrangements in Japan, Europe and the United States, (25–26 August 2000), W.E. Upjohn Institute for Employment Research.

ILO (1996), *World Employment 1996/97: National policies in a global content*, Geneva.

ILO (2000), *World Labour Report 2000: Income security and social protection in a changing world*, Geneva.

Katz, L.F. and Krueger, A.B. (1999), 'The High-pressure U.S. Labor market of the 1990s', *Brookings Papers on Economic Activity* (1:1999), editor's summary by Brainard, W.C. and Perry, G.L.

Larsson, A. (1999), *National strategies for employment policy: Responding to the challenges of the 21st century*, address by the Director General of the European Commission DG V to the IIRA National Policy Forum (17–19 June 1999), Washington, D.C.

Nickell, S. (1997), 'Unemployment and Labour Market Rigidities: Europe versus North American', *Journal of Economic Perspectives*, Vol. 3, pp. 55–74.

OECD (1986), *Labour Market Flexibility*, Paris.

OECD (1996a), *Employment Outlook*, Paris.

OECD (1996b), *Policies and Practices for Enhancing Enterprise Flexibility* (DEELS/ELSA/ED(96)2), Paris.

OECD (1998), *Employment Outlook*, Paris.

OECD (1999), *Employment Outlook*, Paris.

OECD (2000), *Employment Outlook*, Paris.

Oxley, H., Dang, T.-T. and Antolín, P. (2000), 'Poverty Dynamics in Six OECD countries', *OECD Economic Studies No. 30* (2000/I), pp. 7–52.

Reuters (2000), 'Demand for Information Tech Workers to Exceed Supply', press release, 10 April 2000.

Sarfati, H. (1999), *Flexibilité et Création d'Emplois: Un défi pour le dialogue social en Europe*, L'Harmattan, Paris (a succinct summary of the main findings is contained in Sarfati, H. (1999), *The European Job Crisis and the Role of Labour Market Flexibility and Social Dialogue*, New Work Guest Commentary, Brave New Work World, http://www.newwork.com).

Supiot, A. (ed.) (1999), *Au-delà de l'Emploi: Transformations du travail et devenir du droit du travail en Europe*, Flammarion, Paris.

The Economist (2000), 10 June.

Trades Union Congress (2000), *The Future of Work*, TUC, London.

United Nations Population Division (2001), *World Population Prospects: The 2000 revision: Highlights* (ESA/P/WP,165), 28 February, www.un.org/esa/population/wpp2000h.pdf.

Wilkinson, F. (1994), 'Equality, Efficiency and Economic Progress: The case for universally applied equitable standards for wages and conditions of work', in Sengenberger, W. and Campbell, D. (eds), *Creating Economic Opportunities: The role of labour standards in industrial restructuring*, International Institute for Labour Studies, Geneva.

Chapter Two

Different Routes to Improved Employment in Europe

Jørgen Goul Andersen, with Jan Bendix Jensen

Introduction

During the 1990s, many economic experts and policy-makers came to agree that unemployment in Europe is mainly a structural problem rooted in the insufficient adaptation of European labour markets and welfare states to the new challenges of globalization and technological change. In broad terms, it is possible to speak of a dominant philosophy or 'standard interpretation' which explains the unemployment problems in Europe in terms of the inflexibility and disincentives of regulated labour markets, compressed wage structures and generous welfare states. Such *policies against markets* allegedly become counterproductive in a globalizing economy. The proposed solutions not only include active labour market policies, but also point to deregulation and wage flexibility as imperative elements. *Wage flexibility* means lower *de facto* minimum wages, not least aimed at creating more service jobs for low-skilled workers. Lower minimum wages, in turn, presuppose less generous social protection. In short, European welfare states are facing a trade-off, or at best a dilemma between equality and employment (OECD, 1994 and 1997; Esping-Andersen, 1999, pp. 180–84).

This *standard interpretation* was stimulated by the situation in the mid-1990s, when high unemployment was a nearly universal phenomenon in Europe. Since then, however, quite a few European countries have experienced a significant decline in unemployment. Moreover, they include countries that have adopted rather different strategies. There therefore seem to be more routes to improved employment than have generally hitherto been recognized. This points to a need to examine such alternative routes more carefully. Indeed, the experience of the mid-1990s gave rise to overly pessimistic interpretations concerning the overall sustainability of European welfare arrangements which were coloured by the effects of the tightening of fiscal policies to meet the convergence criteria for Economic and Monetary Union. Such *sound* policies may be beneficial in the long term, but undoubtedly aggravated the employment crisis in the short run. Assertions concerning the flexibility of the United States economy also deserve attention. This chapter examines variations between European countries, highlights alternative routes and discusses the compatibility between maintaining generous social protection and improving employment.

The *Standard Interpretation* of Structural Unemployment

According to the standard interpretation outlined in Figure 2.1, unemployment in Europe is a *structural* problem which has its roots in inflexible labour markets. Even high economic growth will only improve unemployment up to the threshold of structural unemployment, which is defined in terms of compatibility with price or wage stability.[1] If actual unemployment comes below that level, employers will start competing for skilled workers who are already employed, rather than hiring unemployed people with low skills and low productivity. This, in turn, leads to rising prices, reduced competitiveness and renewed recession.

The core problem is the gap between wages and productivity for less skilled workers. Logically, there are three solutions to this problem:

- *wage flexibility* through lower minimum wages and less compressed wage structures that reflect differences in productivity. This presupposes less generous social protection in order to secure lower *reservation wages* (that is, the lowest wage for which the individual is willing to accept a job) among the unemployed. If the distributional consequences for the working poor are unacceptable, this may be alleviated through some kind of tax compensation. Not surprisingly, the labour movement prefers to bridge the gap by:
- *higher qualifications*, both among the labour force in general, and the unemployed in particular. Finally:
- *the costs of low-productive service labour may be reduced* through a variety of direct or indirect subsidies (such as reducing value added tax for particular services).

Figure 2.1 The *standard interpretation* of structural unemployment: problem definitions and possible solutions

Problem	Solution
1 Gap between wages and productivity for low-skilled workers	1.1 More wage flexibility: Less compressed wage structures/lower reservation wages * this presupposes less generous social protection * inequality may be alleviated by tax compensation
	1.2 Higher productivity * activation of the unemployed * education/qualification
	1.3 Subsidize low-productive services
2 Inflexibility and distortions prevent smooth functioning of markets	2.1 More flexible employment protection 2.2 More flexible working time 2.3 Avoid distortions/disincentives in tax/welfare system 2.4 More strict work test/welfare

There are also other disturbances to the smooth functioning of markets which lead to higher structural unemployment and/or lower competitiveness (see points 2.1–2.4 in Figure 2.1). These include: over rigid employment protection; inflexible working hours; disincentives in the tax/welfare system; and overly easy access to unemployment benefits. Once again, the main proposed solution is deregulation and improved work incentives. Structural unemployment is basically seen as a question of the disturbance of market forces and most solutions, such as wage flexibility, flexible employment protection and flexible working time, are intended to restore market flexibility. Together with general measures to stimulate growth and productivity, the solutions sketched out in Figure 2.1 reflect, among others, the interpretations and proposals of the OECD Jobs Strategy (OECD, 1994 and 1999e), which recommends a mix of systemic changes to promote greater flexibility, less generous social protection, activation and stricter tests of the availability of the unemployed for work. Although more active labour market policies are also part of the package, it should be noted that the OECD did not make many country-specific recommendations for the United States (OECD, 1999a).

Employment is not impeded by globalization and technological change as such. Instead, these processes reduce demand for low-skilled labour and, at the same time, limit the range of policy alternatives that can be used to address the problem. This makes it difficult to escape the trade-off between equality and employment. To some extent, this view has even been accepted by sworn supporters of the welfare state (Esping-Andersen, 1996 and 1999; however, Esping-Andersen and Regini, 2000, emphasize that they are referring to adjustments at the margin), whereas prominent sociologists (Giddens, 1998 and 2000; and Gilbert, 1995) have endorsed the argument that a side effect of social protection may be the development of a *dependency culture* among benefit recipients that is passed on from one generation to another (Murray, 1984; for criticism of this argument see, for example, Dean and Taylor-Gooby, 1992).

More than anything, this diagnosis achieved credibility on the basis of a comparison between Europe and the United States (see Figure 2.2). For more than two decades, unemployment rates in the United States had been around twice the European average. But since the mid-1980s, it has been the other way round, with European unemployment rates around twice the level in the United States. Indeed, from an economic perspective, employment rates were even more alarming. In the United States, employment rates showed a nearly constant increase, while in Europe they declined or stagnated because of attempts to combat unemployment by reducing labour supply, especially through early retirement. This generated an image of *Eurosclerosis*, that is of European welfare states being caught up in structures of inflexibility, in which the attempts of the welfare state to combat unemployment were of little effect in the short term and made the situation even more unsustainable in the long term.

European Variations by 2000: a Different Picture

While aggregate data for Europe and the United States still confirm the standard interpretation, as described above, country variations increasingly indicate that there are many different routes to improved employment and reduced unemployment in Europe. Before considering

Figure 2.2 Unemployment and employment rates in Europe (EU 15) and the United States, 1960–96

Employment rates 1960–96
(total employment as a percentage of population from 16 to 64 years)

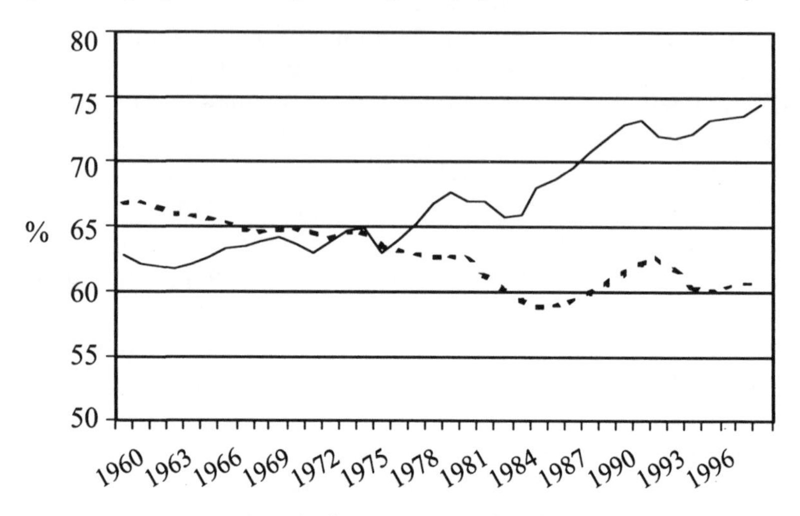

Unemployment rates 1960–96
(unemployment as a percentage of total labour force)

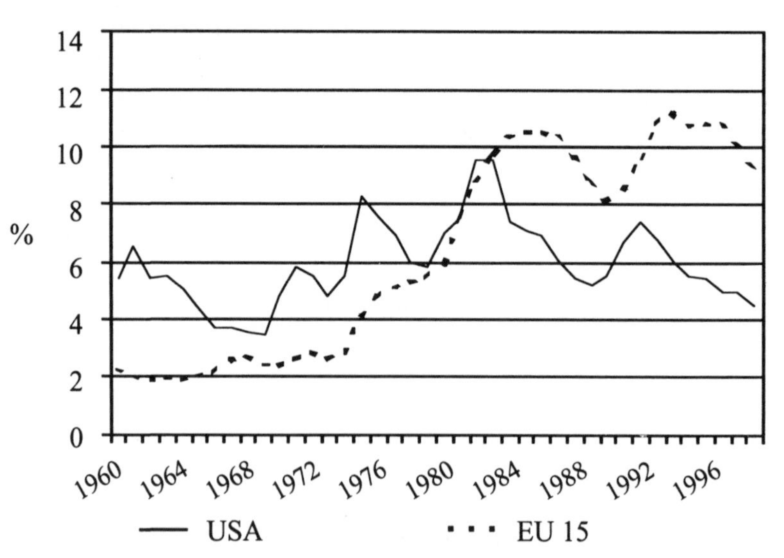

Source: OECD Historical Statistics, 1999 (CD-ROM) and OECD (2000) *Economic Outlook.*

some of the arguments and the empirical evidence vis-à-vis the standard interpretation more systematically, this and the following section explore the labour market situation in the United States and Western Europe in a little more detail.

For descriptive purposes, the point of departure is taken from Esping-Andersen's well-known distinction between three ideal-typical welfare state regimes: liberal, conservative and social democratic (Esping-Andersen, 1990). These models find their closest empirical counterparts in the Anglo-Saxon, Continental European and Scandinavian countries, respectively. A liberal welfare regime is defined by its emphasis on the market and by the deliberately chosen limited role of the welfare state. A conservative regime is a performance-oriented model based on social contributions and a high level of protection, especially for male breadwinners. Within this type, scholars often separate a family-oriented Mediterranean sub-type (Ferrera, 1996; Kuhnle and Alestalo, 2000; Gallie and Paugam, 2000). Finally, the so-called social democratic model is based on universal all-encompassing protection, combined with a high level of public services.

Considering these ideal types in relation to the standard interpretation, it would be predicted that the liberal model would be well-equipped to meet the new challenges, including the provision of low-skilled service jobs, but with the risk of producing a group of working poor, as well as an underclass of welfare recipients with insufficient resources to care for themselves. The social democratic model would tend to produce too few service jobs in the private sector due to high wages, although up to some critical limit this might be compensated by public service employment. Finally, the conservative ideal type, with its strong protection of male breadwinners, would tend to block the entry of women and the young, reinforce insider/outsider divisions and limit the creation of service jobs in both the private and public sectors. To protect breadwinners, this model tends to stimulate early retirement and low employment rates (Esping-Andersen, 1996 and 1999; van Kersbergen, 1995). The conservative model is therefore often assumed to be particularly vulnerable, although it is acknowledged that it tends to produce a highly productive labour force.

By 1994, the division between Europe and the United States largely corresponded with the situation at the level of the individual countries (see Table 2.1). Norway, Switzerland and Luxembourg constituted exceptions which could be explained by their special economies (oil resources, financial centres and immigrants as a buffer). Even Sweden's much heralded *third way* of active labour market policy had failed, with its main effect being to conceal a level of unemployment that was much higher than the official rate of nearly 10 per cent (Sorrentino, 1995, pp. 45–46). However, by 2000, the sharp division between the United States and Europe has been blurred by the success of many European countries (Table 2.1). In Denmark, Ireland, Netherlands and the United Kingdom, unemployment rates declined significantly in the second half of the 1990s, and in 2000/01 even Sweden joined the group of countries with low unemployment rates. To these should be added the *special economies* (Norway, Luxembourg and Switzerland), as well as Austria and Portugal, which in fact maintained fairly low unemployment rates throughout the 1980s and 1990s, but tended to be overlooked in the overall picture. This also means that the *special economies* are not so special any more.

By 2000, Western European countries with unemployment rates around or below 5 per cent in fact outnumbered those with high unemployment. Moreover, among the small open economies, only Belgium, Finland and Greece maintained high unemployment rates by 2000.

This raises the question of what needs to be explained – the successes or the failures? There are at least plausible explanations as to why Belgium, Finland and Greece have performed less well than other small countries. True, the small countries do not count much in aggregate figures, since unemployment has remained high in France, Germany, Italy and Spain. But it would nevertheless appear that there are other solutions than those suggested by the standard interpretation.

Furthermore, considering the unusually tight economic policies applied to meet the convergence criteria for the Euro, even the overall unemployment record of the European welfare states is perhaps not that bad after all. By August 2000, unemployment in European Union countries was down to 8.4 per cent, and this fall is expected to continue in 2001. The issue is also contested as to whether the high German unemployment rate in the 1990s should be ascribed to structural problems in the German welfare/labour market system. Until 1992, Germany was the strong economy of Europe *par excellence*, and there is little doubt that the immense costs of unification, combined with an explosion of opportunities to invest in neighbouring Central European countries, bear part of the responsibility (Manow and Seils, 2000; Ludwig-Mayerhofer, 2000).

Table 2.1 Standardized unemployment rates in Western Europe, 1980–2000 % of the labour force

	1980	1985	1990	1991	1992	1993	1994	1995	1996	1997	1998	1999	Aug. 2000
Portugal	7.7 [1]	8.7	4.6	4.0	4.2	5.7	7.0	7.3	7.3	6.8	5.2	4.5	3.8
Greece	2.8 [1]	7.8 [1]	6.4	7.0	7.9	8.6	8.9	9.2	9.6	9.8	10.7	–	–
Spain	10.5	21.7	16.3	16.4	18.4	22.7	24.1	22.9	22.2	20.8	18.8	15.9	14.5
Italy	5.6	8.3	9.0	8.6	8.8	10.3	11.2	11.6	11.7	11.7	11.8	11.3	10.5
France	5.8	10.1	9.0	9.5	10.4	11.7	12.3	11.7	12.4	12.3	11.8	11.3	9.6
Belgium	9.3	10.4	6.7	6.6	7.2	8.8	10.0	9.9	9.7	9.4	9.5	9.1	8.6
NL	6.1	8.3	6.2	5.8	5.6	6.6	7.1	6.9	6.3	5.2	4.1	3.3	2.7
Luxembourg	0.7 [1]	2.9	1.7	1.7	2.1	2.6	3.2	2.9	3.0	2.7	2.7	2.3	2.2
Germany	2.6	7.2	4.8	4.2	4.5	7.9	8.5	8.2	8.9	9.9	9.4	8.8	8.3
Austria	1.9 [1]	3.6 [1]	–	–	–	4.0	3.8	3.9	4.4	4.4	4.5	3.8	3.2
Denmark	6.9 [1]	7.3 [1]	7.7	8.5	9.2	10.1	8.2	7.3	6.8	5.6	5.2	5.2	4.9
Sweden	2.0	2.9	1.7	3.1	5.6	9.1	9.4	8.8	9.6	9.9	8.3	7.2	5.9
Norway	1.7	2.7	5.3	5.6	6.0	6.1	5.5	5.0	4.9	4.1	3.3	3.2	3.2
Finland	5.3	6.0	3.2	6.7	11.6	16.4	16.7	15.3	14.6	12.6	11.4	10.2	9.7
Ireland	7.3 [1]	16.9	13.4	14.8	15.4	15.6	14.4	12.3	11.7	9.9	7.6	5.7	4.4
UK	6.2	11.5	7.1	8.9	10.0	10.5	9.6	8.7	8.2	7.0	6.3	6.1	5.3
Switzerland	0.2 [1]	0.9 [1]	–	2.0	3.1	4.0	3.8	3.5	3.9	4.2	3.5	–	–
EU 15	–	–	–	8.3	9.2	10.7	11.1	10.7	10.8	10.6	9.9	9.2	8.4
US	7.2	7.2	5.6	6.8	7.5	6.9	6.1	5.6	5.4	4.9	4.5	4.2	4.1

Notes

1 Not standardized rates: based on national definitions.
2 Entries are *standardized unemployment rates*, i.e. unemployment as a percentage of the civilian labour force. Today, these figures are largely comparable across the Atlantic. For details about comparability, see Sorrentino, 2000.

Sources: 1980–1989: OECD, 1999c, 2000a and 2000b.

In terms of European welfare regimes, moderate to low unemployment rates are to be found in both the most liberal regimes (Switzerland and the United Kingdom) and in the Nordic countries (where Finland may legitimately be considered a special case, due to the sudden loss of the Russian market). However, among the Continental European welfare states, Austria and the Netherlands (and perhaps Portugal) stand out as being even more successful, thereby confirming the finding of economic analyses that social insurance-based systems as such do not have any impact on unemployment (Calmfors and Holmlund, 2000).

The Level and Structure of Employment in Europe

Economists have also been concerned about low labour force participation rates in Europe. In 1960, the labour force participation rate was highest in Europe, but in the 1990s the rate in the United States rose to become some 8–9 per cent higher than in Europe (OECD, 2000a).

However, the European pattern is heterogeneous, with dividing lines largely following welfare models. In Scandinavia and Switzerland, the figures were around 80 per cent for the 15–64 age group in 1999, which was even slightly higher than in the United Kingdom and the United States. In Greece, Italy and Spain, the figures were 60–64 per cent. The other countries of the European Union fall in between, from a low of 65 per cent in Belgium to 74 per cent in the Netherlands, which is dissociating itself from the Continental European pattern of *inactivity*. Countries with a high labour market participation rate also tend to have low unemployment. This is not surprising, but clearly argues against the once popular philosophy that the reduction of the labour force would reduce unemployment.

That philosophy has contributed to the declining labour force participation rates of European men, particularly in Belgium, France and Italy, where it was below 75 per cent in 1999, compared with 84–85 per cent in Denmark, Norway and the United States. Even in Sweden and Finland, the figures have dropped to 81 and 76 per cent, respectively, while male participation rates in the Netherlands increased to 83 per cent in 1999, a rise of 3 per cent since 1995. In most other countries, the trend also reversed at the end of the 1990s. However, the Swiss figure of 89.6 per cent, compared with an average of 78.4 per cent in the

European Union, demonstrates that there is still a significant loss of male labour power in all the other countries.

As pointed out in Chapter One, the rise in the labour force participation rates of women became universal in the 1990s. This has typically been accompanied by an increase in part-time employment, most significantly in the Netherlands, although less so in the Mediterranean countries. However, higher part-time employment among women is *not* a universal phenomenon. In Denmark, Norway and Sweden, which were the first countries to introduce part-time employment on a massive scale, it has declined significantly, for example, from 29.6 per cent in 1990 to 22.7 per cent in 1999 in Denmark. The United States also experienced a decline, from 20 to 19 per cent. This would tend to indicate that part-time employment may be only a first step towards full integration, but it remains to be seen whether the new one-and-a-half breadwinner families in Europe will eventually become two-breadwinner families.

At any rate, part-time employment modifies the picture of some European *job miracles*. Unfortunately, comparability is bad, but as country differences are very large, it is possible to obtain a very rough comparison of the total amount of work per capita across European countries by multiplying national estimates of average working hours with employment rates for the population aged 15–64 (OECD, 2000a). This leaves Italy as the country with the lowest level of paid labour, with a mere 865 hours worked per capita in 1999 for the population aged 15–64. In Germany, the estimate is 1010 hours, which is roughly equivalent to the Netherlands, where short-time labour gives an exaggerated picture of work performance (van Oorschot, 2000). In Sweden, the figure is 1191 hours, while in Switzerland and the United Kingdom it is well above 1200 hours, although still far below the figure for the United States of 1460 hours per capita for the working age population. As noted above, these figures should be interpreted only as rough indications, although they neatly summarize the difference in work efforts across the Atlantic. Whether they are at the same time an indicator of sustainability, however, is questionable.

Nevertheless, the most interesting question is still who works and who does not. In particular, an examination will be made of the exclusion of young and older workers, as well as the protection of prime age groups. To avoid conflating the effects of rising female labour market participation rates with other underlying trends, Tables 2.2 and 2.3 focus

Table 2.2 Labour force participation rates for men, by age group

	15–19[1]		20–24		25–34		35–44		45–54		55–59		60–64	
	1983	**1999**	**1983**	**1999**	**1983**	**1999**	**1983**	**1999**	**1983**	**1999**	**1983**	**1999**	**1983**	**1999**
Portugal	66.2	28.3	88.8	71.3	96.5	93.2	96.0	94.7	90.4	90.9	76.9	74.5	62.7	54.5
Greece[2]	31.8	18.8	76.7	70.1	96.5	95.2	97.3	97.2	91.8	90.6	78.7	71.7	69.8	45.4
Spain	51.5	32.2	82.9	66.8	95.4	92.2	96.4	94.9	91.8	90.7	81.7	74.9	58.9	39.8
Italy[3]	30.6	21.9	73.8	64.2	91.6	81.0	98.2	95.0	97.1	95.0	82.0	68.4	36.8	31.3
France	22.5	11.1	79.7	55.1	96.5	93.2	97.8	96.1	93.7	93.0	71.0	67.7	33.7	16.7
Belgium	19.8	10.6	72.8	60.4	96.0	94.1	96.5	94.7	90.3	86.1	65.0	53.4	28.6	20.3
Netherlands[2]	28.4	56.2	76.3	81.0	94.6	94.9	93.5	95.1	86.9	90.8	69.2	66.7	37.4	23.2
Germany	44.3	35.0	78.2	77.4	89.4	91.9	98.3	96.5	95.5	93.2	81.4	76.4	40.3	29.7
Austria[2]	–	47.7	–	74.4	–	92.4	–	96.3	–	91.1	–	63.2	–	13.2
Denmark	52.2	66.5	86.9	86.8	94.4	93.1	95.6	94.5	91.9	90.5	83.8	80.4	50.1	42.0
Sweden	47.7	29.8	84.4	70.1	94.4	88.7	96.3	91.5	94.4	90.8	–	–	–	–
Norway	49.3	50.5	82.1	79.3	91.6	91.7	98.2	93.0	96.4	90.7	84.0	84.7	76.8	61.1
Finland	39.7	30.8	81.9	68.9	95.0	91.8	95.8	92.9	88.2	87.2	64.2	62.7	41.1	25.0
Ireland	43.1	33.1	89.4	78.0	97.1	93.8	96.4	93.1	92.2	87.2	–	–		
UK	71.6	64.1	90.2	81.2	95.8	93.3	96.5	92.9	93.5	88.2	82.8	75.2	57.5	50.3
EU 15[4]	38.9	34.6	78.8	71.7	92.1	91.3	95.3	95.8	91.8	92.4	74.2	70.1	41.0	30.2
US	56.2	52.9	84.8	81.9	94.2	93.3	95.3	92.8	91.2	88.8	81.9	78.4	57.0	54.81

Notes

1 For Norway, Spain, Sweden, United Kingdom and United States, this age category is 16 to 19.
2 Figures for 1999 refer to 1998.
3 Age categories are: 15–19, 20–24, 25–29, 30–39, 40–49 and 50–59.
4 EU 15 average weighted by total population, excluding countries with missing data.

Source: OECD, 2000c.

on men only. Table 2.2 shows the labour force participation rate of men, by age group. The figures for the young are very high in Denmark, Netherlands, Norway, United Kingdom and United States. First and foremost, this reflects the fact that students with a second job are formally counted as members of the labour force. However, from a social perspective, this provides a quite biased image of the labour market. Danish register-based data show that aggregate participation rates (for both sexes between the ages of 15 and 64) decline from 82.5 to 73.4 per cent if students are not included (Goul Andersen, 2000).

In most other countries, higher education rates contribute to a lower level of labour market participation, as does early retirement. Indeed, in the 1980s and 1990s, a very significant decline may be noted among the 60–64 age group, and to some extent among the 55–59 age group, in contrast with the situation in the United States. But European figures also diverge widely, from 51 per cent among the 55–59 age group in Belgium to 87 per cent in Norway.

Prime age men are traditionally the main target of social protection in Continental European welfare states. Because in some countries quite a few students are in the 25–34 age category, it has been necessary to choose the 35–54 category as the 'prime age' group. As can be seen from Table 2.2, labour market participation rates in this group are higher in Europe than in the United States, despite aggregate differences. It may also be noted that, for this group, even the United Kingdom and Scandinavia are below the European average, whereas figures are extremely high among Continental European countries. The job protection of prime age men is also reflected in their low unemployment rates (see Table 2.3). In Italy, unemployment among men aged 35–54 was close to zero in 1991, due to the former priorities of Italian employment offices, which allocated jobs with a strong preference to male breadwinners (Ferrera and Gualmini, 2000). Even in Spain, unusually high job protection has secured low unemployment rates for prime age men (Moreno, 2000). By 1991, only a handful of European countries had unemployment rates for this group that were as high as those in the United States. However, the protection of prime age men deteriorated in Europe in the 1990s, and by 1998 even Italy was no longer able to maintain full employment for this category any longer. The combination of high labour force participation and low unemployment meant that employment among prime age men used to be higher in Europe than in the United States. As shown in Table 2.3,

Table 2.3 Unemployment and employment rates by age, men only, 1991 and 1999: percentages of labour force by population group

	Unemployment rates				Employment rates			
	35–44		45–54		35–44		45–54	
	1991	1999	1991	1999	1991	1999	1991	1999
Greece[1]	2.6	4.4	2.1	4.2	94.0	92.9	88.1	86.8
Portugal	1.7	3.0	1.2	3.4	95.2	91.9	89.3	87.8
Spain	7.5	7.8	7.5	6.9	89.1	87.5	84.5	84.4
Italy[2]	4.0	6.8	2.0	3.9	93.2	88.5	94.3	91.3
France	5.0	7.7	5.2	7.5	92.2	88.7	88.0	86.0
Belgium	3.2	5.4	3.2	5.9	92.0	89.6	83.7	81.0
Netherlands[1, 3]	3.7	2.6	4.1	2.7	91.7	92.6	85.2	88.3
Germany	3.9	6.9	4.0	7.6	93.4	89.8	90.7	86.1
Austria[1]	2.5	3.8	3.2	4.1	–	92.6	–	87.4
Denmark	7.2	2.6	7.1	4.2	88.2	92.0	87.3	86.7
Sweden	2.3	6.9	1.7	5.5	93.4	85.2	92.6	85.8
Norway	3.7	2.6	3.1	2.1	90.5	90.6	87.6	88.8
Finland	6.2	7.1	5.6	8.0	88.2	86.3	82.5	80.2
Ireland	13.1	5.7	11.2	6.0	80.7	87.8	78.4	82.0
UK	6.7	5.2	6.3	4.9	89.2	88.1	85.7	83.9
EU 15	4.9	6.3	4.5	5.9	90.0	90.1	88.6	86.3
US	5.5	2.8	4.8	2.6	88.9	90.2	86.2	86.5

Notes

1 Figures for 1999 refer to 1998.
2 Age categories are 30–39 and 40–49.
3 Age categories are 25–39 and 40–49.

Source: OECD, 2000c. Note that figures are not standardized.

this is no longer the case, although the difference is now negligible. Until the mid-1990s, Continental European welfare states therefore remained superior in fulfilling their main rationale, namely securing employment for prime age men. As pointed out by Buchele and Christiansen, non-employment among prime age men is the only truly comparable figure across countries (Buchele and Christiansen, 1999). However, it does not follow that this is the only figure that matters.

Structure of Unemployment

What is achieved in terms of employment protection for prime age men is often lost for other population groups. As pointed out in Chapter One, unemployment in Europe has a strong but declining gender bias. On average, the ratio between female and male unemployment declined from 1.6 to 1.3 in the 1990s (see Table 2.4 below). In Southern Europe, Belgium and the Netherlands, the ratio was 1.9 or higher in 1990, but had weakened a great deal by the late 1990s. In Austria and Germany, the gender bias is very small, as it is in Scandinavia, where a systematic gender bias is only found in Denmark. In the United Kingdom, women's unemployment rates are even systematically below those of men.

Table 2.4 Unemployment rates for women relative to men, for young relative to prime age persons and for the long-term unemployed (LTU) as percentages of the labour force, 1999

	Women/ men	15–24 years/ 25–54 years	LTU (12 months or more) as percentage of labour force
Portugal	1.3	2.2	1.9
Greece	2.3	3.3	6.0
Spain	2.1	2.1	8.2
Italy	1.8	3.5	7.2
France	1.3	2.5	4.8
Belgium	1.4	3.1	5.3
Netherlands	1.8	2.5	1.5
Germany	1.1	1.1	4.5
Austria	1.0	1.3	1.5
Denmark	1.3	2.3	1.1
Sweden	.9	2.3	2.4
Norway	.9	4.0	.2
Finland	1.1	2.6	3.0
Ireland	.9	1.6	3.3
UK	.8	2.5	1.8
Switzerland	1.3	2.2	1.2
EU 15	1.3	2.1	4.4
US	1.1	3.1	0.3

Source: Calculated from OECD, 2000a. Unemployment rates not standardized.

Long-term unemployment also mirrors the job protection enjoyed by prime age men. In Southern Europe, with the exception of Portugal, between 6 and 8 per cent of the labour force has been unemployed for more than one year. In Belgium, France and Germany, the figure is 4–5 per cent. In other European countries, it is 1–3 per cent, although only Norway compares with the figure of 0.3 per cent in the United States.

Youth unemployment also belongs to the seamy side of the job protection of insiders. In Italy and Spain, youth unemployment varied between 25 and 45 per cent during the 1990s, while it was between 20 and 30 per cent in Belgium and France. Youth unemployment is above the average unemployment rate in all countries except Germany (see Table 2.4). In Scandinavia, however, this depends on definitions. According to the ILO definition, under the terms of which students seeking a job are counted as unemployed, youth unemployment in Denmark and Sweden is about twice the general level. But if students are excluded, youth unemployment in Denmark is significantly below average. In Sweden, using the ILO definition, students inflate the country's total employment figures by almost 2 percentage points in comparison with the national definition, which does not count full-time students as being unemployed (Sorrentino, 2000, p.19).

It is worth noting that highly regulated countries, such as Austria and Germany, have been more successful in fighting youth unemployment than the United Kingdom and the United States, despite market-oriented reforms targeted at the young (Clasen and Taylor-Gooby, 2000). According to the standard interpretation, market-oriented systems would be expected to be particularly well-equipped to reduce youth unemployment. Moreover, such systems should be most efficient in avoiding unemployment among the low-skilled. But the empirical data provided in Table 2.5 show that the effect of education on employment levels is even stronger in the United States than in Europe. In 1998, there was a variation of between 8.5 and 2.1 per cent between education groups in the United States. In Europe, the variation is between 10.6 to 6.0 per cent. Of the European countries, the educational bias seems broadest in the *flexible* United Kingdom. Furthermore, educational biases are above average in *activation-oriented* Scandinavia, and lowest in Southern Europe, where *passive* policies prevailed until recently.

These data are open to multiple interpretations, although it would appear that, contrary to theoretical expectations, enormous wage differences, such as those in the United States, do not solve the

Table 2.5 Unemployment by educational attainment for persons aged 25–64, 1996 and 1998

	1998				1996
	Less than upper secondary education	Upper secondary education	Tertiary level education	Low/ high ratio	Low/ high ratio
Portugal	4.3	4.3	2.6	1.7	2.0
Greece	6.5	9.6	7.3	0.9	0.8
Spain	17.0	15.3	13.1	1.3	1.4
Italy	10.8	8.7	7.0	1.5	1.3
France	14.9	9.5	6.6	2.3	2.2
Belgium	13.1	7.4	3.2	4.1	3.7
Netherlands	6.2	3.2	2.3	2.7	2.0
Germany	16.6	10.8	5.6	3.0	2.7
Austria[1]	9.0	5.8	3.3	2.7	2.6
Denmark	7.0	4.6	3.3	2.1	3.0
Sweden	10.4	7.2	3.6	2.9	2.3
Norway[1]	4.0	3.1	1.7	2.4	1.9
Finland[1]	15.6	11.9	6.5	2.4	3.0
Ireland	11.6	4.5	3.0	3.9	4.0
UK	10.5	5.0	2.6	4.0	3.1
Switzerland	5.6	2.8	2.8	2.0	2.4
EU 15	10.6	9.1	6.0	1.8	2.1
US	8.5	4.4	2.1	4.0	4.5

Note

1 The 1998 figure is for 1997.

Source: OECD, 2000a. Not standardized rates.

unemployment problems of low-skilled people. Furthermore, there is a low propensity to move up from low wage groups (OECD, 1998). It would also appear that on both sides of the Atlantic the greatest improvement during the 1996–98 economic upturn was achieved among the lower educated. This again questions the standard interpretation, which sees structural unemployment as an expression of *sedimentation,* whereby the structurally unemployed are those who cannot return to work, even during an economic upswing. In practice, the data would tend to indicate a simple *creaming* effect, as a result of which, during recessions, employers prefer the better skilled, who even take over the jobs of the less skilled. Yet this is an old and well-known effect which is not tantamount to structural unemployment and does not dictate any market-oriented reforms.

Policy Change and Policy Effects

Few alternatives have been elaborated to the standard interpretation, although some current explanations of policy successes implicitly rest on quite different interpretations. For instance, corporatism is a key factor in recent attempts to explain the *Dutch miracle* (Visser and Hemerijck, 1997), as well as the differences between Austria and the Netherlands, on the one hand, and between Belgium and Germany, on the other hand (Hemerijck, Unger and Visser, 2000; Hemerijck, Manow and van Kersbergen, 2000; Hemerijck and Visser, 2000; see also Bonoli, George and Taylor-Gooby, 2000, ch. 7). However, this explanation implicitly seems to rest on the assumption that competitiveness and wage moderation are the key problems in a global competitive economy. Indeed, wage moderation is exactly the policy goal that corporatism is designed to obtain. This is explicitly acknowledged in Hemerijck, Unger and Visser, who endorse the interpretation of the Dutch Central Planning Bureau that:

> wage moderation has been the single most important weapon in the Dutch adjustment strategy (...) *two-thirds of job growth between 1983 to 1996 should be attributed to wage moderation.*

They also conclude that:

> looking back on twenty-five years of policy adjustment, one is struck by the ongoing importance of wage restraint for maintaining competitiveness (...) Apparently there were no alternative policy options in economies exposed to international competition (Hemerijck, Unger and Visser, 2000, pp. 228 and 252).

From the point of view of the standard interpretation, corporatism would seem to be part of the problem (van Oorschot, 2000). Even if corporatism is less immovable than once believed, solidaristic wage policy and compressed wage structures (as well as generous social protection) should tend to be the corollary of wage moderation. They should aggravate structural unemployment problems because of the gap between minimum wages and productivity for low-skilled workers.[2] If corporatism proves to be efficient, it would therefore tend to challenge the standard interpretation of unemployment.

Wage moderation is part of the traditional economic policy tool kit, but is not a policy directed towards structural reforms. Figure 2.3 presents a tentative classification of policy options in accordance with their underlying assumptions about the nature and causes of unemployment. It also represents a historical development (and a learning process) from traditional macroeconomic steering rooted in variants of Keynesianism, to structural (supply side) strategies aimed at modifying market distortions and restoring incentives (strategies 4–6).

From Demand Strategy to Competitiveness

When the first oil crisis hit Western economies in the mid-1970s, the routine reaction of most governments was to stimulate aggregate demand. In most cases, this strategy came to be seen as inefficient, leading to stagflation, unless combined with a very tight incomes policy (Scharpf, 1987; Hemerijck, Unger and Visser, 2000). Another negative side effect was the increase in state debt, which became a structural problem in many countries as the expected economic recovery failed to materialize. In the early 1980s, Belgium and Denmark were prototypical illustrations of the problem of the accumulation of deficits and increasing interest payments on state debts (Goul Andersen and Christiansen, 1991). Moreover, a strategy of devaluation, which had been widely used in small European economies, was given up in many cases. These strategies proved counterproductive in a globalized economy.[3] For small countries, there was no alternative to a fixed currency policy, anti-inflationary policies and balanced state budgets.

In the 1990s, the convergence criteria for joining the Euro were welcomed as an opportunity to shift the blame for carrying out such policies. Nevertheless, the simultaneous tightening of state budgets throughout Europe in the 1990s had a negative impact on employment,

Figure 2.3 A tentative typology of (un)employment policies

Stimulate domestic demand	1 *Demand strategy*: stimulate aggregate demand, or increase public sector employment
Competitiveness	2 *Competitiveness strategy*: devaluations wage moderation (corporatism, incomes policy) lower corporate taxes, social contributions, higher subsidies
Redistribution of labour	3 *Reduction/redistribution of labour supply*: early exit shorter working hours/longer holidays leave programmes
Structural strategies	4 *Activation/qualification strategy*: education, job training
	5 *Marketing/incentive strategy*: lower minimum wages less generous social protection (lower benefits, shorter duration, tighter eligibility criteria) stronger work incentives: lower income taxes more flexible employment protection more flexible working-time service strategy: subsidies to household services, lower VAT
	6 *Stronger controls/stronger requirements*: stronger work test and mobility requirements 'workfare': duty to work in return for benefits

and the constraints that apply to individual countries do not necessarily apply to entire economic regions acting jointly. If there is one common denominator for nearly all countries with a positive record in relation to unemployment, it seems to be the adoption of *sound* economic policies. Even the German record on unemployment before and after reunification, respectively, seems to confirm this proposition (Ludwig-Mayerhofer, 2000). And the Swedish crisis in the 1990s was strongly aggravated by a partly unfinanced tax reform in 1990, inspired by the idea of the dynamic effects of work incentives (Furåker, 2000).

For small open economies, emphasis on competitiveness, including wage moderation, came to be seen as mandatory. But two questions remain. How can this be obtained? And is it sufficient? In relation to the first question, empirical findings indicate that both strongly centralized and strongly decentralized wage formation have positive effects on wage formation and employment (Calmfors and Holmlund, 2000). The United Kingdom is an illustration of this latter path (Clasen and Taylor-Gooby, 2000), while the former is demonstrated by Austria, Netherlands and Sweden. However, the standard interpretation tends to see wage moderation as basically a dependent variable which, due to wage drift, is almost impossible to control if structural unemployment is high.

Reduction/Redistribution of Labour Supply

As other means seemed inefficient, nearly all European countries came to adopt a series of policies aiming at a redistribution or reduction of labour supply. This was rarely rooted in any philosophy that new technology would lead to a permanent reduction in the need for labour (see, for example, Gorz, 1981 and Offe, 1996), but tended to be dictated more by urgent political needs and often took the form of temporary measures. Once in action, however, such measures proved difficult to reverse. These measures include a large variety of early exit arrangements, leave programmes, shorter working hours and longer holidays. Together, they added up to what critics dubbed a *politics of inactivity*, perhaps most visible in the case of the *Dutch disease* in the mid-1980s (van Kersbergen, 1995; Esping-Andersen, 1996).

According to the standard interpretation, measures such as early retirement are ineffective or counterproductive, especially when seen from a dynamic perspective and taking into account higher wage increases and their behavioural effects, as both employers and employees invest less in maintaining qualifications. On the other hand, early retirement has been a means of enhancing productivity and supporting flexibility in countries with high employment protection. Nevertheless, in the 1990s, concern about ageing populations and dependency ratios placed such arrangements under pressure, with most countries taking action to reverse the trend.

Structural Strategies

A common feature of the above strategies is the assumption that sustainable economic growth (or the redistribution of labour) will over time be able to eliminate, or at least reduce unemployment. According to the standard interpretation, this will not happen under even the most favourable economic growth conditions, as wage drift is inevitable when unemployment reaches the level of structural unemployment. This is the foundation for the structural strategies of activation, flexibility, incentives and stronger controls.

However, the effects of these policies would not appear to be particularly convincing. In the case of activation most, although by no means all programmes seem to have measurable effects, even though it is very uncertain whether they would pass any test of cost-effectiveness (Martin, 2000; van Oorschot, 2000; Larsen, 2000). The effects of lowering minimum wages are largely unknown, since few countries have been willing to take such action. Indeed, the OECD notes that most policy changes have gone in the opposite direction (OECD, 1999a). With regard to social protection, the level of unemployment benefits does not appear to have much effect on unemployment, although the duration of benefits plays a more significant role (Calmfors and Holmlund, 2000; Goul Andersen, 1995). But the question arises as to whether it is preferable for the unemployed to be forced to seek any job as soon as possible, or to be left more time to find an appropriate job.

On the question of tax incentives, while a number of countries have reduced marginal tax rates, the effects seem to have been small (Atkinson and Mogensen, 1993; Gallie, 2000). In terms of flexibility, employment protection is generally believed to have little effect on the *level* of unemployment, but some impact on the *structure* of unemployment, for example in such areas as insider/outsider divisions (Calmfors and Holmlund, 2000; Bertola et al., 1999; OECD, 1999b, p. 88). What may be gained in *external flexibility* may be lost in *internal flexibility,* if employers have fewer incentives to provide in-service training or alternative work, for example for older workers. These are some of the findings of the predominantly economic literature that systematically examines such effects, variable by variable. The question of whether such a context-stripped research strategy is at all feasible, or if such evaluations can only be contextual, remains a matter of dispute.

Table 2.6 Relative poverty rates in households where the head of the household is unemployed, 1988

	(%)
Denmark	3
Netherlands	23
Belgium	28
France	35
Italy	36
EU 12	38
Germany	44
UK	48

Source: European Commission, 1995.

In general terms, many of the effects claimed by the standard interpretation seem to rest more on strong theoretical grounds than on hard empirical evidence, which is moreover difficult to obtain. The social and economic costs and side effects also need to be taken into consideration. For example, although the social costs of activation are small, the economic costs may be quite disastrous during recessions (Furåker, 2000). A side effect of workfare may be the development of quite a large permanently subsidized sector of the economy. Lower minimum wages and less generous social rights run a substantial risk of creating an underclass where such policies fail to achieve the goal of labour market integration. Even where they succeed, there is the risk of creating a group of working poor. If employment is seen as a means (of ensuring social citizenship and economic sustainability), rather than as a goal, such arguments must be given careful consideration.

There seems to be little empirical evidence that market-oriented strategies are particularly efficient. To take another illustration, as indicated in Tables 2.6 and 2.7, Denmark and the Netherlands were the two countries in the European Union in 1998 with the lowest incidence of poverty among the unemployed, and two of the countries with the lowest wage dispersion. Equality and social protection do not seem a precondition for success in the field of employment, but nor do they appear to be an obstacle, as illustrated by the case of the United Kingdom at the opposite end of the scale. The Danish case is also remarkable in two other respects. In the first place, it has turned out that the level of qualifications has increased faster than the demand for qualifications, with the effect that the decline in unemployment has been largest among the lower educated (Finansministeriet, 2000). Moreover, it appears that Denmark used to be the country among the rich OECD nations with the smallest private services sector, and with the smallest increase in the services sector (Goul Andersen, 1993). This may indicate that employment in services is an *essential side-effect* of low unemployment, rather than a cause of it (OECD, 2000a).

Turning to activation, Danish and Swedish evaluations indicate that the most efficient measures may be those which rest at least as much on sociological insights as on an economic rationale, such as private job training and other measures which establish networks and close contacts between the employer and the unemployed (Madsen, 1999; Larsen, 2000; Furåker, 2000). This may also be an important instrument for the integration of immigrants, who account for a large share of the unemployed. The logic of economic incentives seems to be of surprisingly little value, both for analytical and prescriptive purposes.

Conclusion

The positive record of a large number of European countries in combating unemployment by 2000 has changed the premises of the discussion about *inflexible* European labour markets and welfare states. European welfare states do not appear to be badly adapted to globalization and technological change. Indeed, many of them have been able to achieve unemployment rates that are far below the previously estimated limits of structural unemployment, without following the core recommendations of what has been labelled here as the *standard interpretation* of (structural) unemployment problems in Europe.

Table 2.7 Earnings dispersion in selected OECD countries

	9th decile/5th decile ('how rich are the rich')			5th decile/1st decile ('how poor are the poor')		
	1979	**1986**	**1995**	**1979**	**1986**	**1995**
Italy	150	143	160	196	175	175
France	194	196	199	167	162	165
Germany	–	164	161	–	158	144
Netherlands	–	162	166	–	155	156
Austria	178	180	182	194	193	201
Denmark	152	155	–	141	142	–
UK	165	178	187	169	174	181
US	–	–	210	–	–	209

Source: OECD *Economic Outlook*, 1996, quoted in Bertola et al., 1999.

Conversely, the system in the United States does not appear to be as flexible as expected. It does not appear superior in terms of protecting prime age men, nor does it appear to be superior in avoiding the concentration of unemployment among the lower educated, despite the huge wage dispersion. It certainly results in people working a great deal, but it is questionable whether this should be considered an advantage. The diagnosis made in the 1990s of the problems of European labour markets and welfare states simply seems to be far too pessimistic.

It is more difficult to formulate positive visions of what could or should be done. The countries with the most positive record on unemployment by 2000 (Austria, Denmark, Ireland, Luxembourg, Netherlands, Norway, Portugal, Sweden, Switzerland and United Kingdom) do not have much in common, nor are there many common denominators in the strategies that they have adopted.

The short conclusion is that there are many routes to improving the employment situation. The United Kingdom has moved the furthest along a liberal path; the Netherlands has adopted some reforms leading in this direction, but a large part of the Dutch miracle seems to rest on simple wage moderation; the same holds for Austria, where there is little structural change; Denmark has implemented a more active labour market policy, but the causal relationship with improved employment is weak; and Sweden's recent recovery has been obtained without any significant *qualitative* changes at all.

Most countries have been reluctant to follow the core recommendations of the standard interpretation and, apart from activation, have preferred marginal adjustments, although often out of economic necessity (Kalisch, Aman and Buchele, 1998). Moreover, the association between such tightening and improved employment is uncertain. The extent to which policy experiences are transferable from one country to another remains an open question. Context-stripped systematic analyses have not found many convincing associations.

A few lessons may perhaps be tentatively drawn. Although econometric analyses have found no significant association between the methods of financing welfare and (un)employment performance, it does seem that by 2000 high and persistent unemployment is found mainly among the conservative welfare states, even though Austria and the Netherlands are *success stories* in this group. Clear associations have also been found between flexibility and the *structure* (rather than level) of unemployment. It would also seem that tight economic policies may be costly in the short term, but are beneficial in the long term, and that competitiveness (for example, through wage moderation, improved qualifications and technological innovation) is more important than ever.

But such approaches belong to the traditional policy tool kit and *sound* economic policies are not at odds with generous social protection, equality or labour market regulation (Goul Andersen, 1997). For small open economies, competitiveness has always been mandatory. Indeed, this may be one of the reasons why the success rate is highest among these countries. However, it would also appear that countries should seek out (moderate) measures to promote activation, flexibility and greater competitiveness which fit into the specific national institutional context. And, most importantly, there is nothing to indicate that it is necessary, or even economically beneficial, to sacrifice generous social protection systems.

Notes

1 Labelled NAIRU or NAWRU, respectively: non-accelerating inflation (wage) rate of unemployment, estimated on the basis of econometric analyses of the relationship between unemployment and inflation.

2 Austria seems to form an exception, since corporatism has not prevented high wage dispersion. There may also be changes in this direction in the Netherlands (Hartog, 1999; but see Table 2.6).

3 For small open economies that are used to acting within balance of payment constraints, there is little that is new in the strong emphasis on competitiveness that is often associated with globalization (Bonoli, George and Taylor-Gooby, 2000, ch. 3). But free capital movements and rational expectations jointly limit the applicability of traditional macroeconomic steering instruments. Basically, in a system with free capital movements, rational expectations mean that the negative effects of inflation or devaluations (especially increased interest rates) tend to be felt before their positive effects.

References

Atkinson, A.B. and Mogensen, G.V. (1993), *Welfare and Work Incentives: A North European perspective*, Clarendon Press, Oxford.

Bertola, G., Boeri, T. and Cazes, S. (1999), *Employment Protection and Labour Market Adjustment in OECD Countries: Evolving institutions and variable enforcement*, Employment and Training Paper No. 48, ILO, Geneva.

Bonoli, G., George, V. and Taylor-Gooby, P. (2000), *European Welfare Futures: Towards a theory of retrenchment*, Polity Press, Cambridge.

Buchele, R. and Christiansen, J. (1999), 'Do Employment and Income Security Cause Unemployment?', in Christiansen, J., Koistinen, P. and Kovalainen, A. (eds), *Working Europe: Reshaping European employment systems*, Ashgate, Aldershot, pp. 33–56.

Calmfors, L. and Holmlund, B. (2000), 'Den Europeiska Arbetslösheten', in *En Strategi for Sysselsetting og Verdiskaping. NOU 2000:21*, Vedlegg 4, NOU, Oslo.

Carling, K., Holmlund, B. and Vejsiu, A. (1999), *Do Benefit Cuts Boost Job Findings?*, Working Paper 1999:20, Department of Economics, Uppsala University.

Clasen, J. and Taylor-Gooby, P. (2000), *Unemployment and Unemployment Policies in the UK*, paper presented at a seminar in COST A13 Working Group Unemployment, Brussels (3–4 November 2000) Department of Sociology, Tilburg University.

Dean, H. and Taylor-Gooby, P. (1992), *Dependency Culture: The explosion of a myth*, Harvester Wheatsheaf, London.

Esping-Andersen, G. (1990), *The Three Worlds of Welfare Capitalism*, Princeton University Press, Princeton, NJ.

Esping-Andersen, G. (1996), 'After the Golden Age? Welfare State Dilemmas in a Global Economy', in Esping-Andersen, G. (ed.), *Welfare States in Transition: National adaptations in global economies*, Sage, London, pp. 1–31.

Esping-Andersen, G. (1999), *Social Foundations of Postindustrial Economies*, Oxford University Press, Oxford.

Esping-Andersen, G. and Regini, M. (eds) (2000), *Why Deregulate Labour Markets?*, Oxford University Press, Oxford.

European Commission (1995), *Employment in Europe 1994*, Brussels.

Ferrera, M. (1996), 'The "Southern Model" of Welfare in Social Europe', *Journal of European Social Policy*, 6 (1), pp. 17–37.

Ferrera, M. and Gualmini, E. (2000), 'Reform Guided by Consensus: The welfare state in the Italian transition', in Ferrera, M. and Rhodes, M. (eds), *Recasting European Welfare States. West European Politics*, 23 (2) (special issue), pp. 187–208.

Finansministeriet (Ministry of Finance, Denmark) (1998), *Availability Criteria in Selected OECD Countries*, Working Paper No. 6 (Nov. 1998), Copenhagen.

Finansministeriet (2000), *Finansredegørelse 2000*, Copenhagen.

Furåker, B. (2000), *Unemployment and Welfare State Arrangements in Sweden*, paper presented at a seminar in the COST A13 Working Group Unemployment, Brussels, (November 2000), Department of Sociology, University of Gothenburg.

Gallie, D. (2000), *Unemployment, Work and Welfare*, paper presented at the seminar 'Towards a Learning Society: Innovation and Competence Building with Social Cohesion for Europe', Lisbon (28–30 May 2000).

Gallie, D. and Paugam, S. (2000), 'The Experience of Unemployment in Europe: The debate', in Gallie, D. and Paugam, S. (eds), *Welfare Regimes and the Experience of Unemployment in Europe*, Oxford University Press, Oxford, pp. 1–22.

Giddens, A. (1998), *The Third Way: The renewal of social democracy*, Polity Press, London.

Giddens, A. (2000), *The Third Way and its Critics*, Polity Press, London.

Gilbert, N. (1995), *Welfare Justice: Restoring social equity*, Yale University Press, New Haven.

Gorz, A. (1981), *Adieu au prolétariat: au delà du socialisme*, Seuil, Paris.

Goul Andersen, J. (1993), 'Skal Ledigheden Bekæmpes ved at Satse på Servicesektoren?', *FA Årsberetning*, Finanssektorens Arbejdsgivere, Copenhagen, pp.12–17.

Goul Andersen, J. (1995), *De Ledige Ressourcer*, Mandag Morgen, Copenhagen.

Goul Andersen, J. (1997), *Beyond Retrenchment: Welfare policies in Denmark in the 1990s*, paper prepared for the ECPR Round Table on 'The Survival of the Welfare State', Bergen (18–21 September 1997), working paper, Department of Economics, Politics and Public Administration, Aalborg University.

Goul Andersen, J. (2000), *Work and Citizenship: Unemployment and unemployment policies in Denmark, 1980–2000*, paper prepared for a seminar in COST A13 Working Group Unemployment, Munich, (31 March–2 April 2000), CCWS Working Paper No. 18, Department of Economics, Politics and Public Administration, Aalborg University.

Goul Andersen, J. and Christiansen, P.M. (1991), *Skatter uden Velfærd. De Offentlige Udgifter i International Belysning*, Jurist-og Økonomforbundets Forlag, Copenhagen.

Hall, P. (1993), 'Policy Paradigms, Social Learning and the State', *Comparative Politics*, 25, pp. 275–96.

Hartog, J. (1999), *The Netherlands: So what's so special about the Dutch model?*, Employment and Training Papers No. 54, ILO, Geneva.

Hemerijck, A. and Visser, J. (2000), 'Change and Immobility: Three decades of policy adjustments in the Netherlands and Belgium', in Ferrera, M. and Rhodes, M. (eds), *Recasting European Welfare States, West European Politics*, 23 (2) (special issue), pp. 229–56.

Hemerijck, A., Manow, P. and van Kersbergen, K. (2000), 'Welfare without Work? Divergent Experiences of Reform in Germany and the Netherlands', in Kuhnle, S. (ed.), *Survival of the European Welfare State*, Routledge, London, pp. 106–27.

Hemerijck, A., Unger, B. and Visser, J. (2000), 'How Small Countries Negotiate Change: Twenty-five years of policy adjustment in Austria, the Netherlands and Belgium', in Scharpf, F.W. and Schmidt, V.A. (eds), *Welfare and Work in the Open Economy. Vol. II. Diverse Responses to Common Challenges*, Oxford University Press, Oxford, pp. 175–263.

Kalisch, D.W., Aman, T. and Buchele, L.A. (1998), *Social and Health Policies in OECD Countries: A survey of current programmes and recent developments*, Labour Market and Social Policy Occasional Papers No. 33, OECD, Paris.

Krugman, P. (1996), *Pop Internationalism*, MIT Press, Cambridge, MA.

Kuhnle, S. and Alestalo, M. (2000), 'Introduction: Growth, adjustments and survival of European welfare states', in Kuhnle, S. (ed.), *Survival of the European Welfare State*, Routledge, London, pp. 3–18.

Kvist, J. (2000), *Activating Welfare States: Scandinavian experiences in the 1990s*, paper presented at the conference 'What Future for Social Security? Cross-National and Multidisciplinary Perspectives' (15–17 June 2000), University of Stirling.

Larsen, Ch.A. (2000), *Employment Miracles and Active Labour Market Policy: Summarising the Danish effect evaluations*, paper presented at research seminar Unemployment, Early Retirement and Citizenship, (8–10 December 2000), CCWS Working paper 19/2000, Department of Economics, Politics and Public Administration, Aalborg University.

Ludwig-Mayerhofer, W. (2000), *System Description of Unemployment and (Un)employment Policies: Germany*, paper presented at a seminar in COST A13 Working Group Unemployment, Brussels (3–4 November 2000), Department of Sociology, Ludwig-Maximilians University, Munich.

Madsen, P.K. (1999), *Denmark: Flexibility, security and labour market success*, Employment and Training Papers No. 53, ILO, Geneva.

Manow, P. and Seils, E. (2000), 'The Employment Crisis of the German Welfare State', in Ferrera, M. and Rhodes, M. (eds), *Recasting European Welfare States, West European Politics*, 23 (2) (special issue), pp. 137–160.

Martin, J.P. (2000), 'What Works among Active Labour Market Policies: Evidence from OECD countries' experiences', *OECD Economic Studies No. 30* (2000/I), Paris.

Moreno, L. (2000), 'The Spanish Development of Southern European Welfare', in Kuhnle, S. (ed.), *Survival of the European Welfare State*, Routledge, London, pp. 146–65.

Murray, C. (1984), *Losing Ground: American social policy 1950–1980*, Basic Books, New York.

OECD (1994), *The OECD Jobs Study: Evidence and explanations*, Paris.

OECD (1997), *Implementing the OECD Jobs Strategy: Member countries' experiences*, Paris.

OECD (1998), *Employment Outlook*, Paris.

OECD (1999a), *Economic Outlook*, Paris.

OECD (1999b), *Employment Outlook*, Paris.

OECD (1999c), *Historical Statistics 1960–1997*, CD-ROM, Paris.

OECD (1999d), *Quarterly labour force statistics*, Paris.

OECD (1999e), *Implementing the OECD Jobs Strategy: Assessing performance and policy*, Paris.

OECD (2000a), *Employment Outlook*, Paris.

OECD (2000b), *Main Economic Indicators*, available on http://www.oecd.org/media/new-numbers/index.htm#Standardised Unemployment Rates.

OECD (2000c), *Labour force statistics, 1979–1999*, Paris.

Offe, C. (1996), 'Full Employment: Asking the wrong question?', in Oddvar Eriksen, E. and Loftager, J. (eds), *The Rationality of the Welfare State*, Scandinavian University Press, Oslo, pp. 120–33.

Scharpf, F (1987), *Sozialdemokratische Krisenpolitik in Europa*, Frankfurt.

Sorrentino, C. (1995), 'International Unemployment Indicators, 1983–93', *Monthly Labor Review*, 118 (8) (August), pp. 31–50.

Sorrentino, C. (2000), 'International Unemployment Rates: How comparable are they?', *Monthly Labor Review*, 123 (6) (June), pp. 3–20.

Van Kersbergen, K. (1995), *Social Capitalism: A study of Christian Democracy and the welfare state*, Routledge, London.

van Oorschot, W. (2000), 'Work, Work, Work: Labour market participation in the Netherlands: A critical review of policies and outcomes', paper presented at a seminar in COST A13 Working Group Unemployment, Brussels, (3–4 November), Department of Sociology, Tilburg University.

Visser, J. and Hemerijck, A. (1997), *A Dutch Miracle: Job growth, welfare reform and corporatism in the Netherlands*, University of Amsterdam Press, Amsterdam.

Feature No. 1
Employment Stability and Flexibility in Industrialized Countries: the Resilience of the Long Duration Employment Relationship

Peter Auer and Sandrine Cazes

Labour markets in the industrialized countries are said to have changed dramatically over recent years. According to the *end-of-work* gurus, long-term jobs with one employer are a feature of the past: job stability has gone and is not going to return. The future seems to belong to a labour market offering mostly short-term and unstable jobs, of both high and low quality in terms of wages, skills and working conditions. Individuals are being told to prepare for a flexible labour market, with numerous transitions between jobs, or between jobs and other activities and inactivity. This *new* labour market will need constant adaptation through lifelong education and learning and a general preparedness for change. Indeed, individuals are told to behave like *entrepreneurs* and to manage their careers efficiently and maintain a constant status of *employability*, with a view to allowing them to change jobs easily, both internally and externally. Linked to this image is the strong likelihood that traditional social protection, based on (continuous) participation in the labour market, is not sufficient to protect the growing contingent of retirees and a more volatile workforce. New systems therefore have to be designed in which the broken link between employment and social protection is acknowledged and rights derived from work are replaced by rights attached to individuals independently of their working status, or at least in which individuals will take over a much larger share of risk-sharing (and/or of paying for the insurance of the risk) than before (see Jepsen and Meulders, Chapter Three).

Popular conceptions include 'Americans are realizing that the great American Job is gone', we can 'forget any idea of career-long employment with a big company' (Neumark, Polsky and Hansen, 1998, in a critical review of such statements) or 'Japan is struggling to adjust to the end of jobs for life' (*Financial Times*, 2 June 1999). The same vein of media reporting is also to be found for Europe.

But does this hold true when more serious data on job stability are examined?

What picture emerges when such images and stereotypes are compared with objective indicators of job flexibility and job stability? To go straight to the point, research based on an investigation of job stability over the last 10 years shows that in the industrialized countries (and only in those!) job stability as measured by employment tenure has not decreased but has been rather stable or has even increased. However, we do not equate stable jobs with good jobs and we do not claim either that those on stable jobs perceive their jobs as being secure. While a good job is more often than not associated with a stable job, some stable jobs might be undesired, but low employability or economic conditions do not allow for job changes. And perceived job security is based on general and specific economic and labour market conditions, such as the developments of lay-offs and unemployment, rather than on the past stability of employment.

The results presented below are based on an exploitation of data provided by EUROSTAT, supplemented by national data from Japan and the United States. The subject has been treated periodically by researchers and international organizations, such as the OECD and the ILO, which have basically reached the same conclusions (OECD, 1993 and 1997; ILO, 1996). The present study has to be seen as continuing and updating these works. In this feature article, it is only possible to present the most salient figures. However, the authors' study shows that overall stability does not suggest that all groups of the population have the same stable employment relationship (Auer and Cazes, 2000). In particular, mobility rates are much higher among young persons than older people. Average job tenure for young people across all countries is only just below two years, and country variances are low for this population group. The variation is much greater for adults (with averages of about 8 years), and in particular for those above the age of 45, whose average tenure is over 17 years. While age is one of the factors, gender (with women having lower – but increasing – average tenure than men), firm size (with larger firms showing longer tenure than small firms) and sectors (with public administration and utilities having the highest tenure) are also influential factors. Country differences are also remarkable.

Figure F1.1 Average tenure (years) and share of those with more than 10 years of tenure (% of all employed)

					More than 10 years	
Country	**1992**	**1995**	**1998**	**1999**	**1995**	**1998**
Belgium	11.0	11.3	11.6	11.7	43.6	46.5
Denmark	8.8	8.5	8.5	8.5	29.1	33.5
Finland	n.a.	10.7	10.6	10.0	39.6	42.5
France	10.4	10.7	11.3	11.3	42.0	45.0
Germany	10.7	10.0	10.4	10,4	35.4	38.3
Greece	13.5	13.4	13.2	13.0	39.9	51.2
Ireland	11.1	10.8	10.1	9.6	33.1	37.7
Italy	11.9	12.1	12.1	12.2	45.6	49.2
Japan	10.9	11.3	11.6	n.a.	42.9	43.2
Luxembourg	10.1	10.6	11.2	11.3	37.8	44.2
Netherlands	8.9	9.1	9.4	9.5	31.7	36.5
Portugal	11.1	12.3	11.6	11.5	41.6	43.0
Spain	9.9	9.9	10.0	10.1	34.2	39.8
Sweden	n.a.	10.6	11.9	11.9	39.7	47.8
United Kingdom	8.1	8.2	8.2	8.3	26.7	32.3
United States	6.7	6.7*	6.6	n.a.	25.8	25.8
Average	10.2	10.4	10.5	10.6	36.8	41.0

Notes

1 * = data refer to 1996.
2 n.a. = non available.

Source: Auer and Cazes, ILO, based on Eurostat and national sources.

There has been little change for men and an increase for women, resulting in a general stability or slight increase of average tenure in almost all countries under review, except for Finland, Greece and Ireland. In Germany average tenure decreased, probably because of mass lay-offs following reunification, but it has since increased.

Indeed, the patterns tend to differ between men and women. In almost all European countries, average tenure for women employees is shorter than for men (except Portugal, and also the Scandinavian countries, where it is about the same) but generally, female employment tenure has been increasing. This reflects the changing career patterns of women, notably women's increased participation rates and their increased access to more qualified jobs, which generates longer careers and a trend towards stabilization of jobs, even if they are often part-time.

The empirical analysis of the secular evolution of employment tenure has very often focused on male tenure, as it is likely to be less influenced by such changes. However, average tenure for men has remained broadly stable in most European countries, in some countries (e.g. France) it has even increased.

In Ireland, the fall in average job tenure for both sexes, but especially for men, is considerable: tenure has been decreasing since 1993. As this fall is in parallel with strong job creation, the fall is most probably due to the fact that if many newcomers with low tenure join the labour market, average tenure is expected to fall.

However, these patterns have to be analysed more carefully, as trends in job tenure may also reflect changes in the demographic composition of employment and in the business cycle. Average tenure in any given economy is highly dependent on the demographic structure of the working population. Young people tend to have low tenure everywhere. Moreover, econometric analysis, taking into account age composition, has revealed some changes in tenure for the young. This means that those who already had the most flexible employment relationships have seen a further decrease in employment tenure, thus pointing to the increased segmentation of labour markets.

Our evidence suggests that labour markets in general show more stability than is usually assumed and over a longer period. Earlier findings on the subject can also be confirmed, since job stability, as measured by employee tenure, seems to be fairly stable, even taking into account the latest data available for 1999 covering the great majority of industrialized countries. There is a marked difference in job stability between the United States and Europe (around 4 per cent on average). There are also European countries with a relatively low average employee tenure, such as Denmark, Netherlands and United Kingdom. However, these differences are very stable over time, pointing to the fact that labour market institutions and the employment behaviour that they shape are a major explanatory factor in tenure rates.

While there are therefore differences among countries, the distribution between countries and the average tenure within countries remain astonishingly stable. One exception to this trend is Ireland (and on a lower level the United States), where tenure is falling in all age categories, although only slightly. This may be due to strong job creation, rather than structural changes in the labour market. But the overall picture of stability prevails.

A growth has been noted in contingent employment (which is only crudely measured by overall stock data), but even in this case there appears to be no alarming trend towards the demise of stable employment relationships, with the exception of the fall in employment tenure for the young. There is also evidence that temporary jobs are of great importance in terms of job flows (both in and out of employment). But many of these jobs tend to be transformed into permanent jobs, thereby contributing to the relatively low total numbers of temporary employment relationships (see Sarfati, Chapter One).

The results of our research show that it is not possible to speak of a broken bond between workers and their firms. As Neumark notes, the bond may be weakened, but not broken (Neumark, 1998). It would also appear that we are in the presence of segmented labour markets, in which the core is still the dominant form of employment, while the periphery, although growing, still constitutes a marginal form of employment, at least from the long-term perspective of the professional trajectory of most individuals. At this end of the labour market, there seems also to be some concentration of flexible jobs among specific groups of workers, such as young persons, women and the unskilled.

But what does the image of a fairly stable labour market, with flexibility growing at the margins, signify in terms of the new forms of security that, it is claimed, should accompany a changing labour market?

A first conclusion would be that the search for such new forms of security should be very careful and avoid radical solutions that are not adapted to a system that is changing only marginally. It therefore follows that the solution to introduce social protection decoupled from employment, as suggested by some, are premature or even unsuited in the light of our results. If we agree that participation in paid employment should be the main target of labour market policies (e.g. the European Employment Strategy, which targets higher employment to population rates) than we should strive to bundle all efforts to create jobs with derived rights (of social protection, of leave, etc.) Needless to say that these are not the short-term temporary jobs, but the longer term jobs, which eventually still form the core of the industrialized countries' labour markets.

Of course, reforms need to be made but they should target the financial problems related to the ageing of the population by designing systems of partial retirement and new mutual funds, rather than individualizing the whole system. Other areas requiring attention include the provision of coverage for those excluded from stable employment and the redesign of policies for full employment based on a more permanent attachment to the labour force.

There seem to be many good reasons for the continued stability of the employment relationship on both the supply side and the demand side. The ageing of the workforce will trigger greater demand for stable jobs. Investment in human resources will grow in the era of information and communication technologies, which will in turn give rise to a need for companies to retain their workforce. Moreover, companies will have a special incentive to seek higher levels of stability in their workforce when labour markets become tighter. The same will also happen when younger firms mature. Although both numerical and functional flexibility are here to stay (and especially the latter in tighter labour markets), nothing seems to point towards such a dramatic shift in the employment system as to require social protection systems to start again from scratch.

References

Auer, P. and Cazes, S. (2000), 'The Resilience of the Long-term Employment Relationship: Evidence from the industrialized countries', *International Labour Review*, Vol. 139, No. 4.

Auer, P., Cazes, S. and Vincenzo Spiezia (2001), 'Has Job Stability Decreased in Industrialized Countries?', Employment Paper, ILO.

ILO, *World Employment (1996/67): National policies in a global context*, Geneva.

Neumark, D. (2000), *On the Job: Is long term employment a thing of the past?*, Russel Sage Foundation, New York.

Neumark, D., Polsky, D. and Hansen, D. (1998), *Has Job Stability Declined Yet? New Evidence for the 1990s*, National Bureau of Economic Research, Working Paper No. 6330, Cambridge, MA.

OECD (1993), *Employment Outlook*, Paris.

OECD (1997), *Employment Outlook*, Paris.

Chapter Three

The Individualization of Rights in Social Protection Systems

Maria Jepsen and Danièle Meulders

Introduction

European social protection systems were mostly developed at the end of the Second World War, at a time when states wished to encourage women to return home so that men could take back the jobs they had left during the war. The family model was a single-income family, with the woman staying at home to bring up the children. It was logical in this context, even in social insurance systems, to develop mechanisms through which the protection generated by the contributions paid by the husband was extended to his wife and children. This is the context and family model which gave rise to the family modulations of social benefits and derived rights which still exist in current social protection systems, without ever having really been questioned.

But social structures have undergone considerable change. In the great majority of couples, the two spouses now exercise an occupational activity, cohabitation is increasingly frequent and single-parent families are numerous. It would therefore appear paradoxical that these social changes have been ignored in the reforms that are being adopted in the different countries: in the current debate over the future of pension systems, for example, there is practically no question of survivors' or dependants' pensions, despite the fact that in certain countries they account for one-third of the cost of retirement benefits.

Economic theory and analysis have done nothing to remedy these shortcomings. Intra-family relations and the distribution of resources between members of the family unit have not been covered by substantive analysis. For neoclassical economists, the household or the family is a black box and it matters little who produces or who consumes resources, since their distribution is regarded as either a technical issue or a question of preferences which is not addressed by economic analysis. In their view, the situation of households is characterized by a common income and overall consumption managed by an altruistic head of household, who safeguards the interests of the family and behaves as a rational economic agent.

This simplistic vision is found in most comparative analyses of poverty and income inequalities undertaken at the European level. The hypotheses advanced is of the equal sharing of income between the members of the household: a poor individual belongs to a poor household. Households are characterized by the age, occupation, sector of activity and educational level of the head of the household. It is rare for the composition of the household to be taken into account, other than through the simplistic application of a scale of equivalence.

Nevertheless, certain studies have emphasized the importance of power in the distribution of income and consumption within households, and not only preferences and capacities, which are the only elements to be taken into account in the reasoning of economists. Recent empirical research confirms that the allocation of resources between family members depends on age and gender. Studies carried out in Asia and Africa have emphasized the high rates of female mortality due to the systematic denial of resources to women in households which are not poor (Sen, 1989).

In one of the rare studies of distribution within American households, Lazear and Michael demonstrate that the division of consumption between parents and children changes radically with the number of adults in the household: as their number increases, the children's share decreases by the same proportion (Lazear and Michael, 1988). Moreover, access to remunerated work considerably changes the distribution of power within the household. Women who have a wage tend to have more decision-making power within the family, and this power increases with the level of their income (England and Kilbourne, 1990, pp. 163–8).

Findlay and Wright have measured the manner in which the unequal distribution of resources within households affects the measurement of poverty in Italy and the United States (Findlay and Wright, 1996). There can be no doubting their conclusions: traditional methods for the measurement of poverty in households have the effect of systematically underestimating the poverty of women and overestimating the poverty of men.

The development of social systems and their analysis have been and remain broadly influenced by this simplistic economic conception of the household.

In the first section of this chapter, an examination is made of concepts relating to the individualization of rights. The second section is devoted to analysing pension systems. In the third section, family modulations in unemployment compensation systems are considered, while the fourth section covers inequalities and injustices linked to these family modulations and their cost. Finally, recent developments in terms of the individualization of rights are outlined in the fifth section.

1 Concepts Relating to Derived Rights

In practically all the Member States of the European Union, social security systems take into account the composition of the household to which an individual belongs in determining the level of social benefits provided to that individual. This may affect the level of the benefits to which the individual is entitled, either positively (for example, in the form of a supplement to retirement benefits granted as a function of the number of dependants), or negatively (for example, a reduction in the unemployment allowance in the event of cohabitation, as is the case in Belgium).

The individualization of rights implies the elimination of any reference to the composition of the household or life style in the provision of social security benefits. All adults must be entitled to social rights in their own capacity, irrespective of their relation with third persons. According to Peemans-Poullet, the individualization of social security rights is designed to eliminate derived rights and replace them, where appropriate, with rights based on an individual's own contributions (Peemans-Poulet, 1995, p. 6).

In countries in which social protection systems are based on social insurance, *direct entitlements* are acquired by an individual on the basis of the contributions paid to the social security system. Individuals acquire rights as workers through the contributions paid in the context of their occupational activity. In contrast, direct rights are acquired in other countries on the basis of a right of universal access to social security. It is sufficient to be resident in the country to be entitled to social security benefits. All residents are covered by the social security system, irrespective of their labour market status.

Moreover, certain benefits are granted simply on the basis of the relationship between an individual and a beneficiary of direct rights.

These consist of *derived rights*. Beneficiaries of direct rights may receive additional benefits for dependants and certain members of their family may be granted benefits due simply to the existence of a family relationship uniting them with the beneficiary of direct rights. These benefits, which are related to the composition of the household and are not dependent on the contributions paid, are known as derived rights. Such rights are granted without any counterpart, since they do not arise out of any specific contribution, or additional contribution. They are noncontributory benefits.

Derived rights are intended to extend social protection to people who do not exercise an occupational activity. They are based on the relationship with a beneficiary of direct rights. This relationship may be based on family ties, alliance or cohabitation:

- *family relations* are relations of descendancy or ascendancy which bind parents and children, as well as collateral relations between brothers and sisters;
- *relations of union* give rise to derived rights based on marriage; and
- *relations arising out of cohabitation* are relations based on belonging to a household, without any bond of union or family relationship.

The impact of derived rights on the level of social benefits is, in theory, the same for men and women, since the legislation of the Member States of the European Union excludes direct discrimination. However, derived rights are a source of indirect discrimination in view of the inequalities which exist on the labour market and the asymmetrical roles within the family. These sources of discrimination are themselves relayed and even amplified by social security systems.

In this respect, emphasis should be placed on the dichotomy which exists between civil and political rights, which are individualized, and social rights, which give rise to derived rights. In the past, derived rights existed in electoral law, which granted a person as many votes as he had dependants. Marie-Thérèse Lanquetin has demonstrated this dichotomy between all branches of law in which individualization prevails, and social security and taxation, where derived rights persist (Lanquetin, 1999). Another contradiction should also be noted. Even though social security contributions and labour law are individualized, the benefits arising out of them are not. Despite these contradictions, derived rights and family modulations are to be found in nearly all European countries.

In general terms, in universal systems, such as those in Scandinavian countries, derived rights are of a low level and are subordinate to a series of circumstances. Survivors' (or dependants') pensions, for example, are only granted for strictly limited periods of time, while derived rights are rapidly replaced by individual rights. They are therefore both limited in both their level and their duration. It should, however, be noted that in these countries supplementary occupational schemes are important and that they grant derived rights. Despite the importance of this aspect of the question, it was not considered possible to include supplementary retirement schemes within the limited purview of the present chapter.

In other European countries, where systems are based on the insurance principle, derived rights are more frequent and more significant. Dependants' pensions are generally not limited in time and may be accumulated with individual rights.

Derived Rights in Retirement Systems[1]

In 1995, derived rights in pension systems in European countries took on the following different forms:

- positive or negative variations of benefits arising out of the existence of a spouse, either in the form of a supplement to the retirement pension, or through the application of a special rate for the calculation of benefit (Austria, Belgium, Greece, Ireland and Netherlands). Such variations do not exist in Finland, Germany, Italy or Luxembourg.
- the provision of a pension to a surviving spouse. This consists of an important derived right which makes it possible for a person who has never paid contributions to receive retirement benefits solely on the basis of the contributions paid by the deceased spouse. Most of the Member States provide pensions to surviving spouses, although their levels and conditions vary substantially. In this respect, retirement schemes based on the universal model differ significantly from schemes based on the insurance principle. In *insurance* type schemes, derived rights give entitlement to a pension for surviving spouses whose occupational activity does not allow them to obtain a retirement pension in their own right (or in the event that their occupational retirement pension is lower than their survivors' pension) and the provision of this benefit is not limited in time

(Belgium, Luxembourg, Spain). In countries in which the system is universal, retirement benefits for surviving spouses are subject to time limits: they are paid while the surviving spouses do not have a pension of their own, or in other words until they reach the retirement age (Denmark, Netherlands, Sweden).

- a specific form of derived right is entitlement to a pension granted to a divorced spouse. The benefit is based on a relationship which has ceased to exist. This type of derived right exists in Belgium, Germany, Luxembourg and the Netherlands.

The most significant derived right, in terms of both the number of beneficiaries and the cost, is the pension provided to surviving spouses. Figure 3.1 compares the gross replacement rates in 13 European countries of the pension of single persons with an occupational pension (full career and the wage level of an average worker, according to the OECD definition) with the gross replacement rate enjoyed by a widow who has exercised an equivalent occupational activity and whose deceased spouse exercised an occupational activity with a high wage level (1.5 times the wage of the average worker).

With the exception of Ireland and Denmark, all the Member States provide a supplement to a widow or a widower. This supplement is based on the occupational activity of the deceased spouse. As shown in Figure 3.1, a widow or a widower receiving a retirement benefit based on an average wage and a surviving spouse's pension (assuming that the deceased spouse earned a higher income), receives a higher benefit than a single person who exercised an identical occupational activity.

With regard to the level of benefits, it is in Luxembourg, Netherlands and Portugal that the advantage enjoyed by widows is the highest (200 to 300 per cent). In the eight other countries, the gross replacement rate is also higher for widows (the replacement rates are between 40 and 100 per cent higher). Figure 3.1 therefore shows the advantage inherent in accumulating a retirement pension and a survivors' pension.

When the replacement rates for widows who have not exercised an occupational activity, but whose deceased spouse was in an activity providing a high wage, are taken into consideration, the graph shows very much the same profile. In eight of the 13 countries examined,[2] widows and widowers receive a higher pension than single persons with a full career (at an average wage). In the five other countries, the survivors' pension is less than the retirement pension received by a single person.

Figure 3.1 Gross replacement rate of retirement benefits for single persons and widows/widowers in 1995 (average wage)

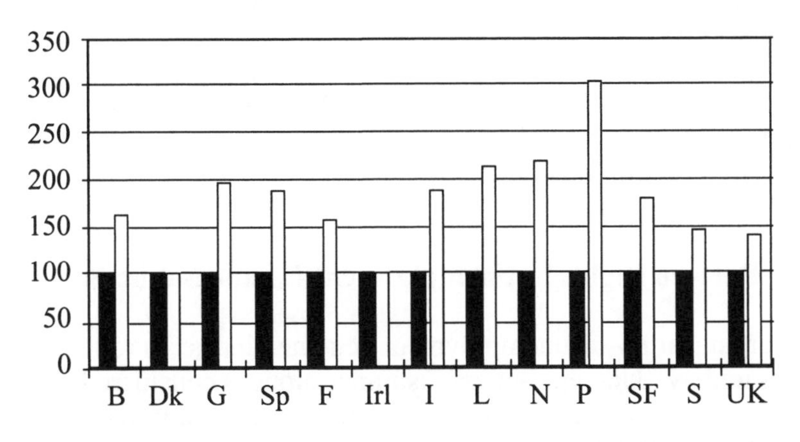

Figure 3.2 Gross replacement rates of retirement benefits for single persons (average wages) and widows/widowers (not having exercised an occupational activity), 1995

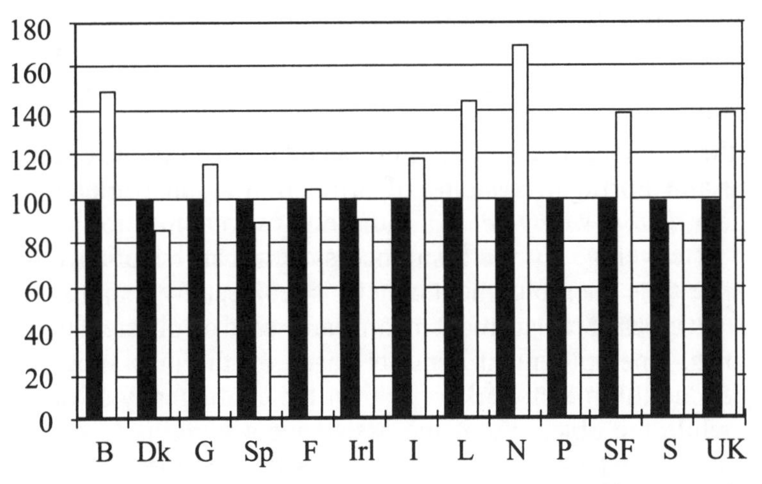

In general, a widow receives higher benefits than a single person. This result is evidently influenced by the hypothesis that the deceased spouse completed a full career at a high wage level (1.5 times the wage of the average worker).

Based on these hypotheses, it would appear that benefits vary very little as a function of family situation in Denmark and Sweden. In these countries, the universal basic pension accounts for an important proportion of retirement benefits.

2 Derived Rights in Unemployment Compensation Schemes

The organization of unemployment schemes in the European Union varies widely. (Unemployment insurance alone is considered below, to the exclusion of unemployment assistance.) Ten countries out of 15 have contributory schemes, or unemployment insurance schemes, for which the main financing is provided through contributions on wages.[3] Only two countries, namely Denmark and Luxembourg, finance their unemployment scheme through taxation, while three countries (Finland, Netherlands and United Kingdom) use a mixed system financed through both contributions and taxation. The level of benefits and the period of coverage also varies from one country to another, with the shortest period being four months (France and Spain) and the longest unlimited (Belgium). In ten countries out of 15, eligibility for unemployment benefits and the duration of the benefits depend on age, the number of days worked, family situation and, in certain cases, the economic situation in the region.[4]

In the Member States of the European Union, with the exception of Greece and Portugal, systems of protection against unemployment provide a *double safety net*. An individual who comes to the end of a period of coverage by the insurance system can benefit from social assistance. The unemployment benefit is replaced by social assistance. These two types of replacement income are based on different underlying principles. Unemployment benefits based on the insurance principle are intended to protect workers against the contingency of unemployment, while the objective of the assistance scheme is to guarantee a minimum subsistence income to the poorest categories.

Even though they are based on the occupational history of the individual, unemployment benefits are not completely individualized.

In many countries, the system takes into account the composition of the individual's household. Table 3.1 shows the manner in which the composition of the household is taken into account in each country.

Table 3.1 Derived rights in unemployment schemes, 1995 (EU 15)

Country	Coverage of the household	
	Dependent adults or children	Cohabitation with a person earning income from work
Belgium		x
Denmark		
Germany	x	
Greece	x	
Spain	x	
France		
Ireland	x	x
Italy	x	
Luxembourg	x	x
Netherlands	x	
Austria	x	x
Portugal		
Finland	x	
Sweden		
United Kingdom	x	x

In 11 of the 15 countries examined, the existence of dependants affects the level of unemployment benefits. Furthermore, in Austria, Belgium, Ireland, Luxembourg and the United Kingdom, the replacement rate is influenced by the occupational income of cohabiting persons.

The countries may be classified into four categories according to the impact of household composition on benefit levels:

1 In Denmark, France, Portugal and Sweden, no supplement is granted for dependants and benefits are not related to the income of cohabiting partners: these are individualized systems.
2 In Spain, and to a lesser extent in the Netherlands, the system is almost individualized. The income of cohabiting partners does not

affect the calculation of benefit levels. The manner in which dependants are taken into account differs from one country to another: in Spain, the minimum level of benefit is calculated with reference to the composition of the household, with benefit amounting to 100 per cent of the minimum income where there are dependent children, and 75 per cent in the absence of dependent children; in the Netherlands, the non-individualization of the benefit is shown by the provision of a supplementary allowance (CW) in cases where the unemployment allowance is lower than the social minimum income, with this allowance amounting to 30 per cent of the minimum wage for a couple, 27 per cent for single parents and 21 per cent for a single person.

3 Countries could be classified into a third group which systematically provides supplements for dependants without taking into account the income of cohabiting partners. These are Finland, Germany, Greece and Italy. In Germany and Finland, the mere existence of dependent children gives entitlement to a supplement. In Greece, all dependants (adults and children) give rise to a supplement which is proportional to the wage. In Italy, unemployment benefit is supplemented by a *housing allowance.*

4 In Austria, Belgium, Ireland, Luxembourg and the United Kingdom, the level of unemployment benefit varies according to the situation of the cohabiting spouse. In Belgium, the three situations of head of family, single person and cohabiting person give rise to different replacement rates. Moreover, the provision of the allowance is limited in duration for cohabiting partners and there is no supplement for dependants. In Luxembourg, the income of the spouse is taken into consideration in the level of the unemployment allowance and the supplement for a dependent child is only provided for a single parent. In Ireland and the United Kingdom, if the two spouses are unemployed the sum of the unemployment benefit is equal to the amount provided to an unemployed person with a dependent adult. In Ireland, all dependants give rise to a flat-rate supplement, while in the United Kingdom only dependent adults are taken into account. In Austria and Ireland, the supplement for dependent children depends on the financial situation of the head of family.

With a view to illustrating the influence of derived rights in the unemployment branch, taking typical cases as a basis, Figure 3.3 shows

Figure 3.3 Gross replacement rate for an unemployed person according to the situation of the spouse and the number of children in 1995

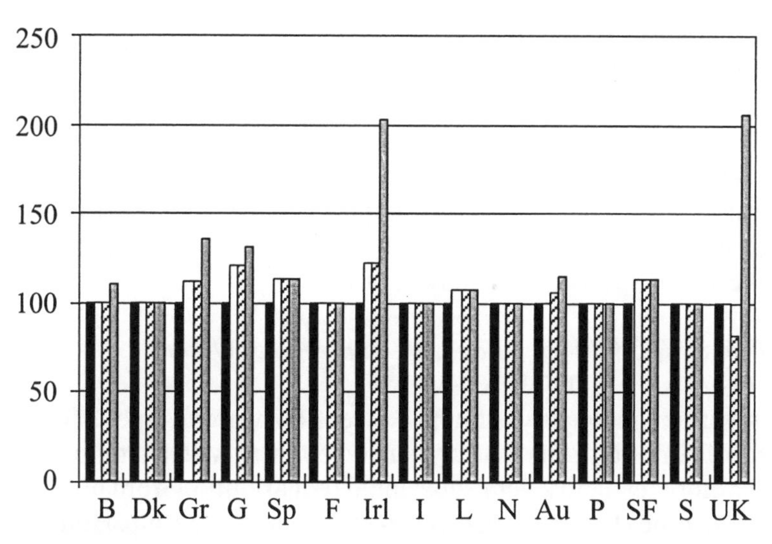

how gross replacement rates vary according to the situation of the spouse and the presence of children. The reference individual, whose gross replacement income is taken as 100, is an unemployed person married to a person working full time, without children. The unemployed person had an average wage in the previous employment and the spouse receives a low wage. The differences between the replacement rates are shown for nine of the 15 countries examined.

In particular, it should be noted that there is a major increase in the gross replacement rate in Ireland and the UK when the spouse does not work. In these countries, the presence of a dependent spouse practically doubles the replacement rate. But measures of this type do not therefore act as incentives to go out to work for spouses who could only obtain a low-paid job.

In contrast, in other countries in which the existence and the situation of a spouse have an effect on gross replacement rates, the variations are generally relatively low. The fact nevertheless remains that the provision of a supplement for a dependent adult does not encourage spouses to seek work, particularly when they could only find low wages.

3 Non-individualization and Inequalities

The non-individualization of rights in the field of social protection gives rise to three forms of injustice: it favours couples over others; it discourages women from working and encourages the development of atypical forms of employment; and it increases the risk of dependence and poverty for spouses who stay at home.

- *Family Modulations Favour Couples over Others*

The first form of inequality is found between the various types of couples. Systems of derived rights favour married couples with a single income. They therefore result in a very substantial redistribution from households with two incomes towards households with a single income. Households with two incomes pay two sets of contributions (since contributions are individualized), and receive benefits which are at best equal (they are sometimes lower) than those provided to a single-income household. This inequality is compounded by a vertical inequality due to the income ceilings which influence the calculation of contributions. These ceilings favour high incomes, since the contributions on these incomes are relatively lower than those paid on lower incomes, which are not subject to the ceiling effect.

Non-individualization also gives rise to inequalities between married couples and cohabiting partners, as well as between single-income households and single persons. Single persons generally receive a lower rate of benefit than beneficiaries who are married with a spouse who stays at home, or indeed the benefit received by such a spouse. Vertical inequality also exists between couples with two low incomes who finance the derived rights of couples with a single high income. Moreover, derived rights generally increase as the income of beneficiaries of direct rights rises.

- *Non-individualization is an Employment Trap*

Any measure providing supplements for dependent adults is likely to encourage withdrawals from the labour market. The participation in the labour market of spouses who are not beneficiaries of direct rights (mostly women) may in practice give rise to the loss of benefit supplements and result in a loss of income for the household. The marginal effective tax rate[5] is particularly high for unemployment benefit where supplements are provided for dependent spouses. The supplements which are paid on condition that the spouse is dependent encourage women not to seek work: the additional income resulting from work does not always cover the loss of the additional benefit and the spouse's participation in the labour market gives rise to additional costs in such areas as childcare, transport and clothing. Supplements of this type have been found likely to encourage women to leave the labour market in Belgium, Ireland and the United Kingdom. The effects of the non-individualization of unemployment benefit on the labour supply of women are reinforced in unemployment assistance systems where benefits are means-tested and the resources taken into account are those of the household as a whole. In such cases, the husband generally receives unemployment assistance benefits and the woman is considered to be a dependant. The loss of unemployment assistance or other benefits (such as housing benefit, health benefits and children's allowances) may have an important dissuasive effect on the labour supply of women. Effects of this type are found in Germany, Ireland, Netherlands and United Kingdom.

Survivors' pensions raise a similar problem when they are provided to women who have not yet reached the retirement age. In most such cases, the provision of the pensions is subject to the absence of occupational activity or to not exceeding a certain ceiling of occupational income. In itself, a survivor's pension is not an incentive to enter the labour market. Indeed, a survivor's pension granted on the basis of a higher income (the husband's income) may in practice be higher than the occupational pension provided on the basis of an average income (the woman's income).

- *Non-individualization Leads to the Marginalization of Women Workers, the Development of Part-time Work and other Atypical Forms of Employment, as Well as Work in the Informal Sector*

Women accept small and informal jobs because they are covered by their husband's social protection. Social security schemes, rather than correcting the inequalities occurring on the labour market, tend to prolong and amplify them.

- *Non-individualization Results in Dependency and the Risk of Poverty*

The characteristics of the labour market situation of women, who are confronted with social security systems based on the model of single-income families and a complete full-time career, give rise to situations of dependence on the spouse in the field of social security. The male partner in the household is the beneficiary of social security rights and the woman is considered to be his dependent spouse.

Derived rights are a source of discrimination and inequality, as well as giving rise to insecurity for the dependent person:

1 if the beneficiary of the direct rights loses the rights, all those benefiting from the derived rights also lose their rights;
2 in the event of the break-up of the household or of death, certain beneficiaries of derived rights lose their entitlement to health care and retirement benefits.

Attention needs to be drawn to the following paradox. In many European countries, regrets are expressed that single women with dependent children are often in a precarious situation. But the roots of their problems lie in their previous situation when they were either housewives and lost their derived rights as a result of divorce; or they were in partial occupational activity and their direct rights are inadequate. Marriage resulted in the ending of their economic independence, and the end of marriage means the loss of their social rights (Peemans-Poulet, 1995).

4 The Cost of Derived Rights

The cost of non-individualization is high. On its own, it constitutes an important item in social security budgets in several European countries. Various estimates have been made of this cost for specific branches using static micro-simulation models. Some of the results are given below.

In Belgium, the cost of derived rights in the retirement system has been estimated by adding together the cost of survivors' pensions and the difference between the sum of all retirement benefits paid at the *household rate* (that is, the benefits provided to retirees whose spouse does not have an income) and the total of retirement benefits calculated at the *single rate*. In 1995, this cost amounted to 138 billion Belgian francs, or 35.2 per cent of the total cost of the retirement branch.[6]

In France, only taking into account the general retirement scheme, the cost of the principal derived rights amounted to 57.5 billion French francs in 1994:[7] the supplement of 10 per cent of the pension provided to retirees with three or more children amounted to 10.6 billion French francs; the cost of the supplement of two years of insurance per child, which only concerns retired women, was estimated at 13 billion French francs; the supplement for a dependent spouse and the widow's pension (provided to a surviving spouse under 55 years of age) were estimated at 1 billion French francs. Finally, as in most EU Member States, the cost of survivors' pensions is the highest and was estimated at 33 billion French francs, or 57 per cent of the total cost of derived rights.

The third country analysed is Finland. The retirement benefits paid under the Finnish system consist of the national flat-rate retirement pension and the occupational pension, which is proportional to previous income. The estimate of the cost of derived rights was undertaken with the assistance of the SOMA micro-simulation model.[8] The gross cost is estimated to be 5.7 billion Finnish markka, or 8.5 per cent of total social expenditure. The significant decline in retirement benefits has, however, been compensated by an increase in assistance supplements and a decline in tax revenue. In other terms, the net cost of non-individualization amounts to 2.7 billion Finnish markka, or 4 per cent of the total cost of retirement benefits.

The cost of derived rights in retirement systems is therefore considerable, particularly in countries where the systems are based on the insurance principle.

An estimate of the cost of derived rights in the unemployment branch has been carried out for Belgium, Finland and the United Kingdom. Derived rights in the unemployment branch are of three types: the supplements provided on the basis of the status of the unemployed person (Belgium); supplements for dependent adults (United Kingdom); and supplements for dependent children (Finland).

In Belgium, it has been noted that derived rights result in a difference between the benefits provided to heads of households, single persons and cohabiting couples. The suppression of derived rights in Belgium (or the harmonization of the status of unemployed persons) results in a reduction of 22 per cent in the benefits provided to heads of households and an increase of 29 per cent in benefits for cohabiting partners. The Belgian unemployment scheme has the specificity of conferring a derived right on heads of households, who are mainly men, and withdrawing part of the rights of cohabiting persons, who are principally women. The individualization of entitlements to unemployment benefit would therefore be equivalent to a reallocation of benefits, with an estimated cost of 2.9 billion Belgian francs, or 2.2 per cent of total current expenditure.[9]

In the United Kingdom[10] and Finland,[11] the cost of supplements for dependants amounts, respectively, to 5.5 and 5.9 per cent of the cost of benefits. However, the suppression of supplements for family dependants would be balanced by an increase in various types of assistance for households with low incomes. Taking into account the rise in the cost of assistance, an estimate of the net cost of derived rights in Finland and the United Kingdom amounts respectively to 2.9 and 2.0 per cent of total expenditure.

5 Recent Developments

Even though several reforms, some of them major, have been made to social security systems in the countries of the European Union, the individualization of rights does not appear to have been one of the priorities. Without claiming to be exhaustive, the purpose of this last section is to indicate briefly the reforms which have had an effect on derived rights in retirement and unemployment systems.

In the United Kingdom, the unemployment system was profoundly modified in 1996 (see also Millar, Chapter Ten). The unemployment benefit became a contributory jobseekers allowance and a means-tested jobseekers allowance. The contributory benefit is a flat-rate benefit which, in contrast with the former system, does not include any supplement for dependants. Where two members of a couple are unemployed, they therefore each receive the benefit and not, as they did previously, the benefit with a supplement for the dependent spouse. The means-tested benefit depends on the number of hours worked by the partner. This means that unemployment benefit has been individualized in the case of the contributory allowance, but quite the contrary for the means-tested system. Since October 2000, the two members of the couple have to make their application together to obtain the jobseekers allowance. With regard to pensions, a minimum pension guarantee was introduced in 1999, the amount of which differs according to whether it is provided to a single person or a couple. A system of pension sharing has also been introduced for divorced couples, which is tending towards the non-individualization of rights.

In Finland, the reform of the pension system envisages the suppression as of 2001 of supplements for dependent spouses and children in the case of retirement pensions.

Sweden is also engaged in substantial reforms of its social security system which have an impact on survivors' pensions. The transitional period for the provision of these pensions has been reduced from twelve to six months and the surviving widow's pension provided by the general pension system (*folkpension*) is means-tested after a certain period.

In France, two major reforms should be mentioned. The public health system now provides a universal right to basic health care. The widow's pension has also been substantially changed, and it is no longer possible to combine earnings and pension benefits in the same year. The period for which the pension is provided is limited to two years for persons who were under 50 when they were widowed, and up to the age of 55 at the latest for people who are over 50 when they lost their spouse.

In the Netherlands, the pension system was changed in 1996. The survivors' pension has become a separate system in that the benefit is only provided if a special contribution has been paid previously. Moreover, the eligibility conditions have been strictly limited. This therefore constitutes an example of the individualization of the survivors' pension, without going as far as its suppression, as in the case of Denmark.

An important element of the individualization of social rights is the granting of a credit for periods during which a person has cared for dependants. This credit is principally designed to provide women with the possibility of receiving a full old-age pension. This right is included in pension systems in Austria, Germany, Luxembourg and United Kingdom.

It must therefore be concluded that, despite the various reforms of social security schemes undertaken in the countries of the European Union, the issue of the individualization of social rights has rarely been broached. Most reforms include a number of measures along these lines, such as the suppression of supplements for dependants, or the imposition of stricter rules governing the provision of survivors' pensions. However, these have much more to do with the objective of reducing social security expenditure than according individual rights. The strengthening of the pension rights of divorced spouses is an example of non-individualization.

Conclusion

Social protection systems in the countries of the European Union are still influenced by a traditional and outmoded image of personal life styles. They are studded with family measures designed to provide coverage for wives who are dependent on their husbands. These measures have the effect of radically complicating systems, as well as giving rise to injustices and perverse effects, including injustices between people who, depending on their life style, receive different levels of benefit, or the employment trap effect which reduces the supply of women workers and encourages them to accept small jobs, which keep them in a situation of dependency in relation to their spouses.

The non-individualization of social rights, combined with the persistence of gender inequalities on the labour market, mean that women are dependent for their social protection and may encourage them to leave the labour market, or never enter it. It is therefore necessary to advocate the progressive replacement of derived rights by individual rights and for the suppression of specific family modulations. Each time that a reform is undertaken in a specific branch of social security, or a new provision is introduced, it should be scrutinized, in the same way as European employment policy, with a view to preventing or reducing insofar as possible any discriminatory effects to which the new policy may give rise.

Notes

1 The data and information contained in sections 2 and 3 are taken from Jepsen, Meulders, Plasman and Vanhuynegem, 1997.
2 Belgium, Finland, France, Germany, Italy, Luxembourg, Netherlands and United Kingdom.
3 Austria, Belgium, France, Germany, Greece, Ireland, Italy, Luxembourg, Portugal and Spain.
4 Austria, Belgium, France, Germany, Greece, Italy, Luxembourg, Netherlands, Portugal and Spain.
5 The OECD defines the marginal effective tax rate as being the rate at which benefits are withdrawn and taxes and social security contributions are increased as earnings rise (OECD, 1996, p. 43).
6 MODETE model, Dulbea, Brussels.
7 The authors wish to thank Mrs M. Tourne of the National Old-age Insurance Fund, France, for her assistance.
8 Calculated using the SOMA model. The authors wish to thank Mrs Anita Haataja for her assistance.
9 The MODETE model, Dulbea, Brussels.
10 Calculated using the POLIMOD model. The authors wish to thank Professor Holly Sutherland of the University of Cambridge.
11 Calculated using the SOMA model.

References

England, P. and Kilbourne, B. (1990), 'Marriages, Markets and other Mates: The problem of power', in Friedland, R. and Robertson, A.F. (eds), *Beyond the marketplace: Rethinking economy and society*, De Gruyter, New York.

Findlay, J. and Wright, R.E. (1996), 'Gender, Poverty and the Intra-household Distribution of Resources', *Review of Income and Wealth*, 42 (3).

Jepsen, M. and Meulders, D. (1997), 'Gender Inequalities in European Unemployment Benefit Systems', *International Social Security Review*, 50 (4), pp. 43–61.

Jepsen, M., Meulders, D. and Plasman, O. (1997), 'Protection Sociale: Le rôle des droits dérivés?', *Les cahiers du MAGE*, (3 April 1997), pp. 81–98.

Jepsen, M., Meulders, D., Plasman, O., and Vanhuynegem, P. (1997), *Individualisation of the Social and Fiscal Rights and the Equal*

Opportunities between Women and Men, DULBEA, Brussels.

Lanquetin, M-T. (1999), 'Individualisation/Familialisation des Droits: Pour une problématique', presentation to the Labour Market and Gender Group (MAGE), Brussels.

Lazear, E.P. and Michael, R.T. (1988), *Allocation of Income within the Household*, University of Chicago Press.

OECD (1996), *Employment Outlook*, Paris.

Peemans-Poullet, E. (1995), 'Flexibilité du Travail et Sécurité Sociale: Quelles conséquences pour les femmes', *Atypische Arbeid en Huishoudens: Recente bevindingen*, Steunpunt Women's Studies-LUC, Anvers.

Peemans-Poullet, E. (1994), 'L'Individualisation des Droits dans l'Assurance Maladie-invalidité des Travailleurs Salaries', study prepared for the Ministère de la Prévoyance sociale, Université des Femmes, Brussels.

Peemans-Poullet, E. (1995), *The Individualisation of Social Protection*, introductory report on the question of the individualization of rights and equal opportunities, Université des Femmes, Brussels.

Sen, A. (1989), 'Women's Survival as a Development Problem', *Bulletin of the American Academy of Arts and Sciences* (43).

Chapter Four

Employment Standards and Social Protection Standards: the Impact of Diversified Working Arrangements (Trends in Western Europe)

Jacques Freyssinet

1 The Problem

In historical terms, social protection systems developed in response to the problems of interruptions in income and exclusion caused by the functioning of labour markets. The variety of forms taken by these systems reflects the different approaches adopted to developing coherence between employment standards and social protection standards.

If the typology proposed by Gøsta Esping-Andersen is accepted, the articulation between the rules which apply to social protection and those applying to the employment relationship is more evident in systems which he qualifies as *conservative-corporatist* and which have developed from the Bismarckian tradition (Esping-Andersen, 1990). In these systems, access to benefits is directly conditional on current or former employment status. In principle, this link is not explicit in the two systems inspired by the principles of the Beveridge model, namely *liberal* and *social democratic* systems. In the former case, access to benefits is selective and related to a situation of poverty, while in the latter access is universal, based on citizenship or residence in a national territory. Access to benefits is not legally dependent on employment. However, in practice, the difference between these two types of systems is less marked in terms of the significance of employment status.

The various forms of *welfare state* reached their zenith in periods when wage employment was the broadly dominant form of participation in production. Their development was consistent with a model of rapid growth nearing full employment. Benefits were designed, explicitly or implicitly, with reference to work or the loss of employment, which constituted the normal model of social participation, if not for the population as a whole, at least for heads of households.

The manner in which employment standards have been challenged over the past quarter of a century by the slower growth rate and the transformation in the forms of growth has affected two branches of social protection most directly, namely unemployment compensation and retirement pensions. In the three types of systems distinguished by Esping-Andersen, these benefits are related to the characteristics of former periods of employment. In parallel, when the other two principal components of social protection are examined, namely family benefits and protection against health risks, it can be seen that countries with a Bismarckian tradition have a strong tendency towards universal coverage.

The question which currently arises is whether the main distinction is between coherent national social protection schemes (whether they are conservative-corporatist, liberal or social democrat), or between the major components of social protection systems. On the one hand, unemployment compensation and retirement pensions are related to previous employment status and their development is increasingly closely linked to that of employment policy. On the other hand, family benefits and health protection are increasingly universal and unrelated to employment.[1] The development of these latter schemes depends principally on demographic and macroeconomic variables. The analysis below therefore focuses on benefits which are directly related to employment standards and policies.

From this point of view, a second type of distinction must be reconsidered, namely the traditional distinction between *insurance* and *assistance* schemes. In logical terms, the former are based on employment, while the latter respond to the situations of individuals suffering long-term exclusion from employment. The historical relevance of this distinction is open to debate (Tuchszirer, 1999). What is certain at the present time is that, with the persistence of massive unemployment and the expansion of precarious forms of employment, the relation between assistance and insurance mechanisms has been profoundly modified. Insurance is tending to be confined to the hard core of stable employment, while assistance is expanding to *peripheral* categories of employment and to unemployed persons threatened with social marginalization. Insurance and assistance cannot therefore be seen as two isolated systems fulfilling different functions, but as two interrelated mechanisms united simultaneously by their relations of complementarity and competition. They must always be taken into account simultaneously in any analysis of the relations between employment standards and social protection standards.

Within the framework of this general issue, this chapter focuses on a transformation which is giving rise to major tensions in the coherence of employment standards and social protection standards. The latter were developed with reference to a stabilized standard working arrangement in the population and over the life cycle. Their balance is now being undermined by the dual growth by the heterogeneity and variability of working arrangements. The depth of the resulting dysfunctions is making it necessary to redefine the relations between the different working arrangements and forms of social protection. Although the diagnosis is robust, the possible developments are not predetermined. Several competing scenarios will depend on the strategies adopted by the social actors.

The analysis set out below is based principally on the case of France, but also draws comparisons with the often analogous trends observed in other Western European countries.

2 A Stabilized Standard Working Arrangement

By accepting inevitable simplifications, it is possible to identify the structure of a standard working arrangement which, born of the trade union struggles of the industrial society, came to be generalized during the period of high growth rates and almost full employment which followed the Second World War (Supiot, 1999).

- The law and case law developed a definition of wage employment based on the *relationship of subordination*. Problems concerning the dividing lines between different types of employment existed, but were of little numerical significance. The growth in the rate of wage employment among active workers strengthened the legitimacy of its use as the basis of social protection.[2]
- The progress achieved in the field of compulsory education and retirement rights came to be generalized in a *three-tiered model of*

the life cycle (school – wage employment – retirement), in which the period of wage employment generated direct and indirect rights for the two other periods in the life cycle. The *standard* length of working life (from 14 to 65 years of age after the Second World War) and the low average life expectancy at age 65 gave rise to a strong ratio between contributors and inactive benefit recipients. This ratio was further reinforced by the low rate of unemployment, and then by the rise in the activity rate of women.
- The generalization of *full-time permanent employment* provided a favourable basis for the calculation of cash benefits (sickness and invalidity, unemployment and retirement benefits). With some exceptions, the replacement incomes provided by social protection systems were very much above the minimum levels guaranteed by social assistance.

In practice, the latter two characteristics of this model only applied to men. Women remained outside paid employment for long periods, or only entered the labour market before and after the period of child-bearing and child-rearing, or indeed only worked part-time. The continuity of their social protection was ensured through the indirect rights generated by the male breadwinner (see also Jepsen and Meulders, Chapter Three). In this framework, male full-time wage employment for the whole of working life therefore provided a clear reference which was deemed to be socially equitable and economically appropriate for the definition of social protection rights.

3 Dysfunctions and Incoherencies

The transformations which have emerged or accelerated over the past quarter of a century have undermined the coherence and viability of the model which was consolidated during the period of strong growth.

3.1 Contents and Dividing Lines between Working Arrangements

The polarization around wage employment alone meant that the variety of working arrangements identified by surveys of the time schedules of households were overlooked. Without getting into a philosophical debate, work may be defined as the series of activities designed to produce socially useful effects (or values), in contrast with periods of rest, leisure or social activities, whose purpose is self-evident.[3] In this context, a distinction has to be made between various forms of work, including:

- work which is remunerated because it directly produces goods and services;
- work in the form of training which generates productive capacities;
- benevolent work, or activism, which produces socially useful products, but is not remunerated; and
- domestic work, which produces values that are useful within the family.

As shown by many authors, attempts to tie the genesis of social protection rights merely to wage employment (or even paid work) are becoming increasingly unrealistic (Supiot, 1999, Chapter II). If wage employment is designated in terms of the relationship of subordination and actual working time, under the terms of the law, such as the time during which employed persons are available to the employer and are required to carry out her/his orders without being freely able to attend to their own personal affairs, growing inconsistencies may be observed:

- the expansion of forms of subordination outside the employment relationship (pseudo self-employment);
- the remuneration as wage employment of time outside a relationship of subordination (such as continuing vocational training outside the enterprise and the time allocated for staff representation);
- the expansion of the periods during which workers are at the disposal of the employer outside working hours (the development of on call work and changes in working time or intermittent work with very brief periods of notice); and
- the emergence of measures for the transition to part-time work or progressive pre-retirement, including the attribution of rights for time which is not actually worked in order to maintain the level of benefit entitlements.[4]

Moreover, traditional forms of social protection associated with homework (such as allowances for housewives) have been replaced by new rights based on the same logic, such as parental allowances for bringing up children and allowances for caring for disabled or dependent family members.

Finally, the issue arises of the social protection of certain forms of benevolent work, including its compatibility with the provision of unemployment benefit.[5]

It is only through a series of relatively artificial assimilation measures that the principle of determining social protection entitlements with reference to a period or duration of employment is maintained.

3.2 The Life Cycle

During the course of the twentieth century, it progressively became clear that the lengthening of the initial period of schooling and the lowering of the retirement age were seen as progress for workers made possible by the development of social protection (family benefits and retirement pensions). This understanding needs to be questioned, because it was not the view of theoreticians or the leaders of workers' movements during the earlier stages of industrialization. By placing work at the centre of the process of human development and socialization, they were fighting to transform its content and status, but certainly not to shorten the length of working life.

Subsequent events have made this approach seem obsolete, but the current period gives good grounds for its careful reconsideration. With the persistence of massive unemployment, the shortening of working life at its two extremities takes on the appearance less of a continuous progress, than as a means of managing employment shortages. In France, the period of full activity tends to be shortened to the age range between 25 and 55 years (prime age). According to an employment survey published by INSEE in July 2000, the activity rate of young persons between the ages of 20 and 24 in March 2000 was 51 per cent (with an unemployment rate of 21 per cent). The activity rate of persons aged between 55 and 59 was 59 per cent (with an unemployment rate of 9 per cent), while the activity rate of prime-aged persons was as high as 86 per cent (with an unemployment rate of 9 per cent). Similar trends, although less marked, can be observed in most European countries (Sarfati, Chapter One and Andersen, Chapter Two, this volume). The consequences of such developments are evident for a system of social benefits based on contributions related to periods of remunerated employment. The deterioration of the ratio between contributors and inactive benefit recipients or the unemployed is undermining the financing mechanism.

Solutions have generally been sought through the combination, to varying degrees, of different measures, such as reducing the level of benefit, increasing contribution rates, expanding the contributory base (beyond wages) and lengthening the period for which contributions are paid, or in other words, the number of years devoted to paid work. The latter approach would not be very realistic in the context of the continued logic of the three-tiered life cycle; the aspirations of workers and the requirements of enterprises in terms of the skills of the workforce are incompatible with a reduction in the duration of initial training and with an extension of periods of full-time work for *ageing* workers. In contrast, innovative solutions can be envisaged through changes in working arrangements at the two extremities of working life.

With regard to young persons, the positive aspects of an indefinite lengthening of initial full-time education are being criticized in many quarters. The quality of the education and the socialization of young persons is more fully guaranteed by an intermediary phase of alternating between work and training. However, the institutional structure adopted is decisive. If they retain their *student status*, young persons are still classified as being inactive and the work performed does not generate social protection rights for them (although their families can continue to receive family benefits). If their status is assimilated to an employment relationship (for example, an apprenticeship arrangement), the young persons are directly integrated into the social protection system as contributors and beneficiaries. It can therefore be seen that the definition of the status of such new forms of work is directly related to social protection standards.

With regard to *ageing* workers, the proposals made concern the introduction of the progressive reduction of working time in stages (see, for example, Taddei, 2000). Under this new form of part-time work, the nature of the employment status is just as decisive from the point of view of social protection standards. Either it consists of progressive pre-retirement (with the statutory retirement age remaining unchanged) and the question arises as to the pension rights acquired during this period (pro rata with working time or through assimilation to full-time work?). Or is the objective to delay retirement through the transition to part-time work, in which case it is necessary to decide whether additional pension rights are acquired. Finally, insofar as recourse to these formulae is left to the choice of the individual, financial incentives may be developed which, depending on the labour market situation, encourage progressive pre-retirement or the extension of working life through part-time work. Working arrangements and methods of social protection are articulated in such cases in new ways, while changes in entitlement to social benefits are becoming an instrument of employment policy.

3.3 Forms of Employment

The multiplication and development of so-called atypical forms of employment (that is, all forms which differ from the traditional model of full-time permanent employment) are undermining the coherence of social protection as it relates to direct wages and assistance. The growth of part-time work and jobs for specific periods (fixed-term contracts and temporary jobs) is having a triple effect on social protection rights:

- it is reducing the total duration or interrupting the continuity of reference periods which serve as a basis for the calculation of entitlements;
- it is contributing to the expansion of categories of the population on very low wages, with a direct effect on the level of their future benefits;[6]
- in certain countries, it is leading to an increase in the number of persons who are not covered by social protection because their period of employment or their wage level is below a minimum threshold.[7]

The impact is also now perceptible on unemployment schemes. During the 1990s, reforms were adopted in many Western European countries to make eligibility conditions more stringent (European Commission, 1998; Freyssinet, 1998). They resulted in the lengthening of periods of previous work required to be entitled to unemployment benefit, or the increase in the minimum number of hours of work which had to have been performed during the reference period. Another tendency was to exclude participation in employment policy measures (such as training and socially useful jobs) from periods generating benefit rights. These measures directly affect workers who have been in precarious or part-time jobs. A similar effect will be experienced subsequently by the same categories of workers when they reach retirement age. They will have paid contributions for shorter periods and/or on lower wages. These developments are giving rise to a series of interdependent imbalances.

In the first place, the nature of the minimum wage is being undermined. In historical terms, the minimum wage was conceived with reference to a minimum subsistence budget for a working family. In many countries, for legal reasons, it is defined as an hourly rate even though, from the point of view of covering needs, it is only meaningful with reference to regular full-time work. This did not raise problems while this type of employment was the standard for almost all workers. However, today, in the case of workers in intermittent and/or part-time work, the minimum wage has ceased to guarantee a minimum subsistence income. As a result, certain people who are in work may at the same time be receiving assistance benefits. The minimum wage merely amounts to the minimum price to be paid by employers for an hour of work.

Secondly, reductions in rights to unemployment benefit and restrictions on access to benefit have reduced the duration for which benefit is provided and the percentage of the unemployed receiving benefit. This has lead to a rising proportion of the unemployed only having access to means-tested assistance schemes. They are therefore no longer being provided with benefits because they have lost their job, but on the basis of poverty criteria, even if they have had a job and are recognized as being jobseekers. Instead of fulfilling a specific social function, assistance measures are becoming a substitute for inadequate compensation schemes.

Thirdly, as the labour market now only offers low-paid jobs (and particularly part-time jobs) to certain categories of jobseekers (particularly the long-term unemployed and the low-skilled), the paradox is emerging that is hardly worth their while in financial terms to take up work once again in view of the benefits and tax exemptions that they would lose as a result. These are the phenomena which are designated by the terms *unemployment trap, inactivity trap* and *poverty trap* (see also Belorgey, Chapter Twelve, this volume). It has therefore been necessary to invent *run on* measures, under which the wage itself is supplemented by the partial maintenance of former benefits, or by specific benefits or tax incentives associated with a return to low-pay work. Forms of social benefits or tax exemptions targeted at low wages are therefore being developed, with the clear risk that employers will take advantage of them to expand the corresponding types of jobs.

Changes in social protection standards are designed to make deteriorating employment standards socially acceptable. Once again, social protection is becoming an instrument of employment policy.

* * *

In global terms, employment policy objectives and measures have had multiple effects on social protection systems, both through changes in labour law and the introduction of new measures relating to unemployment and employment:

- the development of atypical forms of employment, in both the private and the public sectors, has created categories of workers who, due to the intermittent nature or short duration of their jobs, are only eligible for a reduced level of social protection;
- exemptions from social contributions have been used to reduce the cost of labour, to encourage job creation, particularly low-skilled jobs. The result has been both pressure on the level of social expenditure and the need to seek new sources of financing (through taxation); and
- social benefits, or tax incentives, have been used as a financial incentive to encourage the unemployed and certain categories of inactive persons to accept low-paid work.

As a result, the coherence of social protection has been undermined by the far-reaching changes made in employment standards.

4 What Scenarios for the Future?

'In the welfare state model, work was the locus of a basic exchange between economic dependency and social security' (Supiot, 1999, p. 10). *Work* meant full-time long-term wage-earning employment. The diversification of the forms of employment and working time arrangements, combined with the blurring of the frontiers of salaried employment, have progressively destroyed this coherence and it is difficult to see how it could be rebuilt along identical lines. Current changes in the regulation of labour markets, in employment policies and in collective bargaining point to various scenarios. For the sake of simplification, two scenarios will be described below which are as contrasted as possible. Evidently, real situations will not be as contrasted and are likely to consist of compromises. It is nevertheless useful to compare the two logics of social organization which are present in these scenarios.

4.1 The First Scenario Consists of a Dichotomy between the Economic *and* Social *Spheres*

The economic sphere consists of individuals or households, with their capacity for rational calculation, optimise their periods of paid employment, their working arrangements and the time that they devote to other non-commercial activities over their life cycle as a function of their preferences in terms of consumption and leisure. At the same time, they adopt approaches which ensure them a regular income, taking into account voluntary or involuntary interruptions which they foresee in their paid work. Protection against risks is a matter for their own responsibility and for individual freedom of choice. These strategies are only available to individuals who are *employable*, taking into account the situation on the labour market.

The social sphere caters for those who, over a specific period, are recognized as being *unemployable*. It consists of a *safety net* providing a subsistence income under certain resource conditions. It reflects either the moral values of solidarity, or the will of society to protect itself against the risks of insecurity arising out of situations of extreme poverty. The provision of benefits is conditional either upon verification of inaptitude for work, or on really seeking employment. The level of benefits has to be far enough below income from work to prevent any *disincentive to work* or any *dependency trap*.

This dichotomy does not exclude the existence of social protection schemes, but it considerably reduces their scope. In the first place, collective schemes have to be established for risks which cannot be insured against on the basis of an individualized market logic (such as unemployment). Secondly, the responsible state can *protect* individuals who are not sufficiently forward-looking, for example by making it compulsory to pay contributions to a freely chosen pension fund. Finally, representative organizations can, through free negotiation, establish schemes to protect their members. In all these cases, the principle of the payment of contributions has to be applied in the strict sense of the term, respecting a strict actuarial balance between the foreseeable return on contributions and individual benefits.

4.2. *The Second Scenario is based on the Hypothesis of the Interdependence of Social Cohesion and Productive Efficiency*

The conditions for coherence between these two objectives have now changed in nature in comparison with the *Fordist-Keynesian* period:

- productive efficiency is based less and less on individual performances in jobs juxtaposed within rigid organizations, and increasingly on capacities for cooperation within work teams organized in the form of continually changing networks, in which awareness of solidarity is essential;
- the continuous transformation of production techniques, the organization of work and the nature of products and services means that the performance of workers is dependent on their capacity to learn, adapt and be mobile; such capacities are only acquired and their use agreed to when guarantees of security are provided in occupational trajectories;
- the diversification of life styles and individual preferences in terms of working time arrangements and types of activity throughout working life can only be assured if collective guarantees set the framework within which individual choices are made the risk of precarious situations is avoided.

The coherence between employment standards and social protection standards must be founded on the fulfilment of these requirements. It must make it possible to diversify trajectories over the life cycle through a combination or alternation of heterogeneous but complementary forms of working time arrangements, whether paid or benevolent, as well as training and periods of domestic activity.

A group of experts under the direction of Alain Supiot, in a report for the European Commission, proposed the definition of an *occupational status* to 'encompass the diversity of forms of employment experienced during human lives' (Supiot, 1999, p. 86). This would require the reconstitution of social legislation (combining labour legislation and social security legislation) consisting of four concentric circles:

- universal social rights, granted to all members of society, irrespective of whether or not they work;
- rights based on nonoccupational work, or in other words non-paid work;
- rights arising out of occupational activity, under whatever form it is performed; and
- rights confined to wage-earning employment, characterized by subordination.

The objective is to ensure the continuity of collective guarantees throughout diversified individual itineraries by recognizing the complementarity of socially useful activities and those related to personal development. This is only one illustration, and other proposals have been made based on comparable approaches (see, for example, the concept of *transitional labour markets* developed by Schmid and Gazier, 2000).

The implementation of these approaches, which are already reflected in the social protection systems and employment policies of certain European countries, would require a very broad debate between the public authorities and the social partners to define the rules by which certain fundamental principles are to be applied:

- certain fields of social protection, and principally health and family benefits, are of a universal nature (according to the logic of the *social democratic* system, within the meaning of Esping-Andersen). They benefit the whole of the population, irrespective of whether or not they are in paid work;
- social benefits related to paid work (principally unemployment insurance, retirement pensions and coverage against occupational accidents and incapacities), are defined on the basis of the effective recognition of the right to employment. They cover not only those who have jobs, but all those who are actively seeking employment and are available for work. This implies the need for an explicit definition of the concept of suitable employment, or in other words the legitimate demands that workers can make with regard to the quality of their jobs;
- the diversification and discontinuity of forms of work (including atypical forms of employment, the right to lifelong training and the right to leave for socially useful activities) mean that rights to benefits

must be ensured continuously over life-span, irrespective of the diversity in the legal status of the activities undertaken.

It remains to be determined, depending on specific national conditions, the extent to which these schemes need to be established through legal rules or generally applicable collective agreements. The central issue of the debates and negotiations would be the definition of a new basic link between rights to social protection and the exercise of diversified working time arrangements in societies which effectively recognize the right to work.

Notes

1 With the exception, in certain countries, of benefits for persons with disabilities, which are used as substitutes for unemployment benefit, or benefits for housewives, which are intended to encourage withdrawal from the labour market.
2 Schemes for the self-employed were developed by analogy.
3 This definition of the principle clearly leaves entirely aside the problems of dividing lines and overlap.
4 In several European countries, public programmes or collective agreements to encourage the voluntary transition of older workers to part-time work have envisaged that they will continue to build up (in whole or in part) entitlements to retirement benefits as if they were continuing to work full time.
5 In certain states of the United States, under the name of *workfare*, the opposite relationship has been introduced, namely the maintenance of certain social benefits may be made conditional upon the performance by beneficiaries of unpaid socially useful work. In a gentler form, similar measures were introduced in Belgium, the Netherlands and the United Kingdom during the 1990s.
6 If *very low wages* are defined as those which are lower or equal to half of the median wage, the percentage of workers in this situation rose, in France, from 5.0 per cent in 1983 to 10.1 per cent in 1997. Part-time work is the principal factor in this change (Concialdi and Ponthieux, 1997; Ponthieux and Concialdi, 2000).
7 This phenomenon is particularly significant in the United Kingdom. In Germany, a reform introduced in this field in 1999 (the abolition of

exemption from social contributions for *menial jobs*) was violently criticized by employers' organizations (Hege, 1999).

References

Bosco, A. and Hutsebaut, M. (eds) (1997), *Social Protection in Europe: Facing up to changes and challenges*, European Trade Union Institute, Brussels.

Boulin, J.-Y. (2000), 'Cycle de Vie et Protection Sociale: Quelle compatibilité?', in Charpentier, F. (ed.), *Encyclopédie Protection Sociale: Quelle refondation?*, Editions Liaisons, Economica, Paris, pp. 183–94.

Charpentier, F. (ed.) (2000), *Encyclopédie Protection Sociale: Quelle refondation?*, Editions Liaisons, Economica, Paris.

Concialdi P. (1999), 'Pour une Économie Politique de la Protection Sociale', *La Revue de l'IRES*, 30, pp. 177–218.

Concialdi, P. and Ponthieux, S. (1997), *Les Bas Salaires en France 1983–1997*, Document d'étude, DARES (October).

Daniel, C. (1999), 'L'Indemnisation du Chômage depuis 1979: Différenciation des droits, éclatement des statuts', *La Revue de l'IRES*, 29 (Winter 1998–99), pp. 5–28.

Daniel, C. and Tuchszirer, C. (1999), 'Assurance, Assistance, Solidarité; Quels fondements pour la protection sociale des salariés?', *La Revue de l'IRES*, 30 (1999/92), pp. 5–32.

Esping-Andersen G. (1990), *The Three Worlds of Welfare Capitalism*, Polity Press, Cambridge.

European Commission (1998), *Social Protection in Europe 1997*, Luxembourg.

European Commission (2000), *Evolution de la Protection Sociale dans les Etats Membres de l'Union Européenne*, DGV – Missoc Info., Luxembourg.

European Commission (2000), 'Débats et Enjeux Autour des Retraites', *L'année de la Régulation*, 4, La Découverte, Paris, pp. 171–207.

Freyssinet, J. (1998), 'L'Indemnisation du Chômage en Europe: Entre l'activation des dépenses pour l'emploi et la garantie de minima sociaux', in Conseil d'Analyse Économique, *Pauvreté et Exclusion*, 6, La Documentation Française, Paris, pp. 69–92.

Freyssinet, J. (2000), 'La réduction du taux de chômage: les enseignements des expériences européennes', in Fitoussi, J.-P., Passet, O. and Freyssinet, J. (eds), *Réduction du Chômage: Les réussites en Europe*, Rapport de Jean-Paul Fitoussi, Olivier Passet and Jacques Freyssinet, Conseil d'analyse économique, La Documentation Française, Paris.

Freyssinet, J. (2000), 'Travail en Miettes: Quelles logiques de protection sociale?, in Charpentier, F. (ed.), *Encyclopédie Protection Sociale: Quelle refondation?*, Editions Liaisons, Economica, Paris, pp. 233–9.

Hege, A. (1999), 'Allemagne: Petits emplois, bas salaries – abus ou nécessité?', *La Chronique Internationale de l'IRES*, 59 (JULY), pp. 18–25.

Join-Lambert, M-T. (1999), 'La Protection Sociale est Inadaptée au Marché du Travail', *L'Économie Politique*, 2, pp. 6–22.

Maurice, J. and Brocas, A.-M. (2000), *Emploi, Négociations Collectives et Protection Sociale: vers quelle Europe sociale?*, Commissariat Général du Plan, La Documentation Française, Paris.

Morel, S. (2000), *Les Logiques de la Réciprocité: Les transformations de la relation d'assistance aux Etats-Unis et en France*, PUF, Paris.

Observatoire Nationale de la Pauvreté et de l'Exclusion Sociale (2000), *L'Observatoire Nationale de la Pauvreté et de l'Exclusion Sociale: Rapport 2000*, La Documentation Française, Paris.

Ponthieux, S. and Concialdi, P. (2000), 'Bas Salaires et Travailleurs Pauvres: Une comparaison entre la France et les Etats-Unis', *La Revue de l'IRES,* 32, pp. 5–32.

Schmid, G. and Gazier B. (eds) (2000), *The Dynamics of Full Employment: Social integration by transitional labour markets*, Edward Elgar, Aldershot.

Supiot, A. (ed.) (2000), *Au-delà de l'Emploi: Transformations du travail et devenir du droit du travail en Europe*, Flammarion, Paris.

Taddei, D. (2000), *Retraites Choisies et Progressives*, Conseil d'Analyse Économique, La Documentation Française, Paris.

Feature No. 2
Gender and Social Protection Reforms

Jay Ginn

Reforms intended to cut state social protection programmes and promote private sector provision have an unequal impact on the various population groups, with their effects differing according to gender and age cohort, as well as ethnicity and class. Pensions, as a major component of welfare, illustrate the gender impact of cuts in state benefit provision for both older and working age individuals.

Gender Inequality in Pension Income

Public pensions have been reduced in many OECD countries, often by changing the indexing formula, while private pensions have been promoted. Because of gender differences in such areas as employment history, earnings and the ability to build up private pensions, the effects on women are much more serious than they are for men. As a consequence, women generally have substantially lower income in retirement and are more vulnerable to poverty. Combined with the longer life expectancy of women, these problems are important, not only for the individual and the family, but also for the economy and public policy.

In the United Kingdom, for example, some redistribution towards women is achieved through the flat-rate basic pension, especially as this pension is protected during years devoted to caring. Yet, since 1980, the pension has been indexed to prices only and has fallen to only 15 per cent of average earnings, each year dropping even further below the poverty level. At the same time, income from private (occupational or personal) pensions is rising. Most older men have some private pension income, but two-thirds of older women in the United Kingdom receive pensions only from the State. As a result, gender inequality in the income of pensioners has widened (Ginn and Arber, 1999a). In the United States too, where economic inequality among pensioners is exceptionally high and increasing, older women are twice as likely to be poor as older men. Proposals to privatize social security in the United States would exacerbate women's economic vulnerability in later life, especially in the case of women with medium to low earnings (Williamson, 1999).

Disadvantage in private pensions reflects the past family caring responsibilities of women. In the United Kingdom, the fact of having two children typically halves a woman's lifetime earnings, while caring for ageing relatives also impairs the earnings capacity of women in midlife. Because of such past caring responsibilities, the minority of older women who have some private pension income receive relatively small amounts. Older women are therefore far more reliant than men on redistributive state pensions, and their financial security is more severely affected by a shift in public resources from state to private pension provision.

Pension Costs of Caring among Working Age Women

Many women work part time in order to accommodate their family caring commitments, either for children or for frail relatives. Part-time employment is associated with low hourly pay, poor conditions and prospects, insecurity and a lack of fringe benefits, such as occupational pensions. The timing of part-time employment is also important. For women, part-time work is common in the prime earning years, which are the most important for building entitlements through the purchase of private pension schemes. For men, in contrast, part-time employment is mainly confined to their early 20s and late 50s, at either end of their working life. Part-time work during prime earning years can have long-term effects and trap women in low status poorly paid jobs.

In the European Union as a whole, only 37 per cent of working age women are employed full time, with 14 per cent of them working part time (under 30 hours a week). The comparative figures for men are 67 and 4 per cent, respectively. Women's rates of full-time employment range from the lowest levels in the Netherlands, Italy and Spain (27–30 per cent), through medium levels in the United Kingdom, Germany, France and Switzerland (38–39 per cent) to the highest in Denmark and Sweden (52–54 per cent) (OECD, 1999). The gendered allocation of responsibility for family caring accounts for much of the difference in full-time employment rates for women and men, as shown by Harkness and Waldfogel's research using Luxembourg Income Study data for seven industrialized countries. For example, within the category of women between the ages of 24 and 44 in the United Kingdom, some 76 per cent of women without dependent children are employed full time, compared with only 26 per cent of those with children. Of lone mothers of pre-school children, only 9 per cent are employed full time. A similar *gender gap* and *family gap* in women's full-time employment is apparent in Australia, Canada, Germany and the United States. However, in Sweden and Finland the gap is much smaller (Harkness and Waldfogel, 1999).

Despite equality legislation, the gender gap in hourly pay remains substantial in most countries, with women who have children suffering a further significant loss of earnings. Harkness and Waldfogel show the extent of gender and family gaps in the hourly earnings of employed adults in the seven countries that they examined. Both are greatest in the United Kingdom, where women's average hourly earnings are 75 per cent of men's in overall terms. The earnings of women without children are 82 per cent of the average for men, while the earnings of women with children are only 70 per cent of those of men. Even when account is taken of factors such as age, education and occupation, the fact of being a mother of two children incurs a pay penalty of 24 per cent in relation to comparable woman without children.

In some countries, good quality publicly-subsidized childcare and other family services enhance the opportunities for women to maintain full-time continuous employment and gain lifetime earnings approaching those of men. In others, such as the United Kingdom, the choices of mothers are limited by the lack of affordable childcare, so that only a minority of highly qualified professional women (with high-earning partners) are able to maintain full-time employment throughout their reproductive years (Glover and Arber, 1995). The net cost of childcare for two children under the age of three, as a proportion of average family income, is 9 per cent in France, 11 per cent in the United States and Denmark, 16 per cent in Sweden, 28 per cent in the United Kingdom and 39 per cent in Italy (Esping-Andersen, 1999). Variations in the cost of childcare may partly explain why the rate of full-time employment for women in the United States stays at around 60 per cent between the ages of 25 to 54, while women in the United Kingdom show a bimodal pattern by age, with full-time employment dipping below 40 per cent in the prime earning years (Ginn and Arber, 2001).

Data for the United Kingdom for the mid-1990s illustrates the effect that childcare constraints on women's labour market participation and status can have in terms of reducing their coverage by private pension schemes (Ginn and Arber, 1999b). Overall, about one-third of women between the ages of 20 and 59 contributed to a private pension, compared with 62 per cent of men. But women who had never had a child were most likely to make private pension contributions (just over half), while about one-third of those with a child aged over 10 did so, compared with only one-fifth of women with two children at home, one of which was under the age of 10. This differentiation in private pension cover according to parental status is maintained within two broad age groups of women, 20–39 and 40–59.

Among employees in the United Kingdom, occupational class also affects membership of private pension schemes, with 90 per cent coverage of both men and women full-time professionals or managers employed in large organizations, compared with a rate of 57 per cent for unskilled men and 37 per cent for unskilled women. Women part-time workers have lower rates of coverage than full-time workers in each occupational group, although nearly 70 per cent of women part-time professionals or managers contribute to a private pension, a rate which is almost as high as that of full-time women workers in routine non-manual jobs. The private pension coverage of women therefore depends not only on their type of occupation, but also on the interaction of occupational category with hours of work. Women's hours of work, hourly earnings and occupational category are all related to the extent of their unpaid family caring commitments.

Family Policy and Pension System Sustainability

The viability of both state pay-as-you-go and private funded pensions depends on maintaining long-term fertility rates (and therefore limiting the dependency ratio of the elderly), as well as on high employment rates for both men and women. Yet the ageing of the population does not appear to have stimulated governments to provide the infrastructural support required to enable women to combine child-rearing with paid employment. Variations among OECD countries in terms of *collectivism* (when the state assists families with caring) compared with *familialism* (when states rely on the principle of subsidiarity) do not show any relationship with the dependency ratios of the elderly. This dimension of policy is, however, related to the type of welfare regime. Esping-Andersen shows that the provision of good quality affordable childcare and other family services in (mainly) Nordic states results in high employment rates for women and high fertility rates. In contrast, *familialistic* Italy, where childcare is expensive, has a very low fertility rate and a rapidly ageing population. Interestingly, France and the United States (with different types of welfare regime) both have high full-time employment rates for women. In France, this has been achieved through state-subsidized and regulated childcare, and in the United States through a deregulated labour market and low wage rates for private childcarers (including illegal immigrants, who lack economic leverage). Despite relatively cheap childcare in the United States, low-skilled low-paid mothers (especially those without a partner's income) remain disadvantaged in buying the childcare needed for full-time employment. The roots of the polarization to be found in the employment rates of mothers in the United Kingdom (Glover and Arber, 1995) are therefore also to be found in the United States.

Increasingly high divorce rates and the declining popularity of marriage make reliance on a partner's pension a risky strategy. While pension sharing ordered by divorce courts may provide inadequate compensation for the years spent by women in child-rearing, cohabitees are totally excluded. It is therefore important for women to have their own pensions. As has been discussed, for the majority of women, short employment records, periods of part-time employment and low hourly earnings prevent them from building adequate pensions through the market. State schemes have the potential to ensure that the pension costs of family caring are fairly shared between those who undertake such tasks and those who do not. Private pensions, in contrast, allow the costs to lie where they fall mainly on women in later life. The market cannot fulfil the social function of protecting the pensions of those who raise the next generation.

Future Gender Equality in Pensions?

The effect of the retrenchment of public pensions in terms of gender inequality in pension income will depend crucially on the extent to which women are able to maintain full-time employment throughout their working lives. It is possible that women will increasingly adopt a norm of continuous full-time employment, with a corresponding gender equalization of pension income. Yet the available data on women's employment rates give no grounds for assuming that such a scenario will materialize. Most of the increase in women's employment over the past two decades in OECD countries has been in part-time work. A rise in the full-time employment rates of women between 1990 and 1998 is only to be found in a few countries, such as the United States and Denmark, and (from a very low base) the Netherlands. Other countries, including the United Kingdom, Canada, Australia, New Zealand, Ireland, France, Germany and Sweden, show no increase in women's full-time employment in the 1990s (OECD, 1999, Tables B and E).

Until a generation of women retires with lifetime earnings comparable to those of men, the pension penalties incurred by family caring will be reinforced by the retrenchment of public pension systems.

A reassessment by policy-makers of the way in which pension systems treat those who provide family care is essential. If the pattern of past gender inequality in pensions is not to be perpetuated, state pensions which recognize unpaid work must be maintained at an adequate level and the trend towards pension privatization reversed.

References

Esping-Andersen, G. (1999), 'The Household Economy', in Esping-Andersen G., *Social Foundations of Postindustrial Economies*, Oxford University Press, Oxford, ch. 4.

Ginn, J. and Arber, S. (1999a), 'Changing Patterns of Pension Inequality: The shift from state to private sources', *Ageing and Society*, 19 (3), pp. 319–42.

Ginn, J. and Arber, S. (1999b), 'Women's Pensions and the Impact of Privatisation in Britain', in INSTRAW (ed.), *Ageing in a Gendered World: Women's issues and identities*, INSTRAW, Santo Domingo, pp. 49–74.

Ginn, J., Street, D. and Arber, S. (2001), *Women, Work and Pensions: International issues and prospects*, Open University Press, Buckingham.

Glover, J. and Arber, S. (1995), 'Polarisation in Mothers' Employment', *Gender, Work and Organisation*, 2 (4), pp. 165–79.

Harkness, S. and Waldfogel, J. (1999), *The Family Gap in Pay: Evidence from seven industrialised countries*, CASE paper 29, Centre for Analysis of Social Exclusion, London.

OECD (1999), *Employment Outlook*, Paris.
Williamson, J. (1999), *Effects on Women of Privatisation of Social Security*, http://www.bc.edu/crr.

Chapter Five

The Future of Employment in Europe: Elements for Analysis Drawn from the Case of France

Hugues de Jouvenel and Alain Parant

The configuration of socioeconomic systems in the most developed countries since the Second World War has been based principally on two axes: employment, and to a very slightly lesser degree, the family, mentioned here only in passing, but which has also undergone very far-reaching changes over the past 40 years (see also Sarfati, Chapter One).

In France, even more than in other modern societies, employment is the keystone of the edifice. Abundant and well-paid, it is a source of individual prosperity and public generosity. When it is rarer and/or precarious and badly paid, it becomes a factor of severe blockages in society as a whole.

The French system of social protection, which closely combines assistance and insurance functions, is characterized in practice by a method of financing which is, to a very large extent, based on employment, with social contributions financing almost two-thirds of total social expenditure. As a result, the slow-down in growth which commenced in 1973, followed by the decline in the share of wages in added value, had the effect of narrowing the contributory base, at a time when the extension of the population covered by social protection, the ageing of the population, the rise in health care expenditure and the growth of unemployment were tending to increase financing needs. Despite the exemptions on employers' contributions granted to encourage access to work by certain categories of the population, or to safeguard threatened jobs, this *pincer movement* has resulted in a significant increase in contribution rates, which has limited the scope of the recovery in the labour market over the past three years.

Over the next 20 years, the smaller ranks of the generations born since the mid-1970s will continue to arrive on the labour market and replace the very numerous cohorts of the baby boom. All things being equal, employment should therefore grow increasingly slowly.

The deterioration in the dependency ratio (the number of retirees for every 100 active persons), the rising deficits of pension schemes and the increase in the total burden of old age (pensions plus health care) as a proportion of GDP, whether or not economic growth continues, will make certain changes inevitable in terms of the ages and duration of occupational activity, types of employment and skills needs, as well as in systems of remuneration. But it will be even more necessary for the values related to work to develop in a commensurate manner.

In the first place, a brief review will be made of the past with a view to identifying some of the main trends and focusing on a number of elements which have broken with the past. An overview will then be provided of employment prospects. Based on an analysis of a number of the major determinants of the demand and, in a more cursory manner, the supply of employment, this will be developed on the basis of the French example, although it could easily be extended to other European countries.

1 Past Trends

From a longer historical perspective, and in particular comparing the trends since the beginning of the century, the past 30 years constitute an undeniable break with the past. They have been marked by a formidable growth in the active population, clearly resulting from the baby boom and the high rate of immigration during the three post-war decades, but also the rise in the activity rate of women. However, the past 30 years have also been characterized by a major explosion in unemployment and the stagnation of employment.

A Rapid Increase in the Active Population

Although it had been roughly stable at around 20 million since 1910,[1] thereby marking a long pause after the increase of around 7 million recorded in the 19th century, the number of active persons once again rose, at first slowly in the 1960s, and then much more rapidly starting from the 1970s. It has now reached the figure of around 27 million.

The contribution of women has been a determining factor in the growth of the active population by 6 million over the past 30 years. The number of active women has increased from 7 to 12 million. The gains have essentially been in employment in the services sector (which now, in total, accounts for around 70 per cent of active workers, or more than four out of five women, and three out of five men). The active male population, principally as a result of the decline in the industrial sector (which now only occupies around 25 per cent of the total active population, or 35 per cent of working men and as few as 15 per cent of working women), has only grown to a limited extent.

The fact that women are once again in overall terms as active as at the beginning of the century in France (with a general activity rate very close to 50 per cent) is primarily due to a very large rise in activity rates (at least until recently) in the intermediary age ranges of between 25 and 54 years. For women, in the same way as for men, activity rates have in contrast undergone a very significant contraction at the extremities of the age range. These must be seen as a result, on the one hand, of the substantial extension (from the ages of 14 to 16) of compulsory education and, on the other hand, the broad success of the very many measures adopted to encourage older workers to leave work at ever younger ages.

Relative Stagnation of Employment

As shown in Figure 5.1, there has been a significant hiatus since the 1970s between the growth in the active population and the numbers of persons actually working.

It should also be noted that, although the total number of active persons in employment has grown by 1 million, this is in overall terms due to the increase in the number of jobs in both the market and non-market sectors which are subsidized (that is, which benefit from public subsidies and/or partial or total exemption from social contributions), which very regularly overcompensated (up to 1996) for the fall in the number of unsubsidized jobs (from which the remuneration provides the basis for social contributions paid at the normal rate).[2]

In accordance with the widely held idea that all the capacities of individual workers necessarily decline with age, and under the mistaken pretext that the quantity of work is necessarily limited, leading to the erroneous conclusion that an older worker can only take a job which might otherwise be occupied by a young worker, many measures have been developed since 1972 to move aside older workers (including

Figure 5.1 France: active population (trends since 1973)

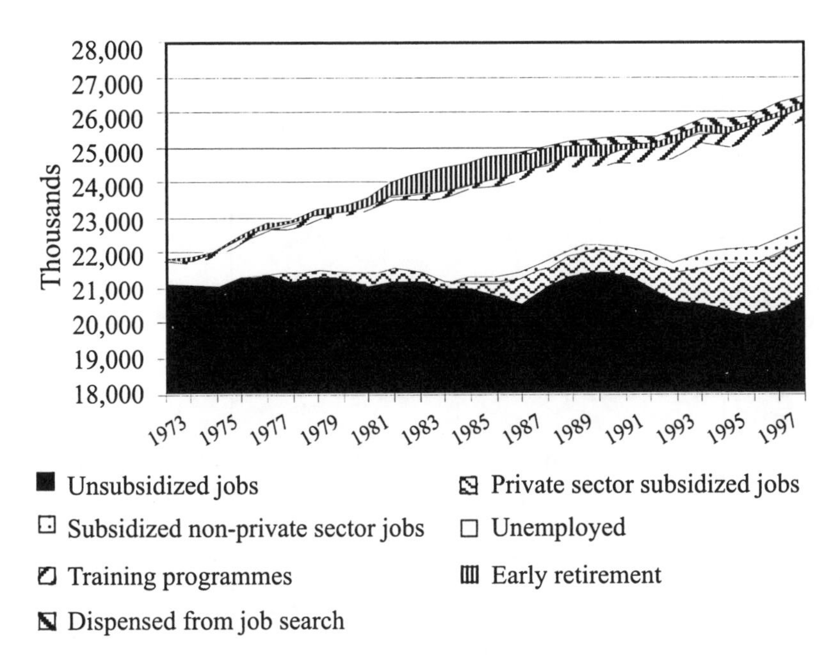

income guarantees in the event of dismissal or resignation, collectively agreed solidarity allowances, the special allowance of the National Employment Fund, early retirement and the lowering of the statutory retirement age).

These various measures have not prevented an explosion in unemployment. From the beginning of the 1970s until 1996, the number of unemployed in practice grew from fewer than 750,000 to 3 million. The unemployment rate rose from under 3 per cent to over 12 per cent. The average duration of unemployment increased from under nine months to over 15 months (Marchand, Thélot and Bayet, 1997) (see Figure 5.2).

The measures adopted have not even succeeded in limiting unemployment among younger workers, whose employment rates have remained at an extremely low level in Europe (Figure 5.3), despite the undeniable recovery in the labour market since 1997 (with the creation of some 1.5 million subsidized and unsubsidized jobs in four years).

In the same way as the measures taken to assist non-market jobs, the various measures adopted have undoubtedly contributed to economic growth through the distribution of the income supplements provided.

Figure 5.2 France: unemployment rates by sex and age (1968 to 1996)

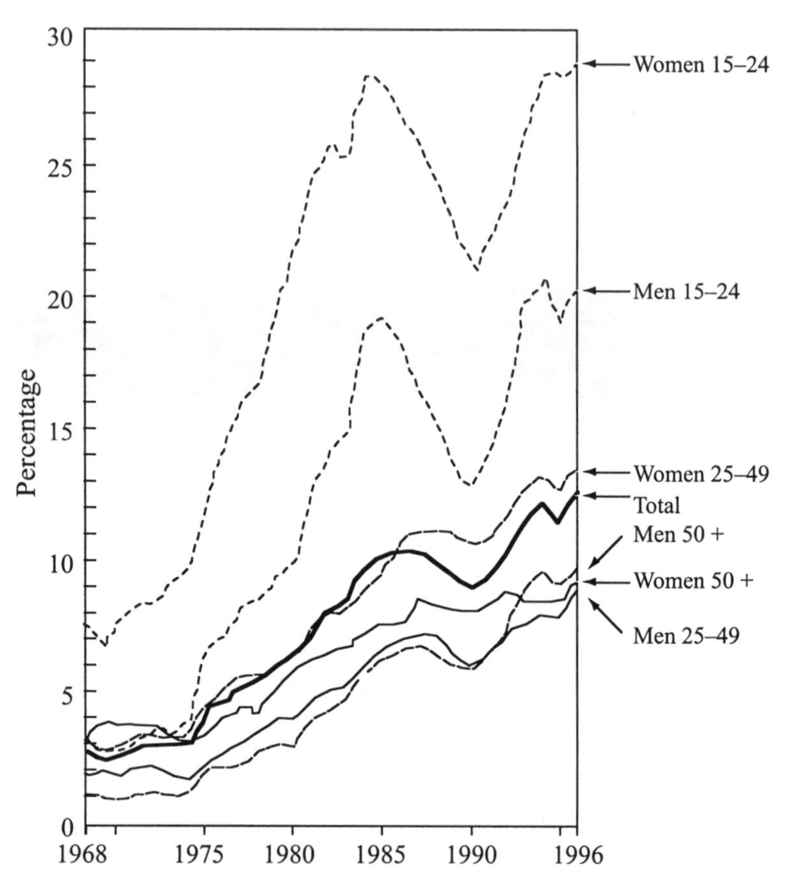

Source: Marchand, Thélot and Bayet, 1997.

Nevertheless, over the longer term, they have exacerbated tensions on the labour market and have aggravated the financial needs of social protection, thereby inhibiting growth and employment itself. They have also completely undermined the situation with regard to withdrawal from work, by facilitating the development of mechanisms and regulation measures other than traditional retirement, by contributing to the very substantial lengthening of the period during which workers are likely to withdraw from the labour market and by introducing a certain flexibility and disorder in the hitherto very ternary life cycle, as well as greater insecurity with regard to social entitlements and the level of protection provided (see also Freyssinet, Chapter Four).[3]

Figure 5.3 Europe: employment rates for 15–24 year olds (trends since 1990)

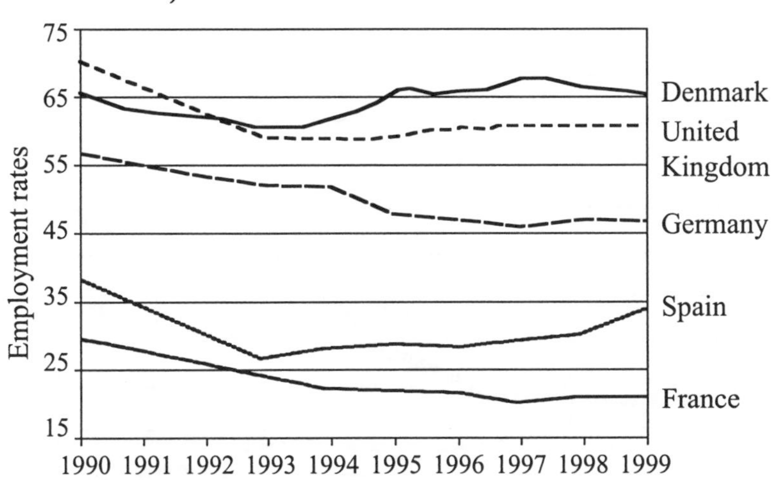

Source: Futuribles graphic presentation on the basis of data from OECD, *Employment Outlook*, 1999.

The question may therefore be raised as to whether the rise in unemployment and the relative stagnation of employment in France were as unconnected with the oil shocks, globalization and the emergence of new technologies as has often been claimed. This thesis is certainly untenable when judged on the basis of a number of international comparisons.

In the first place, it has to be said that there is a remarkable contrast between the United States and Europe. Indeed, the United States created 37 million jobs between 1975 and 1995, while over the same period the five major European countries, which together have a population equivalent to that of the United States, only created 2.4 million jobs.

As shown extremely clearly by Figure 5.4, adjustments were made in the United States by means of wages, while in Europe they were carried out through underemployment.

The contrast is not only great between the United States and Europe. It is just as wide between the countries of the European Union. By way of illustration, in 1997, before the general economic recovery started, the unemployment rate was only 5.6 per cent in the Netherlands, 6.2 per cent in Austria and 7.6 per cent in Denmark, while it had reached the level of 11.4 per cent in Germany, 12.4 per cent in France and 20.8

Figure 5.4 Employment and real wages in the European Union and the United States (trends 1980–98 – base 100 in 1980)

A European Union

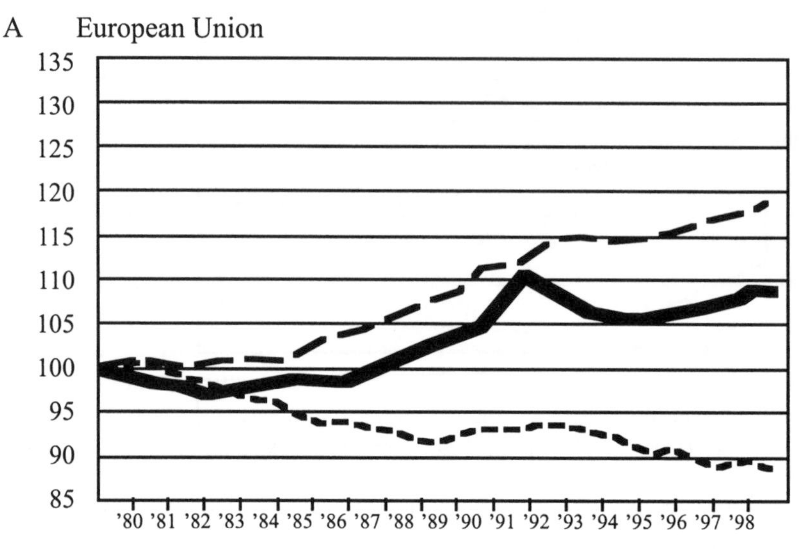

B United States

Note: *Wage costs* means the proportion of the value added of enterprises accounted for by wages. *Wages* means real wages per capita.

Source: as Figure 5.3.

per cent in Spain. Nevertheless, all these countries experienced comparable demographic trends[4] and were faced with the same external situation and the emergence of the same new technical and economic paradigm.

A more in-depth comparison between France and the Netherlands, where a reduction in working time was embarked upon at the beginning of the 1980s, combined with wage compression, which did not have the effect of redistributing poverty but, on the contrary, resulted in a virtuous circle in the economy, shows the extent to which unemployment and underemployment are a result of the policies adopted and the overall dynamics of societies (Boulin and Cette, 1997).

Another break with the past in the development of employment in France over the past 30 years relates to the nature of the new jobs created.

Since the middle of the 1980s, there has been a significant increase in atypical forms of employment, such as temporary jobs (interim work and short-term contracts), part-time work (more or less involuntary) and, as emphasized above, subsidized jobs (see Figure 5.5).

Admittedly, permanent full-time employment remains predominant, even though it has lost ground in overall terms (with the exception of certain specific sectors, such as information technology, where real and worrying shortages of labour have been experienced for several years) (see also Auer and Cazes, Feature No. 1). From 1975 to 1998, the share of permanent full-time work in total employment fell from 77 to 69 per cent (or from 72 to 56 per cent, if part-time permanent jobs are excluded). Moreover, these new forms of employment, despite their contribution to the growth in the number of jobs and the flexibility that they offer on the labour market, are characterized by occupational and financial insecurity, which is very far from being well received in all cases.

2 Determinants of Future Employment Supply and Demand

Underemployment is particularly high among young persons, who are being strongly encouraged to prolong their studies before entering the grey area (the anti-chamber of employment) which consists of courses that provide them with some sort of training and small jobs, which are often very unattractive. Underemployment may be even more involuntary at the other extreme of working life, when employed persons are encouraged, and even constrained to give up work before the statutory

Table 5.1 France and the Netherlands: comparison of certain major macroeconomic indicators

	France	Netherlands
Unemployment rate (% of active population):		
… in 1982 and 1983	8.0 and 8.3	8.5 and 11.0
… in 1996 and 1997 (third quarter)	12.4 and 12.5	6.7 and 5.6
Number of hours worked (employees, including part-time workers) in 1982 and 1996	1567 and 1529	1552 and 1372
Number of hours worked, change 1982–96 (%)	-2.4	-11.6
Active population growth, 1982–96 (%)	7.0	20.5
Total employment growth, 1982–96 (%)	1.9	22.9
Total productivity growth, per employed person, 1982–96 (%)	27.9	17.1
GDP growth, 1982–96 (%)	30.3	44.0
Real wage growth, per private sector employee, 1982–96 (%)	14.9	6.1
Part-time employment (% of total employment), in 1982 and 1983	9.1 and 1.6	19.8 and 36.5
Employed persons working less than 30 hours per week (% of total employment) in 1982 and 1983	8.9 and 12.5	18.5 and 29.3

Source: Boulin and Cette, 1997.

Figure 5.5 France: precarious forms of employment (trends since 1982)

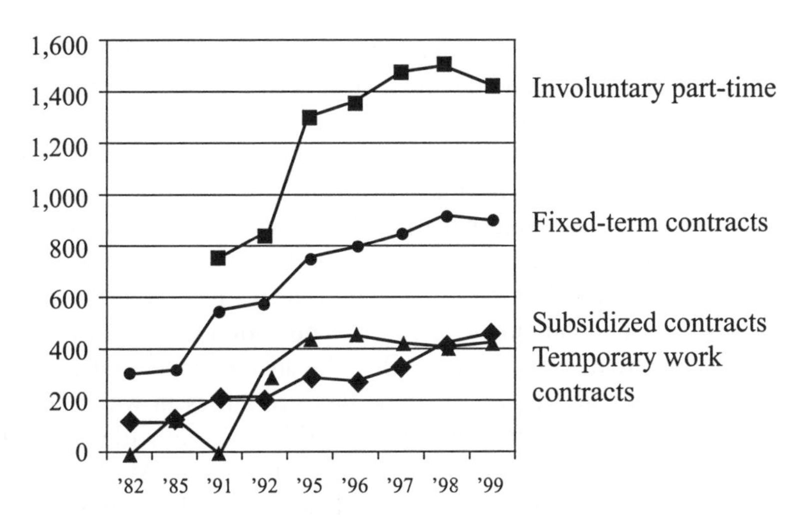

Source: INSEE, Première, March 2000.

retirement age, often at the age of 55 or earlier, whereas people in this age category are seeing their life expectancy lengthen and their state of health is tending to improve.

How might matters develop in the future? Will we see the extension of current trends, or will we, on the contrary, as affirmed by many analysts, see the dawn of a new rising Kondratieff curve, with the improvement in the economy and in employment achieved over the past two years ushering in a new era of lasting prosperity?

Extrapolations hurriedly developed from the latest available indices cannot replace prospective analysis, and it is proposed to the examine below some of the most significant variables in terms of the development of the future demand and, in a more cursory manner, the supply of jobs.

Future Demand for Jobs

The development of the potentially active population, that is those who could go out to work, will in the first place depend on:

- general demographic trends; and

Box No. 1

The unemployment rate and the employment rate: two measures of the labour market situation

The unemployment rate, which is the relation between the number of unemployed persons and the number of active persons in employment or who are seeking a job, has long been the inevitable and unique indicator of the labour market situation and trends. The unemployment rate is still a very widely used indicator. However, it is becoming increasingly common to calculate and analyse the level and trends in the employment rate, which is the proportion of the number of active persons in the working age population who are in work, and which reflects the intensity with which the total labour force of a population is being used and as such is a more relevant indicator than the unemployment rate.

By way of illustration, imagine three countries in which the total population and the population of working age are identical. The unemployment rate in these countries is 10 per cent. As shown in the table below, the number of unemployment nevertheless varies between 345 and 445 persons, with the working age population varying between 3135 and 4015 persons. It is in country C, where the number of unemployed persons is highest, that the number of active persons in work and the employment rate (such as in the case of Sweden in 1996) are also highest. In contrast, it is in country A that the number of unemployed persons is lowest and that the number of active persons in work and the employment rate (close to that of Belgium and France in 1996) are also lowest. Country B occupies an intermediary position with an employment rate of 66 per cent (equal to that of Germany in 1996).

Age	Occupational status	Country A	Country B	Country C
0–19 years		2,500	2,500	2,500
	Active in work	3,135	3630	4015
	Employment rate (%)	*57*	*66*	*73*
20–59	Unemployed	345	405	445
years	*Unemployment rate (%)*	*10*	*10*	*10*
	Other inactive persons	2,020	1,465	1,040
60 years	+2,000	2,000	2,000	
Total	10,000	10,000	10,000	

> In this example, it is clear that country C has hardly any reserves of working age population (1040 inactive persons who are not unemployed) and that, confronted with a recovery or acceleration in its economic growth, it would need to have recourse before the two others to the solution of immigration to endeavour to contain an almost generalized shortage of labour. In the event of a rapid rise in social protection expenditure (linked, for example, to an accentuation of the ageing of the population), the additional burden placed on each active person in work would be proportionally lower (assuming an identical structure of compulsory contributions) than the requirements placed on active persons in countries A and B.

- the development in attitudes and activity rates, particularly for young persons, the elderly and women.

However, other more qualitative factors, and particularly skills levels and the overall attractiveness of employment, also have to be taken into account.

Demographic Perspectives

The demographic projections developed by the National Institute of Statistics and Economic Studies (INSEE), based on the results of the general population census of 1990, for the specific needs of a recent study by the French Economic and Social Council, will be used as a basis for this analysis (Lebatard, 1999).

These projections are based on future values of three variables which determine the rhythm and scope of the renewal of the population. The values used are more contrasted (and they could have been even more so) than those of the projections on which recent works of prospective analysis have been based (Quang-Chi Dinh, 1995).

In a general context of the rapid ageing of the population, with a strong acceleration in the phenomenon in the years 2006–2010, due to the arrival at the age of 60 of the numerous generations of the baby boom, and a slowdown in the growth (or even a decline) of the total population, the category of the population which could in future contain most, if not all active persons, namely between the ages of 15 and 64, will undergo even more brutal and marked changes.

By 2020, the baby bust generations (born since 1975) will be very fully represented on the labour market. Aged under 40, they will be very far from replacing each unit of the much more numerous baby boom generations. This situation will prevail even in the hypothesis of massive recourse to immigration.

The generations of the three post-war decades will have progressively moved on to higher age categories, with their ranks very substantially greater than those of the older generations born between 1920 and 1945, and will in their great majority have withdrawn from the labour market (unless there is an extraordinary rise in the age which forms the dividing line between work and retirement).

Beyond 2002, the tendency for age categories to be smaller in size starts to affect higher age groups, unless there is a vigorous and lasting rise in the fertility rate or a very sustained and lasting level of net immigration, two hypotheses which are easier to assume than to put into effect.

This very low rate of the renewal of the generations will very logically be reflected by a very high rate of internal ageing of the population between the ages of 15 and 64 (Table 5.3).

Box No. 2

CES/INSEE demographic projections for metropolitan France

The hypotheses

- for mortality, two hypotheses have been developed. The first envisages that progress in delaying death will continue at the same pace as during the 1970s and 1980s (or, approximately, one year of life gained on average every four years). Life expectancy at birth for men and women would therefore be, respectively, 77.9 and 86.4 years in 2020 and 82.2 and 90.4 years in 2050. The second hypothesis, which reflects the central hypothesis assumed by the *Central Bureau voor Statistics (CBS)* of the Netherlands for its 1996 projections for Eurostat, assumes a slow down in the very long term in gains in life expectancy, affecting women in particular. In 2020, the life expectancy at birth of men and women would be respectively 78.2 and 85.3 years and, in 2050, would reach 80 and 87 years.
- for the fertility rate, three levels have been envisaged for the future: an average of 1.4 children per woman (more or less the current value of the fertility indicator in the European Community); an average of 1.7 children per woman (the value around which the fertility indicator

fluctuates in France); and an average of 2.1 children per women (a level which, under current mortality conditions, would ensure the replacement of the generations of women of child-bearing age).
- in terms of net migratory flows with the rest of the world, two variants have been selected (with a zero migratory balance being judged *a priori* unlikely): 50,000 net entries (the extension of current trends); and 150,000 net entries (the high hypothesis, justified by the reversal of the demographic situation in 2006 and the need to maintain the active population at an adequate level to respond to economic needs).

The results

At the end of the period covered by these projections, metropolitan France could have between 56 and 71.5 million inhabitants, made up of:
- 9.2 to 17.5 million aged under 20 years (or between 16.5 and 24.5 per cent of the total population);
- 26.7 to 32.8 million aged between 20 and 59 (or between 46 and 48 per cent of the total population);
- 20.2 to 21.2 million aged 60 or over (fluctuating between fewer than 30 and over 36 per cent of the total population).

The Population of Working Age

This population consists approximately of all those persons who are older than the age at which school is compulsory and have not yet reached the retirement age. In France, the accumulation of social progress[5] over the past 30 years has tended to reduce this category of the population to those aged between 20 and 59, compared with an earlier age range of between 15 and 64.

In the future, a rather simplistic extrapolation of the most recent trends results in the assumption of a population of working age essentially made up of persons aged between 20 and 54 years. Based on CES/INSEE projections (see Table 5.2), the population of working age could therefore be composed of between 27.4 million (CES/INSEE 1) and 28.7 million (CES/INSEE 2) persons in 2020. By 2040, the range would evidently be much wider, namely between 22.9 million (CES/INSEE 1) and 28.9 million (CES/INSEE 4). However, in view of the probability that the future ageing of the population will make it necessary to review the management of human resources, and still based on CES/

INSEE projections, it may be estimated that the population of working age in 2020 will be between 35.4 million (CES/INSEE 1) and 36.7 million (CES/INSEE 2). In 2040, the figures would range between 30.3 million (CES/INSEE 1) and 36.3 million (CES/INSEE 4).

Employment Rates

As traditionally calculated for the population between the ages of 15 and 64, employment rates in Europe are very much below those in the United States and Japan. Moreover, in the European context, France is well behind the Scandinavian countries and the United Kingdom, where the employment rate is over 70 per cent and is tending to increase.

Indeed, over 40 per cent of the population between the ages of 15 and 64, or 15 million people, are not in employment in France. There are therefore important reserves of labour which could be activated, including the unemployed (of course), but also persons aged between 15 and 24, those aged between 55 and 64 and women, as well as persons who were marginalized from the labour market while the situation was not favourable, but who could return to it if the improvement continues and if obstacles relating to skills, aspirations and costs were to be reduced. On the basis of a population of 38 million persons aged between 15 and 64, the active population in work in France could vary between 22.6 million (at the current overall employment rate in France) and 28.5 million (at the Danish employment rate of 75 per cent), or a difference of almost 6 million!

However, coming back to current figures, based on CES/INSEE projections and assuming a working age of between 20 and 55 and an employment rate of 60 per cent, the active population in work could vary in 2020 between 16.4 and 17.2 million. If the employment rate rose to 75 per cent, this range would be between 20.5 and 21.5 million. If the working age was between 20 and 64, with an employment rate of 60 per cent, the number of active persons in work could fluctuate between 21.2 million and 22 million, while the range would rise to between 26.6 and 27.5 million with an employment rate of 75 per cent.

The threat which is currently being brandished of general shortages of labour does not therefore appear very credible, unless for reasons related to skills and/or attitudes the French labour force, although substantial, was not capable of meeting the needs of the labour market.

The Future Supply of Jobs

The quality of the jobs available will depend very largely on the scale of contemporary social transfers (based on the capacity of active persons to pay contributions) and longer-term commitments (which are closely related to the duration and arrangements of working life).

Although economic growth is often classified as the primary determining factor in the future supply of jobs, greater importance is given here to enterprise strategies and the impact of public policy.

Through their decisions concerning the establishment and closure of enterprise sites, the anticipation of labour needs and the management of human resources, and the choices made in the remuneration of production factors, enterprises have played a major role in the fall in employment rates in France over the past quarter of a century.

Moreover, the public authorities have made a major contribution to this through their policies. In the first place, reference may be made to the many measures adopted to promote retirement, although the action taken (or postponed) in the field of land-use planning and local development have also had a real, if unseen, impact.

Economic Growth

There are currently two opposing theories, with the most optimistic being supported by the higher level of growth and the fall in unemployment since 1997.

According to this optimistic scenario, the combination of a favourable international environment and a new generation of technologies (ICT) means that we are going flat out into a new economy (the e-economy). We are at the beginning of a new rising Kondratieff curve which should result, after the three meagre decades at the end of the 20th century, in a new era of prosperity, which will be all the more sustainable since the sources of wealth are now immaterial (intelligence and knowledge) and are therefore, in contrast with physical resources, *a priori* inexhaustible. The recovery achieved over the past three years, and the performances in terms of job creation (which are unprecedented over the past 30 years) provide undeniable proof of the turnaround in the cycle which is already giving rise to sectoral labour shortages, and which merely foreshadow the general shortages from which France, in

Table 5.2 France: the ageing of the population aged 15–64 from 1995 to 2040, in thousands and as a per cent

CES/INSEE Projection 1 (Mortality: CBS; fertility: 1.4; net migration: +50 000)

	1995		2020		2030		2040	
15–19 years	3,774	10.0	3,087	8.0	2,853	7.9	2,616	8.0
20–24 years	4,320	11.4	3,401	8.8	2,919	8.1	2,772	8.4
25–39 years	12,897	34.1	11,754	30.5	10,365	28.9	9,004	27.4
40–54 years	11,130	29.4	12,232	31.8	11,621	32.4	11,079	33.7
55–59 years	2,828	7.5	4,115	10.7	4,157	11.6	3,842	11.7
60–64 years	2,916	7.7	3,924	10.2	3,986	11.1	3,565	10.8
Total	37,865	100.0	38,513	100.0	35,901	100.0	32,878	100.0

CES/INSEE Projection 2 (Mortality: INSEE; fertility: 1.7; net migration: +150 000)

	1995		2020		2030		2040	
15–19 years	3,774	10.0	3,770	9.3	3,743	9.3	3,757	9.5
20–24 years	4,320	11.4	3,928	9.7	3,788	9.5	3,826	9.7
25–39 years	12,895	34.1	12,360	30.6	12,193	30.4	11,893	30.0
40–54 years	11,129	29.4	12,417	30.7	12,164	30.4	12,454	31.4
55–59 years	2,826	7.5	4,088	10.1	4,198	10.5	4,012	10.1
60–64 years	2,915	7.7	3,889	9.6	3,965	9.9	3,672	9.3
Total	37,859	100.0	40,452	100.0	40,051	100.0	39,614	100.0

Table 5.2 cont'd

CES/INSEE Projection 3 (Mortality: INSEE; fertility: 1.7; net migration: +50 000)

	1995		**2020**		**2030**		**2040**	
15–19 years	3,774	10.0	3,595	9.1	3,455	9.1	3,364	9.3
20–24 years	4,320	11.4	3,753	9.5	3,491	9.2	3,424	9.4
25–39 years	12,895	34.1	11,838	30.1	11,301	29.8	10,643	29.3
40–54 years	11,129	29.4	12,193	31.0	11,576	30.5	11,500	31.7
55–59 years	2,826	7.5	4,088	10.4	4,127	10.9	3,822	10.5
60–64 years	2,915	7.7	3,889	9.9	3,951	10.4	3,544	9.8
Total	37,859	100.0	39,356	100.0	37,901	100.0	36,297	100.0

CES/INSEE Projection 4 (Mortality: INSEE; fertility: 2.1; net migration: +50 000)

	1995		**2020**		**2030**		**2040**	
15–19 years	3,774	10.0	4,180	10.3	4,220	10.4	4,365	10.7
20–24 years	4,320	11.4	4,141	10.2	4,185	10.3	4,276	10.5
25–39 years	12,895	34.1	11,956	29.6	12,382	30.6	12,666	31.1
40–54 years	11,129	29.4	12,193	30.1	11,576	28.6	11,995	29.5
55–59 years	2,826	7.5	4,088	10.1	4,127	10.2	3,822	9.4
60–64 years	2,915	7.7	3,889	9.6	3,951	9.8	3,544	8.7
Total	37,859	100.0	40,447	100.0	40,441	100.0	40,668	100.0

Table 5.2 cont'd

CES/INSEE Projection 5 (Mortality: CBS; fertility: 1.7; net migration: +50 000)

	1995		**2020**		**2030**		**2040**	
15–19 years	3,774	10.0	3,589	9.1	3,447	9.1	3,353	9.2
20–24 years	4,320	11.4	3,749	9.5	3,484	9.2	3,414	9.4
25–39 years	12,895	34.1	11,865	30.1	11,321	29.8	10,653	29.3
40–54 years	11,129	29.4	12,232	31.0	11,621	30.6	11,531	31.7
55–59 years	2,826	7.5	4,115	10.4	4,157	10.9	3,842	10.6
60–64 years	2,915	7.7	3,924	9.9	3,986	10.5	3,565	9.8
Total	37,859	100.0	39,474	100.0	38,016	100.0	36,358	100.0

Note: figures in thousands.

Source: Conseil Économique et social, 1999.

the same way as Germany, Ireland, Netherlands and Switzerland, is liable to suffer within ten years.

The proponents of the second hypothesis interpret the current recovery somewhat in the same way as the recovery at the end of the 1980s (1986–90). While recognizing that, at the international level and in particular in the dominant economies, we are seeing the emergence of a new technical and economic paradigm, they doubt the power of the new technologies to carry the rest with them and consider that French domestic demand (in the same way as European internal demand) will remain low or, at best erratic, for a number of reasons, including the ageing of the population. Based on the view that competition on international markets will be increasingly harsh, these sceptics consider that public expenditure, particularly on employment and training, could well face increasing constraints. Over and above fluctuations in the economic situation, they do not believe that the conditions exist for strong and lasting growth. In particular, they refer to the fact that structural obstacles to growth, and particularly the rigidities of French society (although the theory applies equally to German and Italian society) have not been overcome and that none of the essential reforms (for example, of the state) have been undertaken.

Care will be taken here not to come down on one side or the other in this debate. However, it will be pointed out that economic growth is something which happens, rather than being ordered at will, and that in historical terms the hopes that have periodically arisen of being on the threshold of indefinite eras of self-sustaining prosperity, fuelled by a number of specific recoveries (in the 1920s, or the 1960s, for example) have regularly been disappointed.

Moreover, even though strong economic growth would today seem to be beneficial for employment, it should nevertheless be recalled employment levels can be very variable at any given level of growth, with enterprise strategies and labour regulations giving rise to a redistribution of jobs which may or may not be egalitarian.

Enterprise Strategies

Globalization is not in itself a new process. Yet, at a time of increased technological sophistication, characterized by the rapid integration of immaterial elements, the extremely rapid transition from goods to services and from the real to the virtual economy, it is nevertheless undergoing very rapid acceleration.

Faced with the extension of *McWorld*, enterprises have been obliged to react, and particularly those in competitive sectors (Barber and Schutz, 1995).

Those that have not yet done so are reviewing their structures through, among other measures, *downsizing*, subcontracting (which has grown rapidly in France since the introduction of the 35-hour week) and the development of project teams. Large enterprises are increasingly tending to become federations of small and medium-sized enterprises (SMEs), while SMEs are becoming federations of self-employed workers. Employment relations which were previously governed by labour law are progressively entering the sphere of commercial law, with the scope of labour legislation being reduced by the practice of subcontracting (see also Belorgey, Chapter Twelve). In parallel, new forms of employment are developing which, although admittedly offering an increasingly high degree of flexibility in the operation of the labour market and contributing in one way or another to the creation of jobs, are not however welcomed in most cases insofar as they appear to be substitute jobs in the form of degraded and degrading types of work. It may be surmised that these *atypical* jobs, which have even reached the public sector, foreshadow the jobs of the future much more than the open-ended employment contracts which characterized the three post-war decades.

Moreover, enterprises, and particularly those in sectors exposed to external competition, are also adapting their geographical strategies. This is true in the industrial sector, with the example of car manufacturers which do not fear to close historical production sites and at the same time establish completely new ones several thousand kilometres away, while others continue to design their future products in the same locations, but have the components produced abroad, leaving only the assembly of the various jigsaw pieces to be carried out at their headquarters. This is all the more true in the services sector, which is prone to greater volatility. French or European managers of databases or files find it extremely advantageous to have basic data entry carried out while their employees sleep, through piecework performed by cheap labour on the other side of the world.

Although these practices contribute to a certain extent to the co-development of the industrialized and developing countries, at first sight they also tend to reduce the employment content of growth in the developed world.

But the employment benefits of high growth rates also depend greatly, as seen over the past 20 years, on the strategies adopted by enterprises to the sharing of the fruits of growth between their workforce and their shareholders, as well as on their management of human resources.

With regard to the latter, and leaving aside the globally negative long-term impact of the completely artificial and short-term rejuvenation of the labour force resulting from the eviction of older workers (combined with the fact that employment offices mostly close their doors to the youngest workers), the absence of a *human accountancy*, for which Alfred Sauvy once pleaded so effectively, is without any doubt very harmful for the overall supply of employment. Without forecasts over five or ten years (the minimum period necessary to develop training and/or suitable international recruitment policies) of the future labour needs of enterprises (in overall terms or by types of employment and skills), it will be absolutely impossible to forecast sectoral labour shortages. There are various sectors in the French economy, as well as in the German, Italian and Dutch economies, which could today employ more people if a real prospective analysis of employment needs were carried out on a regular basis, at least in the major sectors, if not in all enterprises. These include construction (builders, machine operators), metal manufacturing (welders, steel producers), transport (drivers), food production and services (information technology, representatives, catering). In particular, in the information technology, construction and transport sectors, no one can deny that the current shortages were not foreseeable, at least in part.

Perhaps the lesson will be learned from the cruel experience of current sectoral labour shortages that a high unemployment rate is no defence against such shortages.

Public Policies

Very different elements of public policy, through their impact on the volume of jobs available, may have a determining effect and be capable of undermining, in more or less serious and lasting terms, the effects of a vigorous economic recovery.

Initial and continuing training policies are not neutral in this respect. They make an essential contribution to the renewal of skills, as well as, to a greater or lesser extent, to determining the duration of working lives. To these should clearly be added employment policies (including certain aspects of policy respecting the elderly, and particularly the setting of the retirement age), as well as assistance policies, which may create very real obstacles to the recovery of employment levels.[6]

But there are also other policy areas whose influence on employment, although less immediate, is no less important. Reference may be made in particular to *land-use planning policy* and *immigration policy*.

The Case of the Saint-Nazaire Dockyards

In the case of the former, it should be pointed out in the first place that in local terms, in the absence of any real corrective policy measures, the dynamics of demographic development have transformed metropolitan France into a mosaic of areas where the population is over-concentrated and more or less absolute human deserts, as well as into a space that is increasingly segregated in terms of age and economic activity. A particularly interesting example in this respect concerns the renewal of the dockyards in Saint-Nazaire (see Guihéneuf, Guilbaudeau and du Crest, 2000).

Although the Saint-Nazaire basin had for many years been the black spot in the Pays-de-Loire region, with the highest unemployment rate and the feeling of an inexorable decline in the dockyards (which had previously produced the liner *France*), everything changed brutally over a two-year period following the launching of a plan of action designed to make the dockyards into the biggest global producer of passenger liners.

To respond to the increased demand for labour (over 10 passenger liners currently on order), the Saint-Nazaire dockyards have already recruited over 700 workers in two years and still need to recruit 500 in 2000–01, with recruitment forecasts being at the level of 250 a year beyond that date to ensure the renewal of the workforce (at a constant level). Despite their new image, certain very specific areas of initial training are providing very few recruits and the dockyards have had to widen their recruitment criteria, to the point of opening recruitment to women. Even so, recruitment by the dockyards has created a depression. Although the leading enterprise has finally been able to meet its needs, the same is not true of subcontractors and temporary work agencies, which have been obliged to raise wages and bonuses, thereby running the dire risk of undermining their objective of reducing overall production costs. The situation is so bad that the influx of population has rapidly revealed the limits of the available housing stock, with the market for rented property being completely saturated and hotels (which had become used to closing in the winter during the crisis) once again opening all year round and the caravans in camping sites being fully occupied. Prices are soaring everywhere. And the situation will continue, with the shortage of affordable housing being very far from resolved. The calls for tender issued by the city for the construction of public low-rent housing (HLM) have not been successful, with the offers made by major construction firms exceeding the envisaged budgets, among other reasons due to their incapacity to recruit workers at their usual wage levels.

It is essential for the city of Saint-Nazaire and, in broader terms, the region as a whole, to focus attention on the problem of the housing supply. But the situation is also revealing in terms of the potential impact of overlooking factors which indirectly (because they are more in the domain of planning policy) contribute to the recovery of employment. In other areas, other mismatches between living conditions and aspirations, including shortcomings in public and private services, affect large parts of the country, which as a result are losing their population, with their future survival thereby being placed in jeopardy. In the same way as the transformation of trades, good land-use planning is a long-term matter which is undermined by the failure to take a sufficiently broad prospective view and by an orchestration that is too partial and slow.

Immigration

In the past, immigration has often been a ready solution for sectoral and structural labour shortages. Although put on the backburner during the last quarter of the 20th century, immigration can once again offer a solution, although undoubtedly to a less massive extent, since the current situation differs fairly radically from that of the three post-war decades.

The recent publication of a report by the United Nations Population Division has shown that the solution to the problems which will undoubtedly be faced over the next half century by an ageing and declining population, such as the French population, is not principally to be found in the development of replacement immigration (United Nations, 2000, see also Sigg, Feature No. 7). There are certain areas in which replacement cannot be ensured by immigration from abroad (such as maintaining the ratio between active persons and retirees at its level in France of 4.4 in 1995, which is the reference year for United Nations Population Division simulations). Hopes should not therefore be unduly raised. Indeed, in many ways, replacement immigration is more of a trap than a real remedy.

Even assuming that France limited its aspirations in terms of immigration and only saw it, at the very most, as a means of maintaining its working age population at a constant level, such an objective would nevertheless require the entry of almost 5.5 million foreign nationals between 1995 and 2050.

All of the most developed countries appear to be in an identical situation, thereby giving rise almost immediately to bitter competition, with the least attractive countries being left at a disadvantage.[7] The level of development and the labour needs of these countries are relatively similar. While all potential immigrants are not equally welcome in the societies in question, some are particularly sought after everywhere. In one way or another, it is these latter immigrants who will be able to raise the stakes. Although its image and reputation is of a country that has traditionally welcomed immigration, France will also have to take up this challenge, although with resources (and particularly financial resources) that are more limited than those deployed by competing countries, and it will therefore have to replace its broad and undifferentiated receiving policy by a policy of targeted quotas.

This scenario, which had not been foreseen by French society, is now a reality. Finding itself in a hard place, France will rapidly have to review its employment policy and its policy towards the various age groups, as well as its social policies.

Notes

1 Based on current concepts and a reconstitution based on the results of general population censuses (Marchand, Thélot and Bayet, 1997).

2 While subsidized jobs amounted to fewer than 3 per cent of total employment in 1972, their share had risen to 23 per cent in 1996.

3 Indeed, when they become entitled to their pension benefits, two future retirees out of three under the general social security scheme (employed persons in the private sector) are no longer active workers, but are in

unemployment, pre-retirement, incapacity, sickness, are receiving the minimum integration income, or are jobless and not seeking work.

4 Even though the intensity and timing of the baby boom and the *baby bust* were not precisely the same everywhere.

5 Including, in particular, the lowering of the retirement age from 65 to 60.

6 Two factors intervene in the relationship between income and employment and in the development of possible *unemployment traps*:
   - the gap between the minimum income (for example, the minimum integration income in France) and the lowest wage level. Globalization and competition tend to have the effect of reducing this gap by compressing low wage levels, thereby making the corresponding jobs less attractive and increasing unemployment through marginalization. Economic recovery tends to give rise to wage claims which may, in turn, lead to certain enterprises moving production elsewhere and an increase in structural unemployment.
   - the conditions under which the minimum guaranteed income is provided. The incidence of *unemployment traps* has been found to be much higher unless the receipt of minimum benefit levels is accompanied by conditions as to their duration (such as, for example, in the United Kingdom, see Millar, Chapter Ten) or the requirement to accept the jobs which are offered (as in the policy of *workfare* in, for example, Denmark, see Madsen, Chapter Nine).

7 Of the eight countries covered by the report (France, Germany Italy, Japan, Republic of Korea, Russian Federation, United Kingdom and United States), the total immigration needed to meet such an objective would be in the order of over 150 million.

References

Barber, B.R. and Schutz, A. (eds) (1996), *Jihad vs. McWorld: How globalism and tribalism are reshaping the world*, Ballantine Books, New York.

Boulin J.-Y. and Cette, G. (1997), 'Réduire la Durée du Temps de Travail: L'exemple des Pays-Bas', *Futuribles*, No. 222, pp. 13–21.

Boulin J.-Y. and Cette, G. (1997), 'La Réduction du Temps de Travail aux Pays-Bas', *Futuribles*, No. 226, pp. 61–5.

Charpin, J.-M. (1999), *L'Avenir de nos Retraites*, Collection Rapports officials, Commissariat général du Plan, La Documentation Française, Paris.

Guihéneuf, C., Guilbaudeau, C. and du Crest, A. (2000), 'Chantiers navals: Le renouveau', *Futuribles*, No. 254, pp. 33–8.

Lebatard, C. (1999), *Les Perspectives Socio-démographiques à l'Horizon 2020–2040*, Conseil Économique et Social, Les Éditions des Journaux Officiels, Paris, p. 311.

Marchand, O., Thélot, C. and Bayet, A. (1997), *Le Travail en France, 1800–2000*, Collection Essais et Recherches, Nathan, Paris.

Quang-Chi Dinh (1995), 'Projection de la Population Totale pour la France Métropolitaine, Base RP 1990: Horizons 1990–2050', *INSEE Résultats*, No. 412 (August 1995), Paris.

United Nations (2000), *Replacement Migration: Is it a solution to declining and ageing populations?*, United Nations Population Division, New York.

Feature No. 3
Creating Service Jobs: Lessons from Extra-European Experiences

Pascal Ughetto

Services are associated with a significant potential for the development of new jobs. But these jobs are often stigmatized as being low-skilled, badly paid, precarious and subject to arduous working conditions (including pressure from clients and schedules adapted to clients rather than the quality of life of employees). Nevertheless, the experience of the United States since the 1990s shows that jobs created in service activities are not only of this sort, but can also include highly-paid skilled jobs with good working and employment conditions (OECD, 2000). But the implications of the development of the services sector in terms of policy-making are still controversial. The focus is often on the problem of labour costs. A study by Piketty maintains that the excessive labour costs of low-skilled jobs are responsible for a crucial gap in the creation of jobs in France, compared with the United States, particularly in services, and more precisely in large food stores and hotel and catering (see also Sarfati, Chapter One). According to this study, if France had the same employment rate in these activities as the United States, it would have nearly 3 million more service jobs. The study suggests that differences in labour costs between the two countries explain this gap (Piketty, 1998).

The methodology of analysis is of great significance in this respect because, by shifting from a purely economic hypothesis to a socioeconomic approach, Gadrey et al. come to very different conclusions. According to them, Piketty's proposals for France would not necessarily produce the expected effects of automatically raising the level of employment in the activities under consideration. In their view, decisions by firms to create jobs are taken at the meeting point between production strategies and societal factors. Production strategies have an important effect on the creation of jobs, depending on the approach adopted by firms with regard to performance objectives. In

France, in contrast with the United States or Japan, stores dramatically focus on cutting costs of every sort in order to survive in a context of harsh price competition, even though this implies reducing the quality of the services provided to clients. Their American and Japanese counterparts are seemingly less efficient, but this reflects a choice to develop and enrich all types of services. They create more jobs because they use more staff and provide better service for longer shop opening hours. They are also more efficient in the sense that they offer a higher value-added service (Gadrey et al., 1999).

Lower labour costs are certainly a factor in this sector in the United States and Japan. However, the strategies of firms and the importance of cost criteria in improving competitiveness could lead to efforts in France to cut costs and prices, rather than to develop jobs which provide services to clients. It should nevertheless be pointed out that the propensity of stores in the United States and Japan to generate more jobs is not solely based on labour cost criteria. Rather, it depends on an interaction between societal factors and the organization of work, based on:

i) the strategies of firms;
ii) the industrial relations situation and the legislation, which make it possible for employers to create service jobs under special wage and employment conditions;
iii) the tendency of women and students to offer their labour for part-time contracts at certain hours of the day, or on certain days of the week, in accordance with the organization of their life, their role in the family and the significance of their income for their family.

More generally, life styles are of crucial importance. A feature of the United States, and even more so of Japan, is the number of small shops which are open all day long. In Japan, this is due to the lack of space and the difficulties involved in storing large amounts of food in small houses. It may be presumed that the European way of life, and the organization of space and time at the level of the family, does not provide comparable incentives. Moreover, in some European countries, restrictive legislation on opening hours creates other obstacles to the development of these types of jobs. In Germany, for example, the industrial relations system has not up to now made it possible to change the law to offer more opportunities to employers.

This is not to say that Europe would definitely not be favourable to service jobs on the grounds that social attitudes are too rigid. In Sweden, for example, which is a welfare state that pays great attention to the living conditions of families, a major contribution is made to the development of services designed to improve the quality of life (such as childcare services). The corresponding jobs are a result of opposing forces: on the one hand, the opportunities offered to women or men to adapt their working time over various periods (week, year, life ...) make it possible for families to produce the services that they need themselves (such as taking care of their children). On the other hand, the high standard of living (fuelled by redistribution, public services and relatively high wages) offers the means to have recourse to services outside the household. This is why reducing working time is sometimes regarded as favouring employment, provided it is accompanied by changes in the organization of life and the corresponding services (du Tertre, 1999). Another example is the efforts made by Italian cities to improve the quality of transportation services, which both change the quality of life and act as an incentive to job creation (various authors, 1997).

The methodological aspects of these issues have clear policy implications. The development of jobs devoted to services is determined less by pure economic logic than by specific societal interactions between the dominant choices of firms in terms of production strategies and the socioeconomic characteristics of life style. However, a crucial aspect is that, as analysed by Gadrey et al., the development of these types of jobs in food stores is associated with a clear differentiation in employment and wage conditions. Better service means higher production costs.

In Japanese and American food stores, this is supported by both clients (through higher prices) and by workers (in the form of lower wages). Hence, more service jobs would in the first place appear to be linked to the capacity of clients to pay for the additional value. From this perspective, increasing the purchasing power of households (through higher wages and public redistribution measures) could be of great importance in providing people with the capacity to avail themselves of more services. Moreover, the possibility of avoiding badly paid work would appear to be dependent on both what is permitted by law and the industrial relations system and on the capacity of clients to pay for more of the added value (so that workers bear less of the burden).

However, such conclusions have to be tempered by the propensity of European countries to think in terms of promoting social inclusion, rather than merely creating more jobs. Europe generally does not consider poor workers as a preferable alternative to unemployment. This means that additional service jobs have to offer opportunities for the improvement of skills, thereby providing workers with the opportunity to move out of unskilled jobs. In more general terms, the problem also involves a shift from improving the job content of economic activities, to increasing the proportion of skilled workers in the total workforce.

References

Gadrey, J., Jany-Catrice, F. and Ribault T. (1999), *France, Japon, Etats-Unis: L'emploi en détail: Essai de socio-économie comparative*, Presses Universitaires de France (PUF), Paris.

OECD (2000), *Employment Outlook*, Paris.

Piketty, T. (1998), 'L'emploi dans les services en France et aux Etats-Unis: Une analyse structurelle sur longue période', *Économie et Statistique*, 318, INSEE, Paris.

Tertre, C. du, (1999), 'Intangible and Interpersonal Services: Toward new political economy tools', *Service Industries Journal*, 19 (1), Frank Cass Publishers, Ilford.

Various authors, (1997), 'Territorial Excellence: Time and quality in the cities', *Transfer*, 3, Issue 4/1997, Keesing Publishers, Antwerp.

PART II

SOCIAL PROTECTION AND LABOUR MARKET TRAJECTORIES IN SELECTED COUNTRIES AND WORLD REGIONS

Chapter Six

Social Protection and Labour Market Outcomes in Australia

Raymond Harbridge and Prue Bagley

Introduction

This chapter examines the intersections between the labour market and social security. The first section describes the changes in the labour market. These include the increased participation of women, the dramatic expansion of casual and part-time work and the rapid growth of unemployment. These changes have placed stress on a system that was predicated on female financial dependence within the confines of the nuclear family and full-time permanent employment for men of working age. The second section discusses how Australian governments in the 1990s have attempted to respond to these changes, for example by means of labour market assistance, changes to social security allowances and the introduction of a national employment-based superannuation scheme.

Changes in the Labour Market

Women's Participation

The dramatic growth in the number of women participating in the labour force is one of the most important changes in the postwar era. In 1966, the reported participation rate was 41.3 per cent for all women and 30.9 per cent for married women. By 1980, these figures stood at 52.9 per cent and 46.9 per cent, and by 1999 they had reached 65.8 per cent and 63.8 per cent, respectively (Australian Bureau of Statistics, 1986 and 1996). Not only is the participation rate for all women increasing, but the gap between all women and married women is disappearing.[1]

Over a similar period, the participation rate of men has declined from 90.9 per cent in 1966, to 86.9 per cent in 1980 and 83.2 per cent in

1999.[2] It is unlikely to be a simple matter of one group replacing another. Pech and Innes argue that the decline in the participation rate of men 'was not caused by women displacing men in the labour market – the Australian workforce remains one of the most gender-segregated in the world' (Pech and Innes, 1998, p. 4). Factors that explain this increase in women's participation probably include: a change in occupational composition, with a growth in employment areas which traditionally employed women and a concurrent contraction of industries that employed men (Wilson, 1994; Department of Social Security, 1993); the increased level of educational attainment of women and a greater willingness amongst employers to employ women (Bacon, 1999); and legislation prohibiting discrimination and promoting equal opportunities (Pech and Innes, 1998). There have also been significant changes in personal and family relationships and in women's expectations of career prospects.

The data in Table 6.1 show that, despite the enormous growth in the participation rate of women, there is still a sizeable gap in the participation rates of men and women. Much of the increased participation of women is due to the expansion of atypical forms of employment (Mangan and Williams, 1999, p. 40). This change in participation rates has policy implications for the Government because it calls into question traditional assumptions about women's financial dependence on men.

Casual Employment

The Australian Bureau of Statistics (ABS) defines casual employees as those who do not receive paid sick or holiday leave. Despite having some limitations, the strength of this definition is that it captures one of the most important aspects of casual employment, namely non-entitlement to benefits (Campbell, 1996). There has been an enormous growth in the proportion of casual labour. Casual employment in Australia now stands at 27 per cent of all employees. This casualization of the workforce has been wide ranging and 'has applied to both full-time and part-time employees ... the private and public sector ... all industries ... all occupations and all sizes of workplace' (Campbell, 1996, p. 576).

As the data in Table 6.2 indicate, the proportion of casual employees rose in the decade up to 1998. What is notable is the increase in casual

Table 6.1 Australia: participation rates by gender, 1966–99*

Year	Males	All women	Married women	Total
Aug. 1966	90.9	41.3	30.9	66.4
Aug. 1970	89.9	45.1	37.6	67.7
Aug. 1975	87.9	49.1	44.1	68.7
Sept. 1980	86.9	52.9	46.9	70.0
Sept. 1985	85.0	55.1	50.3	70.2
Sept. 1990	85.5	62.4	60.0	74.0
Sept. 1995	84.6	64.8	62.9	74.8
Sept. 1999	83.2	65.8	63.8	74.5

* Includes only persons aged 15–64, producing a higher participation rate than some other figures that include all persons aged over 15 years.

Sources: Data for 1966–77: *Labour Force Australia 1966–1984* (ABS, 1987, Cat. No. 6204.0); data for 1978–95: *Labour Force Australia 1978–1995* (ABS, 1996, Cat. No. 6204.0); data for 1996–99: *Labour Force Australia* (monthly) (ABS, various issues, Cat. No. 6203.0).

Table 6.2 Australia: casual and other employees by gender

	Casual '000		Other '000		Proportion of casual (%)	
	1988	1998	1988	1998	1988	1998
Men	415.7	894.1	3,127.8	3,064.1	11.7	22.6
Women	737.3	1,052.0	1,821.2	2,234.6	28.8	32.0
Total	1,152.9	1,946.1	4,949.0	5,298.7	18.9	26.9

Source: ABS, 1999a.

work amongst men. While both the proportion and actual number of women in casual employment is greater than that of men, the rate of change for women has been lower.

Romeyn notes some distinctive features of casual work. In contrast to permanent work:

- casual workers tend to have left school early and not studied further;
- casual workers receive less in-house and external training;

- few casual workers have a career structure available to them;
- casual workers have low levels of eligibility for superannuation, paid study leave and long service leave;
- many of the occupations in which casual workers are concentrated tend to be relatively low-skilled;
- despite *casual loading*,[3] casual employees tend to have lower average earnings (Romeyn, 1992, p. 38).

There is debate about the status of casual employees. Norris and Wooden claim that the distinctive feature of the casualization of labour in Australia is the extent to which workers are protected by regulations governing the terms and conditions of their employment. They argue that this distinguishes Australian casual workers from temporary workers in other countries (Norris and Wooden, 1996, p. 13; see also Dawkins and Norris, 1990, p. 171). In contrast to Romeyn, Norris and Wooden say that the impact of casual loading is that 'multivariate research has invariably found that part-time workers in Australia receive higher average hourly earnings than do otherwise similar full-time workers' (Norris and Wooden, 1996, p. 13). Recent research tends to indicate that casual workers are often in a less than desirable position. Analysing data from the survey of employment and unemployment patterns conducted by the ABS, Dunlop identified the risk factors associated with being low paid. She found that:

- casual employment is positively associated with the probability of low pay;
- those in full-time employment and those in permanent work have a greater chance of upwards earning mobility than casual workers or those employed part-time;
- casual workers have a higher chance of exiting employment after one year (Dunlop, 2000).

The debate regarding the status of casual employees remains unresolved. For example, in the latest literature, Wooden sees casualization as a sign of increasing flexibility (Wooden, 2000), while Watson views it as one of the indicators of the worsening health of the labour market (Watson, 2000).

Part-time Work

Part-time employment has increased. As illustrated by the data in Table 6.3, the differences between employed men and women are marked. For both categories, the increase in actual numbers has been nearly fivefold over the past three decades. While the total number of women employed is less than that of men, the number of women working part-time has always exceeded the number of men over the same period. The other striking pattern that appears in the data is the shift in composition of the total employed labour force. As the data in Table 6.3 show, male part-time employment was less than 5 per cent in 1966. But, by 1999, it had more than doubled. Women's part-time employment grew by a similar magnitude.

An important factor in the growth in part-time work is the extent to which those working part-time choose to do so. Part-time work may suit family commitments, and there is a link between the growth of part-time work and the increase in the participation of married women in the labour force (Pech and Innes, 1998). However, there may be some people who work part-time because they are unable to find full-time employment. ABS data indicate that the proportion of people working part-time who would rather work more hours has changed over time. It is interesting to note that the figure peaked in 1983 (20 per cent) and again in 1993 (28.1 per cent). A comparison with unemployment figures shows that they also reached new highs in those two years. While *would prefer to work more hours* does not translate directly into *would rather work full-time*, it does illustrate a degree of underemployment.

Self-employment and Contracting

While self-employment is often mentioned in discussions about the dynamic nature of the Australian labour market, it has not been subject to the same degree of analysis as either part-time or casual employment. The growth in self-employment is often reported as one of the forms of nonstandard employment that has increased in Australia.

The ABS defines a self-employed person as someone who 'operates his or her own economic enterprise or engages independently in a profession or trade and the business is not incorporated, either with or without employees'. As shown by the data in Table 6.4, although the actual number of self-employed people has increased, the rate of self-

Table 6.3 Australia: part-time employed by gender

Year	Employed full-time '000	Employed part-time '000	Total employment '000	Employed part-time (per cent)
Men				
Nov. 1966	3,248.10	125.00	3,373.10	3.71
Nov. 1970	3,524.80	126.70	3,651.50	3.47
Nov. 1975	3,678.40	156.90	3,835.30	4.09
Sept. 1980	3,806.60	214.80	4,021.40	5.34
Sept. 1985	3,925.30	264.10	4,189.40	6.30
Sept. 1990	4,235.40	378.70	4,614.10	8.21
Sept. 1995	4,210.80	523.40	4,734.20	11.06
Sept. 1999	4,387.70	622.00	5,009.70	12.42
Women				
Nov. 1966	1,117.40	363.20	1,480.60	24.53
Nov. 1970	1,313.90	485.50	1,799.40	26.98
Nov. 1975	1,404.00	705.50	2,109.50	33.44
Sept. 1980	1,513.40	825.20	2,338.60	35.29
Sept. 1985	1,648.60	976.70	2,625.30	37.20
Sept. 1990	1,975.40	1,316.00	3,291.40	39.98
Sept. 1995	2,072.70	1,533.70	3,606.40	42.53
Sept. 1999	2,165.00	1,733.20	3,898.20	44.46

Sources: Data for 1966–77: *Labour Force Australia 1966–1984* (ABS, 1987, Cat. No. 6204.0); data for 1978–95: *Labour Force Australia 1978–1995* (ABS, 1996, Cat. No. 6204.0); data for 1996–99: *Labour Force Australia* (monthly) (ABS, various issues, Cat. No. 6203.0).

Table 6.4 Australia: self-employment and total employment

	Self-employed '000		All employed '000		Self-employed (per cent)	
	1978	**1996**	**1978**	**1996**	**1978**	**1996**
Men	641.7	830.7	3,890.1	4,732.6	16.5	17.6
Women	241.6	391.3	2,123.5	3,584.0	11.4	10.9
Total	883.3	1,222.0	6013.6	8,316.6	14.7	14.7

Source: ABS *Labour Force Australia*, January 1997, Cat. No. 6203.0.

employment (as defined by the ABS) has remained almost static for two decades.

Noting that the self-employed are a diverse group of workers, VandenHeuvel and Wooden attempted to analyse the component parts of the self-employed workforce to distinguish between independent and dependent contractors. They found that self-employed contractors accounted for 7.5 per cent of non-farm employment and that of those,[4] 61.7 per cent can be described as independent of the hiring organization (in the sense that they regularly provide services to more than one organization ... [and] 38.3 of self-employed contractors or 2.9 per cent of the total non-farm work force are treated by employers as contractors but in practice may be difficult to distinguish from wage and salary earners (VandenHeuvel and Wooden, 1995, p. 273).

Unemployment

Unemployment, and people's experiences of unemployment, have changed markedly over the past three decades in Australia. The numbers of unemployed people have risen dramatically. The length of time a person may expect to be unemployed has increased and the number of people unemployed long term has grown.

Table 6.5 Australia: unemployment rate by gender, 1966–99[5]

Year	Men (per cent)	Women (per cent)	Total (per cent)
Nov. 1966	0.9	2.8	1.8
Nov. 1970	1.1	2.5	1.8
Nov. 1975	3.8	7.0	5.4
Sept. 1980	5.0	7.7	6.3
Sept. 1985	7.6	8.6	8.1
Sept. 1990	7.3	7.4	7.3
Sept. 1995	8.9	7.7	8.3
Sept. 1999	7.5	7.4	7.4

Sources: Data for 1966–77: *Labour Force Australia 1966–1984* (ABS, 1987, Cat. No. 6204.0); data for 1978–95: *Labour Force Australia 1978–1995* (ABS, 1996, Cat. No. 6204.0); data for 1996–99: *Labour Force Australia* (monthly) (ABS, various issues, Cat. No. 6203.0).

The data in Table 6.5 illustrate the significant rise in unemployment over the past three decades. In 1966, the rate was less than 2 per cent, while by September 1999 it was 7.4 per cent, having reached double digits three times in the intervening years (1983, 1992 and 1993). It should be noted that the actual number of unemployed people may be higher than the figures above suggest, as they do not include discouraged jobseekers, a rather depressingly self-descriptive term. In addition to the increase in the actual numbers of the unemployed, the nature of unemployment has changed. The average duration of unemployment has increased markedly since 1978, when the average length of time spent unemployed was about 28 weeks for both men and women. In 1999, unemployed men were out of work for an average of 60.2 weeks and unemployed women for an average of 41.7 weeks (ABS, Cat. Nos. 6204.0 and 6203.0).

It is estimated that the unemployment rate for indigenous Australians is about 26 per cent (Aboriginal and Torres Strait Islander Commission, undated). This is much higher than total Australian unemployment and it could be even higher in practice. Significant numbers of indigenous people are employed on Community Development Employment Project (CDEP) schemes (about one quarter of all employed). Without these schemes, the unemployment rate would be likely to be as high as 40 per cent (Taylor and Hunter, undated).

Government Responses to Changes in the Labour Market

The last two governments in Australia, the 1993 Labor government and the Liberal-National coalition government elected in 1996, have responded very differently to the challenges arising at the intersection of a considerably changed labour market and a welfare system under pressure. It is valuable to review some of the initiatives of the two governments, as they illustrate an interesting contrast in political approaches driven by differing philosophical explanations of how labour markets and social security systems do (or should) operate.

Social Security History

Australia's system of social security developed incrementally during the 20th century. The means-tested old age pension was first introduced nationally in 1909.[6] In the 1940s, the system was extended to include family allowances (in 1941), the widow's pension (in 1942) and the unemployment allowance (in 1945). The supporting parents allowance (for sole parents) was introduced in 1973. The role of the Australian state in the provision of welfare was not limited to the payment of cash benefits. It also involved direct intervention in the labour market through wage regulation. This has been called the *wage-earner welfare state*. In this regard, Castles notes that:

> In Australia, wages policy, in large part, substituted for social policy ... welfare state through state expenditure was, in quite large part, pre-empted by a welfare state through wage regulation (Castles, 1994, p. 124).

This policy revolved around the nuclear family. Everything possible was done to guarantee that a *fair wage* was paid to adult men which would ensure that the male breadwinner was able to support himself and his dependent wife and children (Castles, 1994, p. 124). Although some authors have, with justification, been critical of social security systems because of the manner in which they have institutionalized women's financial dependence on men, it would be fair to say that the *wage-earner welfare state* was a product of its time.[7]

In common with social security systems in other countries, the Australian welfare state has come under increasing pressure as the rate of dependency has risen. This rate increased from 12 per cent in 1954, to still only 12.1 per cent in 1971, to 18 per cent by 1981 and 21.3 per cent by 1993 (Jones, 1996, p. 81).

The 1993 Labor Government Response

The Labor government's response to the changes in the labour market and the stresses on the social security system were contained in the policy programme known as *Working Nation,* which was introduced in 1994 and only partially implemented, as Labor lost power early in 1996. In the context of this chapter, two components of the Working Nation policy are important: the reform of labour market assistance and the changes to income support incentives.

Reform of Labour Market Assistance

The primary focus was on those who had been unemployed for 18 months or longer.[8] The government believed that economic growth alone would not deliver jobs to all the unemployed. At the heart of these reforms was a job guarantee, known as the *Job Compact.*

Placements for those in the Job Compact were to come from the expansion of the *Jobstart* programme and the introduction of a new job creation scheme called *New Work Opportunities* (NWO).[9] It was anticipated that smaller existing schemes would be expanded. The bulk of the 160,000 placements were to come from Jobstart. It is important to note the major differences between the Jobstart programme and the other initiatives. Jobstart was designed to provide placement in a subsidized job, while the other programmes generally offered places in *brokered programmes,* in which a third party funded by the Government supplied training and work experience. In the brokered programmes there was no expectation that work would be extended beyond the life of the programme. Much of the planning centred around this difference:

> … the 70/30 balance between subsidized jobs and brokered placements was vital in terms of programme efficiency and cost. Employer placements were more likely to lead to regular jobs, and on average would cost about A$4,600. Average NWO places, by contrast, were projected to cost about A$11,400 per place' [10] (Finn, 1997, p. 28).

Jobstart wage subsidies to employers were thought to be generous enough to encourage them to employ the long-term unemployed. The longer a person had been unemployed the greater the subsidy. To encourage longer retention, employers who kept workers on at the end of the 12 month period would be entitled to a A$500 bonus.

Delivery

The long-term unemployed were to receive intensive *case management.* Initially, all case management was to be provided by a government agency, the Commonwealth Employment Service (CES). However, the government intended to introduce competition into the provision of this service and planned from 1995 to allow community and private sector agencies to bid for case management contracts.

Income Support Incentives

The reforms were to include:

- spouses of unemployed people would receive payment *in their own right* according to their activity;
- the income test for couples would be modified so that it was largely based on the income of each individual;[11]
- the allowance income test would be modified;
- the Department of Social Security would modify its administrative processes to further encourage unemployed people to take up part-time and casual work opportunities (that is to make it easier to advise the Department of earnings and to ensure that allowances were reinstated without difficulty when a full-time casual job ended) (Working Nation, 1994b, pp. 144 and 154).

These initiatives were designed to encourage unemployed people to take up part-time and casual or temporary work. They were also designed to encourage persons (mainly women) with spouses who were in receipt of unemployment allowances to enter the labour market.

Evaluation

Social policy initiatives such as Working Nation are notoriously difficult to evaluate. It is difficult to establish the outcomes that might have occurred had the programme not been implemented. The Labor government's loss of power early in 1996, midway through Working Nation's planned life, confounds the picture further, since Working Nation was largely abandoned by the Liberal-National coalition government.

Labour Market Assistance

Jones is critical of the government for embarking on such a large-scale active labour market programme when research has shown that such policies are not as successful as was first thought. Jones identifies the possible unintended outcomes from initiatives such as Working Nation as: the displacement of one group of unemployed by another (for example, the short-term by the long-term unemployed); and the deadweight cost where a worker who would have been employed anyway ends up in a subsidized job. He also notes that participants may become permanently dependent on assistance programmes and employers may become dependent on subsidized labour (Jones, 1996, pp. 171–2).

Finn is more generous and regards Working Nation as a core part of the government's effort to modernize the beleaguered welfare system. He claims that the government did have evidence to support its belief that intensive assistance would be the most effective way to help the long-term unemployed and that, initially at least, the signs for Working Nation were good, with a 20 per cent drop in long-term unemployment by June 1995 (Finn, 1999, p. 59). However, the data are problematic. The ABS, in its monthly *Labour Force Survey*, from which much of the data regarding the labour market are drawn, does not provide a separate category for those involved in labour market programmes. As a result, many of the participants in the Job Compact may show up as *employed* in official statistics, thereby creating an artificial picture. In addition, and perhaps of more consequence, there was the problem of *churning*. The government had decided that Job Compact participants who were unsuccessful in obtaining work at the end of the programme would no longer be considered to be long-term unemployed because of their 'substantial intervening job experience' (Working Nation, 1994b, p.129). This *churning*, or *recycling*, meant that many of the most disadvantaged unemployed disappeared from official sight as they joined the pool of the short-term unemployed.

The biggest obstacle that Working Nation faced, a factor which had been underestimated, was the aversion of employers to hiring the long-term unemployed. The government had anticipated that the incentive of graduated wage subsidies would overcome this problem. This was not the case. Employers had negative attitudes towards the long-term unemployed. They believed they were not *job ready*, were lacking in skills and motivation and had poor attitudes towards work. These perceptions were compounded by the belief that Australia's legislation regarding unfair dismissal would make it difficult for employers to dismiss unsuitable workers (Department of Employment, Education, Training and Youth Affairs, 1996, pp. 47–8). In the first year (1994–95), the number of placements in Jobstart was about 16,000 (28 per cent) lower than had been anticipated, and indications were that the number of available placements would continue to drop. The government was forced to expand the number of placements in the brokered programmes, which was a more expensive alternative and provided less opportunities for the client to find work after the end of the programme.

Table 6.6 Australia: employment outcomes for Job Compact clients, February 1996

Programme	**Proportion of Job Compact clients in unsubsidized employment (per cent)**
Jobstart	41.1
Jobskills	29.8
New work opportunities	21.6

Source: Department of Employment, Education, Training and Youth Affairs, 1996, p. 53.[12]

To add to the woes of Working Nation, the number of people feeding into the programme (the newly long-term unemployed) increased. This meant that, while the total numbers in the Job Compact were declining, they were not dropping as substantially as had been anticipated. This added to the pressure on available placements. The Department believes that this happened as a result of Working Nation's exclusive focus on workers who had been unemployed for 18 months or more. Some of the help which had previously been available to persons who had been unemployed for less than 18 months had been withdrawn as the focus shifted (Department of Employment, Education, Training and Youth Affairs, 1996, p. 53).

The Department's evaluation therefore found that Job Compact had achieved only limited success in reaching its goals. While the figures for the long-term unemployment had fallen, it was difficult to establish the extent to which the programme had positively helped participants, rather than merely recycling them through the programme and into short-term unemployment. On balance, the Department did not think that Jobstart constituted the most suitable first programme for the long-term unemployed. These findings are contested. Junakar and Kapuscinski argue that Working Nation was successful in aiding the long-term unemployed. They claim that 'it was a very valuable social experiment which was aborted for political reasons' (Junakar and Kapuscinski, 1997, p. 1).

Income Support Incentives

Saunders believes that these reforms represent a significant change in philosophy and, irrespective of how successful they were as a work incentive, deserve to be applauded on the grounds of equity. What is not clear, as Saunders illustrates, is how successful the measures were in encouraging women to work. He suggests that factors other than disincentives in social security payments play a role in determining the labour market status of women whose partners are unemployed (Saunders, 1995).

The changes to the income test were designed to encourage unemployed people (married and single) to take up part-time and casual work by reducing the high effective marginal tax rates (EMTRs). High EMTRs act as a disincentive to work. Working Nation attempted to tackle this problem, and Saunders commends the approach as one 'which recognizes that the longer-term benefits of increased labour supply and reduced benefit dependence can outweigh these short-run costs' (Saunders, 1995, p. 13). However, he concludes that the policy was likely to be less effective than the government anticipated. Finn reports that the new rules were 'plagued by ambiguities'[13] and that 'the problems experienced in negotiating the income test rules reflected the overall stress the social security system was under as it implemented a bewildering array of reforms and rule changes' (Finn, 1997, p. 55).

The 1996 Liberal-National Coalition Government Response

In March 1996, a Liberal-National coalition government replaced Labor. The coalition had a greater faith in the ability of the market to ease unemployment and a stated antipathy for government interference in the workings of the market. While space precludes documenting every aspect of the new government's policies, some aspects are of particular interest. These are the *Work for the Dole* scheme and the introduction of competition into employment placement. A review of the major piece of industrial relations legislation, the 1996 Workplace Relations Act, is of interest in view of the government's commitment to introducing labour market flexibility.

Work for the Dole

The policy of *mutual obligation* was introduced in 1998. The policy initially targeted young people, but has since been extended to include:

- 18–19 year old school leavers who have been receiving the youth allowance for three months;
- 18–24 year olds receiving the unemployment allowance for six months or more; and
- 25–34 year olds receiving the unemployment allowance for 12 months or more.

An unemployed person's *mutual obligation* may be fulfilled by undertaking voluntary or part-time work, or education or training. Alternatively, people must accept a place in the Work for the Dole scheme as such places become available. Failure to comply results in reductions in allowances. This type of scheme is not new. However, Work for the Dole does represent a major expansion. In this context, it has been promoted as a *social exchange* rather than a labour market programme.[14]

Macintyre argues that Work for the Dole 'represented a clear shift in the underlying culture of Australian welfare away from rights based entitlement and towards a system based on a form of mutual obligation' (Macintyre, 1999, p. 103). This is an explanation that sits comfortably with the government's philosophy of social security. As the government ministers declared, 'the concept of mutual obligation has gained strong public acceptance through its aim of encouraging self-reliance and personal responsibility' (Reith and Newman, 1999).

The government's evaluation of the Work for the Dole scheme found that the programme had been successful in developing positive work habits in young people. It found that 34 per cent of participants were working three months after leaving the programme and that a further 23 per cent had some employment in the three months since leaving the programme (Department of Employment, Workplace Relations and Small Business, 1999). As with all evaluations, it needs to be read with some caution. Hawke notes that 'the specifications for evaluation of the "Work for the Dole" scheme are general, value laden and highly subjective' (Hawke, 1998, p. 401). Comparing outcomes for 1994–95 and 1999, both boom years for employment, the Australian Council of

Social Service found the scheme was much less successful than work experience programmes under Labor's Working Nation package. Only 33 per cent of former participants were in unsubsidized work three months after leaving the programme, compared with a success rate of 59 per cent achieved by the axed Jobstart programme. It was also found to be somewhat less successful than the current intensive assistance services provided through the Job Network which have achieved an employment rate of 36 per cent. The Council acknowledges that the Work for the Dole scheme offers some positive benefits, such as social contact and the restoration of work habits. But its employment success has been limited by the lack of formal training, its two-day-a-week duration over six months in mostly non-mainstream jobs and its failure to lift participants out of poverty (Australian Council of Social Service, 2000). Work for the Dole may well be politically popular, but in reality it may amount to little more than window dressing.

Competition in Employment Placement

The concept of building competition into employment counselling and placement were included in Working Nation. However, the new plans represent a significant extension. The new government introduced the *Job Network,* which now consists of about 200 private, community and government organizations which provide job matching and job search training. In addition, they provide intensive assistance to the long-term unemployed and those at high risk of becoming long-term unemployed. The organizations receive a fee from the government for every person placed in employment. This is paid on a differential fee scale, with those who are the most difficult to place attracting a premium fee. Some regard this as a theoretically and fiscally sound policy that promotes choice and competition (see, for example, Department of Employment, Education and Training, 1998). Others regard it as the inappropriate privatization of unemployment (see, for example, Goodman, 1997).

The 1996 Workplace Relations Act

The new government introduced changes in the industrial relations system, in the form of changes to the existing award system and through the 1996 Workplace Relations Act. There is debate about the degree to which this marks an extension of Labor's policies, or a significant break with the past.

Historically, most workers were covered by awards negotiated by trade unions at the industry level. Changes to Australia's centralized system began before the election of the coalition government. In 1991, the Accord included an agreement to begin introducing enterprise bargaining, that is single-employer negotiation.[15] Campbell and Brosnan see this as the first decisive step towards deregulation (Campbell and Brosnan, 1999).

Since the election of the coalition, the pace of deregulation has quickened markedly. The key objective of the 1996 Workplace Relations Act is:

> ... ensuring that the primary responsibility for determining the relationship between employers and employees rests with the employer and employees at the workplace or enterprise level (Department of Employment, Workplace Relations and Small Business, 1998).

The focus is now on negotiating employment contracts (Australian Workplace Agreements) at the enterprise level. Although awards continue to exist, the government views their role as one of a safety net of minimum standards. Their coverage has been restricted to 20 so-called *allowable matters*, and they may not set terms or conditions beyond these areas.[16] However, changes to the labour relations system may not be occurring as swiftly as the government intended, as illustrated by the data in Table 6.7, although there is a clear difference between the public and private sector.

Table 6.7 Australia: percentage of employees covered by the various payment systems

	Awards only	Overawards/ unregistered agreements	Registered collective agreements	Other pay arrangements (inc. AWAs)*
Private sector	26	30	29	15
Public sector	13	1	76	10
All employees	22	22	42	14

* Australian Workplace Agreements.

Source: Department of Employment, Workplace Relations and Small Business, 2000.

The government believes that it is appropriate for it to play only a minimal role in setting the wages and conditions of Australian workers. In contrast, the Australian Council of Trade Unions sees the Act as 'part of a deliberate strategy to shift the balance of bargaining power significantly in favour of employers' (Australian Council of Trade Unions, 1997). There is clearly tension between mechanisms of social protection, as traditionally provided by the labour relations system, and the efforts of the government and employers to reduce labour costs.

Superannuation

Australia's population is ageing. The ABS projects that by 2051 about 25 per cent of the population will be aged 65 years and over (ABS, 1999b). Traditionally, Australia has had a two-tiered system of retirement income: the *age pension* and voluntary savings. The age pension is universal (subject to a means test) and is funded from general taxation. It is payable to men aged 65 years and over and to women aged 61 years and over.[17]

The ageing population profile resulted in concern about the affordability of the age pension and the subsequent establishment of the so-called *third pillar* in Australia's retirement income system. The *superannuation guarantee* was therefore introduced in 1992. This consists of a mandatory scheme requiring employers to contribute an amount calculated as a percentage of each employee's earnings. Castles believes that the development of this type of retirement income scheme is in keeping with earlier developments in the Australian wage earner welfare state. It came into effect while a Labor government was in office and has its genesis in the agreements reached between the government and the trade unions (the Accord) (Castles, 1994, p. 135).

The percentage of employees receiving superannuation benefits has increased since 1993. There is still a difference between the proportion of men (89.7 per cent in 1998) and women (87.6 per cent in 1998) receiving superannuation benefits through employment, although it has grown smaller (ABS, undated, *Labour-Superannuation*). There have been some concerns about the equity of the system, which is built around the notion of full-time permanent work. The result may be that those who work on a part-time or casual basis,[18] or those with fractured work histories,[19] do not receive the full benefit of the superannuation guarantee (see Olsberg, 1997).

Bateman suggests that the changes in labour force participation over the past three decades (the reduced participation rate of older men and the increased participation of older women) indicate that men have begun retiring earlier and women later (Bateman, 1999, p. 46). However, work done by the Retirement Income Modeling Unit at the Department of the Treasury argues that it is conceptually incorrect to equate changes in the participation rate with changes in retirement practice:

> Our estimates indicate that the retired only make up some 60% of those classified as Not in the Labour Force ... RIM estimates that, since 1978, around 25% of the fall in participation rate for males aged 45–54 was due to early retirement ... we estimate that the increase in participation rate of females aged 45–54 was reduced some 5% by early retirement and reduced by around 25% for females aged 55–59 ... results suggest that the increases in early retirement have slowed and might even have stabilised (Bacon, 1999, p. 9).

As the superannuation guarantee policy is less than a decade old, it is difficult to assess its impact on labour supply.[20] Research undertaken for the OECD identifies two possible areas in which the superannuation guarantee may affect the labour market. Firstly, mandatory employer contributions may lead to short-term wage rigidity. Secondly, once the superannuation guarantee matures, earnings from it will impact on age pension entitlements. The report concludes that, although there is little evidence on which to judge the impact of the superannuation guarantee, most agree that in the long term these impacts will be minor (OECD, 1997, p. 60).

Conclusion

There have been legislative responses by the various governments to the challenges arising out of changes in the Australian labour market. The 1993 Labor government introduced Working Nation, which represented considerable government intervention in the labour market. The government attempted to ameliorate long-term unemployment through investment in labour market programmes. There is debate about the efficacy of this programme. On balance, it was probably not as effective as the government had hoped. Attempts to encourage people receiving social security allowances to take up the increasingly available part-time and casual work also faced difficulties. Although amendments to allowable income levels did provide some encouragement, they were constrained by the complex system of entitlements and abatements. Working Nation addressed the increased labour market participation rate of women through changes that sought to remove the notion of female financial dependence. As discussed above, these changes had some merit on the grounds of increased equity, regardless of how successful they were in other terms (Saunders, 1995). Finally, the Labor government introduced a national employment-based retirement income scheme, the super-annuation guarantee. This built on Australia's tradition of the wage earner welfare state and has increased the proportion of workers receiving superannuation benefits. Somewhat ironically, it is based on traditional forms of employment. As a result, those who work part time, in casual employment or who have fractured employment histories will receive less benefit than persons who have been employed in full-time permanent work for the duration of their working lives.

The Liberal National coalition government, which was elected in 1996, has also grappled with the changes in the labour market. Its response has focused on the individual and on notions of individual responsibility. These themes are consistent with neo-liberal philosophy. The coalition government introduced Work for the Dole as part of a package of mutual responsibility. The unemployed are required to give something back to the community that supports them. This is primarily a social exchange agreement, rather than a labour market policy. In addition, the coalition government has contracted out employment services for the unemployed. This is in keeping with the belief that competition reduces costs and promotes choice. It has also reduced the government's direct provision of services for the unemployed. Finally, the government has introduced changes designed to deregulate industrial relations. The coalition government considers that the market is the most appropriate way to deliver a number of social policy outcomes. As a result, it believes that changes to workplace relations will encourage flexibility and lead to increases in employment. Some have argued that in many of these areas the coalition government has followed policy initiatives first introduced by its Labor predecessor.

Notes

1 The Australian Bureau of Statistics (ABS) includes both *de jure* and *de facto* marriages in the married category.
2 All figures are for people aged 15–64.
3 *Casual loading* is an additional amount paid on top of the hourly rate to compensate for non-entitlement to benefits, such as sick leave and annual leave.
4 They excluded self-employed agricultural workers from their survey. As the ABS figures discussed above show, these account for a significant number of the self-employed.
5 ABS advises that from April 1986 a new definition of *employed persons* was used. This extended the existing definition to include persons who worked without pay between 1 and 14 hours per week in a family business or on a farm. Previously these people had been defined as either unemployed or not in the labour force, depending on whether or not they were actively looking for work.
6 It existed in some states before that date.
7 For example, see Shaver for an interesting analysis of the interaction between the liberal welfare state, gender and social policy in Australia (Shaver, 1995 and 1996); and Pateman for the relationship between the welfare state and patriarchy (Pateman, 1989).
8 In most Australian literature, and in Australian Bureau of Statistics figures, the long-term unemployed are those unemployed for a year or longer. *Working Nation* drew a somewhat artificial line at 18 months or more. This had consequences downstream.
9 NWO was to include regionally developed community projects, environmental projects and human services, such as care for the elderly.
10 Using figures supplied by Stretton Stuart, 1994.
11 The reform set a level at which a joint income test was applied to ensure that one person in a high income couple did not, as a result of the changes, become eligible for income assistance.
12 Using data from the post programme monitoring survey conducted three months after the participants left the programme.
13 The 1995 Annual Report of the Social Security Appeals Tribunal said that 'many recipients, having attempted to correctly declare their income, feel aggrieved when the DSS takes action to recover what has suddenly become an overpayment' (quoted in Finn, 1997, p. 55).

14 That is the notion that unemployed people should return something to the community that supports them.
15 The Accord consisted of agreements between Labor and the Australian Council of Trade Unions.
16 *Allowable matters* include: classifications of employees, hours of work, rates of pay, annual/long-service/carers/sick/family/bereavement/compassionate/parental leave provisions, public holidays, allowances, loadings for overtime/casual/shift work, penalty rates, redundancy pay and notice of termination, stand-down provisions, dispute settling procedures, jury service, type of employment, superannuation, pay/conditions for outworkers.
17 The age at which women become eligible is being increased by six months at two yearly intervals until 2013, when it will reach 65.
18 For example, people who are employed on short-term casual contracts or those who work part time for more than one employer may fall below the earnings threshold.
19 This may include parents (usually women) who leave the workforce to care for children, as well as people who experience unemployment.
20 The scheme will be fully mature by 2040 (Atkinson and Creedy, 1997, p. 21).

References

Aboriginal and Torres Strait Islander Commission (undated), *Issues: Employment and economic status*, www.atsic.gov.au.

ABS (various issues), *Labour Force Australia*, monthly survey, Catalogue No. 6203.0, Commonwealth of Australia, Canberra.

ABS (1986), *Labour Force, Australia 1966–1984*, Catalogue No. 6204.0, Commonwealth of Australia, Canberra.

ABS (1996), *Labour Force, Australia 1978–1995*, Catalogue No. 6204.0, Commonwealth of Australia, Canberra.

ABS (1999a), 'Labour: Casual employment', in *Australia now: A statistical profile* (July), http://www.abs.gov.au/.

ABS (1999b), 'Population: Australia's older population: Past, present and future', *Australia Now: A statistical profile* (June), http://www.abs.gov.au.

Atkinson, M.E. and Creedy, J. (1997), 'The Choice of Early Retirement Age and the Australian Superannuation System', *Australian Journal of Labour Economics*, 1 (1), pp. 1–23.

Australian Bureau of Statistics (ABS) (undated), 'Labour-Superannuation', *Australia Now: A statistical profile*, http://www.abs.gov.au/.

Australian Council of Social Service (2000), *Does Work for the Dole Lead to Work for Wages?*, Sydney.

Australian Council of Trade Unions (1997), *The Legislative Framework: Unions – and collective bargaining rights resolution*, ACTU Congress, http://www.actu.asn.au/national/about/policy/97legisb.htm.

Bacon, B.R. (1999), *Ageing in Australia: Some modelling results and research issues*, Retirement and Income Modeling Unit, Department of Treasury, www.treasury.gov.au.

Bateman, H. (1999), 'Perspectives on Australian Retirement Income Policy', *Australian Social Policy*, 1, pp. 31–59.

Campbell, I. (1996), 'Casual Employment, Labour Regulation and Australian Trade Unions', *Journal of Industrial Relations*, 38 (4), pp. 571–99.

Campbell, I. and Brosnan, P. (1999), 'Labour Market Deregulation in Australia: The slow combustion approach to workplace change', *International Review of Applied Economics*, 13 (3), pp. 353–94.

Castles, F. (1994), 'The Wage Earners' Welfare State Revisited: Refurbishing the established model of Australian social protection, 1983–1993', *Australian Journal of Social Issues*, 29 (2), pp. 120–45.

Dawkins, P. and Norris, K. (1990), 'Casual Employment in Australia', *Australian Bulletin of Labour*, 16 (3), pp. 156–73.

Department of Employment, Education, Training and Youth Affairs (1996), *Working Nation: Evaluation of the employment, education and training*, EMB Report 2/96, Australian Government Printing Service, Canberra.

Department of Employment, Workplace Relations and Small Business (1998), 'Principal Object of the Act', *Workplace Relations Act, Update*, January 1998, http://www.dewrsb.gov.au/group_wra/userguide/.

Department of Employment, Workplace Relations and Small Business (1999), *Evaluation of the Work for the Dole Program*, http://www.dewrsb.gov.au/group_lmp/files/Work_for_Dole_evaluation/evaluation_of_work_for_the_dole.htm.

Department of Employment, Workplace Relations and Small Business (2000), *Award and agreement coverage survey*, July, www.dewrsb.gov.au/workplaceRelations/publications/Aacoverage/brochure.pdf.

Department of Social Security (1993), *Meeting the Challenge: Labour market trends and the income support system*, Australian Government Printing Service, Canberra.

Dunlop, Y. (2000), *Labour Market Outcomes of Low Paid Adult Workers*', Australian Bureau of Statistics Occasional Paper, Catalogue No. 6293.0.00.005., www.abs.gov.au/.

Finn, D. (1997), *Working Nation: Welfare reform and the Australian job compact for the long term unemployed*, Australian Council of Social Services, New South Wales.

Finn, D. (1999), 'Job Guarantees for the Unemployed: Lessons from Australian welfare reform', *Journal of Social Policy*, 28 (1), pp. 53–71.

Goodman, J. (1997), 'New Deals and Privatising Unemployment in Australia', *Journal of Australian Political Economy*, 40, pp. 27–43.

Hawke, A. (1998), 'Work for the Dole – A Cheap Labour Market Program? An Economist's Perspective', *Australian Journal of Social Issues*, 33 (4), pp. 395–405.

Jones, M. (1996), *The Australian Welfare State: Evaluating social policy*, Allen and Unwin, Sydney.

Junankar, P. and Kapuscinski, C. (1997), *Was Working Nation working?*, Australian National University, Canberra.

Macintyre, C. (1999), 'From Entitlement to Obligation in the Australian Welfare State', *Australian Journal of Social Issues*, 34 (2), pp. 103–18.

Mangan, J. and Williams, C. (1999), 'Casual Employment in Australia: A further analysis', *Australian Economic Papers*, 38 (1), pp. 40–50.

Martin, J. (2000), 'What Works among Active Labour Market Policies: Evidence from OECD countries' experiences', *OECD Economic Studies No. 30* (2000/I), Paris.

Norris, K. and Wooden, M. (1996), 'The Changing Australian Labour Market: An overview', in Norris, K. and Wooden, M. (eds), *The Changing Australian Labour Market*, Australian Centre for Economic Performance, Canberra.

OECD (1997), *Private Pensions in OECD Countries: Australia*, Labour Market and Social Policy Occasional Paper, Paris.

Olsberg, D. (1997), *Aging and Money: Australia's retirement revolution*, Allen and Unwin, Sydney.

Pateman, C. (1989), 'The Patriarchal Welfare State', in Pateman, C. (ed.), *The Disorder of Women*, Polity Press, Cambridge, pp. 179–209.

Pech, J. and Innes, H. (1998), 'Women in the Australian Labour Market 1966–1996: The impact of change on the social security system', *Social Security Journal*, 2, pp. 3–30.

Reith, P. and Newman, J. (1999), *Strengthening and Extending Mutual Obligation*, press release, 11 May, www.dewrsb.gov.au/ministers/reith/mediarelease/1999/pr49_99.htm.

Romeyn, J. (1992), *Flexible Working Time: Part-time and casual employment*, Department of Industrial Relations, Canberra.

Saunders, P. (1995), *Improving Work Incentives in a Means-tested Welfare System: The 1994 Australian social security reforms*, Social Policy Research Centre, Discussion Paper No. 56, University of New South Wales, Sydney.

Shaver, S. (1995), 'Women, Employment and Social Security', in Edwards, A. and Magarey, S. (eds), *Women in a Restructuring Australia: Work and welfare*, Allen and Unwin in association with the Academy of Social Sciences in Australia, St Leonards, New South Wales, pp. 141–57.

Shaver, S. (1996), 'Liberalism, Gender and Social Policy', Social Policy Research Centre, Discussion Paper No. 68, University of New South Wales, Sydney.

Stretton, A. and Stuart, A. (1994), 'The Job Compact and Reform of Delivery Arrangements', paper presented at the Conference of Australian Economists, Gold Coast, September.

Taylor, J. and Hunter, B. (undated), *The Job Still Ahead: Economic costs of continuing indigenous employment disparity*, Centre of Aboriginal Economic Policy Research, The Australian National University, Canberra, www.atsic.gov.au/issues/employment/contents.htm.

VandenHeuvel, A. and Wooden, M. (1995), 'Self-employed Contractors in Australia: How many and who are they?', *The Journal of Industrial Relations*, 37 (2), pp. 263–80.

Watson, I (2000), 'Beyond the Unemployment Rate: Building a set of indices to measure the health of the labour market', *Australian Bulletin of Labour*, 26 (3), pp. 175–90.

Wilson, S. (1994), 'Labour Market Trends and Unemployment Patterns', in Disney, J. and Briggs, L. (eds), *Social Security Policy: Issues and options*, Australian Government Printing Service, Canberra.

Wooden, M. (2000), 'The Changing Skill Composition of Labour Demand', *Australian Bulletin of Labour*, 26 (3), pp. 191–8.

Working Nation (1994a), *Working Nation: The White Paper on employment and growth*, Australian Government Publishing Service, Canberra.

Working Nation (1994b), *Working Nation: Policies and programs*, Australian Government Publishing Service, Canberra.

Chapter Seven

Labour Market Reform in New Zealand

Raymond Harbridge and Pat Walsh

The Regulated Labour Market

The Industrial Conciliation and Arbitration Act 1894 marked the beginning of government regulation of industrial relations in New Zealand. At the heart of this legislation were the tenets of compulsory conciliation and arbitration. As Woods notes, this rested on core principles, including: the setting down of minimum terms and conditions through employment awards; the so-called *subsequent party* clause, which extended the coverage of negotiated awards to include specified industries or occupations; compulsory trade union membership; and compulsory arbitration in cases where conciliation was unsuccessful (Woods, 1963).

Different levels of wage fixing evolved under this system. At the most basic level, there were statutory protections which set a safety net of minimum terms and conditions for all workers. Alongside this, the minimum terms and conditions for specific groups of workers were set by both negotiated awards and by the Arbitration Court (in cases where parties had not been able to reach agreement independently). Brosnan and Rea estimate that most of those not covered by this system of awards (about 40 per cent of workers) where white collar workers (Brosnan and Rea, 1991). On top of the negotiated awards was a so-called *second tier* of collective agreements which provided pay and conditions above award level. The final level involved individual contracts between a worker and his or her employer. These also provided for pay and conditions above award level.

By the 1960s, this highly regulated system was beset by problems and was increasingly criticized by both unions and employers. The unions became increasingly frustrated by the arbitration system. They pursued a form of enterprise bargaining with growing vigour through the 1970s and early 1980s. This gave them some flexibility and they used it to the advantage of skilled workers (where it restored wage relativities) and then to sidestep wage controls introduced by the government. The increase in *second tier* agreements added to the dissatisfaction felt by employers towards the system. Government attempts to overcome the shortcomings of the system were largely unsuccessful and, by the late 1970s, unable to make structural changes, it intervened directly and overturned agreements that it considered to be excessive. Then, in the early 1980s, in response to this and other problems, the Government introduced a freeze on wages and prices. This was in keeping with the ethos of direct government involvement in all aspects of the economy.

Deregulation

New Zealand's highly regulated labour market existed in a wider environment of regulation. The government maintained high levels of intervention in areas such as imports and exports, money markets and banking. The fourth Labour government was elected in 1984 and began a rapid programme of deregulation and liberalization. The policies pursued have since become familiar the world over. Traditional Keynesian economic theory, which saw a role for government in mediating market outcomes, was replaced by so-called *New Right* economic theory and a belief in the market as the mechanism for delivering the best outcomes. Government intervention then became an unwarranted interference in the operation of market forces. What makes the New Zealand experience remarkable is the speed and degree to which these policies were implemented. In less than a decade, New Zealand changed from one of the most regulated economies in the world, to become one of the least regulated (OECD, 1990).[1] Galt argues that this philosophical change was supported by more practical concerns (Galt, 1989). The highly protectionist stance towards industry was costing the country as an increasing deficit fuelled inflation.

With respect to labour market deregulation, Bray and Neilson note that the government was 'relatively cautious' compared to its 'extravagance in other areas of economic and social policy' (Bray and Neilson, 1996, p. 69). However, the restructuring did have significant impacts on workers. In an attempt to make local industries internationally competitive, many import tariffs were reduced or removed. In addition, the size of the public service was reduced. Smaller government was believed to be more efficient and restructuring was promoted in an attempt to reduce government spending. These policies had far-reaching effects as 'the consequent rapid decline of manufacturing, combined with moves to 'downsize' the state sector, produced dramatic increases in unemployment and declines in Government popularity' (Bray and Neilson, 1996, p. 76). The number of people in receipt of unemployment benefit gives some indication of this. In 1980, some 20,850 people received an unemployment allowance. By 1990, that figure had increased sixfold to 139,625 (Statistics New Zealand, 1997).

Traditional links between the Labour Party and the union movement may account for the government's restraint in the area of industrial relations. However, there were calls for changes. Employers argued that greater labour market flexibility was essential if New Zealand's industries were to compete internationally. Initially, Labour attempted some form of compromise. The centralized occupationally based award system remained. The government introduced legislation designed to encourage the growth of bargaining at the enterprise level, while at the same time ensuring that unions would be able to operate effectively in the changed environment. The Federation of Labour[2] was concerned by calls from the New Zealand Employers' Federation for the introduction of the principle of a *single set of negotiations*. In practice, this principle would mean that each employer would be covered by only one set of negotiations (either an occupational/industry award or an enterprise agreement). The Federation of Labour was concerned that this would result in a constituency divided into those with strong negotiating power and those with relatively little negotiating might.

Walsh notes that, by 1987, the Labour government had accepted the need to encourage enterprise bargaining at the expense of employment awards, but had still not resorted to the radical deregulation that characterized other aspects of its administration (Walsh, 1989). The position of both the Employers' Federation and the Federation of Labour had hardened. The former, which had previously accepted the need for both levels of bargaining, now supported enterprise level bargaining only. In contrast, fears about the impact of the single set of negotiations principle resulted in escalating support for centralized award bargaining among the member unions of the Federation of Labour. This support was evident, even among those unions which had earlier been actively involved in enterprise bargaining. In this climate, the Labour government introduced the Labour Relations Act 1987.

In a guide to the new Act, the Minister stated that the aim was to encourage, rather than impose enterprise bargaining (Roger, 1987). As a result of the Act:

- the single set of negotiations principle would apply;
- unions determined whether groups of employees were covered by awards or enterprise agreements;
- once covered by an enterprise agreement, employees could not later return to award coverage without employer agreement;
- enterprise bargaining would stand alone and would not be underpinned by awards; and
- all settlements would be registered with the Arbitration Commission (this would eliminate *second tier* bargaining).

Allowing unions to determine whether their members were covered by occupational/industry awards or enterprise agreements meant that unions controlled the pace of change. The Minister believed that the Act would see an increase in enterprise bargaining and a concomitant decline in multi-employer awards (Roger, 1987). However, this did not happen. It was apparent from the first wage round under the new legislation in 1987/88 that it was giving rise to unintended outcomes. Harbridge and McCaw noted that in that first round the number of documents registered with the Arbitration Commission had declined by 25 per cent in comparison with the previous year.[3] This decline was a result of a reduction in the number of enterprise agreements negotiated. In addition, the number of composite agreements also declined.[4] Industry, rather than occupational bargaining had failed to develop any further. This trend continued. At the end of the 1989/90 wage round, only 23 per cent of all workers governed by registered awards and agreements were covered by enterprise agreements. A significant majority of workers were still covered by multi-employer award settlements. Furthermore, the majority (82 per cent) of those who were covered by enterprise agreements were public sector employees (Harbridge, 1991; Harbridge and McCaw, 1992). The single set of negotiations principle therefore resulted in private sector unions largely rejecting enterprise bargaining.

Despite the failure of the legislation in this respect, there is evidence to suggest that there were increases in labour market flexibility, even though the period has generally been characterized as one of labour market inflexibility. The issue of inflexibility is a consistent theme in the publications of lobby groups, such as the New Zealand Business Round Table (NZBRT), and government advisors, including the New Zealand Treasury (see, for example, NZBRT, 1987 and 1998; and Treasury, 1990). However, it is challenged by analyses of the collective employment agreements during this period. Brunhes, Rojot and Wassermann developed a four point framework for examining flexibility, consisting of:

- wage flexibility;
- external numerical flexibility (levels of employment, deployment of part-time and casual work);
- internal numerical flexibility (working time arrangements); and
- functional flexibility (degree of delineation between job classifications) (Brunhes, Rojot and Wassermann, 1989).

This framework was used to examine the flexibility contained within collective agreements. Various wage rounds were examined from the period 1984/85 to 1990/91.[5] These reviews (Harbridge and Rea, 1992; Harbridge and McCaw, 1990; Harbridge, 1990) reveal a great degree of flexibility in both wages and working times. The level of flexibility was greater than anticipated and existed despite claims of market rigidity.

The Employment Contracts Act

The Labour government was defeated in the general election in 1990. The newly-elected Conservative National government was quick to implement its labour market reforms. While the Employment Contracts Act 1991 represented a substantive break with the tradition of industrial relations in New Zealand, it was in keeping with the philosophy that had driven deregulation in other sectors of the economy since 1984. The belief in the market as the mechanism to deliver the best outcomes was extended to employment relations. As a consequence, the relationship between workers and employers was to be viewed as any other business relationship. Bray and Neilson characterize the Act as 'the most radical withdrawal of the state from labour market regulation in the developed world' (Bray and Neilson, 1996, p. 82).

For nearly one hundred years, trade unions had enjoyed a privileged role in industrial relations in New Zealand, in that they alone had represented workers in collective negotiations. The 1991 Act ended this. It completely avoids using the term *trade union* and refers instead to *employee organizations*. Trade unions could continue to represent workers, but only as an *employee organization*. Their automatic access to, and rights in the workplace ceased to exist. Employee organizations do not enjoy any of the traditional rights exercised by trade unions. Membership of employee organizations was voluntary and it became illegal to discriminate in employment on the grounds of membership or non-membership of such an organization. Workers could choose whether or not they wanted to act collectively through membership of an employee organization.

Compulsory membership of trade unions had been a contentious issue since its inception in 1936. At different times, this compulsion had been revoked (by Conservative governments) and reintroduced (by Labour governments) (Szakats, 1972; Howells, 1983; and Walsh, 1983). However, the 1991 Act did more than simply end compulsion.

The peak union body, the New Zealand Council of Trade Unions,[6] complained to the International Labour Organization. It argued that the Act breached several of the ILO's eight fundamental Conventions. The ILO upheld the complaints in respect of the Freedom of Association and Protection of the Right to Organise Convention, 1948 (No. 87), and the Right to Organise and Collective Bargaining Convention, 1949 (No. 98) (Haworth and Hughes, 1995). The report noted that, while the Act allowed collective bargaining, it did not promote or encourage it:

> ... problems of incompatibility between ILO principles on collective bargaining and the Act stem in large part from the latter's underlying philosophy, which puts on the same footing (a) individual and collective employment contracts, and (b) individual and collective representation (ILO, 1994, para. 254).

The data in Table 7.1 illustrate the impact that the Employment Contracts Act has had on the actual number of unions, their membership and the density of union membership (that is the number of union members as a percentage of the total employed workforce), thereby

Table 7.1 New Zealand: unions, membership and density, 1953–98

Year	Unions[1]	Private sector membership	Private and public sector membership[3]	Density[2] %
Dec. 1953	412	290,149	n.a.	n.a.
Dec. 1963	382	333,911	n.a.	n.a.
Dec. 1973	309	427,692	n.a.	n.a.
Dec. 1983	248	527,683	n.a.	n.a.
Dec. 1985	259	n.a.	683,006	43.5
Sept. 1989	112	n.a.	648,825	44.7
May 1991	80	n.a.	603,118	41.5
Dec. 1991	66	n.a.	514,325	35.4
Dec. 1992	58	n.a.	428,160	28.8
Dec. 1993	67	n.a.	409,112	26.8
Dec. 1994	82	n.a.	375,906	23.4
Dec. 1995	82	n.a.	362,200	21.7
Dec. 1996	83	n.a.	338,967	19.9
Dec. 1997	80	n.a.	327,800	19.2
Dec. 1998	83	n.a.	306,687	17.7

Notes

1 'Unions' means private sector registered unions only for the period to 1985. From 1989 to May 1991, it denotes public and private sector registered unions. Since December 1991, data are reported from unofficial surveys of unions as reported by Crawford, Harbridge and Walsh (1999).
2 In reporting union density, the surveyed level of union membership is indicated as a proportion of the total employed workforce, as measured by the Household Labour Force Survey (Statistics New Zealand, 1998). This method of calculating density is likely to understate the true density figure, as it makes no differentiation between full and part-time employees, nor does it take account of the number of full or part-time small entrepreneurs working as self-employed persons included in the employed workforce figure. Thus, the denominator tends to be overstated. At the same time, union membership is primarily reported on a full-time equivalent basis, thus understating the numerator.
3 As no reliable estimates can be made of public sector service organization membership prior to 1985, and as the Household Labour Force Survey

was only commenced around that time, it is inappropriate to speculate on union density levels prior to 1985.

Sources: Department of Labour, *Annual Reports* (various years); Crawford, Harbridge and Walsh, 1999.

indicating the dramatic consequences of the legislation. The density of union membership has halved in the decade since 1991.

Annual surveys of unions undertaken by the Industrial Relations Centre at Victoria University of Wellington have attempted to track changes in union membership by industry. The changes over the period from 1991 to 1998 indicate that some industries have been more vulnerable to change than others. While union membership in agriculture, fishing, hunting and forestry declined by a staggering 94 per cent, membership in public and community services declined by 24 per cent. Although this second figure is much smaller, it still represents a loss of nearly one quarter of all members.

Even though the Employment Contracts Act 1991 has had a substantial negative effect on trade unionism, the decline of trade unions in New Zealand has been largely consistent with international experience. International studies have highlighted the impact of structural changes in employment, and specifically the shift in employment from the traditionally strongly unionized manufacturing sectors to weakly organized service sectors (see Bamber and Lansbury, 1998; Jones, 1992; OECD, 1994; Peetz, 1999). However, it is easy to overstate the case, especially over the relatively short term, as suggested by the data in Table 7.2. What is perhaps more important in the New Zealand context is the changing share of public and private sector employment. The declining share of employment in large and medium-sized workplaces, and especially the concentration of employment growth in workplaces with fewer than 10 employees, is also likely to be significant in any analysis (see Peetz, 1999, for a discussion of the Australian experience). The impression is therefore that the Employment Contracts Act 1991 had a massive shock effect in the first 18 months following its introduction, within the context of a longer-term declining trend, due in large part to structural changes in the economy.

As noted above, industrial relations had been built round a system of awards (generally bargained collectively) and compulsory conciliation and arbitration. The Employment Contracts Act abolished the Arbitration

Table 7.2 New Zealand: union membership by industry (Dec. 1991–Dec. 1998)

Industry	Dec. 1991	Dec. 1998	Decline 1991–98 (%)
Agriculture, fishing, hunting and forestry	14,234	911	94
Mining and related services	4,730	796	83
Manufacturing	114,564	70,490	38
Energy and utility services	11,129	5,150	54
Construction and building services	14,596	3,704	75
Retail, wholesale, cafés and accommodation	64,335	12,415	81
Transport, communication and storage	52,592	35,552	32
Finance and business services	32,219	20,235	37
Public and community services	205,925	157,436	24
Total	514,324	306,687	40

Source: Crawford, Harbridge and Walsh, 1999.

Court and the conciliation councils. Awards were replaced by employment contracts. As noted elsewhere, 'a highly decentralized system with bargaining taking place predominantly at the level of the enterprise quickly replaced the concept of a highly centralized industrial relations system with multi-employer bargaining taking place at the national level. Deunionization and decollectivization were inevitable outcomes of the new system' (Harbridge and Crawford, 1997, p. 238). The dramatic decline in collective bargaining was notable from the first year of the coming into force of the Employment Contracts Act, when an estimated 300,000 workers moved from collectively negotiated agreements to individual employment contracts. These trends have continued. They have been summarized in Harbridge and Crawford (1997) and Crawford and Harbridge (1998), who report, *inter alia*:

- a continued decollectivization of the workforce, with some 300,000

employees ceasing to be covered by collectively bargained contracts (while collective contracts continued to cover some 420,000 employees);
- a virtually total collapse of multi-employer bargaining;
- enterprise bargaining is the dominant form of collective bargaining;
- industrial disputes have diminished and can now be characterized as rarer, shorter and less costly; and
- applications to the Employment Tribunal have increased dramatically, more than doubling during the period 1992–98 (Department of Labour, 1998).

Flexibility was once again measured using the four point framework developed by Brunhes et al. (1989). This revealed:

- increased downward wage flexibility;
- relative wage flexibility between industries;
- the achievement of internal flexibility through radical changes in working time arrangements, particularly in those industries engaging labour for all seven days of the week. In many cases *clock hours*, in the sense of specified ordinary hours of work, have been removed from contracts. Penal rates for work outside standard hours have also disappeared from a large number of contracts;
- external numerical flexibility was achieved through the ease of engaging part-time and casual employees outside the terms of any relevant collective employment contract; although
- less external numerical flexibility was achieved in the area of terminations, with restrictions on dismissals and uncertainty over redundancy payments remaining controversial; and
- functional flexibility was achieved through the collapse of occupational demarcations between job classifications.

This flexibility, which in effect meant a reduction in employment benefits for many workers, was said to encourage long-term growth and employment. Kelsey argues that it failed in this regard (Kelsey, 1997). She notes that while unemployment dropped dramatically in the first years of the Act, it reached a plateau of around 6 per cent in 1996. In addition, she concludes that the growth in employment was driven by a disproportionate growth in part-time work and she questions the 'quality and sustainability of new jobs' (Kelsey, 1997, p. 272).

Social Security Reform

The changes wrought by the Employment Contracts Act were accompanied by changes in New Zealand's welfare system. New Zealand has a unique social welfare system which expanded, in stages, during the twentieth century. The system provides a range of cash benefits to supplement inadequate or nonexistent personal income. The system is funded from general taxation rather than from targeted contributions and, in this respect, is unlike the social security systems in most other countries. The rates of benefit are applicable to all individuals who meet the relevant qualifying criteria (usually income, residence and benefit specific criteria). Unemployment benefit is payable to any unemployed individual who is available for work and is actively looking for suitable employment.

Several other benefits should also be noted in view of their effects on the composition of the labour market. The domestic purposes benefit is paid 'to a parent caring for children without the support of a partner, to a person caring for someone at home who would otherwise be hospitalised, and in some cases, to an older woman alone'. A similar benefit is paid to widows. Invalids benefit is paid to persons who are '16 years old and over who have a permanent sickness or disability which stops them working or makes it difficult for them to work', and sickness benefit is paid to those 'over the age of 16 who are incapacitated for work through sickness or accident, and as a result suffer a loss of earning' (Statistics New Zealand, 1999).

More recently, changes to the benefit structure have seen the introduction of a community wage. From 1 October 1998, persons receiving unemployment benefit, sickness benefit, a training benefit, a 55+ benefit or a young jobseekers allowance have received a benefit known as the *community wage*. In return for receiving the community wage, recipients are expected to:

- search for work;
- meet with Work and Income New Zealand when asked to do so;
- take a suitable work offer; and
- take part in activities to improve their chances of finding a job.

The data in Table 7.3 illustrate how the number of people in receipt of these benefits has increased over the past two decades.

In 1991, the National government introduced a number of changes to New Zealand's social security system. Policy statements issued by the Minister of Social Welfare indicated several of the principles driving these changes. The government wanted to reduce spending generally and believed that welfare was one area where this could be achieved. In addition, and perhaps more importantly, the government wished to address the issue of *welfare dependency*, which appears in international debates about the welfare state. The Minister believed that 'we must reform policies so they promote growth, encourage employment and continue to offer protection and support that is sustainable to those in genuine need' (Shipley, 1991, pp. 1–2). According to this view, welfare benefits create dependency amongst recipients and act as a disincentive to seeking appropriate work. Cuts in benefit rates can therefore be proposed as a means of reducing welfare dependency and encouraging people to seek employment.[7] The links between the Employment Contracts Act and the changes to the welfare system are indicated by the comments of the then Finance Minister:

> Benefit reductions together with changes to employment contracts law should improve both the opportunity and incentive to move from welfare to work (Richardson, 1991, p. 44).

The data in Table 7.4 indicate the changes in the rates of unemployment benefit. The figures show that some people experienced reductions of up to 25 per cent in their income.

Other changes were also introduced to counter welfare dependency. The *stand-down* period (during which a benefit is not payable and people are expected to manage on their existing independent resources) was extended from 6 to 26 weeks for those who were voluntarily unemployed,[8] or who failed the *work test*. The work test was designed to address the problem of individuals who were in receipt of an unemployment benefit but not actively seeking employment. Economist Paul Dalziel has argued that these changes to the welfare system were in effect a tax on the poor. He believes that they had a weak effect in terms of encouraging people into paid employment, but a significant effect on income distribution in New Zealand (Dalziel, 1993).

Table 7.3 New Zealand: persons in receipt of selected social welfare benefits

Year	Unemployment	Training	Sickness	Invalids	Domestic purposes	Widows	Total
1980	20,850	–	7,504	15,647	37,040	16,120	9,7161
1985	38,419	–	9,627	21,464	56,548	13,557	13,9615
1990	139,625	9,453	19,511	27,824	94,823	12,676	30,3192
1995	136,496	11,665	34,037	39,686	104,027	9,007	33,4918
1998	151,897	7,915	35,172	49,419	113,029	9,361	36,6793

Source: Ministry of Social Policy, 1999.

Table 7.4 New Zealand: changes in unemployment benefit rates

	Pre-1991 (NZD)	1991 Rates (NZD)	Percentage change
Single 18–19 years	114.86	108.17	-6
Single 20–24 years	143.57	108.17	-25
Single 25 years and older	143.57	129.81	-10
Married couple	223.22	216.34	-3
Single (1 child)	213.14	185.93	-13
Married couple (1 child)	255.08	229.88	-10

Sources: Buurman, 1992; Stephens, 1992.

The Labour/Alliance Coalition Government

A Labour/Alliance coalition government was formed following the elections in November 1999.[9] Once again, industrial relations have been the subject of government attention. In the lead up to the election, the Labour Party declared that fairness in labour market relations would be one of its key policies. On 13 March 2000, the Employment Relations Bill was tabled in parliament. The Bill has since been passed into law and came into effect in October 2000. It has repealed the Employment Contracts Act.

In direct contrast with the Employment Contracts Act, the new law recognizes inequalities in the bargaining power of employers and employees. The Labour Party says that the legislation aims to build productive employment relationships through the promotion of mutual trust and confidence in all aspects of the employment environment, and therefore:

- recognizes that employment relationships must be built on good faith behaviour;
- acknowledges and addresses the inherent inequality of bargaining power in employment relationships;
- promotes collective bargaining;
- protects the integrity of individual choice;
- promotes mediation as the primary problem-solving mechanism; and
- reduces the need for judicial intervention.

The new Act reinstates the special role played by trade unions in industrial relations in New Zealand. Unions which are able to satisfy the Registrar of Unions that they operate independently of employers, are democratic, financially accountable and governed by appropriate rules will, once again, be registered. Unions are able to represent both individuals and groups. Membership of a union is sufficient to authorize the union to act on that member's behalf. Only unions are able to negotiate collective agreements on behalf of workers. New employees are covered by the terms and conditions of existing collective agreements for the first 30 days of their employment. During this time they may negotiate additional terms and conditions, providing that they are not inconsistent with the existing collective agreement. At the expiration of the 30 day period, new employees may either join the union or negotiate directly with their employer for any changes to their terms and conditions of employment.

In addition, the Employment Relations Act provides that unions are able to enter workplaces to:

- negotiate or enforce employment agreements;
- deal with safety and health matters affecting members;
- provide information about unions; and
- recruit new members. It also provides for at least two paid union meetings a year for union members.

The Act also makes provision for industrial action. Where the parties have negotiated unsuccessfully for 40 days (in pursuit of single or multiparty collective agreements), employees may strike and/or employers may lock workers out.

The legislation has been the focus of some discontent amongst business lobby groups. Prior to the 1999 election, the Employers' Federation argued that repealing the Employment Contracts Act would reduce employment and lead to an increase in industrial action.[10] More recently, a member of the influential lobby group, the Business Round Table, has claimed that 'Margaret Wilson's [the Minister of Labour] belief that the relationship between employer and employee is one of inequality which requires a collectivist response, could have been borrowed from Karl Marx' (Myers, 2000).

The obvious question that arises in the current context is the possible effect of the Employment Relations Act 2000 on union decline and bargaining power. Ultimately, the question of whether or not the new Act will provide a basis for increasing union membership is an empirical one, and the answer will become clearer over time. Already, however, a number of unions have reported spikes in membership enquiries[11] and, if nothing else, the discussion concerning the Act has raised the profile of trade unions. Although it would appear that the legislation offers enhancements to unions that may enable them to recruit and retain members more effectively than was possible under the Employment Contracts Act, there are a number of implications that arise from the new Act which do not lend themselves easily to interpretation *ex ante*.

Unions faced several key problems in bargaining under the Employment Contracts Act. Two key issues were free-riding and non-inclusive bargaining. To some extent, the new Act resolves the latter issue. However, there are inherent problems in dealing with the former. The Employment Relations Act 2000 gives effect to the principle of *join the union, join the contract*, and therefore allows a union to bargain inclusively for its members in a particular workplace, or over a broader area through a multi-employer agreement.

It is difficult to see how the new Act will affect the free-rider phenomenon. It is estimated that free-riding increased under the Employment Contracts Act from around 16 per cent in 1989/90 to around 27 per cent by 1999/2000 (Harbridge and Wilkinson, 2000). Although under the Employment Relations Act 2000, only union members can be bound by a collective agreement, the conditions of the agreement are extended *de jure* to new employees engaged in work that falls within the coverage clause for the first 30 days of their employment. If employees choose not to join the union at the end of the 30 day period, they continue to be covered by the same conditions until or unless an alternate individual employment agreement is negotiated. The Act prohibits the automatic variation of the terms of an individual employment contract upon completion of the initial 30 day period.

As employees are automatically bound by the terms of the collective agreement if they join the negotiating union, there is little reason for employers to offer inferior terms or conditions to employees under individual agreements. In some ways, this situation may exacerbate the free-rider problem.

It is possible that there may be greater fluctuations in union membership under the new Act with, for instance, a surge in membership of the union after the announcement of restructuring in order to gain access to the redundancy protection offered by a collective agreement negotiated by a union. If employees resign from the union, they continue to be bound by the terms of the collective agreement until such time as a new individual agreement is negotiated. The only restriction is that the employee cannot subsequently be covered by a collective agreement negotiated by a different union in respect of the same job until at least 60 days from the expiry of the original agreement.

One of the criticisms made in the ILO's review of the Employment Contracts Act 1991 was that collective and individual employment contracts were treated essentially as equivalent options under the legislation, ignoring the obligation under ILO principles to promote and encourage collective bargaining. The Employment Relations Act 2000 clearly places emphasis on collective bargaining. However, in so doing, it means that the option of whether to pursue collective or individual employment arrangements is no longer cost-neutral to employers. Given that a collective agreement will in practice form the minimum base for the conditions of all employees whose work it covers, irrespective of union membership, employers may incur substantial additional costs from concluding a collective agreement than from a collective employment contract. This may provide an incentive for some employers to adopt strategies to avoid the conclusion of a collective agreement, including strategies aimed at de-unionizing the workplace (which may or may not be within the Act's good faith provisions).[12]

In other respects, some rights are extended to unions that should genuinely assist them in their organizing activities. The extension of union access rights to include access for the purposes of recruitment is a particular example and marks a significant change from the situation under the Employment Contracts Act.

After nine years in the cold climate of the Employment Contracts Act 1991, there may, however, be question marks concerning the capacity of some unions to avail themselves fully of their newly reinstated position in the industrial landscape. Obviously, this will become clearer over time.

Conclusion

New Zealand has had a history of a cradle-to-grave social security system based in particular on the provision of support to families, as well as to individuals, with a view to ensuring an adequate level of income, access to housing, education and health care. For most of the twentieth century, New Zealand's industrial relations were characterized by state-sponsored unionism, collective bargaining and compulsory conciliation and arbitration. From the mid-1980s, under a Labour government, New Zealand underwent a number of wide-ranging neo-liberal reforms which deregulated most sectors of the economy. Industrial relations were largely exempt from these reforms, although Government attempts to legislate in this area in the late 1980s had unintended consequences. In 1991, the Employment Contracts Act, which was enacted by a National government, changed this situation and the government largely withdrew from its traditional role in industrial relations. At the same time, the National government introduced a series of related measures which cut back social welfare payments and tightened eligibility criteria. The National government's labour market and social security changes were clearly designed to enhance labour market flexibility and reduce welfare dependency.

The impact of these measures on trade unions, in terms of their influence and membership, the coverage of collective bargaining and a range of employment conditions, was considerable and negative. The social security changes were associated with a significant increase in income inequality, although this was compounded by the broader economic deregulation begun in the 1980s under the Labour government. A decade later, a new government is in power and there have once again been significant changes to the industrial relations legislation. The new government clearly intends to move away from the neo-liberal policies that dominated the 1990s. Trade unions are being re-legitimized and collective bargaining encouraged. However, this does not signify a return to the highly-regulated industrial relations system that existed prior to 1991. Moreover, there is no suggestion that the social security cuts, also introduced in 1991, are to be reversed.

Notes

1 See also Castles, Gerritsen and Vowles (1996) for a comprehensive review of the policy changes under the Labour administration.
2 An affiliation of trade union organizations.
3 The Industrial Relations Centre of Victoria University of Wellington established a database of settlements negotiated by unions and registered by the Arbitration Commission. The 1986–87 wage round, the last negotiated under the Industrial Relations Act 1973, established a benchmark (Harbridge, 1988b).
4 That is, single employer/multi-union arrangements.
5 The years during which Labour was in office.
6 The New Zealand Council of Trade Unions was formed in 1988 and includes those unions previously affiliated to the Federation of Labour and to the Combined State Unions.
7 As Hyman notes 'an insufficient gap between benefit levels and wage opportunities is said to reduce the incentive to be in paid work and to encourage welfare dependency. But this is a form of double-speak. Incentives to be in paid work in fact become punishments for not being in paid work' (Hyman, 1994, p. 21).

8 That is, those who quit a job without good or sufficient reason.
9 The government is a coalition of the Labour and the Alliance parties and a number of smaller parties, including New Labour, the Democrats, the Greens and indigenous parties.
10 As reported in the *New Zealand Herald*, 'Labour job contracts proposal alarms employer spokesman', 17.11.99, www.nzherald.co.nz.
11 Reported in the *Dominion*, 2 October 2000, p. 7.
12 Studies have suggested that employers may be prepared to offer wages above the union negotiated rates in order to avoid unionization, based on the premise that higher direct wage costs will be more than offset by lower non-wage costs (see Pencavel, 1991). It is interesting to note in this context the union proposal in the draft code of good faith to prohibit an employer from offering terms and conditions in collective agreements which are inferior to those applying to employees under individual employment agreements.

References

Armitage, C. and Dunbar, R. (1993), 'Labour Market Adjustment under the Employment Contracts Act', *New Zealand Journal of Industrial Relations*, 18 (1), pp. 94–112.

Bamber, G. and Lansbury, R. (eds.) (1998), *International and Comparative Employment Relations: A study of industrialised market economies* (3rd edn), Allen and Unwin, St Leonards.

Bollard, A. (1987), 'More Market: The deregulation of industry', in Bollard, A. and Buckle, R. (eds), *Economic Liberalisation in New Zealand*, Allen and Unwin, Wellington.

Bray, M. and Neilson, D. (1996), 'Industrial Relations Reform and the Relative Autonomy of the State', in Castles, F., Gerritsen, R. and Vowles, J. (eds), *The Great Experiment: Labour parties and public policy transfer in Australia and New Zealand*, Allen and Unwin, St Leonards.

Brook, P. (1990), *Freedom at Work,* Oxford University Press, Auckland.

Brosnan, P. and Rea, D. (1991), 'An Adequate Minimum Code: A basis for freedom, justice and efficiency in the labour market', *New Zealand Journal of Industrial Relations*, 16 (2), pp. 143–58.

Brunhes, B., Rojot, J. and Wassermann, W. (1989), *Labour Market Flexibility: Trends in enterprises*, OECD, Paris.

Buurman, G. (1992), 'Social Welfare Benefits and Income Distribution in New Zealand', in Birks, S. and Chatterjee, S. (eds), *The New Zealand Economy: Issues and policies*, Dunmore Press, Palmerston North.

Castles, F.G., Gerritsen, R. and Vowles, J. (eds) (1996), *The Great Experiment: Labour parties and public policy transfer in Australia and New Zealand*, Allen and Unwin, St Leonards.

Crawford, A. and Harbridge, R. (1998), 'External Legitimacy in New Zealand: An update', *Journal of Labor Research*, XIX (4), pp. 711–21.

Crawford, A., Harbridge, R. and Walsh, P. (1999), 'Unions and Union Membership in New Zealand: Annual review for 1998', *New Zealand Journal of Industrial Relations*, 24 (3), pp. 383–96.

Dalziel, P. (1993), 'Taxing the Poor: Key economic assumptions behind the April 1991 benefit cuts', paper written at the request of the New Zealand Council of Christian Social Services, Department of Economics, Lincoln University.

Department of Labour (1998), *Annual Report*, Wellington.

Economic Monitoring Group (1986), *Labour Market Flexibility*, New Zealand Planning Council, Wellington.

Galt, D. (1989), 'Industry and Trade policies', in Walker, S. (ed.), *Rogernomics: Reshaping New Zealand's economy*, Centre for Independent Studies, Auckland.

Harbridge, R. (1988a), 'The Way We Were: A survey of the last wage round negotiated under the Industrial Relations Act 1973', *New Zealand Journal of Business*, 10, pp. 48–65.

Harbridge, R. (1988b), 'Whatever Happened to Second Tier Settlements? A Survey of Settlements under the Labour Relations Act 1987', *New Zealand Journal of Industrial Relations*, 13 (2), pp. 143–56.

Harbridge, R. (1990), 'Flexibility in Collective Wage Bargaining in New Zealand: Facts and folklore', *New Zealand Journal of Industrial Relations*, 15 (3), pp. 241–50.

Harbridge, R. (1991), 'Collective Bargaining Coverage in New Zealand: The impact of the Employment Contracts Bill', *Australian Bulletin of Labour*, 17 (4), pp. 310–24.

Harbridge, R. and Crawford, A. (1997), 'The Impact of New Zealand's Employment Contracts Act on industrial relations', *California Western International Law Journal*, 28 (1), pp. 235–52.

Harbridge, R. and McCaw, S. (1989), 'The First Wage Round under the Labour Relations Act 1987: Changing relative power', *New Zealand Journal of Industrial Relations*, 14 (2), pp. 149–67.

Harbridge, R. and McCaw, S. (1990), 'Registered Settlements and Wage Flexibility in the New Zealand Private Sector 1984/85–1987/88', *The Journal of Industrial Relations*, 32 (2), pp. 224–37.

Harbridge, R. and McCaw, S. (1992), 'Award, Agreement or Nothing? A Review of the Impact of S132(a) of the Labour Relations Act 1987 on collective bargaining', *New Zealand Journal of Industrial Relations*, 17 (2), pp. 175–83.

Harbridge, R. and Rea, D. (1992), 'Collective Bargaining and the Labour Market Flexibility Debate in New Zealand: A review', *Economic and Labour Relations Review*, 3 (1), pp. 126–52.

Harbridge, R. and Walsh, P. (1989), 'Restructuring Industrial Relations in New Zealand: 1984 –1988', *Labour and Industry*, 2 (1), pp. 60–84.

Harbridge, R. and Wilkinson, D. (2000), 'Free-riding: Trends in collective bargaining coverage and union membership levels in New Zealand', paper presented to a National Key Centre for Industrial Relations conference, Melbourne, 12–14 July.

Haworth, N. and Hughes, S. (1995), 'Under Scrutiny: The ECA, the ILO and the NZCTU complaint 1993–1995', *New Zealand Journal of Industrial Relations*, 20 (2), pp. 143–62.

Hector, J. and Hobby, M. (1998), 'Labour Market Adjustment under the Employment Contracts Act 1996', *New Zealand Journal of Industrial Relations*, 22 (3), pp. 311–28.

Holland, M. and Boston, J. (eds) (1992), *The Fourth Labour Government: Politics and policy in New Zealand* (2nd edn), Oxford University Press, Auckland.

Howells, J. (1983), 'For or Against Compulsory Unionism? Recent Ballots in New Zealand', *International Labour Review*, 122 (1), pp. 95–110.

Hyman, P. (1994), *Women and Economics: A New Zealand feminist perspective*, Bridget Williams Books, Wellington.

ILO (1994), 295th Report of the Committee on Freedom of Association, Case No. 1698, Complaint against the Government of New Zealand presented by the New Zealand Council of Trade Unions (NZCTU), *Official Bulletin*, Vol. LXXVII, Series B, No. 3, Geneva.

Jones, E. (1992), 'Private Sector Union Decline and Structural Employment Change, 1970–1988', *Journal of Labor Research* 13 (3) (Summer), pp. 255–72.

Kelsey, J. (1997), 'Employment and Union Issues in New Zealand: 12 years on', *California Western International Law Journal*, 28 (1), pp. 253–74.

Ministry of Social Policy (1999), *Statistics Report*, http://www.dsw.govt.nz/comms/files/MoSP_StatsReport_99.pdf.

Myers, D. (2000), 'Fairness', speech delivered to the ACT annual conference, New Zealand Business Round Table, www.nzbr.org.nz/documents/speeches.

New Zealand Business Roundtable (1987), *Freedom and Employment: Why New Zealand needs a flexible decentralised labour market*, New Zealand Business Roundtable, Wellington.

New Zealand Business Roundtable (1988), *Labour Markets and Employment*, New Zealand Business Roundtable, Wellington.

New Zealand Labour Party (undated), *The Employment Relations Bill Explained*, www.labour.org.nz/erb.

OECD (1989), *Economic Surveys: New Zealand*, Paris.

OECD (1990), *Economic Surveys: New Zealand*, Paris.

OECD (1994), *Employment Outlook*, Paris.

Peetz, D. (1999), *Unions in a Contrary World: The future of the Australian trade union movement*, Cambridge University Press.

Pencavel, J. (1991), *Labour Markets under Trade Unionism: Employment, wages and hours*, Blackwell, Cambridge, MA.

Richardson, R. (1991), *Budget 1991*, Government Print, Wellington.

Roger, S. (1987), Foreword to *A Guide to the Labour Relations Act*, Department of Labour, Wellington.

Rudd, C. (1992), 'Controlling and Restructuring Public Expenditure', in Boston, J. and Dalziel, P. (eds), *The Decent Society: Essays in response to National's economic and social policies*, Oxford University Press, Auckland.

Shipley, Hon. J. (1991), *Social Assistance: Welfare that works: A statement of Government policy on social assistance*, Government Printer, Wellington.

Statistics New Zealand (various issues), *New Zealand Official Yearbook*, Government Printer, Wellington.

Statistics New Zealand (1997), *New Zealand Official Yearbook*, Government Printer, Wellington.

Statistics New Zealand (1998), *Household Labour Force Survey*, Government Printer, Wellington.

Statistics New Zealand (1999), *New Zealand Official Yearbook on the Web (1999)*, www.stats.gov.nz.

Stephens, B. (1992), 'Budgeting with the Benefit Cuts', in Boston, J. and Dalziel, P. (eds), *The Decent Society? Essays in Response to National's Economic and Social Policies*, Oxford University Press, Auckland.

Szakats, A. (1972), 'Compulsory Unionism: A strength or weakness? The New Zealand system compared with union security agreements in Great Britain and the United States', *Alberta Law Review*, 10, pp. 313–42.

Treasury (1990), *Briefing Notes to the Incoming Government*, Wellington.

Walsh, P. (1983), 'Union Membership Policy in New Zealand: 1894–1982', in Brosnan, P. (ed.), *Voluntary Unionism*, Industrial Relations Centre, Victoria University of Wellington.

Walsh, P. (1989), *An Analysis of the Legislative Process: From the State Sector Bill to the State Sector Act*, New Zealand Institute of Public Administration, Wellington.

Walsh, P. (1991), 'Pay Fixing Reform in the New Zealand Public Service', *New Zealand Journal of History*, 25 (1), pp. 18–40.

Whatman, R., Armitage, C. and Dunbar, R. (1994), 'Labour Market Adjustment under the Employment Contracts Act', *New Zealand Journal of Industrial Relations*, 19 (1), pp. 53–73.

Woods, N.S. (1963), *Industrial Conciliation and Arbitration in New Zealand*, Government Printer, Wellington.

Feature No. 4
The New Zealand Reforms: Outcomes and New Directions

Anne de Bruin

New Zealand's welfare state, which had its beginnings in the late 19th century and underwent consolidation during the 1950s and 1960s, was based on the synergy with full employment and a relationship between the state, capital and labour that maintained a fair living wage or 'family wage'. This assured a modest affluence within the nuclear two-parent family. The procurement of welfare was chiefly based on state support for wage and employment security, underpinned by the consensus-based industrial relations regime, and coupled with easy access to State provided education, health and housing services. This was complemented by a social welfare system that needed only to be residual, and could comfortably be funded from general taxation.

The 1970s and early 1980s saw the erosion of the historic compromise between capital and labour which had supported the family wage. The combination of growing unemployment and social and demographic change made the nuclear family less typical, and the foundations of the welfare state began to crumble. A landslide election victory in 1984 provided a mandate to commence radical reform.

There is a significant body of literature on the reform experience in New Zealand over the past 15 years (see Galt, 2000, for a summary of this literature). International interest has also been high since the New Zealand model rigidly conformed to an integrated theoretical line of thinking epitomizing market fundamentalism of the neoclassical paradigm. It was supported by a legislative framework, chiefly composed of 1989 Reserve Bank of New Zealand Act (RBA), the 1991 Employment Contracts Act (ECA) and the 1994 Fiscal Responsibility Act (FRA) that embodied these theoretical principles.[1] The RBA was founded on the rational expectations hypothesis of new classical macroeconomics which essentially predicts no long-run and short-run trade-offs between inflation and unemployment, thus supporting a policy ineffectiveness proposition. The FRA encompassed the beliefs of public choice theorists, who emphasize that the political system and bureaucracy tends to promote excessive public sector growth and who recommend a fiscal constitution to restrict the power of elected bodies.

The RBA focused monetary policy on price stability, with the Bank's autonomy only being limited by a Policy Targets Agreement (PTA) specifying explicit inflation targets. The objectives of the FRA include ensuring that public operating expenses do not exceed operating revenue on average over a reasonable period of time. By stringently circumscribing the conduct of monetary and fiscal policy, the RBA and FRA gave rise to risks of concomitant shortcomings in economic policy. For example, in the late 1980s, critics argued that the Reserve Bank's approach to fulfilling the inflation target was too costly in terms of growth and employment. Although the PTA allows for deviation from the required price stability band in times of supply shock, even in the event of shock such as the impact of the Asian Crisis on New Zealand, the conduct of monetary policy remained single-mindedly focused on containing inflation and was an exacerbating factor. Similarly, the FRA-engendered fixation on budget surpluses was illustrated when the May 1998 budget pared back planned government expenditure and ruled out further immediate tax cuts in response to the Asian Crisis. This aggravated the downturn.

The reform experience cannot be judged a success in view of the raft of unsatisfactory economic and social outcomes. These include wide ethnic disparities in well-being, a poor labour productivity record, rising income inequality and poverty, relatively unsatisfactory real GDP growth and a large current account deficit. The unemployment rates of Maori and Pacific Islanders have, for example, been around three times higher on average than for the majority European population[2] and 'New Zealand now appears to have one of the highest levels of inequality in the OECD' (O'Dea, 2000, p. 9).

Recent research suggests that New Zealand's productivity growth has been quite dismal since 1991, namely in the post-ECA era (Maloney, 1998). If a key objective of labour market deregulation and social security reform was to counter welfare dependency (see Harbridge and Walsh, Chapter Seven), a telling measure of failure is the marked increase in dependence, as well as the higher incidence of poverty and deprivation.[3]

At the beginning of the 21st century, New Zealand begins another era in policy reconfiguration. The change to a centre-left Labour-led coalition government marks an ideological shift and acceptance of a new way of thinking in policy-influencing circles encompassing both social and economic considerations (see, for example, Treasury, 1999; Department of Labour, 1999). The emphasis has therefore changed from the overarching pursuit of a liberalized and globally competitive economy within a pure noninterventionist context as an end in itself, towards the pursuit and perception of such policy goals more in terms of the outcomes that they can deliver to all New Zealanders. The commitment to the growth of an inclusive knowledge society that provides opportunities, enhances skills, is innovative and increases employment, informs broad policy-making under the new government.

In a clear move away from the earlier hands-off policy, active industrial and regional development policies are firmly on the political agenda. The strategy for achieving the government's objectives includes strengthening and working with the community and the voluntary sector as an integral part of employment, education, housing and health policies, especially with a view to reducing disparities for ethnic minorities. Priority is placed on capacity-building to give the Maori and Pacific Islander communities the capability to devise their own economic and social programmes. Several policies focused on job creation have also been identified (Labour Party, 1999a). A change in housing policy will complement these efforts, since high accommodation costs contributed significantly to increased poverty in the 1990s. Market rents have now been changed to income-related rents for tenants of public housing. State social security provision is therefore supported by housing policy with a view to ensuring an adequate level of income adequacy.

The new government has also given a firm policy signal of state provision of an adequate floor for the standard of living of the retired. Politics in New Zealand is marked by the perennial struggle to resolve the issue of security in retirement. The 1993 multiparty superannuation accord confirmed the encouragement of private savings, with the future strategy consisting of a phased reduction of entitlements. Nevertheless, the 1998 attempts to cut superannuation rates proved to be politically unacceptable. Superannuation is again at the political forefront, with Treasurer Cullen's proposed comprehensive pre-funding of state pensions through a dedicated fund, financed from future budget surpluses.[4] The proposal raises questions of inter-generational equity and opportunity costs. The younger generation, which is already carrying the burden of high student debt, will pay higher taxes to support baby boomers in their retirement. The surpluses reserved for superannuation are not available to be spent in other areas of social security or for economic development. The economic success of the scheme also assumes not only a rising rate of national savings to produce adequate budget surpluses, but also that the return on the investment of the dedicated funds will produce high net benefits for the citizens of New Zealand, and not just for the fund management industry. However, the scheme has considerable merit in that it safeguards a comfortable minimum income for the retired that will be sustainable for the next 60 years. This mitigates the possibility in coming years of widening ethnic and gender income inequality resulting from greater reliance on private pension provision.[5]

The focus of New Zealand's welfare state in the 21st century is on enhancing opportunities for economic and social participation. It is a 'capacity-building welfare state' (Labour Party, 1999b). The focus has therefore shifted away from the provision of a *minimum* safety net to alleviate poverty, which was characteristic of much of the 1990s, to poverty prevention through the development of the capacity to adjust to economic, social and global change, as well as the provision of a more comfortable and stable safety net. The Prime Minister, Helen Clark, recently wrote that 'we want a society which is inclusive of all ages, regions, ethnic and socioeconomic groups. We want a society in which everyone can claim a stake. The politics of exclusion and division which have characterised New Zealand for so long will not be practised by any Government I lead' (Clark, 2000, p. A15). Time will tell if the new policy direction will deliver these desired outcomes within the changed legislative policy framework following the repeal of the ECA.

Notes

1 A *Code of Social and Family Responsibility,* formulated in 1998, attempted to extend the legislative framework to the private domain of the family. However, general public disapproval resulted in abandonment of the proposed Code.

2 Maori, the indigenous people of New Zealand, and Pacific Islanders, make up 14.5 per cent and 5.6 per cent, respectively, of the country's population of 3.8 million. A high unemployment rate is only one of the indicators of the labour market disadvantage of these ethnic groups.

3 In 1998, around 14 per cent of New Zealanders aged 15–64 received major social security payments, compared to only 5 per cent in 1981. For further dependence and social exclusion indicators, see Department of Labour, 2000.
4 This will be achieved through the creation of the New Zealand Superannuation Fund, financed by the New Zealand Super-annuation Tax. This tax will not be in addition to existing income tax, but will replace an equal part of the income tax on personal income.
5 See also Feature No. 2 (Jay Ginn) which highlights the serious gender problems of pension privatization.

References

Clark, H. (2000), 'Labour has Delivered and it will Continue to do so', *The New Zealand Herald*, 20 September.

Department of Labour (1999), *Human Capability: A framework for analysis*, Department of Labour, Wellington.

Galt, D. (2000), 'New Zealand's Economic Growth', Treasury Working Paper 00/9, http://www.treasury.govt.nz/workingpapers.

Labour Party (1999a), 'Opportunity: A nation at work (Labour on employment)' (October) http://www.labour.org.nz/infocentre1/policies/employmentpol.html.

Labour Party (1999b), 'Security with Opportunity: Welfare for the 21st century' (September) http://www.labour.org.nz/infocentre1/policies/socialwelfarepol.html.

Maloney, T. (1998), *Five Years After: The New Zealand labour market and the Employment Contracts Act*, Institute of Policy Studies, Victoria University of Wellington, Wellington.

O'Dea, D. (2000), *The Changes in New Zealand's Income Distribution*, Treasury Working Paper 00/13, http://www.treasury.govt.nz/workingpapers/default.htm.

Treasury (1999), 'Towards Higher Living Standards for New Zealanders: Briefing to the incoming Government', http://www.treasury.govt.nz/pubs/bmb/brief99/contents.htm.

Chapter Eight

Central and Eastern European Countries: the Transition from a *Planned* to a *Market* Economy – What Consequences for Social Security?

Henri Lourdelle

The social protection systems in Central and Eastern European countries generally have long traditions, with their historical origins in the *Bismarckian* system of social insurance. In Slovenia, for example, the first mutual benefit association was founded in 1835, even before the implementation under the Austro-Hungarian monarchy of the fundamental principles of German social insurance, which remained in force until 1922. The same occurred in Romania in 1874 with the Health Act. Nevertheless, the integration of these countries into the *Soviet bloc* resulted in three major measures in the field of social security, the consequences of which are still being felt:

- the integration of the social budget into the State budget;
- financing by enterprises or administrations alone; and
- the absence of a ceiling and of the individualization of contributions.

The fall of the Berlin Wall was highly symbolic. It marked the end of a world and of an *époque* and gave rise, for the populations in the countries concerned, to a profound desire for change at both the political and social levels, including social protection systems.

One of the first measures in this respect consisted of giving a certain level of financial independence back to social security systems, even though in some cases, such as Estonia, the social insurance budget remained an *appendix* of the state budget or, as in Hungary or Poland, the state and/or the parliament have retained control of the social security budget. The same applies in certain countries of the European Union, such as Sweden and, most recently, France (in 1996), where the parliaments *approve* or *adopt* the social security budget.

This parliamentary approval is all the more necessary in Central and Eastern European countries where, in view of the realities of the unemployment and economic situation, contributions do not cover the full cost of the benefits provided and the State budget therefore has to make up the shortfall. Indeed, this is in conformity with the ILO's Social Security (Minimum Standards) Convention, 1952 (No. 102), which provides that, as a fundamental guarantee, the state shall accept general responsibility for the financial equilibrium of social security systems.

Another measure has been to associate the social partners with the *management* of the branches of social security covered by social insurance schemes. This is the case, for example, in Poland, where advisory bodies bring together on a tripartite basis the public authorities, employers and trade union organizations. These branches are mainly financed through contributions paid by insured persons and may be distinguished in that respect from the branches which are covered by the social security system and are financed by taxation. The latter cover the whole of the population and include measures which, in the European Union, would be categorized as *social assistance.* These branches of social security are administered exclusively by bodies under the responsibility of the state.

It can therefore be seen that over the past decade social protection systems have been, and are still subject to many initiatives, often under the pressure and *liberal* inspiration of the World Bank and the International Monetary Fund. But the process is still ongoing and the task is immense. The implementation of these reforms has involved above all the high-level officials in the countries concerned, for whom a large number of seminars and technical training courses have been organized, although trade union organizations have not been associated with them. Nevertheless, from *transmission belts* for the orders of the authorities, which they mostly were, the latter have been able to transform themselves and now apparently constitute, with some few exceptions, an independent and dynamic movement which sees itself as defending and furthering the interests of its members.

Indeed, it is essential for the trade union movement to take up and become involved in this field, which is of prime importance for it. Far from being merely a technical field, social protection is a highly *political* issue in the full sense of the term and the reforms which have been initiated will determine the type of society that is being developed. To misquote a proverb, 'tell me who you spend your time with and I will tell you who you are', it might easily be said 'tell me what type of social protection system you are building, and I will tell you the society you are developing!'.

Taking into account the economic and social developments which they have experienced, Central and Eastern European countries currently have to face at least four major challenges:

- *pursuing the reforms undertaken since the change of regime* even though, in the difficult social and economic situation with which they are confronted, these reforms often, and at a very practical level, result in the populations concerned having to make new efforts (such as the raising of the pensionable age and the extension of the period of insurance giving entitlement to a full pension), while at the same time unemployment is rising and *atypical* forms of employment are increasing, such as part-time and fixed-term contracts);
- *finding the necessary financial resources*, particularly since the integration of social security budgets into the state budget had as its principle and most significant consequence the fact that social protection systems now have no financial reserves. It also served to conceal current trends, which would have required the adoption of reforms to address or anticipate them;
- *addressing the consequences of their accession to the European Union*. In addition to the efforts required to achieve budgetary rigour and stability, the reforms that are undertaken have to respect the coherence, or rather convergence of existing systems in order to prevent the development of a new type of dumping, namely social dumping. This requirement is particularly severe since, once these countries have acceded to the European Union, their systems will start to be *coordinated* with the social security systems in other countries, under the terms of Regulation 1408/71, which determines the rules and procedures for this process;
- *confronting the changes in the field of labour*, which amount to a transition from an economy which was admittedly *planned*, but in which everyone worked (irrespective of the quality and economic *value* of the work performed) and benefited from social protection, to a *market* economy, in which social protection is closely related to employment and which, at least initially, is leaving many people

marginalized. This explains the disenchantment demonstrated in recent electoral results.

Finally, it is important to ensure that these reforms do not give rise to new forms of social tension, or to new and important social inequalities. In this context, two of the reforms to be undertaken are of particular significance in view of the constraints that are faced and the challenges to be met, namely: the pensions system and the health system.

1 Pensions: the Urgency of Reforms which Reconcile Needs and Solidarity

If there is one branch of social protection that needs to be *reformed* in these countries, it is undoubtedly the retirement benefits branch. However, the need for reform is unrelated to the essentially demographic reasons often cited in the European Union. Indeed, the proportion of older persons in the total population (and particularly in relation to the population of working age) is around the same, or sometimes lower than that of the European Union (in which there is currently one older person aged 65 or above for every four people of working age, or a rate of 25 per cent, compared with 24.1 per cent in the Czech Republic and 22.5 per cent in Hungary). The demography of Central and Eastern European countries differs from that of the European Union in several respects, which directly affect the financing of pensions.

In the first place, most of them are experiencing a decline in their population as a resulting of a birth/death ratio that is less than one (partly due to the phenomenon of emigration to the European Union). Moreover, and in contrast with the situation in the European Union, life expectancy is declining. Living conditions, stress and alcoholism are the causes most frequently cited. In other words, the higher mortality rate means that the ageing of the population is not as significant and that the problems of the *granny boom*, which is widely feared in the Member States of the European Union, is not as acute in Central and Eastern European countries.

1.1 The Situation of Pension Schemes

An anachronistic generosity in eligibility conditions ...

A feature that is inherited from the former system is that pension schemes in Central and Eastern European countries may appear generous in terms of their eligibility conditions for pension benefits (such as age, length of service and contributions paid) in relation to the rules in force in the European Union. The retirement age is still mainly 60 for men and 55 or 56 for women, depending on their occupational category, and this age may be still lower in such countries as Bulgaria (52 for men and 47 for women). Moreover, with regard to length of service, it is sufficient to have paid contributions for around 20 years (for all insured persons in Hungary and for women in Bulgaria, for example) to be entitled to a full pension.

... but mediocre pensions

Despite this generosity, in real terms the level of statutory pensions is frequently mediocre in relation to prices and the cost of living, which are coming ever closer to the levels in the European Union. Expressed in terms of a percentage of the average wage, the replacement levels may seem attractive. However, in financial terms, the real situation is much more gloomy.

In Slovenia, for example, which is the European Union accession country with the highest GDP (65 per cent of the level in the European Union in 1998), and the highest rates of pensions, the average pension amounts to 69 per cent of average wages, which might appear to be an entirely acceptable rate. However, in real terms, this amounts to 325.41 Euros, or 67,914 tolars (1 Euro = 208.704 tolars) for an average pension. The average wage is 471.17 Euros (98,336 tolars). Moreover, some 37 per cent of retirees in Slovenia receive less than 50,000 tolars a month (around 239.57 Euros), while only 18 per cent of them receive a pension which is higher than the average wage.

In Poland, the average retirement pension was 783.84 zlotys in 1999, or around 200 Euros (1 Euro = 3.91909 zlotys), or 45.9 per cent of the average wage. In Hungary in the same year, the average pension, which amounts to a little less than 40 per cent of the average gross wage, was 116.71 Euros, or 30,588 forints (1 Euro = 262.075 forints). The average wage was 77,187 forints, or 294.52 Euros. In Bulgaria, pensions amount to between 25 Euros for the minimum pension and 50 Euros for the maximum pension.

... and changes in the wage mass which affect the financing of the scheme

In these regions, as has been seen, the contributory capacity of individuals is affected by the major changes on the labour market (including the rise in unemployment and the development of atypical forms of employment). After a spectacular fall in employment rates at the beginning of the 1990s, there has been a weak recovery in recent years in six of these countries (Bulgaria, Latvia, Poland, Romania, Slovakia and Slovenia), which has not, however, been sufficient to compensate for the losses suffered during the previous period. Employment rates, which used to be appreciably higher than those in the European Union (80 per cent in the Czech Republic and over 70 per cent in most of the other countries), have stabilized at around 70 per cent in the Czech Republic (which nevertheless represents a fall of 10 points), 65 per cent in Estonia, Lithuania and Slovenia, 60 per cent in Poland and Slovakia, 55 per cent in Bulgaria and Latvia and hardly more than 50 per cent in Hungary. These are official figures, although it would appear than many employees are not officially registered and are therefore in the informal economy.

Another factor which has to be taken into consideration is the decline in the employment rate of women which, although substantial, was less spectacular than might have been feared in view of the high rate of women's employment in these countries. The unemployment rate for women is higher than that of men practically everywhere, with the exception of Hungary and Estonia. At least three reasons may be advanced to explain this fall in women's employment.

The first may, somewhat shamefacedly, be classified as a traditional factor: when unemployment rises, women are often the principal victims in these, as in other countries.

The second factor is more unexpected. As part of the rupture with the ideology of the former regimes, *feminist demands* have emerged in Central and Eastern European countries, including a call for *femininity* to be recognized. In the countries of the European Union, the *promotion of women* still involves their economic emancipation, and therefore their access to employment (in 20 years, the numbers of women in employment have risen from 40 to 60 million and are continuing to rise, even though the increase is mainly in part-time jobs). This increase is also making it possible to compensate part of the impact of the *granny boom* in the financing of pensions. In contrast, in Central and Eastern European countries, the aspirations of women appear to be oriented more towards recognition of their family work and roles. This aspiration is probably encouraged by the numerous family benefits which are provided in these countries, particularly in the form of *parental* or *family* leave. By way of illustration, in Romania, either parent (although women are the principal beneficiaries) is entitled to paid leave to bring up a child under two years of age. The parents receive 85 per cent of their wages. In Slovakia, parents receive a *parental allowance* for bringing up a child under three years of age, or under seven years of age where the child is seriously disabled or suffering from a long-term illness. Similar provisions are to be found in Hungary, Latvia and Slovenia.

Finally, there is the issue of crèches and kindergartens. Formerly, these services were provided free-of-charge or at a very low cost. Now, many childcare structures are private and involve a substantial financial contribution from the parents. By way of illustration, in Lithuania, the parents have to pay around 60 litas a month, or 17.50 Euros (out of a minimum gross wage of 430 litas, or 125 Euros a month). In Latvia, it costs the parents between 17 and 20 lats a month (between 31.77 and 37.37 Euros), out of a minimum monthly gross wage of 42 lats (78.47 Euros). In Poland, the cost of a crèche is around 1,987 zlotys a month (505.22 Euros), which is shared between the parents and the municipality (the minimum wage is 500 zlotys a month).

1.2 Current Reforms

Timid reforms of statutory pensions

Even though most reforms have concerned the establishment of so-called *second pillar* schemes, to adopt the terminology used by the World Bank, it cannot be said that nothing has been done with regard to statutory schemes, even though these reforms have all been perceived as being *negative*. Depending on the country, they have consisted of:

- raising the retirement age: in the Czech Republic, between now and 2006, it will rise to 62 for men and 61 for women; in Hungary, it will be increased to 62 for everyone in 2009; in Lithuania, it will be raised to 62.5 years for men and 60 for women in 2009;

- increasing the length of insurance: this issue is already under debate in Slovenia;
- eliminating distinctions for particular categories of employment which permit, for certain specific jobs (arduous jobs), a shorter period of insurance to be eligible for a full retirement benefit. For example, Bulgaria is proceeding along this path;
- making the indexation of pensions less favourable. In view of the low level of pensions, this measure is of limited economic significance, although the same cannot evidently be said for its social consequences;
- in contrast, nothing has been done to adjust the level of statutory pensions.

... but giving priority to individual retirement savings accounts

Under pressure from the international financial institutions, such as the IMF and the World Bank, which are very present in these countries, political leaders in Central and Eastern European countries are rushing to set up *individual retirement savings accounts*, commonly and abusively known as *pension funds*, without having any great knowledge of the precise meaning of this term. Nevertheless, the words *pension funds* have had and will perhaps continue to have a magic effect, as if on their own they were able to exorcise all the fears concerning statutory retirement systems. But these savings accounts are principally being established for reasons of economic expediency and are meeting with varying levels of success. For example, in Poland they are compulsory for employees born after 1968, while in the Czech Republic 20 per cent of the active population, or one million employees, are covered by such funds. The coverage rate is less significant in Hungary and is very low in Slovenia and Bulgaria, where such accounts only cover a little less than 6 per cent of employees.

1.3 Issues Raised by These Reforms

This debate on the reform of retirement schemes is not therefore merely a technical matter. In view of the underlying issues involved, it is in practice a real social debate which raises several questions of substance.

Why is dialogue needed?

Although everyone appears to have understood the urgency of the sometimes drastic reforms that are necessary, these are often undertaken by political decision-makers hurriedly and without any dialogue with the social partners. Yet dialogue is indispensable if it is wished to gauge the *acceptability* of reforms to the population, and particularly to employees, who are the principal contributors and those primarily concerned by their effects. In the absence of such dialogue, the social partners, and through them workers, instead of being partners and responsible actors in the reforms, are at best subjected to them, and may actively contest them.

When will the level of statutory schemes be adjusted?

In general terms in these countries the tendency is to put off for as long as possible the reform, and therefore the adjustment of the pensions provided by statutory schemes. However, when the question arises, for example, of increasing contributions with a view to improving statutory schemes, the reaction may well be to turn towards *individual retirement savings accounts*, which are more personal, rather than to other more collective, and therefore less attractive schemes.

What are the consequences for social cohesion?

The first layer, or *pillar,* of retirement benefits is *universal* and offers a higher degree of *solidarity*. The question therefore arises as to whether postponing the reform does not run the risk of further accentuating the tension between the privileged few who will have access to a second pillar, and who will long remain a minority, and all those who have to be satisfied with the mediocre levels of the statutory pension. What effect will this have on solidarity, which is the cement of social cohesion? Admittedly, if the second pillar is made compulsory, as in Chile or Poland, there might be grounds for believing that this risk is limited, or even nonexistent. However, the situation in Chile is anything but reassuring in this respect. Indeed, even though the system there is compulsory, only 50 per cent of potential insured persons (the employees concerned) actually pay contributions to these individual retirement savings accounts. In a country where wages are low and jobs rare or uncertain, there is a major temptation to try and avoid this statutory obligation in any manner possible (such as failing to declare wages, or the payment of contributions on only part of the remuneration received) with the risk of the development of jobs in the *black* economy. This is all the more true as responsibility for paying contributions and declaring wages rests, as it does everywhere, with the employer.

Another question which arises, in terms of social cohesion, is whether it is legitimate to withdraw a portion of the contribution paid to systems based on solidarity and designed to develop solidarity, with a view to their transferral to purely individual systems, particularly in societies in which the gap is widening between those who have access to wealth and well-being, and those who are in precarious jobs, unemployment and even poverty?

Are these measures coherent with the reforms undertaken in the European Union?

Contrary to a widely held view, pensions in the countries of the European Union are not principally provided by private schemes, or in other words by pension funds. The *Green Paper on supplementary pensions in the Single Market,* issued by the European Commission on 10 June 1997, states in this respect that 'currently state pensions (...) account for the bulk of pension payouts (88%)'. In other words, they are provided by schemes financed on a *pay-as-you-go* basis, which are therefore based on solidarity between generations and individuals, despite differences between countries (European Commission, 1997).

It should also be noted that, while nearly all the countries of the European Union have undertaken reforms of their retirement systems (and particularly in Denmark, France, Germany, Italy and Spain), these reforms consist of adaptations of the systems, but do not fundamentally call them into question, in contrast with what has happened in South America, and particularly in Chile, at the instigation of the IMF, with the dramatic consequences that can be seen to be emerging today. In Chile, only half of the population is in practice covered by the new system, which constitutes a veritable social *time bomb*, while the administrative costs account for between 20 and 30 per cent of the contributions paid and only cover administrative, commercial and publicity costs.

Are individual retirement savings accounts becoming the principal system?

In view of the low levels of benefits provided by statutory retirement schemes in the countries under examination, it is legitimate to raise the question of the role that could be played by individual retirement savings systems. In the absence of reforms which are sufficiently far-reaching to make the statutory schemes more *effective*, will such funds in future play a role that is far from marginal?

In these countries, supplementary retirement systems are almost exclusively composed of *defined contribution* schemes, or in other words, individual retirement savings accounts, which means that the income of employees when they retire will practically only consist of what they have actually contributed, and therefore *saved,* during their active lives. However, in view of the low level of wages in Central and Eastern European countries and their particularly high *real* unemployment rates (with the possible exception of certain areas in the Czech Republic and Hungary), which are often double the rates in the European Union, without overlooking the financial risks incurred in the very long term …

The question therefore has to be raised as to whether these reforms have not *put the cart before the horse*? Pensions systems cannot be disconnected from developments on the labour market and the various forms taken by employment in the countries concerned. It is therefore indispensable, before any decision is taken concerning retirement benefits, to consider the situation of workers in atypical, part-time or fixed-term jobs. Women are primarily concerned, but also young persons. What will their *real* possibilities be of subscribing to this type of supplementary scheme, and what rights will they be able to acquire? Do such systems take into account, and are they adapted to the situation of this large number of workers, whose situation is often precarious?

What role will the social partners play in managing these individual retirement savings schemes?

In general, the social partners are no more associated with the management of these systems than they have been with their establishment. What is at issue is not their intervention in the daily management of the schemes, but in supervising the institutions which administer them and in debating the major policy orientations, including investment options. In this respect, once a guarantee has been obtained as to the return on investments, would it not be possible to follow other rules qualified in certain quarters as *socially responsible*, along the same lines as certain major American, Canadian and Swiss pension funds?

Is this not a legitimate claim for a trade union organization? Does the fact that individuals pay contributions to a supplementary retirement system not amount to the same thing as postponing the payment of part of their remuneration, which is already due? Is it such an exaggerated claim that the persons concerned should be able to be involved in what is done with the wages that have been paid in the form of contributions? Furthermore, and particularly through *socially responsible* investments, or *sustainable growth*, why should contributors, through their trade union organizations, be denied the possibility to influence investment choices with a view to promoting employment?

On the issue of investment strategies, it is frequently argued, with the support of the World Bank and the IMF, that the establishment of these systems of individual accounts should contribute to national economic recovery. In other words, they should be limited to the countries themselves. This *nationalist* investment strategy would appear to be a double aberration, firstly in accordance with the principle that *prudent* management presupposes the diversification of risks and the optimization of financial returns. And secondly, because it is difficult to see how national stock exchanges could absorb the whole of this potential source of savings.

2 The Health System: a Difficult Choice between Rationalization and the Temptation of Privatization

Health systems are also very dependent on socioeconomic developments. They are giving rise to numerous debates and choices, some painful, which are bringing into conflict:

- the government, which is trying to contain costs;
- workers, who wish to defend their jobs; and
- users (who are also those providing the financing) and their representative organizations, who aspire to a system that is both effective and nonselective, or in other words, does not give rise to

exclusion and does not accentuate the social tension between those who have the means to obtain (quality) health care and the others.

2.1 *A Situation that is Quantitatively Comparable to that of the EU, but very Different in Terms of Quality*

In most of the countries under consideration, outpatient medical care is free-of-charge, irrespective of whether State, regional or local health systems are used (Bulgaria, Hungary and Lithuania) or health insurance schemes (Czech Republic, Poland, Romania and Slovenia). However, in other countries, a contribution is required from the patient (in Estonia, it is five crowns per consultation).

In theory, hospitalization is free-of-charge for insured persons and members of health systems (except in Latvia, where there is a degressive flat-rate hospital charge, under which the hospitalized patient pays five Latvian pounds for the first day in hospital, and then 1.5 pounds for each additional day – 1 Euro = 0.535 pounds). The drugs prescribed and provided in hospital are also currently free-of-charge, except in Bulgaria, where a bold reform of the health system in its entirety is under way.

With regard to drugs, in the case of outpatient care they may be covered by health insurance schemes (Czech Republic) or the general system (Romania and Slovenia), or may have to be paid for and then subsequently reimbursed more or less at their full cost (Hungary, Lithuania and Poland).

In qualitative terms, the figures for health care and hospital personnel are fairly similar, and even slightly higher than those of the European Union (European Parliament, 1998). Doctors, pharmacists and nurses are available in sufficient numbers. The weakness is the distribution of health care personnel over the national territory, with a high concentration in cities and certain regions, and penury elsewhere. However, this is a problem that is also found in many other countries. In Bulgaria and Latvia, there are 33 doctors for every 10,000 inhabitants, while the number in Hungary is 39, compared with an average of 28.1 in the European Union in 1994 (with variations ranging from 53 in Italy to 15.6 in the United Kingdom).

In contrast, the situation is very different in terms of quality. Hospitals are mostly old, poorly equipped and badly distributed. Radiologists work with equipment that is obsolete, and even sometimes dangerous to them and their patients.

2.2 *Two Tendencies in Reforming the System*

Two tendencies are currently emerging to address this situation. The first reflects the desire of public authorities to rationalize the use of the available means, particularly through a better distribution of existing personnel and facilities.

Several initiatives have been undertaken in this respect in the Czech Republic, Lithuania and Hungary, although they have come up against strong resistance. If they intend to pursue this policy, the governments will certainly have to:

- develop better dialogue with the social partners, users and health professionals before adopting any rationalization measures;
- ensure that they are not confining themselves to a purely administrative and financial logic, but are following a policy of quality public health; and
- act transparently, both in terms of the objectives pursued and the means used.

The second tendency consists of proceeding towards the privatization of health systems, on the pretext of giving users and practitioners greater responsibility and achieving better economic performance, both of which remain to be proved.

For example, in the Czech Republic, Poland and Romania, health insurance contributions are paid to *health insurance funds* which conclude contracts with doctors and specialist health care institutions. This system has not, however, prevented health expenditure from continuing to rise (Czech Republic) and has caused numerous conflicts (Poland) with health care professionals, upon whom increasingly strict profitability criteria have been imposed, as well as with the population as a whole.

In Romania, the system of contributing to health insurance funds has been combined with a health system at three levels (perhaps similar to the retirement system?), which envisages various levels of financial contributions by insured persons. A minimum *package* of care is included in all insurance schemes, based on the compulsory monthly contribution paid to the fund. To this is added another *package* of care, known as *co-payment*, which means that it involves an additional payment by insured persons. Finally, access to high technology care is exclusively financed by the insured person.

Privatization may also take the form, as in the cases of Hungary and Poland, of the opening of private cabinets. It can also affect the hospital sector through the opening of private hospitals. At present, this is only occurring to a moderate level, and particularly in small establishments carrying out benign interventions which do not require the use of substantial and costly equipment or, as in the case of Poland, through the opening of *foundations* within public establishments. However, the reform which is under way in Bulgaria would appear to be going even further, as it will result in health care professionals and hospitals being considered to be health *businesses*. They will therefore have to be inscribed in the *commercial register* and the whole of the hospital system will be privatized.

Irrespective of the form that it takes, *privatization* continues to raise substantive questions affecting the basic principles on which the systems are based. If health is considered to be a universal right, this right cannot be subjected to the laws of the market which, by their very nature, always result in the selection of risks and produce phenomena of exclusion. Moreover, health-related matters cannot be reduced to purely economic terms. They have to be integrated into the broader health policy pursued by the state and the social partners in the country.

In any event, with regard to both methods of financing and the organization of the health system, it is important for the public authorities to take the necessary measures to guarantee the access of all persons to the system. But certain developments, by their very nature, run counter to this objective.

Solidarity, which must not be confused with assistance, also needs to play its role in health systems. These matters amount to a veritable choice of society!

A Clear Conclusion: the Legitimate Role of Trade Union Organizations in Influencing and Redirecting Reforms

Central and Eastern European countries are therefore confronted with very real social problems in relation to their social protection systems, both in terms of basic values, which may or may not have to be defended and promoted, and the issues that are arising and have to be addressed.

The necessary responses are all the more urgent in view of the fact that signs of impatience are emerging and disillusionment is setting in.

It will undoubtedly be said in some quarters that these reforms are costly. This is admittedly the case. But solutions do exist, such as the allocation to the reforms of a proportion of the resources obtained through privatization. Or even by flattening all benefits, as a basis for rethinking the system and redeploying the resources allocated to certain benefits.

All of this implies changes in culture, if only to develop real reactions and instruments of dialogue. It is only at this price that solutions will be found and implemented. In order to do so, it is important that trade union organizations, as well as employers' organizations, should not be afraid of assuming their responsibilities in these areas. Indeed trade union organizations are already doing so.

The involvement of the social partners, and particularly of trade unions, may take on differing dimensions, for example, in the case of pension and health systems. The term *involvement* does not necessarily mean a monopoly of representation. In order to prevent a return to a totally *planned* society, it is important that certain areas of decision-making and dialogue should be open to the representatives of civil society, which includes trade unions.

Finally, trade union organizations will gain in legitimacy when they clarify their objectives and acquire a minimum level of expertise in the relevant areas. Nor should it be overlooked that technical solutions are at the service of social protection policy, and not the reverse, and that social protection exists to serve the interests of individuals, without ever sacrificing them on the altars of results and performance.

References

Council of Europe (1995), *La Protection Sociale dans le Contexte de la Transition Politique et Économique*, report of the meeting, Strasbourg.

European Commission (1997), *Supplementary Pensions in the Single Market: A Green Paper* (COM(97)283 final), Luxembourg.

European Commission (1999), *Employment in Europe 1998*, Brussels.

European Parliament (1998), *Health Care Systems in the EU: A comparative study* (SACO 101).

International Social Security Association (1994), *Restructuring of Social Security in Central and Eastern Europe: A guide to recent developments*, Geneva.

Lourdelle, H. (1999), *Livre Blanc sur la Protection Sociale dans les Pays d'Europe Centrale et Orientale*, ETUC, Brussels.

PHARE Consensus Programme (1999), *L'Évolution de la Protection Sociale en Europe Centrale et Orientale.*

Chapter Nine

The Danish Model of *Flexicurity*: a Paradise – with Some Snakes

Per Kongshøj Madsen

1 The Danish 'Job Miracle'

Over the past seven years, Denmark has experienced a fairly dramatic decline in unemployment. From a maximum of 12.4 per cent in 1993, the official number of registered unemployed dropped to 5.7 per cent in 1999, the lowest level since 1976. For young persons aged between 16 and 24 years, the unemployment rate fell even more, from 12.0 per cent to 3.7 per cent. Not surprisingly, this favourable employment situation has caused international interest and made Denmark a member of the group of small successful European economies (Auer, 2000).

And the economic figures *are* indeed impressive. Overall employment grew by almost 6 per cent, from 2,530,700 in 1993 to 2,678,700 persons in 1999. Of the increase, 75 per cent was in the private sector. This was accomplished without deficits on the external balance of payments (except for 1998) and with rising surpluses for public budgets. A further outstanding aspect of the Danish employment system is the high employment ratio. In 1999, the employment/population ratio was 71.6, among the highest in the OECD area.

To many international observers, Denmark therefore seems to have created a unique combination of stable economic growth and social welfare since the mid-1990s, at a time when liberals were arguing that the classical Scandinavian model was becoming obsolete and was no longer able to face the demands of flexibility and structural change arising out of technological progress and the growing forces of international competition. The term *flexicurity* is used to characterize this successful combination of adaptability to a changing international environment and a solidaristic welfare system, which protects the citizens from the more brutal consequences of structural change. The recent success of the Danish model of *flexicurity* thus points to a third way between the flexibility often ascribed to a liberal market economy and the social safety nets of the traditional Scandinavian welfare state.

However, reality is, as usual, more complex than the portraits of *model societies* found in international discussions of welfare state systems. The purpose of this chapter is to present a brief, as well as critical analysis of the factors behind the recent changes, with emphasis on the knowledge that can be gained from recent evaluations of the reforms made to Danish labour market policy since 1994.

2 A Good Old-fashioned Upswing?

A first factor that should be noted is that the Danish upswing since 1993 is not in itself an *economic miracle*, but a standard example of demand-driven growth. Firstly, an expansion of fiscal policy was allowed in 1993–94. Then came falling international interest rates, rising housing prices and a credit reform allowing home-owners to convert the fall in long-term interest rates into lower housing costs. Private demand was strongly stimulated. In 1994 alone, private consumption grew by 7 per cent in real terms. Investment in housing accelerated. The same happened, after a while, with private investment in general, all according to the standard economic textbook.

Furthermore, the relative reduction in unemployment is less impressive if the inflow into early retirement schemes and leave schemes is taken into account. If gross unemployment is examined, including participation in the above schemes and in active labour market measures, the reduction in unemployment was from 21 per cent in 1994 to 16 per cent in 1999 (measured as share of the workforce). This was nevertheless still a significant reduction.

3 The *Golden Triangle* of the Danish Labour Market

But if a closer look is taken, it can be argued that the Danish *miracle* is not just a trivial mixture of demand-driven growth and the hiding of a large share of the population in various welfare programmes. The most important observation is that the change from economic stagnation to economic growth and rising employment has been possible without the outburst of wage inflation which normally follows a dramatic fall in unemployment. Further investigation is needed in this respect. Has Denmark invented a Scandinavian version of the inflation-free growth economy?

The relative success of the Danish model in recent years has stimulated ideas about the development of a new Danish employment system in the form of the so-called golden triangle shown in Figure 9.1.

The argument underlying the golden triangle theory is that the success of the Danish employment system is due to its unique combination of *flexibility* (measured, for instance, by a high level of job mobility), *social security* (a generous unemployment benefit system) and *active labour market programmes*, all of which support the ongoing transformation of the economy. The golden triangle depicts Denmark as a kind of *hybrid* employment system. Due to employment protection legislation which allows employers to hire and fire workers with short notice, the Danish system has a level of flexibility which is comparable to that of Canada, Ireland, United Kingdom and United States (OECD, 1999b, Chapter 2). At the same time, through its social security system and active labour market programmes, Denmark resembles the other Nordic welfare states.

The following sections look more closely at each of the corners of the golden triangle.

Figure 9.1 The *golden triangle* of the Danish employment system

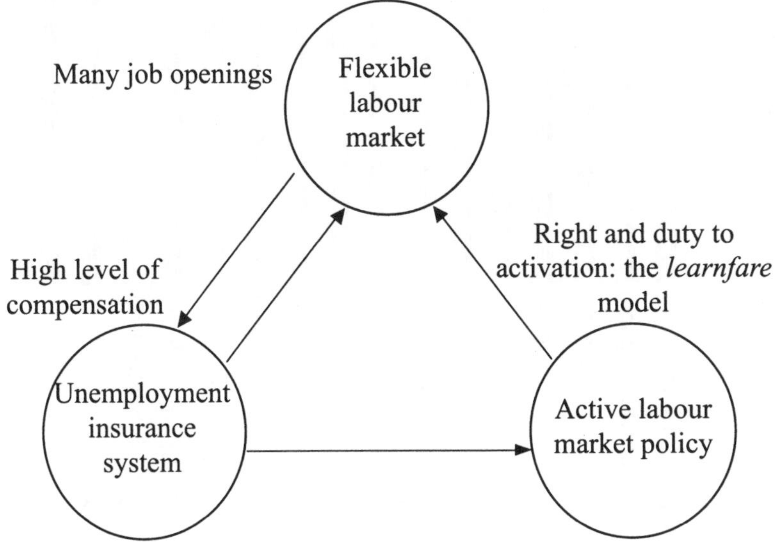

Source: Adapted from Arbejdsministeriet, 1999, p. 7.

4 Job Mobility

Compared to the net changes in employment, the underlying mobility of workers between jobs and the level of both job creation and job destruction are surprisingly high. A recent study concerning hires, separations, job creation and job destruction has found that, on average, the level of worker turnover is about 30 per cent, and in no year less than 25 per cent (Bingley et al., 2000). The level of job turnover (job creation and job destruction) is also much higher than the level of yearly net changes in employment levels. The overall average of job turnover is around 12 per cent.

Another indicator of the high rate of mobility on the Danish labour market is provided by data on the average tenure of employees. Such data were published by the OECD in 1997 and in a recent ILO working paper (OECD, 1997; Auer and Cazes, 2000). Figure 9.2 shows the distribution of employees by tenure in a number of OECD countries.

Figure 9.2 Average tenure (years) of employees in a number of OECD countries

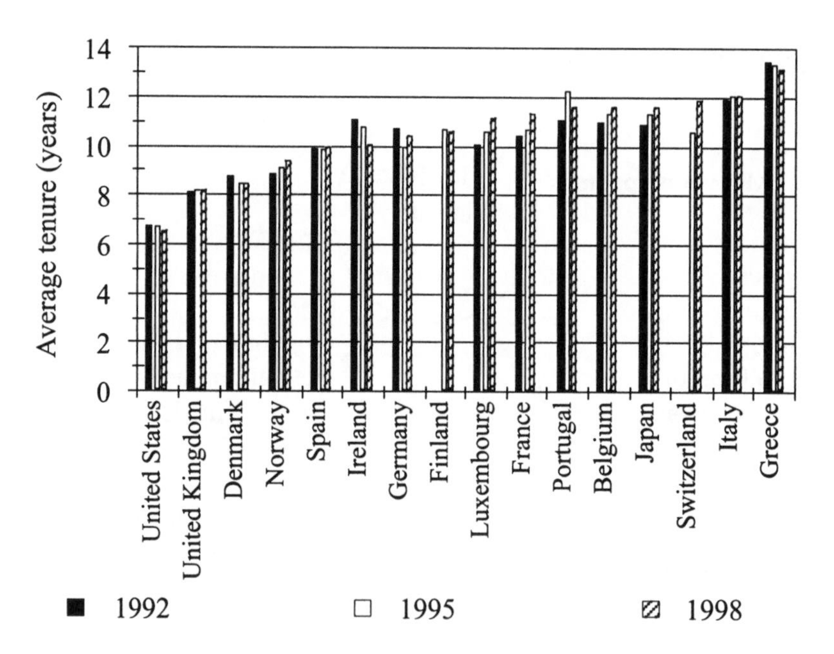

Source: Auer and Cazes, 2000.

Denmark is at the low end of the international scale in terms of average tenure, along with countries such as the United Kingdom and the United States. In contrast, other Nordic countries, such as Finland and Sweden, have much higher levels of average tenure. Sweden is at the top end of the scale, with Italy and Greece. Moreover, it may be noted that the average levels of tenure, in both Denmark and in other countries, are fairly stable over time. The level of average tenure therefore appears to be an inherent structural characteristic of the employment system of each country. Finally, during the time span covered by the data, there are no signs of an overall decline in the stability of the employment relationship in the countries covered by Figure 9.2.

One explanation for the high level of job mobility is the liberal regime of employment protection found in Denmark. A number of studies have compared the level of employment protection in Denmark with that of other countries. Figure 9.3 summarizes the results of the latest OECD study (OECD, 1999b, Chapter 2). As shown by the indicator of employment protection legislation contained in Figure 9.3, Denmark is ranked as having a low level of employment protection compared to most other industrialized countries, and much lower than the other Nordic countries, with which Denmark is commonly grouped.

If a closer look is taken at employment protection in Denmark, the following points may be noted (for a more detailed overview see Cazes et al., 1999; and OECD, 1999b, Annex 2A):

- dismissal is acceptable if it is caused either by the conditions of the enterprise (lack of work) or by the behaviour of the employee (lack of competence, substantial absence without justification, criminal offences, etc.); an employer is not allowed to dismiss an employee on such grounds as sex, religion or pregnancy;
- the length of the notice period is variable, depending on the duration of employment. Furthermore, the notice period differs between white-collar and blue-collar workers. For white-collar workers, there is a general minimum notice period of one month, which increases with the length of employment up to a maximum of six months after nine years of employment. For blue-collar workers, the notice period is normally much shorter and workers who have been employed for less than nine months may be dismissed without notice;
- severance pay is only provided for white-collar workers who have been employed for more than 12 years;

Figure 9.3 Overall strictness of employment protection legislation (EPL) in the late 1990s: average indicator for regular contracts, temporary contracts and collective dismissals (selected OECD countries)

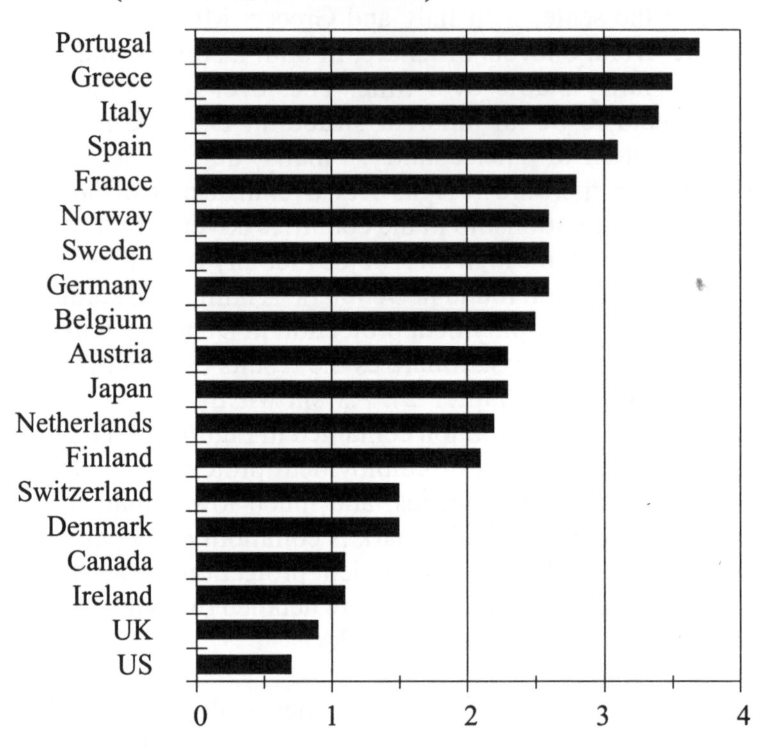

Source: OECD, 1999b, Table 2.5.

- in the event of unjustified dismissal, compensation of up to 12 months pay may have to be paid by the employer. Reinstatement is possible, but rare.

It might be thought that this high level of job mobility and low level of employment protection would lead to a widespread feeling of insecurity among Danish employees. Paradoxically, this is not the case. In a survey conducted in 1996, the proportion of Danish workers *not* strongly agreeing with the statement 'my job is secure' was about 45 per cent, and therefore considerably lower than for all the other countries in the sample. This feeling of job security was found among all subgroups of workers (OECD, 1997, Table 5.2). Although this may also reflect the positive situation on the Danish labour market at the time of the survey, there are no clear indications that Danish workers are reacting to the high level of flexibility with a strong feeling of insecurity. Similar results have also been found in a more recent survey (The Dublin Institute, 1999).

There are at least three explanations for this. One is the predominance of small and medium-sized enterprises (SMEs) in the Danish industrial structure, which implies that strong internal labour markets are less important than in other countries. It is easier to shift from one firm to another due to lower entry barriers at the enterprise level. Furthermore, the general improvement in the Danish labour market situation since 1994 may also have influenced the responses. But a final explanation is the relatively generous unemployment benefits paid to unemployed workers from the first day of unemployment and for a considerable period.

5 The Danish Unemployment Compensation System

The vast majority of unemployed persons who are members of an unemployment insurance fund receive unemployment benefits calculated at the rate of 90 per cent of their previous income, with a ceiling of 145,000 DKK per year. Unemployment benefits may be claimed from the first day of unemployment and for a maximum of four years, including periods of activation.

For low-income groups, this and other income-related benefits, combined with the effects of the rather high level of income tax, result in high net income replacement rates (OECD, 1999a). For an average production worker, for example, the replacement rate is around 70 per cent. For low-income groups, the net replacement rate is around 90 per cent, and is highest for single parents.

In the Danish labour market system, the potential disincentives deriving from these high income replacement rates are addressed by requiring the unemployed to be actively seeking jobs and by offering mandatory full-time activation after 12 months of unemployment for adults and six months of unemployment for young unemployed persons under the age of 25. Activation is therefore seen as fulfilling both a qualification and a motivational purpose.

6 The Active Labour Market Policy

Between 1979 and 1993, the main pillar of the active policy to address long-term unemployment was a programme of job offers, training and support to the unemployed to help them start up in self-employment. However, this programme only showed relatively poor results, with only a minority of the participants becoming employed on the open labour market. This factor, combined with a sharp new increase in unemployment between 1990 and 1993, increased the political pressure to find new measures to break the vicious circle of long-term unemployment. The result was a general labour market reform, which came into force in January 1994, with the following main characteristics:

- the introduction of a two-period benefit system, with an initial *passive* period of four years and a subsequent *activation* period of three years; during the passive period, an unemployed person receives benefits and is also eligible for 12 months of activation;
- a change in the assistance provided to individual long-term unemployed persons from a rule-based system to a system based on an assessment of the needs of the individual (with the introduction of *individual action plans* as an important instrument);
- the decentralization of policy implementation to regional labour market authorities, which are empowered to adjust programme design to fit local needs;
- the ending of the connection between vocational training and the unemployment benefit system, with the effect that employment with a wage subsidy no longer increases the duration of the period for which the unemployed are eligible for unemployment benefits;
- the introduction of three paid leave arrangements for childcare, education and sabbatical leave to encourage job rotation by allowing employed (and unemployed) persons to take leave while receiving a benefit paid by the state and calculated as a fraction of unemployment benefit.

Since 1994, Danish labour market policy has undergone a number of further reforms, mainly involving a shortening of the maximum period for which the unemployed receive benefits (the *passive* period). As noted above, this period was four years in 1994 (with an option of 12 months of activation during this period). In 1996, the passive period was reduced to two years. For young unskilled unemployed persons, the period was reduced to six months in 1996. It was subsequently decided in 1999 to further reduce the passive period to one year for adult unemployed persons. By the end of 2000, Denmark will therefore have fully implemented the first two of the European Union's employment guidelines, which call for early activation for both young and adult unemployed persons.

After the passive period, the activation period begins and still lasts for three years. If full-time activation during this period does not result in the unemployed person obtaining a normal job, she/he loses entitlement to receive unemployment benefit, but may still be eligible for means-tested social security.

The changes in the profile of Danish labour market policy since the mid-1990s have placed Denmark in the upper range of OECD countries in terms of expenditure on both active and passive labour market policy measures. The data in Figure 9.4 illustrate the high level of expenditure on both passive benefits (unemployment benefits and pensions for the unemployed) and active benefits, for which Denmark is ranked second after Sweden.

6.1 Some Early Evaluation Findings

The labour market reform introduced in 1994 was evaluated in 1996–98. The findings of general evaluations of the implementation process and of a number of evaluations of the effects of the various measures have been published (see Madsen, 1998a, for a survey of the findings).

With regard to the measures for the unemployed, the evaluations show a number of remarkable positive results:

- the individual action plans are seen by the unemployed as being positive and relevant instruments to plan their return to normal work;
- the unemployed have generally been satisfied with the programmes in which they have participated (job training, education, etc.);
- it has also been estimated that most of the programmes have reduced subsequent periods of unemployment for the participants. The exceptions are educational leave (decided upon by the unemployed) and some other forms of education. But both private and public job training and education targeted at increasing the employability of

Figure 9.4 Expenditure on active and passive labour market policy, 1998 (share of GDP) (selected OECD countries)

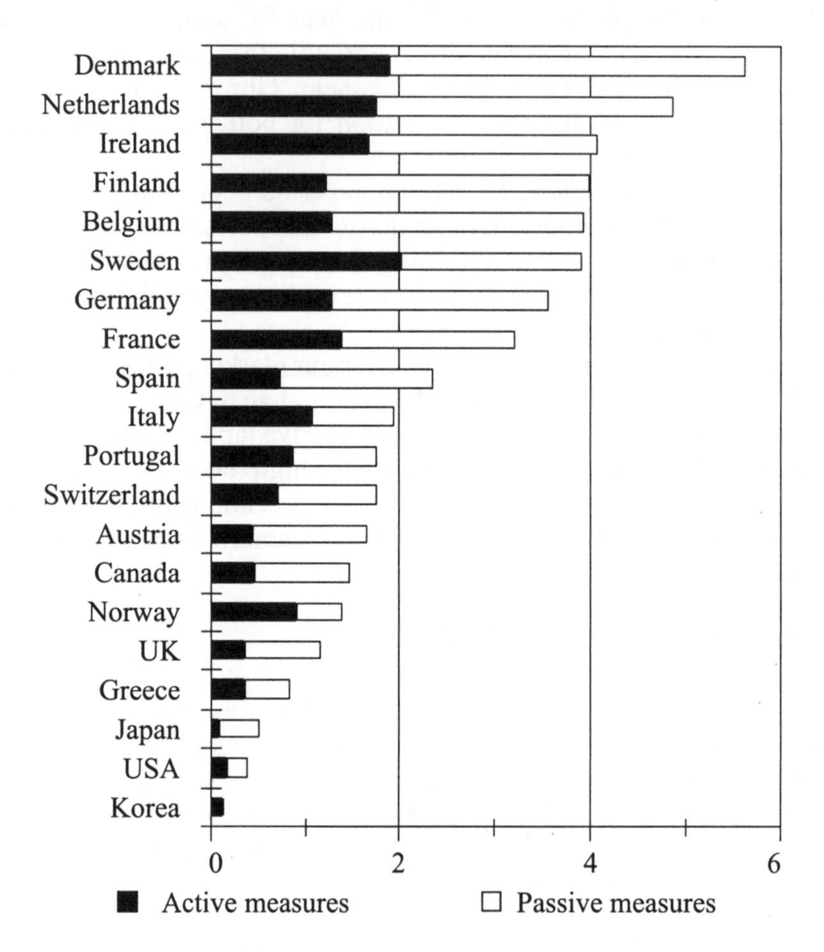

Source: OECD, 2000.

the unemployed have had significant effects as measured by the reduction in subsequent periods of unemployment;

- also, unsurprisingly, the improved state of the macro-economy since 1994 has contributed to the success of the activation programmes; and
- the programmes directed at younger unemployed persons (under 25 years of age) and involving stronger obligations to participate in training and a lowering of unemployment benefits after six months

of unemployment have proven to be successful in the sense that most of the young unemployed in the target group left unemployment either to take an ordinary job or to begin education.

The leave schemes were extensively evaluated in 1996 (Andersen et al., 1996; Pedersen, 1996). The main findings include (Madsen, 1998a and b, 1999a):

- half of the persons taking leave are unemployed and a majority are women. Some 60 per cent of the employed taking leave are from the public sector. The average duration of leave is approximately 200 days;
- educational leave is mostly taken to improve formal qualifications in relation to the current employment situation. Of the employed persons taking educational leave, some 50 per cent do so together with colleagues. Both employers and employees evaluate educational leave very positively;
- childcare leave is mainly taken by women (90 per cent). The attitude of firms is more critical towards childcare leave than towards educational leave;
- on average, about three-quarters of vacant jobs are filled by substitutes. The replacement rate is higher for public employers and smaller firms. When interpreting these figures, it should however be borne in mind that the Danish labour market has experienced a strong upswing since 1994;
- a striking finding of the evaluation is that almost half of the substitutes were *employed* before becoming a substitute for an employee taking leave. Only a minority of 13 per cent reported that they had been unemployed for more than three months. In the case of Danish paid leave arrangements, where the employer controls the hiring of a substitute, the normal recruitment mechanisms have not therefore been changed. Hiring through informal channels and the practice of giving priority to persons with a record of little previous unemployment is still the normal pattern. On the other hand, there is of course the possibility of the paid leave arrangements creating job opportunities for the longer-term unemployed further down the chain (for example, when substitutes gain access to more permanent employment), although this aspect was not investigated in the evaluations.

The estimated effect of the leave schemes on *total unemployment* depends on the manner in which those taking leave are categorized into employed and unemployed persons and on the assumptions that are made concerning the proportion of vacancies that are filled by the unemployed. In the evaluation, it was estimated that the leave schemes reduced open unemployment by 60–70,000 persons in 1995 (compared to an overall level of unemployment of 288,000 persons). Between two-thirds and three-quarters of this reduction was the result of the unemployed taking leave, and therefore not being counted in the official unemployment statistics.

6.2 Recent Evaluations of Active Policy Measures

In a study published in March 2000, the Ministry of Labour presented some of the first results based on a new database which it had developed (Ministry of Labour, 2000). The database contains information on the labour market situation of all individuals, including their participation in labour market programmes and their contacts with the social security system.

The study focuses on the potential micro-level effects of active labour market programmes:

- the *motivation effect* implies that an unemployed person seeks work more actively in the period immediately *before* she or he has to participate in an activation programme. It is therefore assumed that participation is partly involuntary and that the unemployed will try to avoid taking part in programmes by *escaping* into employment (or other activities, such as ordinary education). The strength of the motivation effect is therefore indicated by the change in the probability of leaving unemployment in the period immediately before the person is obliged to take part in an activation programme;
- the *training (or qualification) effect* stems from the rise in the level of qualifications during activation, which should improve the possibilities of finding a job for those who have participated in one of the active programmes.

The following sections summarize the findings for each of the effects.

6.2.1 The motivation effect of activation

As noted above, one of the main changes in Danish labour market policy during the period since 1994 has been the gradual reduction in the period during which the unemployed receive unemployment benefits without having to participate in activation. This has of course resulted in an increase in both the number of persons activated and the *degree of activation* (the number of persons undergoing activation as a proportion of the total numbers engaged in activation and of the unemployed). For example, the *degree of activation* increased from about 15 per cent in the mid-1990s to around 30 per cent in 1999.

The reduction in the period of passive benefits may of course have a number of motives. One could be the argument that long periods of passivity will further reduce the prospects for re-employment because the unemployed lose both general and job specific skills. Another argument is the idea of the motivation effect, as described above. On the other hand, early activation includes the risk that activation measures are offered to unemployed persons who would otherwise have found a job by themselves (the so-called deadweight). A central dilemma of the design of labour market policy measures is therefore to find the right timing for passive and active measures.

The overall conclusion of evaluations of the motivational aspect of active labour market measures in Denmark is that the data show significant effects in terms of the increased probability of taking up employment in the period immediately before having to take part in mandatory activation programmes. However, the specific dilemma posed by this observation should be borne in mind. If it is wished to increase the motivation effect, there may be a temptation to change the content of activation programmes to make them less attractive to participants. But this would also probably imply that the *quality* of the programmes themselves would be lowered in terms of their training content and other activities to improve the skills of the participants. As a result, the overall outcome might be less positive for unemployed persons who are unable to find a job before entering activation.

6.2.2 The training effect of activation

Another potential effect for the individuals taking part in activation programmes is of course that they increase their chance of gaining employment due to the improvement in their qualifications and therefore their employability. In the present study, the improvement in employability is measured by the reduction in the proportion of the year for which the persons concerned receive any form of transfer income (such as unemployment benefit, social security or sickness benefit). A reduction in this proportion is a reliable indicator of a genuine improvement in the employment situation of an individual, either because they have found ordinary employment or taken up some form of ordinary education.

The effects of the various types of labour market programmes are of considerable interest (Figure 9.5). In this respect, the largest reductions in unemployment are found for participants in private job training. Public job training, training in job search and targeted education with support from the employment services show positive, but lower effects. For non-supported education (which typically involves training in very basic skills) and for educational leave, the effects are positive but very small. These findings are in line with international experience (Martin, 2000).

Finally, the results have to be evaluated in terms of the cost of the various measures. A few simple calculations of cost-effectiveness have been made, which show positive budgetary effects for public and private

Figure 9.5 Denmark: reduction in unemployment after taking part in various programmes (averages for 1996–98)

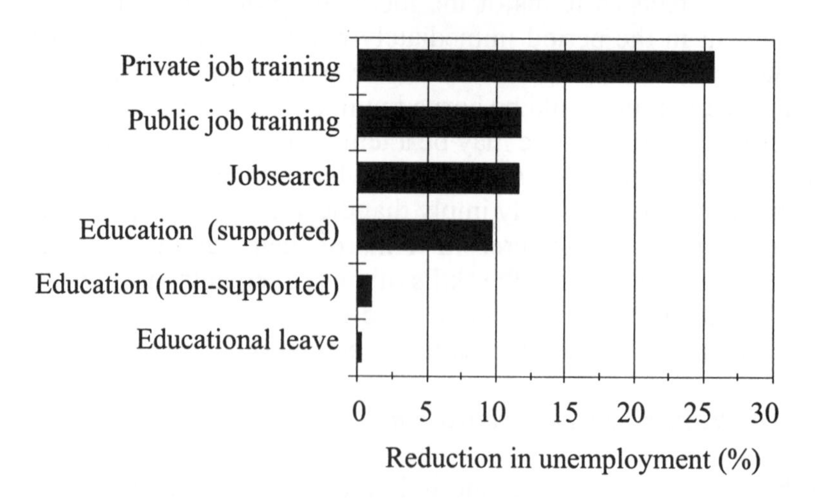

Source: Ministry of Labour, 2000, Appendix 5.1.

job training and (small) negative effects for education. However, the estimates are of a very crude nature and, for instance, only include the impact on public expenditure on unemployment benefits, etc. during the first year after leaving a programme.

7 Labour Market Reforms and the 'Job Miracle'

The evaluation findings discussed above have focused on the micro-level. However, the coincidence of the implementation of the labour market reforms and the dramatic fall in unemployment has of course stimulated discussion about the extent to which the inflation-free macroeconomic upswing can be attributed to the shift in labour market policy in the 1990s. The structural problems on the labour market are often measured by the so-called *Philips curve*, which shows the relation between unemployment and wage inflation. A lowering of the level of wage inflation for a given size of unemployment is taken as an indicator of greater flexibility in the functioning of the labour market. Since 1994, the Danish Philips curve has become almost horizontal, indicating a steep fall in structural unemployment (Madsen, 1999b).

Of course, there could be a number of factors behind these developments. The changing attitudes and behaviour of firms, employees and the social partners could be important. The improvement in the state of the labour market in itself has helped to reduce marginalization. But, based on the many positive evaluation findings for both the process and the effect of the labour market reforms, there is a case for arguing that the change in Danish labour market policy in 1993–94 has made a significant contribution to the improved functionality of the Danish labour market in recent years.

A study by the Danish National Institute of Social Research aims to summarize the findings of the large-scale evaluation programme of the 1994 labour market reforms (Larsen and Langager, 1998; see also Søndergaard, 1998). The general question raised is whether the labour market reforms and the subsequent adjustments in labour market policy have had a positive impact in the functioning of the labour market. Not surprisingly, this question has to be answered with considerable care. However, the evaluation findings concerning the importance of the activation strategy may be summarized as follows (Larsen and Langager, 1998, pp. 34–6):

- the employment goals specified in the individual action plans indicate that there is a *considerable planned mobility* among the unemployed;
- the labour market policy seems to function effectively in the sense that the planned mobility among the unemployed is *greater* in areas where the need for mobility is highest (due to threats of bottlenecks);
- there are *significant positive employment effects* of both vocational training and education for the unemployed; and
- the *effective supply of labour among the insured unemployed seems to have increased* between 1994 and 1997, probably due to the stricter demands made on the unemployed during the second phase of the reform (for instance, the increased demands on the young unemployed).

With regard to the measures directed at firms, there are indications that the reforms have contributed to the absence of bottlenecks since 1994:

- there is a (weak) indication that *the quality of the services provided by employment services to firms has improved* since the reform in terms of meeting the need for skilled labour (although there are also examples of labour shortages in the short term);
- the introduction of new forms of placement services (in the form of *open* self-service placements), together with monitoring activities and regular contacts with employers, has lead to *an increase in the transparency of the labour market,* thereby improving its functioning as a system for matching labour supply and demand.

Whether these effects of the reforms have led to an improvement in the general functioning of the labour market, measured by its ability to adapt to external shocks and to allocate labour efficiently, is harder to evaluate.

The lack of significant shortages of labour since 1994, in spite of the fall in unemployment and the strong growth in employment, could indicate that the functioning of the labour market has improved. Whether this is solely due to the reforms, or also to other factors (including changes in wage-fixing practices) cannot be definitively determined on the basis of the available evidence.

8 The Snakes in the Danish Paradise

As noted in the introduction to this chapter, the dramatic fall in open unemployment in Denmark since the mid-1990s has attracted the attention of international observers. In many respects, there are real grounds for this admiration. But on the other hand, it may be useful to take a closer look at some of the drawbacks and tensions in the Danish model of flexicurity. Returning to the concept of the golden triangle, a number of problems or dilemmas can be identified in the Danish employment system.

Large Groups Expelled from the Labour Market

Firstly, the highly dynamic nature of the labour market, involving a large number of shifts between jobs, also implies a continuous testing of the productivity of employees. One outcome of these ongoing selection processes is that some workers are being gradually expelled from the labour market if they fail to meet the productivity criteria set by employers. The few restrictions placed on employers with regard to lay-offs may of course add to the risk of exclusion from the labour market. There may also be many other, often inter-related, causes of marginalization, such as health problems, lack of formal or informal skills, age or ethnic background.

Figure 9.6 shows the rise from 1978 to 1998 in the number of persons aged between 15 and 64 years in full-time equivalents receiving transfer income. Over this 20-year period, the number almost doubled, from 450,000 to over 800,000 persons. This figure does not include persons covered by active labour market measures for the unemployed, who accounted for another 87,000 persons in 1999, or persons above the age of 67 receiving old-age pensions.

Measured as a proportion of the adult population in the same age category (15–64 years), the group of transfer income recipients grew from around 15 per cent in the late 1970s to some 25 per cent in the late 1990s, with the trend being slightly downwards since 1994 due to the effects of the economic upswing. In a longer-term perspective, the rise is even more dramatic. In 1960, the proportion was as low as 6 per cent.

One of the prices paid for the high level of efficiency of the Danish labour market therefore appears to be that a large number of persons are being gradually excluded from the labour market and placed on

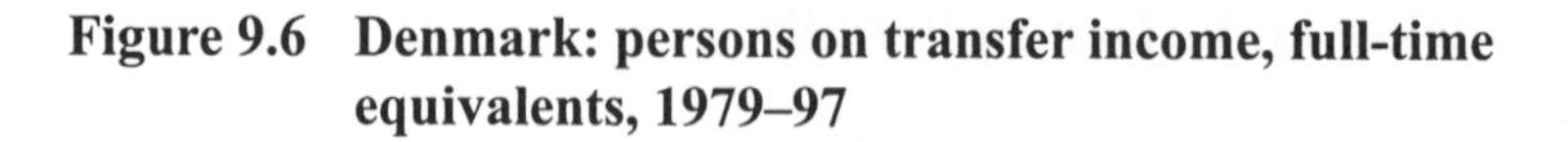

Figure 9.6 Denmark: persons on transfer income, full-time equivalents, 1979–97

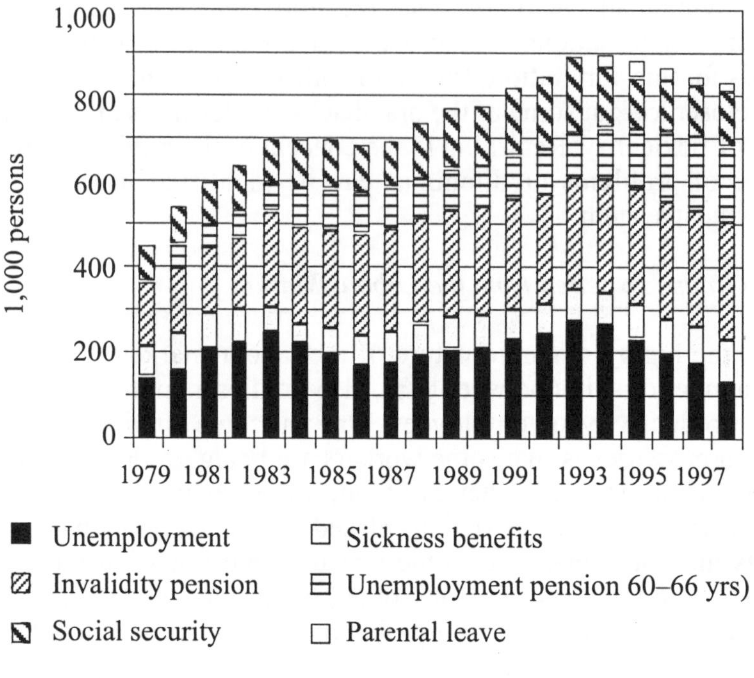

Source: Kvist, 2000.

long-term transfer income. It should be added that the high level of the population receiving transfer income is not a purely Danish phenomenon. All four Nordic countries experienced the growth in the share of inactive adults receiving transfer income up to the level of about 25 per cent in the late 1990s, indicating that the mechanisms involved cannot be attributed solely to special features of the dynamics of the Danish labour market, but also to more general aspects of the interplay between welfare states of the Nordic type, modern labour markets and the business cycle (Nordic Council of Ministers, 2000).

Unemployment Benefits and Poverty Traps

Another debate related to the golden triangle has already been foreshadowed. The high replacement rates in the Danish unemployment benefit system increase the risk of financial disincentives, especially for low-income groups. While such effects are theoretically plausible, they have been hard to verify empirically, at least as being important in their magnitude. Indeed, the general attitude has been to rely on early and intensive activation measures to counter problems related to the potential disincentives of the unemployment benefit system.

Problems of Active Labour Market Policy

Turning to the third corner of the golden triangle, some further critical points may be made. Danish labour market policy has been given a more active profile during a period of economic expansion. In the event of a change in the business cycle, the cost of maintaining the level of ambition to activate the unemployed at an early stage would lead to a sharp increase in public expenditure at a time when revenues would be falling due to the economic downturn. The political pressure to cut active programmes could therefore become overwhelming, and would be compounded by Denmark's *de facto* need to comply with EMU budget criteria.

Furthermore, a number of evaluations have shown examples of *creaming effects*, implying that the most resourceful among the unemployed are obtaining the best quality activation offers. This may be rational from the narrow viewpoint of economic efficiency, as well as being understandable in terms of the practical aspects of the implementation and delivery of services by employment services. But the bias towards the stronger unemployed is still in conflict with some of the declared political objectives of the active labour market policy.

And on the Horizon …

Taking a longer-term perspective, a number of further problems may be identified which could increase the forces that are already causing a rise in the number of persons excluded from the Danish labour market. These include:

- the demographic changes over the coming decades, which imply a growth in the number of older workers, with higher risks of marginalization;
- the rising share of immigrants in the Danish population, with the proportion of persons from non-European countries rising from about 4 per cent today to about 10 per cent in 2020; and

- the increasing wage competition from low-wage countries, also within Europe, which will be strengthened in the event of the accession of a number of Eastern European countries to the European Union.

These challenges to the Danish model will place the need to reduce the upward trend in the numbers of persons left outside the golden triangle high on the Danish political agenda in coming years (Nordic Council of Ministers, 2000).

9 The Transferability of the Danish Experience

The question of the extent to which the positive Danish experiences of recent years can be transferred to other countries is a complex issue (Madsen, 1999b).

On the one hand, it may be observed that the Danish model in its present form is in many respects the outcome of a long historical process and is characterized by the specific combination of the various elements of the Danish economic, social and political structure. These include:

- an industrial structure with many small and medium-sized firms;
- a generous state-financed system of unemployment benefits;
- a welfare state supporting a high participation rate for both men and women;
- a well developed public system of education and training; and
- an industrial relations system which involves the social partners in all policy areas of relevance to the labour market.

Attempting to take isolated policy elements developed within this specific set of institutions and transfer them to other social environments would run a high risk of being unsuccessful. On the other hand, some of the factors behind the current success of Danish employment policy could also be relevant in other contexts.

Firstly, the Danish experience points to the importance of the macroeconomic environment. Labour market policies cannot generate ordinary jobs by themselves. Sufficient pressure from the demand side is a prerequisite. On the other hand, once the upswing is under way, labour market policies play an important role in securing the supply of skilled labour and avoiding bottlenecks.

Secondly, some of the specific elements of Danish labour market policy in recent years could be of relevance for other countries:

- the idea of *decentralization* to adapt labour market policy more closely to local needs;
- the strong involvement of the social partners has proven successful, but can of course only be implemented in the context of a well-developed industrial relations system;
- the concept of the *individual action plan*, which signifies a more flexible and individualized approach to the activation and training of the unemployed; and
- the concepts of *job rotation and leave schemes*, in which upgrading the skills of the workforce in general, or meeting other needs of employees, is combined with the education and training of the unemployed to act as substitutes. One important lesson of Danish experience in this respect is that the spread of such programmes is stimulated by removing strict requirements on the hiring of substitutes. Another lesson is that such programmes may function well in both individual job rotation systems and planned job rotation schemes involving a number of employees from one or more firms.

In addition to these more specific elements, emphasis should finally be placed on the way in which the Danish employment system combines a flexible employment relationship with good coverage by the unemployment benefit system and the principle of the right and duty to activation.

In a number of areas (such as dismissals, labour market education and training and working time regulations), the Danish employment system combines a high level of flexibility with a reasonable level of protection for the individual employee. This has been accomplished, not by imposing strict legal demands on individual employers, but by creating institutions that facilitate both the negotiation of solutions by the social partners and individual flexibility in moving between firms and jobs. The Danish model therefore points to the feasibility of a strategy of negotiated flexibility and individual protection as an alternative to more liberal and market-oriented employment systems.

References

Andersen, D. et al. (1996), *Orlov – Evaluering af Orlovsordningerne*, Socialforskningsinstituttet, 96 (11), Copenhagen.

Auer, P. (2000), *Employment Revival in Europe: Labour market success in Austria, Denmark, Ireland and the Netherlands*, ILO, Geneva.

Auer, P. and Cazes, S. (2000), 'Stable or Unstable jobs: Untangling and interpreting the evidence in industrialized countries', Working Paper, ILO, Geneva.

Bingley, P. et al. (1999), *Beyond 'Manucentrism': Some fresh facts about job and worker flows*, Working paper 99–09, Centre for Labour Market and Social Research, Aarhus.

Cazes, S., Boeri, T. and Bertola, G. (1999), *Employment Protection and Labour Market Adjustment in OECD Countries: Evolving institutions and variable enforcement*, Employment and Training Paper No. 48, ILO, Geneva.

The Dublin Institute (1999), *Employment Options of the Future*, Dublin.

Kvist, J. (2000), *Social Security Recipients in Northern Europe, 1980–2000* (unpublished memo), Danish National Institute of Social Research, Copenhagen.

Langager, K. (1997), *Indsatsen for de Forsikrede Ledige: Evaluering af arbejdsmarkedsreformen I*, Socialforskningsinstituttet, 97 (20), Copenhagen.

Larsen, M. and Langager, K. (1998), *Arbejdsmarkedsreformen og Arbejdsmarkedet*, Socialforskningsinstituttet, 98 (13), Copenhagen.

Madsen, P.K. (1995), 'Orlovsordningerne: Gode nok eller for meget af det gode?', *Samfundsøkonomen*, 1995 (1), pp. 21–8.

Madsen, P.K. (1998a), 'Arbejdsmarkedsreformen: Erfaringer og perspektiver', *Landsarbejdsrådets arbejdsmarkedspolitiske redegørelse 1997*, Copenhagen, pp. 83–159.

Madsen, P.K. (1998b), *Paid Leave Arrangements and Gender Equality: The Danish experience in the 1990s*, Conference Paper presented at a high-level conference organized by the OECD, the Ministry of Children and Family Affairs and the Ministry of Labour and Government Administration, Oslo (12–13 October 1998), OECD, Paris.

Madsen, P.K. (1998c), 'A Transitional Labour Market: The Danish paid leave arrangements', *New Institutional Arrangements on the Labour Market: Transitional labour markets as a new full employment concept*, European Academy of the Urban Environment, Berlin, pp. 68–73.

Madsen, P.K. (1998d), 'Working Time Policy and Paid Leave Arrangements: The Danish experience in the 1990s', *TRANSFER – European Review of Labour and Research*, 4/98, pp. 692–714.
Madsen. P.K. (1999b), *Denmark: Flexibility, security and labour market success*, Employment and Training Papers No. 53, ILO, Geneva.
Martin, J.P. (2000), 'What Works among Active Labour Market Policies: Evidence from OECD countries' experience', *OECD Economic Studies No. 30* (2000/I), Paris, pp. 79–112.
Ministry of Labour (2000), *Effects of Danish Employability Enhancement Programmes*, Copenhagen (http://www.am.dk/publikationer/2000/effects/eodeep.shtml).
Nordic Council of Ministers (2000), *Supply of Labour in the Nordic Countries: Experience, developments and political deliberations*, Copenhagen.
OECD (1997), *Employment Outlook*, Paris.
OECD (1999a), *Benefit Systems and Work Incentives* (1999 edition), Paris.
OECD (1999b), *Employment Outlook*, Paris.
Pedersen, L. (1996), *Orlov, Ledighed og Beskæftigelse*, Socialforskningsinstituttet, 96 (10), Copenhagen.
Regeringen (1999), *Arbejde og Service*, Copenhagen.
Schmid, G. (1995), 'Is Full Employment still Possible? Transitional Labour Markets as a New Strategy of Labour Market Policy', *Economic and Industrial Policy*, No. 11, pp. 429–56.
Schmid, G. and Auer, P. (1998), 'Transitional Labour Markets: Concepts and examples in Europe', *New Institutional Arrangements in the Labour Market: Transitional labour markets as a new full employment concept*, European Academy of the Urban Environment, Berlin, pp. 11–28.
Søndergaard, J. (1998), *Er Arbejdsmarkedet Blevet mere Fleksibelt?*, working paper, Socialforskningsinstituttet.

Chapter Ten

Adjusting Welfare Policies to Stimulate Job Entry: the Example of the United Kingdom

Jane Millar

Since May 1997, when the Labour Party won a landslide victory in t general election, the government has pursued an ambitious programn of welfare reform in the United Kingdom. Central to this policy agen is the idea of the *active welfare state*, in which the main role of policy to enable people to support themselves through paid employment. Tony Blair put it in his first speech as Prime Minister, 'work is the be form of welfare – the best way of funding people's needs, and the be way of giving them a stake in society'. Recreating the welfare sta around paid work is thus the central organizing principle for the vario reforms.

This chapter examines these policy developments. It is organiz into two main sections. The first outlines the key features of the reforn in respect of both labour market programmes and tax/benefit chang The second section then summarizes the research evidence so f available on how these policies are working in practice.

1 Adjusting Welfare Policies: 'Work for Those who Can'

The theme of the importance of work as a route out of poverty and a means of social integration is found throughout the government's poli documents. The first principle of the *new contract for welfare* sta that 'the new welfare state should help and encourage people of worki age to work where they are capable of doing so' (Department of Soc Security, 1998, p. 23). Similarly, the first report on the Governmen anti-poverty strategy summarizes the key policy goal as 'work for tho who can, security for those who cannot' (Department of Social Securi

1999, p. 7). This goal is being applied to people of working age in general, and not just those registered as unemployed. The measures that are being implemented can be divided into two broad categories: measures intended to *make work possible* and to *make work pay*.

1.1 Making Work Possible

Table 10.1 summarizes the key policies that are intended to support employment. These can be grouped into three main categories. First, there are a range of measures, in general coming into effect from 1999/2000, which are aimed in particular at helping parents to combine work and family life. Maternity leave has been increased from 14 to 18 weeks and extended to all employed women, regardless of length of employment. Women who have completed one year's service with their employer (previously two years) are able to take additional maternity leave for up to 29 weeks. Eligibility for maternity allowances has also been extended. Parental leave, unpaid and for up to 13 weeks, has been introduced for the first time for those with at least one year's service with their employer. There are new rights for part-time workers, who make up about a one-fifth of the workforce (6 million people), mainly women. These rights include entitlement to the same hourly rate of pay as full-time workers and the same access to company pension schemes, sick pay, holidays and other leave, and training. Perhaps the most important new programme in this list is the National Childcare Strategy, which was launched in 1998 with a budget of some £470 million. This represents a major departure from previous policy in the United Kingdom, where the provision of child care has traditionally been seen as outside the remit of government responsibility. The aim is to provide quality and affordable care for all children aged 0–14, including after school and holiday care. Local authorities are responsible for implementation, in partnership with private and voluntary groups (see also Cressey, Chapter Thirteen).

Second, there are a number of area-based initiatives, including the New Deal for Communities, which aims to tackle multiple deprivation in the poorest areas. This targets additional resources (a total budget of £800 million) on 17 deprived neighbourhoods in order to reduce worklessness, improve health, reduce crime and raise educational standards. The Employment Zones are aimed at helping the long-term unemployed, particularly those with multiple social problems, to enhance their employability. Prototypes ran in five areas between February 1998 and March 2000 and full programmes have been implemented in 15 areas since April 2000 with a budget of £112 million over two years. They are being operated by a mixture of public/private partnerships. Jobseekers in these areas are able to access *personal job accounts* worth up to £5,000 to help them find jobs, gain skills or set up in self-employment.

Thirdly, and probably the most important of the provisions aimed at helping people into work, are the New Deal programmes, starting with the New Deal for Young People, which was announced shortly after the 1997 election. There are seven different New Deal programmes targeted at different groups which vary in a number of ways: the size of the target group, eligibility rules, conditions of involvement and the type of support offered. However, they share the same underlying assumption about the nature and type of help that people need to get them back into employment. They are all supply-side programmes and are all based on the idea that each unemployed or workless person has their own individual needs and circumstances. Each person will therefore require different types of support. Some people are *work ready* and just need help in finding suitable jobs, while others may need help in gaining skills and confidence before they can start seeking work. The best way to help people into employment is therefore through a tailor-made

Table 10.1 UK: making work possible: measures to support employment

Measures to support employment	• improved maternity rights • parental leave (unpaid) • improved rights for part-time workers • National Childcare Strategy
Area-based policy measures	• 17 New Deals for Communities • 15 employment zones
New Deal programmes	• compulsory for young and long-term unemployed people • voluntary for lone parents, disabled people, partners, older workers, musicians

package that addresses the specific needs of the individual at that particular time. To put this into practice, the participants in each programme are allocated to a personal adviser, who offers individual advice and support. There is, however, variation in the options that personal advisers can offer the different client groups.

Table 10.2 provides greater detail on the six main New Deal programmes, highlighting some of the key differences between them (excluding the very small programme for musicians). The New Deal for Young People is often described as the flagship programme. It is targeted at persons aged between 18 and 24 years of age and who have been unemployed for at least six months. It is compulsory and includes a *gateway* period of advice and support for jobseeking. Those who can find jobs during this period leave the programme. Those who have not found work by the end of the gateway period (four months) are offered one of four options: subsidized employment, full-time education and training, voluntary work or environmental work. These may last for varying periods of time and, if work has still not been found during or at the end of an option, there is a *follow through* period of further advice and support from the personal adviser. The New Deal for Young People has the largest budget, although not the largest target group, and is the most structured and intensive of all the programmes. The other compulsory programme is the New Deal for Long-term Unemployed, which is targeted at persons aged 25 and over who have been unemployed for 12, 18 or 24 months (depending on the area). Personal advisers offer advice and support and participants can take up two main options: subsidized employment and education/training.

Both of these programmes therefore offer a combination of individual advice and support with access to work experience and/or training. Subsidies are provided to employers for taking people on, but the employers must meet training requirements. There is some scope for local variation in delivery, and employers, education providers and voluntary organizations have been involved in planning and implementation at the local level, mainly under the direction of the employment service.

There are four main voluntary programmes (that is, programmes targeted at specific groups, but with no requirement for the individuals to take part in them and no loss of benefits if they refuse). In these programmes, the main help offered is the individual advice, information and support of a personal adviser. The New Deal for Lone Parents is the

Table 10.2 UK: making work possible: summary of the New Deal programmes

Scheme and national starting date	Target group	Approx. no. in target group and original budget	Options
Young people April 1998	Required for: 18-24 years claiming benefit for 6 months; earlier entry for some	400,000 £2,620m	Personal adviser subsidized employment, training, voluntary, environmental work
Long-term unemployed June 1998	Required for: those aged over 25 years, claiming benefit for over 2 years	500,000 £450m	Personal adviser Subsidized employment, training
Lone parents April 1998	Voluntary for: lone-parents with children aged over five, claiming benefit for at least 3 months	500,000 £190m	Personal adviser
Partners February 1999	Voluntary for: partners of people unemployed for at least 6 months NB: required if no children	200,000 £60m	People aged 18–24: access to New Deal for Young People Others: personal adviser
Disabled people April 2000	Voluntary for: those claiming disability-related benefits	900,000 £200m	Personal adviser
Aged 50+ April 2000	Voluntary for those: aged 50 plus and claiming benefits for at least 6 months, also partners of claimants	2 million £270m	Personal adviser plus training grant, employment credit

most well developed. It started up nationally in 1998, following a pilot period in eight areas of the country. The target group is lone mothers who have been on income support for six months or more and with a youngest child aged 5 years and 3 months or over. There is no *menu* of options (as in the New Deal for Young People), although access to training has been extended as the programme has developed. Participants have access to a personal adviser, who can provide help in looking for work, information on such matters as training, benefits and child care, as well as continuing to provide support once the participants are in work. The New Deal for Partners of Unemployed People is aimed at a very new group in terms of labour market policy, namely the partners of unemployed jobseekers. These are mainly women who are married to unemployed men and who receive benefits as dependants of their partners. The scheme is voluntary, but it is intended to make participation compulsory for all childless partners of unemployed jobseekers in the near future.

The two most recent programmes both started up nationally in April 2000. The New Deal for Disabled People is intended to raise awareness among employers of the employment needs of disabled people, as well as helping disabled people find work. There are almost one million potential participants in this programme, with a wide range of circumstances and needs. The New Deal for People Aged 50 and Above is targeted at older workers and their partners who have been receiving benefits for at least six months. A distinctive feature of this scheme is the availability of an employment credit (that is a cash addition to wages) for up to one year. The scheme has a large potential target group, as many older workers and their partners are not employed and workless rates have been rising steadily among this age group.

There are some clear gender differences across the programmes. The target groups for the schemes for young people and the long-term unemployed are primarily men (over 70 per cent). The target groups for the schemes for lone parents and partners are primarily women (over 90 per cent). The schemes for disabled people and older workers have more mixed target groups, although men probably predominate. As would be expected, the compulsory schemes are much better resourced and much more clearly structured than the voluntary programmes. They are focused on improving *employability* and therefore include an emphasis on training and work experience, as well as job placement. The voluntary schemes are more focused on reducing *barriers to work* and are therefore more *work-first* oriented and place less emphasis on developing human capital (Millar, 2000).

Most of the programmes started with pilot or prototype schemes in selected areas of the country and the national programmes have been running for up to three years for some groups, but for much shorter periods in other cases. There has been an extensive programme of evaluation, examining both the ways in which the programmes have been working and the main outcomes. These are discussed below. First, however, the complementary policies aimed at improving the financial returns from working are outlined.

1.2 Making Work Pay

Making work pay, or improving financial incentives to work, is also central to the government's strategy. A range of policy instruments has been used, as summarized in Table 10.3. These may be divided into two main groups. First, there are benefits intended to help support people financially as they make the transition into work. Research has shown that making this move is often difficult, especially for families. Benefits paid to non-working people are relatively low in the United Kingdom, with most workless people receiving means-tested assistance in the form of either the jobseekers allowance or the income support scheme.[1] These provide regular but low levels of benefit and few claimants have any resources to help them while they are waiting for their first wages to be paid. One-off payments (various job grants) and short-term payments (allowing benefits or parts of benefits to run on for the first few weeks of work) are available for some groups of claimants, mainly lone parents and disabled people. Help may also be provided with interview costs and opportunities may be accorded to try out jobs for short periods without loss of benefits.

Secondly, certain measures are intended to boost in-work income on a regular and ongoing basis. These include fiscal measures (reduced starting rates of income tax and national insurance contributions, a new tax allowance for children); the direct regulation of wages (the national minimum wage); new in-work benefits (the working families tax credit and the disabled person's tax credit); and greater opportunities to combine part-time work with the receipt of benefit (but only for lone parents and disabled people). Again, this represents a substantial raft of new policies. The national minimum wage is a clear departure from

Table 10.3 UK: making work pay: main tax and benefit changes

The transition to work – rules apply to some groups of claimants	• jobfinders grant • jobmatch payments • help with interview costs • work trials with no loss of benefit • benefits run-on into work
Increasing incomes in work	• the national minimum wage • working families tax credit • lower starting rates of income tax and national insurance contributions • children's tax credit (from 1 April 2001) • increased earnings disregards for part-time work for lone parents and disabled people

past policies in that it represents the first time that a national minimum wage rate has been set in the United Kingdom (minimum rates used to be set for different sectors and groups of workers, but these were abolished in the 1990s). The national minimum wage came into effect in April 1999 at a level of £3.60 per hour (£3.20 for young workers), which is equivalent to about 36 per cent of median male wages. Over one and a half million workers (about 5 per cent of the workforce) have been entitled to higher pay because of the minimum wage, two-thirds of whom are women. In its assessment of the impact of the first two years, the Low Pay Commission concluded that there was no measurable impact on overall employment and that employment continued to grow in low-paying sectors, while job losses were small (Low Pay Commission, 2000).

The flagship programme in this area, however, is the working families tax credit, which replaced family credit from the autumn of 1999. Family credit was paid to families with children where one parent was in low-paid employment of at least 16 hours per week. It was paid as a cash benefit to the main carer, rather than to the employed partner, and was reduced as earnings rose. The working families tax credit has a similar structure, but is paid at higher rates and to the employed person in the form of an addition to wages. It is being received by about 1.1 million families (Department of Social Security, 2000a) and provides a guaranteed minimum income of about £214 per week, for a family with one earner in full-time work and receiving the national minimum wage (HM Treasury, 2000).[2] The disabled persons tax credit works in much the same way.

2 Stimulating Job Entry

This constitutes an ambitious and wide-ranging set of measures, aimed at a large and heterogeneous section of the working age population, which is being implemented over varying time periods and includes both national and local responsibilities and action. Identifying and disentangling the impact of these measures is therefore complex. At the aggregate level, the picture shows some improvement, although it can be argued that positive labour market trends are providing a favourable environment for the Government's policies, rather than being a direct consequence of them. Employment levels are high, having increased by over a quarter of a million between 1999 and 2000, and by almost one million since 1997. Unemployment levels are falling, with the number of registered unemployed benefit claimants down to about 1.1 million in May 2000. If unemployment continues to decline at the same rate, it is expected fall below the one million mark by early 2001 (Bivand, 2000). The number of children living in households where no-one is in employment has fallen from 17.9 per cent in spring 1997 to 15.8 per cent in spring 2000 (Department of Social Security, 2000a). While poverty rates and other indicators of deprivation have not changed much, most of the available information refers to the period before these measures were introduced (Department of Social Security, 2000a; Rahman, 2000).

2.1 New Deal Statistics

Government statistics (Department for Education and Employment, 2000a and b), drawn from the official New Deal Database, show that just over 546,000 young people had started on the New Deal for Young People by September 2000,[3] and in total about 254,000 had found jobs. Of these, about 195,000 were *sustained* jobs (defined in these statistics as lasting 13 weeks or more). This is equivalent to about 36 per cent of all participants, although the rate is slightly lower for women (34 per cent) and ethnic minorities (27 per cent).

Around 306,000 people had been through the New Deal for the Long-term Unemployed by September 2000, of whom about 56,000 had found jobs. Of these, about 47,000 were sustained jobs (lasting 13 weeks or more). This is equivalent to about 15 per cent of all participants, with the rates being similar for men and women. Two-fifths of those who leave the programme return to benefits.

About 187,000 lone parents had attended an initial New Deal for Lone Parents interview by September 2000, and about 65,000 lone parents had found work. This amounts to about one-third of all those who attended an initial interview, or two-fifths of those who had completed the programme. Almost half of those in employment are continuing to receive support from personal advisers.

There has therefore been a positive effect on entry into work for the groups concerned.[4] The New Deal for Young People has been the most successful, perhaps not surprisingly, since it is the best funded programme. Estimates of *employment additionality* (the number of moves into jobs that would not have happened without the programme) have been estimated at about 50 per cent for the New Deal for Young People and about 20–25 per cent for the New Deal for Lone Parents. The programmes have had quite large start-up costs, but in general look likely to be more or less self-financing (House of Commons Select Committee Report, 2000).[5] There are concerns about the number of people who leave the programmes, but whose whereabouts is unknown (about 30 per cent of those who leave the New Deal for Young People). There are also concerns about the differences in outcomes in different areas of the country, as well as about the fact that the most disadvantaged people may not be receiving all the help that they need. Little is yet known about the longer-term outcomes and the extent to which jobs are sustained beyond 13 weeks. In overall terms, however, the Government has judged these programmes to be successful and is planning to continue and extend them.

2.2 Taking Part in New Deal Programmes

Research evaluations have also provided insights into how these programmes are working in practice and how people are responding to the opportunity (or requirement) to take part in them.[6] The key findings are summarized below and show some common themes across the various target groups, as well as some important differences between and within these groups (Millar, 2000).

These programmes are mainly targeted at persons who have been out of work for at least six months, and longer in some cases. These are people who face a range of barriers to work, including a lack of skills and work experience, low or inappropriate job search, lack of self confidence and a lack of realistic goals, the level and type of job opportunities available in the local labour market, and employer attitudes. For young people, the key barriers are lack of skills and work experience, ineffective job search, low pay and access to and costs of transport. For the long-term unemployed, the key barriers are a mismatch between their skills and the requirements of employers, outdated skills and a lack of transport. For disabled people, the key barriers are special needs associated with their disabilities and employer attitudes. In the case of lone parents, childcare and money issues are paramount. For partners, they also include child care and a concern about role reversal. Each group includes people with multiple barriers and special needs. There are therefore a wide range of circumstances and needs to be addressed.

A wide range of *work-readiness* has also been found. In general, people have been found to have positive attitudes to work - they want to work and are actively seeking work, although many are pessimistic about their chances of finding work. However, this is much more likely to be true for young people and the unemployed than for other groups. Among lone parents, partners and disabled people, it has been found that many are not currently seeking work. This is often related to family responsibilities (in particular, caring for children) or their health condition. Some are discouraged workers who feel that it would be almost impossible for them to find work. Others want to postpone looking for work until their children are older or more settled at school, or for various other reasons. Others want to learn new skills or enter full-time education rather than go straight into work.

The take-up rates for voluntary programmes have not therefore been high – under 5 per cent of disabled people and about one-fifth of lone parents responded to the invitation to take part in the prototype programmes. However, this does not necessarily mean that all the non-participants are actively opting out. These groups (disabled people, lone parents and partners) are relatively new target groups for labour market programmes and this seems to be reflected in the way they have responded to the schemes. At this first stage there have clearly been mixed responses. Many had not heard of the programmes and were therefore unsure what was being offered, whether it was required of them or not, and what impact it might have upon their benefits. Some pre-knowledge, perhaps gained through local publicity, did seem to be helpful in bringing people in. Some of those who did not participate were not actively opting out. They did not remember receiving a letter, the letter came at a time that was difficult for them, or they somehow just did not take up the interview offer. People were more likely to attend if the letters specified an appointment time or were followed up by phone calls. On the other hand, many of those who did attend thought that they were required to do so, or that they would lose benefits if they did not. Attendance therefore also reflected a mixture of negative and positive responses.

Among the participants in the compulsory programmes, most have been found to be positive about taking part in the programme. Compulsion to carry out job search and meet other requirements is not unfamiliar to these groups. However, views about compulsion and about the use of sanctions have been mixed, for both younger and older workers. Fear of benefit loss does seem to help re-motivate some of the younger people. However, older workers have tended to feel insulted by this aspect, although some have also felt that a degree of compulsion is not inappropriate. Those in favour of compulsion argue either that people should not be able to choose not to work, or that the long-term unemployed need a stimulus and have to be required to participate, otherwise they will not do so. Those who are against compulsion consider it to be counterproductive and unfair, or that people will not be motivated if they are compelled to attend.

Overall, participation has led to a positive response for most people. It has boosted confidence, enhanced job seeking and improved skills. But more negative views have been expressed where programmes are felt not to be meeting needs. Training opportunities have sometimes been considered to be too limited and of poor quality. Very strikingly, reactions to the personal advisers have been central to the manner in which people have perceived and valued their participation. This has applied across all the programmes. Effective advisers are seen as friendly, helpful and approachable. Ineffective advisers tend to treat people with a lack of respect and do not have enough of the right sort of information. However, a friendly attitude is not enough in itself; people also want their needs to be identified and practical help offered. Advisers play an important role as intermediaries between the participants and employers, and a key aspect of the programmes (especially the New Deal for Young

People) has involved bringing in employers and helping them to make use of the scheme.

It is hardly surprising that the New Deal programmes have been most effective for young people and for those already closest to the labour market. For other groups, they have so far played more of an advisory and informative role, rather than a role in job seeking or job matching. However, and perhaps especially for groups such as lone parents and disabled people, access to support and accurate information may be an important element in helping people into work. Even those who are otherwise work ready seem to benefit from this type of support. This would suggest that caution needs to be exercised before accepting that there are high levels of dead-weight, since the way in which this is measured may underestimate the value of the programme to those who appear to be work ready.

3 Adjusting Welfare Policies: the United Kingdom as an Active Welfare State?

The United Kingdom has not hitherto been at the forefront in the development of active labour market policies and, indeed, has been a relatively low spender on such programmes compared with many other European countries (OECD, 1997). Nevertheless, the policies and programmes outlined above show the extent to which the country is moving rapidly in this direction. Three important new elements of these programmes stand out in comparison with past approaches.

First, the policies are aimed at *worklessness* rather than unemployment. Worklessness is seen as the key problem because of the clear association between worklessness, poverty and the receipt of benefit. Of the estimated 4.4 million children living in poverty (one-third of all children in the United Kingdom), just over half live in workless households (HM Treasury, 1999). Of the 5 million people of working age who receive state benefits, about half are sick or disabled, one-in-five are lone parents and the remainder are unemployed (Department of Social Security, 2000c). This focus on worklessness means that the target groups of these policies are much broader and much more diverse, with a wide range of work experience, work readiness and work orientation. Many more women are also included than in the past.

The inclusion of these other groups as potential workers opens up new opportunities for people who have been excluded from such support in the past. But it also raises some tensions and potential problems. These include the question of how work obligations for all people of working age can be reconciled with their caring and other responsibilities (Hirsch, 1999). How far is it appropriate to expect or require all people of working age to be available for employment? Should women with (young?) children be expected to work full-time as well as caring for their children? It is not only care work that may suffer from this strong emphasis upon paid work, but also voluntary and community work. Is it possible to continue to value other forms of work and other ways of contributing to society in such a work-based welfare state?

Another very contentious issue that arises out of the work-based focus is the role and extent of compulsion. At present, there are two compulsory schemes and four that are voluntary. However, the government plans to introduce a requirement that all benefit claimants must attend a work-focused interview as part of their claim. Some compulsion will therefore be extended to lone parents and people claiming disability benefits, as well as those registering as unemployed. There are questions about the capacity of the system to deal with such a large number of people. Indeed, many may simply have an interview and be deemed unsuitable for work at that point. Compulsion can mean many different things and the requirement to attend an interview is a relatively mild condition for benefit receipt. But compulsion is controversial and unpopular with the relevant pressure groups, which could give rise to problems for the government.

Another potential problem area is that the policy focus tends to be on workless *households*, rather than workless *individuals*. This means that the goal of reducing levels of worklessness can be achieved by getting one adult into work, which has perhaps understandably been the focus. There is some recognition of the need to support second earners in families, who are targeted by the New Deal for Partners. But the fiscal measures which have been adopted, and particularly the working families tax credit, may be creating financial disincentives for second earners (Dilnot and McRae, 1999). If a second member of a family which is receiving the working families tax credit takes a job, the amount of benefit is reduced pound for pound. The additional benefit paid for those working 30 hours or more per week applies to only one earner, and not to two part-time workers who work 30 hours between them.

Current policy therefore tends to reduce work incentives for partnered mothers (of low-paid men), while increasing them for lone mothers. This may be short-sighted if these women find themselves locked out of the labour market, since having two earners in a family is one of the most secure routes out of poverty.

The second area of change in relation to the past is that there is now a much wider range of policy measures and instruments. Of course, these programmes have not been introduced onto a previously blank sheet. Over the past two decades at least, there has been a steady stream of programmes and subsidies intended to help unemployed people move from unemployment into work (Gardiner, 1997; Hasluck, 1999a and b). These were mainly focused on unemployed people, but even the broadening of the target groups was to some extent foreshadowed by the previous Conservative administration which, for example, also introduced pilot schemes intended to help lone parents move into employment. However, the Conservative approach in the 1980s and 1990s was focused much more strongly on financial incentives to work than on services to support employment, and relied much more on the stick (keeping benefit levels down) than on the carrot (boosting incomes in work).[7] The Labour government has not got rid of the sticks, but has added more carrots, both in cash and in kind. Policy now includes a much stronger emphasis on services, as well as more in-work financial support, of which the measures to develop childcare provision are a good example. There is a much more rounded view of the situations and needs of non-working people.[8]

Nevertheless, these remain measures in the context of a labour supply driven model, and there is still a reluctance to engage with issues such as the unequal geographical distribution of labour demand. Direct job creation schemes are not popular with the government, but there is some interest in the extent to which *intermediate labour markets* (forms of supported and semi-supported employment) may be able to help the most disadvantaged people back into work. There is a need for wider debate about the rights and obligations of employers, especially in respect of training. The issue of whether the focus should be work-first (getting people into jobs and letting the labour market do the rest) or on human capital (improving skills so that people can get better jobs, otherwise they will be stuck at the bottom end of the labour market) remains a crucial debate. Making work sustainable, which involves keeping people in jobs and helping them improve their employment situation, is recognized as an important element of the active labour market. But there is a need for considerable development of measures, such as support for further on-the-job training, financial incentives for the retention of former unemployed workers and more access to in-work mentoring support. This is also true of services. For example, the childcare gap is very large in the United Kingdom and it will take some years before a system can be developed to provide help for all those who need it. These policies will be costly and considerable additional resources have already been allocated to programmes in these areas. The costs of ongoing wage supplementation for large numbers of workers may be steep, especially if it contributes to downward wage adjustments.

The third key area of innovation is that the measures adopted involve significant institutional and cultural change. As noted above, the work of the personal advisers has been crucial to the New Deal programmes across all client groups, and also in relation to employers, education and training providers, and voluntary sector organizations. The personal advisers need a broad range of knowledge and skills. They need caseloads of manageable size and support from other services and agencies. They also have to combine the provision of support and encouragement with the application of sanctions, which may give rise to tension between their welfare and control roles. In general, the personal advisers have provided a good service within the constraints of the programmes, and have themselves welcomed and been committed to their new job descriptions. But there is still major change ahead.

This also applies at the institutional level. Pilot schemes bringing the Employment Service (which is responsible for all aspects of job seeking) and the Benefits Agency (responsible for paying benefits) together into a single service (known as ONE) have been running in twelve areas of the country since 1999. It is now planned to merge these into a single new agency which will deal with all people of working age and will combine the jobseeking and benefit paying roles. This is an important signal of the importance of the work-based welfare model, as well as involving a substantial change in the working practices and culture of both of these government departments. In addition, the responsibility of much of the in-work benefit delivery has been assigned to the Inland Revenue, rather than the Department of Social Security. This represents a major change for the Inland Revenue, which has never before taken responsibility for assessing benefit entitlements or for their delivery.

In overall terms, there have been some very significant changes since 1997. As noted above, these do not necessarily imply a reduction in expenditure and, indeed, in the short term at least, they require increased resources. There is pressure to show high levels of success (particularly with a general election due before 2002), but many of the policies will be slow to show an impact. And even if the policies are highly successful, there will still be many who will need adequate and accessible benefits while they are not working, both as short-term assistance and for longer periods of time. The active welfare state cannot eliminate the need for effective systems of social protection.

Notes

1 The jobseekers allowance replaced unemployment benefit in 1996 and has two forms – contributory and means-tested. The contributory version is only available to those who have made the requisite number of contributions. Most claimants (over 80 per cent) receive the means-tested form, including all those with children, since the contributory benefit is a flat-rate amount with no additions for dependants. Lone parents are not required to seek work and most receive income support. Disabled people may be receiving either income support or incapacity benefit (which is a contributory benefit payable to people unable to work due to incapacity).
2 An unemployed couple with one school age child would receive about £180 a week, and a couple with two children about £200 in benefits, so this guarantee is just above income out of work, depending on family size and housing costs.
3 Which means that the government has fulfilled its election promise of getting 250,000 young people into work within five years.
4 The numbers going through the programmes for disabled people and for partners are still relatively small, as these programmes have not been running for very long.
5 The government puts the figure at around £4,000 per job, but other estimates suggest a much higher cost. In fact, all the New Deal programmes have spent less than the budgets originally allocated, partly because unemployment has been falling and the number of eligible people has therefore been smaller than anticipated.
6 It should be noted that in the case of the programmes for lone parents and

disabled people, the completed evaluations are of the prototype (or pilot) schemes rather than the national programmes.

7 However, the Conservatives did introduce the earnings top-up in 1996, which was a pilot scheme to pay wage supplements to low-paid workers without children (Finlayson et al., 2000).

8 Another important area of policy, not discussed in this paper, is the pledge to end child poverty within 20 years, which is also being pursued through a range of national and local initiatives (Millar, 2001).

References

Bivand, P. (2000), *Labour Trends: Working brief*, The Unemployment Unit, London.

Department for Education and Employment (DES) (2000a), *Statistical First Release: New deal for young people and long-term unemployed people aged 25+*, London.

Department of Social Security (DSS) (1998), *New Ambitions for our Country, a New Contract for Welfare* (Cm 3805), London.

DES (2000b), *Statistical First Release: The new deal for lone parents: Statistics to September 2000*, London.

Dilnot, A. and McRae, J. (1999), *Family Credit and the Working Families Tax Credit*, Institute for Fiscal Studies, London.

DSS (1999), *Opportunity for All: Tackling poverty and social exclusion* (Cm 4445), London.

DSS (2000a), *Opportunity for All: One year on: Making a difference: Second annual report 2000*, London.

DSS (2000b), *Cross-benefit Analysis*, London.

DSS (2000c), *Households below Average Income, 1998/9*, London.

Finlayson, L., Ford, R., Marsh A., Smith A. and White M. (2000), *The First Effects of Earnings Top-up*, Department of Social Security Research Report No. 112, London.

Gardiner, K. (1997), *Bridges from Benefits to Work: A review*, Joseph Rowntree Foundation, York.

Hasluck, C. (1999a), *Employers and the Employment Option of the New Deal for Young People: Employment additionality and its measurement* (ESR Report No. 14), Employment Service, Sheffield.

Hasluck, C. (1999b), *Employers, Young People and the Unemployed: A review of research* (ESR Report No. 12), Employment Service, Sheffield.

Hasluck, C. (2000), *The New Deal for Young People: Two years on* (ESR Report No. 41), Employment Service, Sheffield.

Hirsch, D. (1999), *Welfare beyond Work: Active participation in a new welfare state*, Joseph Rowntree Foundation, York.

HM Treasury (1999), *Supporting Families through the Tax and Benefit System*, London.

HM Treasury (2000), *Tackling Poverty and Making Work Pay: Tax credits for the 21st century, the modernisation of Britain's tax and benefit system*, Paper No. 6, London.

House of Commons Select Committee on Education and Employment (2000), *Eighth Special Report: New Deal for Young People: Two years on*, House of Commons (HC 510), London.

Low Pay Commission (2000), *'The National Minimum Wage': The story so far: Second Report of the Low Pay Commission*, London.

Millar, J. (2000), *Keeping Track of Welfare Reform: The New Deal programmes*, Joseph Rowntree Foundation, York.

Millar, J. (2001), 'Benefits for Children: the UK', in Battle, K. and Mendelson, M. (eds), *Benefits for Children: A four country study*, The Caledon Institute, Canada.

OECD (1997), *Labour Market Policies: New challenges: Enhancing the effectiveness of active labour market policies: A streamlined public employment service* (OECD/GD 161), Paris.

Rahman, M., Palmer, G., Kenway, P. and Howarth, C. (2000), *Monitoring Poverty and Social Exclusion 2000*, Joseph Rowntree Foundation, York.

Chapter Eleven

A Critical View of Incentives to Help Benefit Recipients into Work in the Netherlands

Frans Pennings

Introduction

Until the beginning of the 1990s, Dutch benefit agencies were mainly focused on the payment of benefits to claimants within the relevant time limits and in accordance with the statutory rules (see Pennings, 1990). Although there were some provisions concerning the reintegration of persons with disabilities, and although unemployed and disabled claimants had, of course, to seek work, benefit administrations gave little priority to helping people back to work. In the 1990s, it was found that this system was not functioning well, as it was becoming too expensive and human resources were not being used properly.

Reintegration policies were initially targeted at the unemployed, but have gradually been extended to include measures for the disabled. The reason for this is that the number of persons with disabilities in the Netherlands, in terms of the numbers of persons claiming disability benefits, is relatively high. As the cost of benefits is a major problem in controlling public finances, which is of importance, *inter alia*, in meeting the requirements relating to the Euro, the reintegration of persons with disabilities has become a very pressing issue. Additional arguments for a consistent reintegration policy are that persons with disabilities should also have the opportunity to participate in society and be able to exploit their capacities. A more recent argument is that the shortage of workers on the labour market, where increasing numbers of vacancies cannot be filled, makes the re-employment of disabled persons who are able to work even more desirable.

Consequently, the policy of encouraging benefit recipients to re-enter the labour market has taken on great importance. This chapter discusses the efforts made and the problems which have been experienced. Use is mainly made of Dutch examples of incentive measures. The reason for this is that, in addition to the author's specific knowledge of these measures, they include a variety of incentives which are of recent design. In view of the problems experienced in the Netherlands in relation to disability benefits, it is interesting to note the approaches adopted to encourage benefit recipients to return to work.[1]

In the second section, a general review is undertaken of the policy relating to incentives, followed by a closer examination of incentives in the areas of unemployment benefit, disability benefit and social assistance benefit. In view of the low (official) general level of unemployment, on the one hand, and the greater problems involved in encouraging persons with disabilities to return to work, on the other hand, most of this chapter is concerned with incentive measures concerning persons with disabilities.

1 The Policy of Incentives

1.1 Some Basic Remarks on Incentives

A first type of incentive consists of supplements to the wages of benefit recipients who enter work which is paid less well than their previous employment, or than the level of the benefit to which they would have been entitled. If the only work available for a particular claimant is paid at a lower rate than the wage earned previously, the job offer can be made more attractive through the provision of a wage supplement of this type. The supplement therefore encourages benefit recipients to accept job offers.

A second type of incentive scheme involves the provision of subsidies to encourage employers to recruit benefit recipients. During periods of high unemployment, some categories of the unemployed are not able to compete on the labour market, due to real or alleged deficiencies. For the long-term unemployed and persons with low skills levels, as well as for persons with disabilities, these disadvantages also persist in periods of low unemployment.

Recruitment subsidies are intended to compensate for the deficiencies of these categories of benefit recipients, and particularly their lack of experience and lower production capacity. Real disadvantages in comparison with other workers may consist of a lack of updated skills and work experience, while disadvantages which may principally relate to the prejudice of employers include the age of the candidate, the length of unemployment and the disability.

However, incentive measures may also give rise to side effects. In the manufacturing and services sectors, these are known as *distortion* effects, while in the labour market they are denoted by the terms *substitution* and *deadweight*. *Distortion* means that the normal price mechanism of the private sector of the economy is disturbed by the subsidy. *Substitution* means that an employee is replaced by a subsidized employee. In general, this is an undesirable result for the displaced employee. It is also an inefficient use of public funds, as no additional employment is created. The term *deadweight* is used when an employer recruits a subsidized unemployed person, even though the same employee would have been recruited without a subsidy. This constitutes an inefficient use of public resources. Moreover, the fact of subsidizing an employer who would in any case have been prepared and able to employ persons without a subsidy may involve a distortion of competition. Side-effects on the labour market can be countered by ensuring that the subsidized operation is additional to the enterprise's previous activities. For instance, a subsidy may be payable only in respect of workers who perform tasks which would not be carried out if no subsidy were paid (for an earlier study of this subject, see Rajan, 1985).

1.2 Brief Description of the Development of the Incentives Policy

Prior to the Second World War, reintegration measures in virtually all Western European countries were often of a very low quality. Recipients of social assistance benefits who were able to work had to do so, mainly in order to show that they were willing to work. But it was preferable for this work not to be productive, so that it did not distort competition. The persons concerned were often assigned to useless work (*digging holes*), with the result that relief work gained a very bad reputation.

The post-war period and the 1950s and 1960s were an era of full employment, in which hardly any labour market measures were necessary, with the exception of work created for persons with disabilities and persons who could not be employed on the regular labour market.

When unemployment figures started to rise in the 1970s, a completely new approach was adopted. As unemployment was initially seen as a temporary phenomenon, subsidies were paid to employers on condition that they did not dismiss their surplus employees. Large sums of money were spent in order to increase the demand for products and labour.

In the early 1980s, it became clear that structural causes were at the origins of unemployment. Measures were therefore taken to reduce wage costs. In addition, job creation and training measures were focused on influencing the supply of labour, particularly with a view to improving the skills of the unemployed, providing them with work experience and even encouraging them to accept work at lower wage rates.

In view of the experiences with job subsidy schemes and the great improvement in the economic situation since the 1990s, reintegration measures have come to be focused on beneficiaries of unemployment benefit and of public assistance schemes.

As a result of the improvement in the labour market situation, the numbers of beneficiaries of unemployment benefit have decreased considerably in recent years. Many persons claim this benefit for a short period only. On the other hand, there is also a relatively large group of long-term unemployed (for over a year). This group consists mainly of older persons. Some 23 per cent of the unemployed are over 57 and a half years of age, and 45 per cent of these older workers are in long-term unemployment. In practice, those who are now looking for work consist of persons with few opportunities on the labour market, the disabled and older workers.

Since the mid-1990s, when unemployment levels started to fall, persons with disabilities also started to be targeted by reintegration measures, with the result that the incentive measures now in force for the disabled date from the 1990s.

Reintegration policies have therefore been adjusted over time to take into account new insights, policy objectives and economic developments. Among other consequences, this has had the result that little evidence is currently available on the effectiveness of the measures which have been adopted.

2 Incentives for the Unemployed

2.1 General Remarks

Under the terms of the Dutch Unemployment Benefits Act,[2] only employed persons are insured. To be entitled to benefit, claimants must have worked for at least in 26 out of the last 39 weeks before the first day of unemployment. If they meet this condition, benefit is paid at the rate of 70 per cent of the minimum wage for six months, which amounts to no more than a modest income provision.

Benefit is payable at a higher rate and for a longer period to those who meet the condition that they have received wages over at least 52 days in at least four of the last five years before the year in which they became unemployed. If they fulfil this condition, they receive an earnings-related benefit (70 per cent of their former wage, subject to a ceiling) for a period which depends mainly on their age and varies from six months to five years. The insurance scheme establishes no thresholds, so even persons working short hours in part-time jobs are covered.

The Act is designed so that it does not, in principle, create disincentives for persons who accept a job, even if it is for only a few hours. This is achieved by means of the rule that claimants are entitled to benefit if they lose at least five hours of work in comparison with the average number hours worked for the past 26 weeks before they became unemployed. If beneficiaries take up work, the amount of benefit is reduced in relation to the number of hours of work. As a result, if beneficiaries accept a part-time job, after becoming unemployed from a job involving more hours of work, they retain a partial unemployment benefit. Since benefits only amount to partial compensation for the loss of working hours, beneficiaries are in principle better off accepting work than remaining in benefit.

If claimants become unemployed again within a certain period, the level of unemployment benefit is calculated on the basis of the wage on which the previous benefit was based. As a result, beneficiaries are not paid a lower benefit as a result of accepting temporary work.

The Unemployment Benefits Act allows beneficiaries to participate in training where the training is, in the view of the benefit administration, necessary for the individual. In this case, the beneficiaries retain their entitlement to benefit. The benefit administration has so far applied a rather restricted interpretation of this rule. Training is only considered to be necessary for those with limited opportunities on the labour market, and this provision only covers relatively short training courses. Moreover, these rules do not cover training which is only valid for a single enterprise. Nor are beneficiaries permitted to engage in productive work.

Moreover, no subsidies are payable to beneficiaries under the terms of the Unemployment Benefits Act itself.

2.2 Experimental Measures

In 1999, the Unemployment Benefits Act was amended to allow the possibility of introducing experimental measures for the vocational reintegration of recipients of unemployment benefits. The Act itself does not provide for such experimental measures. However, it empowers the Minister of Social Affairs and Employment to issue decrees respecting experimental measures for the reintegration of unemployed persons. The provisions on experimental measures allow the benefit administration to permit exceptions from the main provisions of the Act for a maximum period of four years, where this is considered useful to facilitate reintegration.

The reason why the form of experimental measures has been chosen is that the immediate structural extension of reintegration measures entails the risk of the substitution of other workers by unemployed persons benefiting from assistance measures, which is considered to be undesirable. It therefore has to be demonstrated that the experimental measures have had the desired effect, without any undesirable side effects.

The government has acknowledged that the reintegration provisions contained in the Unemployment Benefits Act itself (with the exception of the experimental provisions) are insufficient to help persons with limited opportunities on the labour market to find work.

For the purposes of reintegration measures, and therefore also for the experimental measures, unemployed persons are placed in one of the following four categories:

1 unemployed persons who have a good chance of finding work again without help;
2 unemployed persons who have to bridge a relatively short gap in the labour market, which means, for example, that they have to undertake job training or follow a short course to facilitate their placement in a job;
3 unemployed persons who are further removed from the labour market, which means that they have to undergo a relatively long period of training before they are considered ready for placement activities; and

4 unemployed persons who have currently no opportunities on the labour market and first have to be *socially activated.*

The risks of *substitution* and the *distortion* of competition, as discussed above, can be avoided, according to the government, by excluding the first category of the unemployed from eligibility for assistance under the experimental measures.

The provisions on experimental measures allow exemptions from the statutory benefit rules for a maximum duration of four years. The following is an example of a case in which an exemption from the general provisions is considered to be useful. Under the general rules, entitlement to benefit ends when beneficiaries start to work. In cases where beneficiaries give up self-employment after more than one-and-a-half years, they cannot claim any remaining benefit entitlements. A royal decree issued on the basis of the provisions relating to experimental measures may provide for an exemption from this rule. As a result, beneficiaries can become self-employed in their own new enterprises for a maximum period of four years and still apply for the remainder of their unemployment benefit entitlement if the enterprise fails.

The Minister is also empowered to issue a decree respecting experimental measures allowing beneficiaries to engage in unremunerated work for an employer for a specified period while remaining entitled to benefit.

A third type of experimental measure involves allowing beneficiaries to remain entitled to benefit while taking up self-employment, with 70 per cent of the income earned from their activities being deducted from their benefit (see Pennings, 1992).

Under the terms of an experimental measure, eligible persons may, for a maximum period of four years, be awarded a supplement to their wages if they accept a job that pays less than they had been receiving before becoming unemployed.

As can be seen from the above, reintegration incentives are limited to experimental measures. Moreover, these measures still have to be developed. No evidence of the impact of these experimental measures is therefore available yet. The purpose of this experimental facility is to help older unemployed persons who are experiencing labour market difficulties to find work again.

The provisions cover persons who are in receipt of unemployment benefit. In principle, partially disabled persons receiving (partial) unemployment benefit can also claim unemployment benefits under these provisions, provided that they meet the necessary conditions. There are, however, more specific provisions for persons with disabilities, which are discussed below.

The provisions respecting experimental measures also allow the use of funds from the unemployment fund to help unemployed persons find work. Dutch benefit administrations have been reluctant to use funds in this way in the past. However, in accordance with the European Union's employment guidelines, they are obliged to adopt a *conclusive approach*, which means that the government has to ensure that all unemployed persons are offered an opportunity for reintegration within the first 12 months of unemployment, such as training, retraining, work experience, a job or other vocational reintegration measures. The possibility of developing such measures on an experimental basis is designed to meet this obligation gradually.

3 Incentives for Persons with Disabilities

3.1 General Remarks

In the Netherlands, there are currently three different disability benefit laws. The major legislation, the Insurance for Incapacity to Work Act, covers the insurance of employees.[3] For persons who were already disabled before they reached the age of 18, and for students who become disabled, benefits are available under the Disability Provisions for the Young Disabled Act.[4] The third scheme is for the self-employed.[5]

Coverage for this benefit is from the first day of insurance, and there is no link between the period of insurance and the level of the benefit. Nor does the Act set a threshold for coverage, which means that part-time jobs involving only a few hours of work are also covered.

Two steps have to be taken to determine the level of benefit. First, claimants have to be examined by a medical doctor to determine their limitations for work. Subsequently, an expert checks a computer database of job descriptions to establish whether the claimant can still perform a minimum number of jobs. For this purpose, practically any job that exists on the labour market is taken into account, and it is not relevant whether the job is suitable for the claimant. Nor is it relevant whether there are vacancies for the job, since the assessment is of a purely theoretical nature.

The expert selects the three jobs in which the claimant could earn the highest income. The wage levels for the jobs that the claimant could still do are relevant for the determination of the level of the benefit. Therefore, the higher the wage level, the lower the benefit. Moreover, even a relatively low degree of disability (at least 15 per cent loss of earnings capacity) already gives entitlement to a (proportional) benefit. The other two schemes follow the same approach as the employees' insurance scheme, although the benefit rate is calculated on the basis of the minimum wage, rather than of previous wages.

3.2. Background

The Dutch disability benefit scheme has been the subject of close political scrutiny since the beginning of the 1990s. The reason has been the rise in the numbers of beneficiaries of disability benefit, which has been greater than in comparable countries (Aarts and Burkhauser, 1996; see also, Einerhan, Knol, Prins and Veerman, 1995). One of the reasons for this rise is that, until 1987, the scheme allowed benefit offices to take into account the reduced opportunities of the claimant to find work. As a result, even partially disabled persons could receive a full benefit. Although this type of provision is not uncommon in other countries, it was used to a large extent in the Netherlands during the labour market restructuring of the 1970s and 1980s. Workers who had been made redundant were able to claim a full benefit for an unlimited period, that is until their pensionable age. This made disability benefit more attractive than unemployment benefit and the numbers of recipients of disability benefit rose sharply. In the 1990s, the cost of these benefits came to be seen as a major political problem. The eligibility conditions for the benefit were therefore revised. Since 1993, benefits for have been based on a new definition of disability and persons under the age of 50 who were already in receipt of benefits in 1993 have been reassessed. Persons over 50 who were already receiving the benefit have not had their benefit entitlement reassessed and have tended to remain on benefit.

The rise in the numbers receiving disability benefit is also a result of the relatively low threshold, as noted above (15 per cent loss of earnings capacity), for entitlement to a proportional benefit. A second reason is that the productivity rate is very high in the Netherlands. Quite a high proportion of employees appear to be suffering from new diseases, such as *burn-out*. A large proportion of new cases of disability consist of persons suffering from psychological problems.[6]

Table 11.1 Netherlands: disabled persons as a percentage of the working population in 1998

	NL	Germany	Denmark	Sweden	UK
Population 15–64	6.3	3.6	4.3	5.8	4.7
Working population	8.6	5.0	5.4	7.5	6.2

Source: Ministry of Social Affairs, *Sociale Nota 2001*, The Hague, 2000, p. 124.

As noted above, a new definition of disability was introduced in 1993. In general, the relevant provisions are now strictly applied. Even persons with serious limitations on their capacity to work are now often considered still able to do some work. A person with serious back problems, for instance, is considered to be still able to repair coffee machines, on condition that a suitably adapted chair is provided. A blind person can still work as a telephone operator. After the adoption of this new concept of disability, many beneficiaries lost their entitlement to benefit, or their benefit was considerably reduced. They can claim (partial) unemployment benefit if they fulfil the necessary conditions. However, unemployment benefit is less attractive than disability benefit, as it is paid for only a limited period.

The concept underlying this approach is that disabled persons should no longer focus on the work they did before they became incapacitated for work. Instead, they should be forward-looking and seek types of work that they can still do. The rule that the jobs with the highest earnings are taken into account in calculating their benefit levels is not only meant to affect their benefit, but is also designed to encourage them to seek work. In theory, it shows how much they could still earn, or in other words, how attractive it would be to return to work.

When introducing the new rules in 1993, the government announced that the new definition of disability would affect 21 per cent of the disabled. In fact, the consequences were much more serious, with 47 per cent of the disabled having their benefit withdrawn or reduced. In contrast, the objective of reintegration has met with much less success. The government believed that 50 per cent of those who were found to be (partially) capable of work would return to work, but the actual figure turned out to be 22 per cent.

Since the incentive of lowering the benefit for those who could, in theory, work proved to be rather unsuccessful, the Government adopted several measures to promote their reintegration. In this connection, a distinction may be made between three types of incentives, which are discussed below:

- the removal of barriers contained in the Disability Benefits Act for the acceptance of a job or for the hiring of persons with disabilities by employers (section 4.3);
- the provision of incentives for the disabled to enter work and for employers to recruit persons with disabilities. These incentives were reorganized and brought together in a new law, the Act respecting the vocational reintegration of persons with disabilities (section 4.4); and
- the imposition of sanctions on employers if an employee in their enterprise becomes disabled (section 4.5).

3.3 Removal of Barriers to Reintegration

Persons with disabilities may be willing to take up work, but may be uncertain whether they will be able to perform the work. The reasons for not being able to work may relate to the disability or to other reasons, such as uncertainty as to whether they will be able to cope with the organizational aspects of the job. In such cases, the persons concerned may be reluctant to take up the work (and in the event of such uncertainty, they are not required to do so). To encourage them to take the risk of returning to work, the Act provides that their benefit conditions shall not be changed for a maximum period of three years. Instead, the income from their work is deducted from their benefit. As a result, the fact of taking up the work has no permanent consequences on their benefit entitlement and, if the work stops, the full benefit is paid once again.

In the event that a disabled person takes up work which is deemed to be appropriate, the level of benefit is adjusted (a lower level of benefit is provided, or the entitlement to benefit is terminated). If the beneficiary falls ill again, under the normal rules for reclaiming benefit, a waiting period of 52 weeks would apply. As this would discourage beneficiaries from accepting work, a shorter waiting period is applied for former beneficiaries during the first five years after the benefit has been withdrawn. This waiting period is four weeks if the disability is due to the same cause as the previous disability. Where such beneficiaries had started to work for lower wages than they had received before becoming disabled, the subsequent benefit is based on the previous higher wages. It is therefore more attractive for such persons to accept a new job since, in the event of failure, they are once again awarded disability benefit within a short period.

In this respect, it should be noted that it has also been made more attractive for employers to employ persons with disabilities. Under the terms of the Dutch Sickness Benefit Act, sickness benefit is no longer provided to employees who are still covered by a contract of employment and, in the event of illness, the employer has to continue paying wages for 52 weeks.[7] This rule acts as a disincentive for employers to employ people who have been disabled, and who may therefore be expected to fall ill more often than other workers. This is an illustration of the manner in which one incentive, designed to reduce sickness benefit claims, can create disincentives for the recruitment of persons who are frequently ill or who are disabled. With a view to removing this disincentive, the Sickness Benefits Act also provides that former beneficiaries who become ill once again are entitled to sickness benefit for the first five years after the withdrawal of the benefit. As a result, the employer does not have to pay their wages during this period should they fall sick once again.

3.4 Reintegration Incentives aimed at Benefit Recipients and Employers

The incentives mentioned above are designed to remove disincentives to work. However, they are not sufficient to remove all barriers to entering work. A new Act, adopted in 1998, therefore introduced subsidies for employers and employees.[8]

3.4.1 Subsidies for employers

The following subsidies are payable to employers:

- a so-called *replacement subsidy* of up to 8,000 guilders (3.636 Euros) is available for employers who retain employees who become disabled and who have been employed in the enterprise for at least one year. The benefit administration is obliged to pay this subsidy and employers do not have to demonstrate that they have actually incurred any costs. A proportional subsidy is paid in the event of a part-time job. If the sum of 8,000 guilders is not sufficient, the benefit administration can provide a subsidy adapted to the situation;

- the above subsidy concerns employers which retain employees who become disabled. A subsidy is also payable to employers which recruit disabled persons as new employees. To be entitled to the subsidy, employment has to be offered for at least six months. Once again, the benefit administration has no discretion in awarding the subsidy and employers do not have to demonstrate that any extra expenses have been incurred in recruiting the person concerned. The subsidy is 12,000 guilders (5,454 Euros) in the first year, 8,000 guilders (3.636 Euros) in the second year and 4,000 guilders (1.818 Euros) in the third year. These amounts are for full-time jobs. In the case of part-time jobs, *pro rata* amounts are paid. These subsidies have been criticized for being relatively high in view of the fact that no proof has to be provided of the additional costs incurred.

3.4.2 Subsidies for persons with disabilities

As discussed earlier, under the terms of the Disability Benefits Act, the earnings capacity of a claimant is determined by the earnings available in three jobs which the claimant can still in theory perform. The middle wage of the three jobs is taken into account. In the event that claimants accept a job with wages below their theoretical earnings capacity, they receive a wage supplement under the terms of the Reintegration Promotion Act. This is payable for a maximum period of four years and decreases over time. The subsidy is also available for persons starting out in self-employment.

In addition, in three regions, a scheme has been developed on an experimental basis consisting of the provision of personal reintegration subsidies for the expenses necessary for reintegration. In this way, beneficiaries can find their own solutions to the problems with which they are confronted when endeavouring to return to the labour market.

3.4.3 Assessment

When the Act to promote the vocational reintegration of persons with disabilities was introduced in 1998, the government believed that it would lead to an additional 6,500 placements. In total, according to the government's assessment, there would be 63,000 placements a year. These would not all be claimants of disability benefit, but could also include former beneficiaries or persons with disabilities who were not entitled to the benefit.

The assessment currently available only concerns the initial period.[9] It appears that in 1999, only 259 of the 1,600 planned placement projects were implemented during the first nine months of the year. Only 10 per cent of the available resources were used. Projects involving placement activities for 46,000 persons were organized as from July 1998, but only 15,000 persons were placed, half of them with their own employer.

Some 27 per cent of the employers interviewed concerning the projects argued that no persons with disabilities could be placed in their enterprise. Of the employers interviewed, 145 stated that disabled employees are disadvantageous for the work process, while 20 per cent indicated that the complexity of the procedures was a negative element. Almost all of the employers interviewed who had taken up a subsidy under the scheme admitted that they would also have hired the employee without the subsidy (the *deadweight* effect discussed earlier). The reasons given for not making use of the subsidy included lack of knowledge, not having the time to apply for it and not seeing any advantage in taking the trouble to do so.

Experiences of experimental vocational reintegration subsidy schemes have so far been very disappointing. In each of the three regions, about nine persons in total have received subsidies over a period of one year. The reasons for the low take up rate are not known yet.

3.5 Incentives Related to Employers' Contributions (Sanctions)

In 1998, the method of financing the Disability Benefits Act was completely revised. The purpose of the changes is to increase the responsibility of employers for the cost of benefits. Under the new provisions, a *basic contribution* has to be paid which is the same for all employers. In view of the objective of making it more attractive to employ persons with disabilities, this contribution does not have to be paid for disabled employees, provided that at least 5 per cent of the employer's total wage bill is for employees with disabilities. Enterprises are therefore offered a financial incentive as part of the system of financing the benefits.

In addition to the basic contribution, a *differential contribution* also has to be paid, based on the payroll. The differential contribution is based on the number of employees in the enterprise who have become disabled over the past three years. These contributions finance the cost of the disability benefits paid to such employees over the first five years of their benefit entitlement. For a large enterprise, the maximum differential contribution is 3.24 per cent of the payroll.

Employers may also decide, subject to certain conditions, to bear the risk themselves of the payment of disability benefits for the first five years and may purchase private insurance for this purpose, although this is not a requirement. The employees concerned receive the same benefits as those provided under the statutory scheme.

3.6 Placement Incentives

Over the past decade, employment offices and benefit administrations have been heavily criticized for not doing enough to help benefit recipients find work. With a view to changing this situation, the government decided that placement activities would be privatized. Private companies and employment offices could tender for placement contracts by auction. The system is structured so that they are remunerated for each successful placement, and is therefore based on an incentive system.

This change was inspired by the fact that the only success stories concerning the vocational reintegration of benefit recipients have consisted of cases in which private agencies have provided unemployed or disabled persons with full individual attention. This approach is costly, but appears to be necessary to assist persons with few labour market opportunities to find work.[10]

Agencies are provided with incentives to work in this area. However, the provision of incentives to private agencies to assist the unemployed find work also gives rise to problems. For example, private agencies, which have to make profit, may focus on the persons with the best chances on the labour market. Secondly, such measures may attract persons who will take whatever work they can to earn money. It may therefore take some time to identify the best agencies. The selection of the agencies is through an auction system, which is currently a popular system for the attribution of public contracts. Under this system, the agencies have to present proposals and plans. No information is yet available on the criteria and results of this approach.

A third danger of this approach is that the placement agencies and employment offices may not cooperate adequately, for example through failure to exchange the relevant information, perhaps on grounds of privacy or competition.

3.7 Summary

There are therefore a range of incentives for the reintegration of persons with disabilities, combined with disincentives for their dismissal. In the event that a worker becomes disabled, an employer has to pay a differential contribution. If it is decided to keep the employee, the employer receives a placement subsidy, the worker may receive a wage supplement and the employer does not have to pay a differential contribution, and may benefit from a lower basic contribution if other disabled workers are also engaged. As a whole, this would appear to be a generous raft of measures.

However, these measures do not appear so far to have been successful. The available resources are far from being exhausted. There are evidently a number of explanations for this situation. Employers tend to take a considerable amount of time before they become acquainted the provisions respecting new subsidies. Although the eligibility conditions for employers are easy to fulfil (they 'can get a disabled worker for almost nothing' or, in other words, the combined effect of the subsidies and reduced contribution rates mean that the wage costs are very low for the first few years), they appear to be making little use of the facilities offered. The staff of benefit offices claim that they have no time to encourage employers to engage workers with disabilities (on the workload of benefit offices, see Bergsma and Mullenders, 1999, p. 203). In practice, their functions are still confined to calculating the level of benefit.

4 Incentives for Recipients of Social Assistance Benefits

4.1 General Remarks

Social assistance benefits are provided by local communities (most of their cost is reimbursed by the central government) to persons whose income is below benefit rates and who have no or only a low level of assets. Benefit rates vary according to the type of household. They are set at 100 per cent of the net minimum wage for a couple,[11] 90 per cent for a single parent and 70 per cent for a single person. In 2000, the net minimum wage was 2,260 guilders (1,027 Euros) a month.

4.2 Background

Beneficiaries of public assistance benefits are difficult to reintegrate. More than 50 per cent of beneficiaries have been receiving public assistance benefits for over three years. The problem is that, after a period of unemployment, beneficiaries lose their contacts with the labour market and it becomes much more difficult to find work. This is shown by practical experience and supported by statistical data, which demonstrate that there is indeed a correlation between the duration of unemployment and the possibility of finding work again (Van den Berg and Van der Veer, 1993).

Persons receiving public assistance benefits consist mainly of: those who do not meet the conditions for unemployment benefit, or whose benefit entitlements have expired; those who do not qualify for disability benefit because their disability has not been recognized as being medically certified; and divorced women. Older persons, women, members of ethnic minorities and low skilled persons are predominant among the beneficiaries of public assistance benefits.

Local councils have to develop a plan each year covering the assistance that will be provided to recipients of public assistance benefits to help them find work. The plan has to cover the manner in which the community will fulfil its obligation to cooperate with the administrations of insurance schemes for employees, and with employment offices.

A recipient of public assistance benefits who accepts work is paid a benefit of 4,000 guilders (1,818 Euros). This payment is considered necessary on the grounds that beneficiaries who stop claiming benefit are often financially penalized. The benefit is therefore designed to remove the disincentive of employment and poverty traps caused by the loss of means-tested benefits as beneficiaries who return to work begin to earn an income that is slightly higher than the level of their former benefits. The benefit is provided in the form of four annual payments made directly to the beneficiary.

A special law, the Act respecting the vocational reintegration of jobseekers, contains measures to help the long-term unemployed into work.[12] Under the terms of the Act, persons can be given a job with a special local public organization (to be created on the basis of special provisions), or can be posted to a private enterprise or public organization for a limited period, provided that they can acquire relevant work experience in the organization. Childcare facilities can be organized for unemployed parents who accept a job, since the absence of childcare is an important barrier preventing the unemployed, and particularly women, from returning to work. A special Act respecting childcare facilities for the unemployed has also recently been adopted. The wages applicable to persons covered by the scheme are to be determined by collective agreement.

In addition, subsidies are available to employers for the recruitment of unemployed persons who meet the conditions set out in the Act. Bonuses can also be paid to persons engaged on the basis of the Act who complete a training course or find a job on the regular labour market.

Moreover, under the terms of the Act, provision is made for the organization of experimental measures at the local level, under which beneficiaries may exempted from one or more of the obligations set out in the Act so that they can endeavour to find new ways of returning to work.

5 Older Persons

In the Netherlands, very few persons over the age of 60 still work. This is due to the attractive retirement schemes available (although, their conditions have recently been tightened) and the pension system. In addition, many workers have become accustomed to the idea of pre-retirement. Moreover, demands on workers are increasing and many older workers are relieved to be able to retire. A mere 31 per cent of persons aged 55 and over are still working.

It is possible for those who wish to do so to continue working over the age of 60. Those who take this option often acquire a higher supplementary pension. It is also possible to continue working after the age of 65. However, contracts of employment expire at the age of 65. If employers wish to retain such persons, they may do so. Indeed, these employees are cheaper to employ, since statutory social security contributions are no longer paid. The fact that they continue to work has no effect on the statutory old age pension, which is paid in any event. Yet, despite these financial advantages, very few persons are willing to continue in work (in practice, only those with very interesting jobs).

Now that there is a shortage of workers, employers are looking around to find new workers. However, it would appear that they are still not willing to employ older unemployed persons. Indeed, unemployed persons over the age of 45 still experience serious difficulties in finding work.

In view of these problems, up to July 1999, beneficiaries aged 57 and a half and over could be exempted from the obligation to accept a suitable job which was offered to them. From 1 July 1999, they have no longer been exempted from this obligation (*Werkloosheidswet*). Up to now, they have not been required to seek work. This exemption from the rules applicable to younger workers is granted in cases where they are unlikely to have real opportunities of finding work. However, it may be expected that the exemption will be withdrawn in the near future. The provisions covering experimental measures in the Unemployment Benefit Act can also be used to improve the labour market opportunities of this category of workers.

6 Women

The participation rate of women has always been relatively low in the Netherlands. It is now rising and reached the level of 57 per cent in 1997. However, there is still a significant gender gap, since the male participation rate is 78 per cent.

Many women work part time, as a result of which they are able to combine working and caring for their children. One reason for the growth in part-time work is the shortage of adequate childcare facilities. Recent research (which has not yet been reported) shows that women tend to prefer the combination of part-time work and part-time childcare facilities, rather than the option of full-time work. Indeed, there is now a great demand for workers in sectors traditionally employing a high level of women, such as health care and education, but the rise in part-time is continuing.

One cause for concern in this respect is that the proportion of women among new disability benefit claimants is currently considerably higher than that of men. Indeed, the incidence of young women becoming disabled is five times higher than that of men in the same age category. Most of the problems are of a psychological nature. It is not clear yet what the reasons are for this phenomenon, although the question is under investigation.

Conclusions

Experiences with Dutch schemes are, in general terms, similar to those in other Member States of the European Union, namely that policy measures to reduce unemployment based on general subsidy schemes are not seen as offering the right answer. The predominant approach, instead, is to develop individual plans for those with weak opportunities on the labour market.

Disincentives arising out of benefit schemes are being removed, although the rules are still so complicated that even beneficiaries encounter difficulties in understanding the details. The experimental measures which have been adopted are promising, but much depends on the manner in which they are designed and implemented.

Subsidy schemes have been developed for persons with disabilities and are relatively generous. The results have not so far been convincing, although it may take some time for employers and others actors to become fully conversant with the new measures.

Individual approaches would appear to be the most promising. These require a good deal of work for each individual. In the first place, their interests and shortcomings in such areas as education and experience have to be identified. They then have to be convinced that work offers advantages, and that they will be able to acquire these advantages. They then have to follow a training programme. Once this has been completed, an employer has to be convinced that the candidates are of interest to them. During the initial periods of employment, they have to be monitored and any problems have to be resolved before the experiment is brought to an end by the employer or the candidate. All of this is time-consuming and costly. Nevertheless, it would appear that it is the only manner of helping people with few opportunities on the labour market to return to work.

What lessons can be learnt from these experiences? The major lesson is that an individual approach is more appropriate than a general approach. Individuals have to be encouraged to take up work. They need to be provided with assistance to overcome the barriers which exist for the long-term unemployed, older and migrant workers. But, in the second place, once the appropriate schemes have been created, they may still not be particularly successful. Benefit administrations and employment offices often have a very bureaucratic approach and the provision of individual attention to the needs of a claimant is often too difficult for them. It is very easy for employers to find reasons not to employ workers in the above categories. They prefer to import workers from other countries. And the claimants themselves need some time to become familiar with the schemes. In practice, schemes with personal reintegration subsidies are almost ideal, but the take-up rate is still low.

It may be necessary to keep a scheme (almost) unchanged for a long period so that all the parties concerned can become familiar with it. Greater pressure on employers to assume their individual and collective responsibilities may also help. However, real results will only be achieved when there is a strong economic need to employ persons from the above categories.

Notes

1 Issue No. 4 of the *European Journal of Social Security* (on the theme of disability benefits) suggests that disability benefits are also a sensitive issue in other countries. The approaches in the countries described in the *Journal* show many similarities and it would therefore seem that a description of the Dutch system offers a good illustration of the problems encountered when implementing a policy of encouraging the reintegration of benefit recipients into work.
2 *Werkloosheidswet*, Act of 6 November 1986, *Stb.* (Dutch Official Gazette) 1986, 566.
3 *Wet op de Arbeidsongeschiktheidsverzekering* (*WAO*).
4 *Wet Arbeidsongeschiktheidsvoorziening Jong gehandicapten* (*Wajong*).
5 *Wet arbeidsongeschiktheidsverzekering zelfstandigen* (*WAZ*).
6 For literature on the growth in the number of beneficiaries, see Kuptsch and Zeitzer, ISSA, 1998; Freyssinet, 2000 (who compares the performance of the *success story countries* – Denmark, Ireland, Netherlands and the United Kingdom, see particularly his analysis of the Netherlands pp. 168–80); ILO, 2000; den Uijl et al., 2000; Hartog, 1999; and Auer, 2000.
7 *Ziektewet*, Act of 5 June 1913, Stb, 1913, 204, as amended.
8 *Wet op de (re)integratie arbeidsgehandicapten*, Act of 23 April 1998, *Stb.* 1998, 290.
9 *Evaluatiegegevens van de Wet Rea* (Ministry of Social Affairs), 18 January 2000.
10 Statistical data on such projects are scarce and relevant to small areas only. On such projects, see Van den Berg and Van der Veer, 1993, who indicated

that in 1989 the possibility for unemployed persons from ethnic minorities to find a job within one year of registration was 54 per cent through special projects, compared with 38–43 per cent through regular employment offices.

11 Both partners can claim 50 per cent of the benefit, but the right to benefit is not individualized to such an extent that no account is taken of the income of the partner.

12 *Wet op de Inschakeling Werkzoekenden.*

References

Aarts, L.J.M. and Burkhauser, R.V. (1996), *Curing the Dutch Disease: An international perspective on disability policy reform*, Avebury, Aldershot.

Auer, P. (2000), *Employment Revival in Europe: Labour market success in Austria, Denmark, Ireland and the Netherlands*, ILO, Geneva.

Berg, van den, H. and Van der Veer, K. (1993), *Wegen naar Werk*, VU uitgeverij, Amsterdam.

Bergsma, E. and Mullenders, P. (1999), 'Implementing Social Security in a Market System: An analysis of the purchaser-provider relationship in the provision of reintegration services', *European Journal of Social Security*, 1 (2), pp. 203–22.

CTSV (College van Toezicht Sociale Verzekeringen (Social Insurance Supervisory Board)) (1995), *De Werkgever Geprikkeld?: Effectiviteit financiële prikkels voor werkgevers in de ZW, AAW en WAO*, Zoetermeer.

CTSV (1996a), *In en uit de WAO*, Zoetermeer.

CTSV (1996b), *Herbeoordeling van Arbeidsongeschikten*, Zoetermeer.

CTSV (1996c), *Bemiddeling van Herbeoordeelden*, Zoetermeer.

CTSV (1997), *Bemiddeling van Gedeeltelijk Arbeidsgeschikten*, Zoetermeer.

CTSV (1998a), *Het Werkhervattingsproces na een WAO-beoordeling*, Zoetermeer.

CTSV (1998b), *Stoornissen, Beperkingen en Handicaps in de Uitvoering. Over Verschillen in de Implementatie, Interpretatie en de Uitvoering van de Richtlijn Medisch Arbeidsongeschiktheids-criterium, Geïllustreerd aan de Hand van de Problematiek bij me*, Zoetermeer.

CTSV (1999), *Augustusrapportage Arbeidsongeschiktheids-verzekeringen 1999*, Zoetermeer.

CTSV (2000a), *Claimbeoordeling WAO*, Zoetermeer.

CTSV (2000b), *Zicht op Reïntegratie. Een Onderzoek naar de Uitvoering van de Poortwachtersfunctie*, Zoetermeer.

Einerhand, M.G.K., Knol, G., Prins, R., and Veerman, Th. (1995), *Sickness and Invalidity Arrangements*, VUGA, The Hague.

Freyssinet, J. (2000), 'Réduction du Taux de Chômage: Les enseignements des expériences européennes', in Conseil d'Analyse Économique, reports by Fitoussi, J.-P., Passet, O. and Freyssinet, J., *Réduction du Chômage: Les réussites en Europe*, La Documentation Française, Paris.

Gunst van, F. and Pennings, F.J.L. (1995), *Reintegratie van Werklozen. Begeleiding en Bemiddeling van Werklozen, Sociale Zekerheid en Arbeidsvoorziening*, Lemma, Utrecht.

Hartog, J. (1999), 'Country Employment Policy Reviews: The Netherlands', ILO Symposium on Social Dialogue and Employment Success (Geneva, 2–3 March).

ILO (2000), *World Labour Report 2000: Income security and social protection in a changing world*, Geneva.

Kuptsch, C. and Zeitzer, I.R. (1998), 'Public Disability Programmes under New Complex Pressures', Chapter 6 of the Secretary-General's Report to the 26th General Assembly, *Developments and Trends in Social Security 1996–98* (Marrakech, 25–31 October 1998), International Social Security Association, Geneva.

Pennings, F.J.L. (1990), *Benefits of Doubt: A comparative study of the legal aspects of employment and unemployment schemes in Great Britain, Germany, France and the Netherlands*, Kluwer, Deventer.

Pennings, F.J.L. (1992), 'Niederländische und deutsche Arbeitslosen-vericherung im Vergleich', *Zeitschrift für ausländisches und internationales Sozialrecht*, 6 (2), pp. 151–76.

Pennings, F.J.L. (1998), *De Werkloosheidswet*, Deventer.

Pennings, F.J.L. (2000), *De WAO*, Deventer.

Prins, R., Veerman, T.J. and Koster, M.K. (1993), *Work Incapacity and Invalidity in Belgium, Germany, Sweden and the Netherlands*, CTSV, Zoetermeer.

Rajan, A. (1985), *Job Subsidies: Do they work?*, Gower, Aldershot.

Uijl, S. den, Klosse, S., Bahlmann, T. and Schippers, J. (1998), 'Reintegration of Partially Disabled Employees: From market efficiency vs social justice to market efficiency and social justice?', in Hessel, B., Schippers, J. and Siegers, J. (eds), *Market Efficiency vs Equity*, Thesis Publishers, Amsterdam.

[illegible], K., [illegible], G., [illegible], S. [illegible] (1995), [illegible] and [illegible] [illegible], The Hague.

[illegible], E. (2005), [illegible] Les [illegible] des [illegible], in [illegible] (eds) [illegible], Paris.

[illegible] van [illegible] (1998), [illegible] Regelung [illegible] Zeitschrift [illegible]

[illegible] (1999), [illegible] Employment [illegible] ILO Symposium [illegible]

ILO (2000) [illegible]

[illegible] and [illegible] (1999) [illegible] International [illegible]

[illegible] (2003), Fragility of [illegible] comparative study of the legal [illegible] of employment [illegible] Germany, France and the [illegible]

Pennings, F.J.L. (1992) [illegible] Nederland, 6/7, pp. [illegible]

Pennings, F.J.L. (1994), [illegible] Ph.D. [illegible]

Pennings, [illegible] (2006) [illegible] Ed. [illegible]

[illegible], R. [illegible] and [illegible] (eds) [illegible] CISI, [illegible]

[illegible], A. (1993), [illegible]

[illegible], Schoukens [illegible] and Schuppen [illegible] (1998), Pensioenen [illegible] in [illegible], S. [illegible] and [illegible] (eds) [illegible] Publishers, [illegible]

PART III

ALTERNATIVE POLICY MIX SCENARIOS

Chapter Twelve

Can Social Protection Respond to the Challenges of Precarious Jobs, Better Access to Employment and Equitable and Universal Decent Standards of Living? Lessons from the French Experience

Jean-Michel Belorgey

In the same way as in other European countries, workers and their families are the two pillars on which the French social protection system is primarily based. The term *workers* has to be understood in this respect as meaning employed persons enjoying direct rights, and their dependants, such as wives and children, who thereby benefit from derived rights. The origin of the modern right to social protection is therefore to be found in wage employment, as demonstrated by the fact that social protection is financed through contributions based on wages. Leaving aside the major social assistance laws of the beginning of the century, work is therefore central to the social protection system.

This system has evidently been undermined since the beginning of the 1970s by the interruption of the trend, which had up to then been almost constant, of the extension of wage employment and the improvement of the protection provided to wage-earners, as well as by the development on the labour market of increasingly precarious forms of employment. It has also been affected by changes in family composition and models. This has led to a clear maladjustment of the applicable rules on several levels and the emergence of perverse effects, which have frequently been aggravated, rather than resolved by the measures adopted.

One group of the authors, thinkers, economists and sociologists analysing the situation has concluded, frequently in a rather summary manner, that this signifies the *end of work*. Others have deemed that these developments are unacceptable. Still others, or even the same ones, have seen a way out of this dilemma in the establishment of a basic income. It is not possible to outline a new social strategy without first taking up a position in this debate. Moreover, the form which might be envisaged for an income guarantee must in itself be coherent with the principles identified in any such debate.

When endeavouring to draw up recommendations, it is clear in the first place, if an effective social protection policy is to remain or once again become possible, it is important to improve the management of the labour market (which should in turn make it possible to divert some of the resources used for social protection to the most needy, by responding more effectively to the diversity of situations) and to pay greater attention than is currently the case to promoting the access or reintegration into the labour market of those who are currently excluded from it.

1 The Diagnosis: a Social Protection System Undermined by Trends in the Labour Market and in Life Styles

1.1 The Diversification of Forms of Employment

Since the 1970s, the expected trend towards greater stability in the protective status of wage employment has been turned on its head. Atypical forms of employment have grown in importance in response to the demand for flexibility by enterprises, and also sometimes by individuals. These forms of employment have been recognized in labour law. There has also been an increase in part-time work. In more profound terms, wage employment has been undermined on two fronts: the traditional position of employed persons, which was to accept subordination in exchange for protection, is being transformed, as they are being required to take on greater responsibility and to be more polyvalent; while subordination, which was once considered inherent to wage employment, is also being found among the self-employed. In overall terms, the incidence of low wages is rising and the numbers of working poor are increasing.

1.1.1 The development of atypical forms of employment

The standard model of employment which characterized the period of *full employment*, namely full-time permanent wage employment, now only concerns 56 per cent of the active population.

Atypical forms of employment, such as fixed-term and temporary contracts, paid vocational training contracts (including apprenticeship) and *subsidized employment,* alone account for 30 per cent of the population which is in work. Admittedly, not all of these atypical forms of employment are precarious: permanent part-time work is not necessarily precarious, and some people choose and are content in a *career* in temporary work. However, these situations as a whole do not correspond to the ideal model on which our system of social protection was built.

Somewhat paradoxically, the state itself has played an important role in the emergence and diversification of these forms of employment. Since 1982, the legislator, in addition to fixed-term contracts, has defined other types of employment contract, including subsidized employment contracts. Although the legislator in theory sought to limit the conditions under which they could be used (in the case of fixed-term and temporary contracts) to exceptional work not related to the permanent activity of the enterprise, while at the same time ensuring that they are protected in accordance with the principle of equality of treatment, the use of these forms of employment has in practice exceeded forecasts.

1.1.2 The development of part-time work

The increase in part-time work in itself raises numerous problems. Between 1975 and 1995, the overall number of jobs in France rose by one million. Over the same period, the number of part-time jobs grew by 1.7 million, with 90 per cent of them being taken up by women. Part-time employment now accounts for 18 per cent of jobs, compared with 8 per cent at the beginning of the 1970s, and 31 per cent of women's jobs.

In most cases, part-time work is more of a way out of unemployment than a choice of life style. Nevertheless, it does represent a choice for some people wishing to enter the labour market, in certain cases of progressive retirement and for certain skilled women who have opted for part-time work for relatively long hours (80 per cent).

As a result, the development of a single set of binding rules runs the risk of penalizing certain workers. This has been illustrated very recently (May 1999) in Germany, by the bill regulating *small jobs* paying 600 marks, which are covered by a much more flexible regime providing fewer social guarantees than *normal* employment. Originally, these jobs responded principally to the demand of students and housewives wishing to supplement the household income. In both cases, the low level of earnings (economic distribution) was justified by the existence of other family income and by social rights acquired outside employment (as dependants and/or through their status as students). When, in endeavouring to take into account the situation of persons not benefiting from any redistribution through the household, or any social rights, the public authorities wished to confer pension rights upon them and make them contribute to the financing of this protection, a large number of the workers concerned preferred to resign and leave the labour market.

1.1.3 Wage employment and self-employment: the blurring of the dividing lines

New forms of the organization of work, the call for greater autonomy and skills in wage employment, and the development of short contracts for specific tasks, combined with the rising phenomena of integration and economic dependence in networks of enterprises, have also contributed to blurring the dividing lines between wage employment and self-employment.

Intermediary employment situations lying between *pure* wage employment and *pure* self-employment are now multiplying. These situations can be seen more clearly if a distinction is drawn, for purposes of comparison, between the two criteria which traditionally set apart wage and self-employment, namely responsibility for the organization and performance of work, and liability for the risks of the enterprise (being responsible for risks incurred in the provision of services).

Pseudo self-employed workers, who are dependent on a single client and are therefore covered by a *de facto* relationship of subordination in terms of the organization of work, have their counterpart in *pseudo* employed persons, whose status as wage-earners depends on intermediaries (such as courier firms, and to a large extent in such sectors as management consultancy, information technology and training), but who manage their work themselves and bear the risks inherent in the services that they provide.

In contrast, social protection systems, which were established on the basis of occupational activity, have in turn created and hardened these dividing lines. This is particularly true in terms of retirement and unemployment insurance.

1.1.4 The working poor

In parallel with the development of atypical forms of employment and part-time work, and the blurring of the dividing lines between wage and self-employment, or as a result of both of these phenomena, a new category is emerging, namely the working poor. According to *Données sociales 1999*, the proportion of workers earning low wages, defined as wages which are lower than two-thirds of the median wage, rose from 11.4 per cent to 15.1 per cent between 1983 and 1997. There has also been an even greater growth in very low wages, defined as wages which are lower than half of the median wage. Their proportion has risen from 5 to 10 per cent. This is largely due to the development of part-time work which, for the most part, is involuntary.

1.2 The Fragmentation of Lifestyles

Social protection systems based on stable workers and their families have not only been undermined by the increasingly diverse forms of employment and mobility, but also of family composition.

1.2.1 The evolution of family models and composition

Demographic developments (the ageing of the population, the declining number of marriages and the fall in the fertility rate) are leading to a reduction in the average size of families and an increase in the numbers of persons living alone. This is compounded by the instability of family or household composition. In practice, this is a result, less of the frequency with which alliances are breaking up, than of the diversity of cohabitation and living arrangements during the course of a lifetime.

1.2.2 The accumulation of handicaps

Following the decades of growth during which inequalities were reduced, trends have also been reversed in this respect since the middle of the

1980s: unemployment and precarious forms of employment have increased, and even converged on the same households, and in particular have undermined the situation of single persons.

This is occurring to such an extent that a duality is emerging between households which are excluded in the long term from stable employment and those which are well integrated and are working ever harder. The jobless rate for the active population by category of household shows the emergence of this trend. Between 1990 and 1996, while the jobless rate of persons with a working spouse tended to fall (from 27.1 to 21.5 per cent), the rate of jobless single persons of working age rose (from 20.2 to 28.5 per cent), as did that of persons with an unemployed spouse, which increased from 12.9 to 22.4 per cent. The OECD has pointed to the development in several European countries of households in which no one works (OECD, 1999).

1.3 Maladjustments in the Social Protection System

The complexity of situations tends to be reflected in the adoption of complex rules and strategies, both out of a concern for equity and to address the realities of social situations. The brutal application of uniform rules runs the risk of creating exclusion on a broad scale. In contrast, rules which are too flexible and leave decision-makers with margins for interpretation may result in arbitrary decisions, particularly by judges, and especially in the absence of adequate regulations. However, complexity may be no more than a result of the maladjustment of systems, and bear little relation to the needs of users or the general interest. This would appear to be true of recent developments, characterized by a maladjustment of the unemployment compensation scheme and the rules governing retirement benefits, as well as through the combined effect of legislative measures, the emergence of threshold effects and poverty traps, and more generally through a real lack of transparency in the social protection system.

1.3.1 An unemployment compensation system which penalizes the most precarious

Labour market developments, with the almost continuous rise in unemployment, have placed a growing burden on the unemployment benefit system. The unemployment insurance scheme has required several successive reforms to balance its budget. One of the results of these reforms has been to penalize those in the most precarious situations, to the point of excluding them from unemployment insurance. Moreover, the development of different conditions for various occupations since 1988 has resulted in the transfer of many of the long-term unemployed to the minimum integration income (RMI), or more generally to social assistance.

After a period during which benefit rights improved (the creation of the supplementary waiting allowance in 1974, the extension of income guarantees in 1977), the reforms carried out in the 1980s and 1990s have tended to reduce benefit rights and increase contribution rates. Three major reforms have been undertaken since 1979.

In 1982, the creation of special measures for specific occupations gave rise to a distinction in benefit rights based, no longer exclusively on age, but on age and the previous duration of insurance under the scheme. This measure resulted in a major reduction in the possible duration of benefits for workers with limited periods of employment.

In 1984, a major reform resulted in the separation of a so-called insurance scheme, financed through contributions and subject to negotiation by the social partners, intended to provide benefits for a limited period to jobseekers who had previously paid contributions, and a solidarity (assistance) scheme, financed through taxation and controlled by the state, intended to provide unemployment benefits to those excluded from the insurance scheme. This duality broke with the unified scheme of 1979, in which the state participated in the provision of benefits to the unemployed through the payment of a fixed general subsidy. It led to a distinction between several categories of unemployed persons covered by differing schemes and sources of financing, whereas previously jobseekers had benefited from both public assistance (basic benefits) and insurance benefits. This is evidently a source of exclusion, or at the very least of segmentation which stigmatizes beneficiaries.

In 1992, confronted by financial difficulties, the scope of the unemployment insurance scheme was further reduced and beneficiaries who had exhausted their entitlements were covered by the state through the solidarity scheme created previously. But they were subjected to increasingly restrictive conditions: the level of benefits financed by the state was adjusted at a lower level than the benefits of the joint scheme and they lost their initial parity with the basic benefits of that scheme, while the eligibility conditions were also tightened.

The combined effect of changes in rules and developments on the labour market had two major effects:

- *the decrease in the proportion of the unemployed receiving benefits*: 62.4 per cent of registered unemployed persons received benefits in 1992 (including 52.4 per cent under the insurance scheme). This figure fell to 53 per cent in 1998. For the insurance scheme, the coverage rate fell from 52.4 per cent in 1992 to 41.3 per cent in 1998. This was a result, in particular, of the longer periods of unemployment of workers who had been in the scheme for only a short time. Had the rules not been changed, and had they remained as they were in 1990, the fall in the coverage rate of the insurance scheme would have been substantially less (46.5 per cent in 1996);
- *an increased incidence of low rates of benefit*: in 1992, some 12 per cent of unemployment persons receiving benefits were provided with an average monthly level of benefit that was equal to or lower than half of the statutory minimum wage (SMIC), while in 1998 this was the case for 40 per cent of beneficiaries.

1.3.2 A retirement system which duplicates this penalization

The rules in force concerning retirement benefits are also badly adapted to workers who have not been in traditional jobs and whose employment status has varied over their working life. The rules penalize them.

Their first effect is to increase the gap between those who have followed a continuous career covered by the insurance scheme and who benefit fully from the system, and those whose careers have been low paid and intermittent, who are badly covered. Indeed, while periods of unemployment for which unemployment benefit is paid count towards retirement, the same is not true for periods during which the RMI is provided.

Furthermore, certain threshold effects give rise to particular penalties: and especially the requirement of having to have worked 200 hours in a quarter for the full quarter to be taken into account; or the requirement of a minimum period of work covered by a specific scheme for it to be taken into account.

Moreover, workers who finish their careers in self-employment or in the liberal professions are affected by a significant reduction in their entitlements to the supplementary scheme. This rule, introduced during the post-war decades to discourage people from leaving the general scheme, now has perverse effects arising out of the increasingly common constraints of occupational mobility.

Finally, the 1993 reform, which extended the reference period from the 10 to the 25 best years of earnings for the calculation of pensions, will further emphasize the impact of career changes on retirement benefits, while at the same time increasing the period of insurance required to obtain a full pension.

1.3.3 Threshold effects and poverty traps

Income from social transfers is of great importance for those who are on low budgets. Family and housing benefits in certain cases represent three quarters of such budgets, and in many cases over half. However, the rules governing each type of benefit set break-off points or *threshold effects* related to changes of situation such as, in the case of family allowances, the age of the children or, in the case of housing benefits, the effect of no longer receiving the RMI.

These are compounded by other *statutory* effects:

- debts, which are suspended for beneficiaries of the RMI, resurface; and
- exemption is no longer granted from local residence taxes.

A return to work is also discouraged when the level of income earned is not sufficient to compensate both for the decrease in benefits and the rise in costs. To reach this level of earnings, single persons have to earn at least the minimum wage, while those with families have to earn more. Even *run on* benefits do not resolve this situation beyond the period for which they are provided (nine months for half-time work), following which the beneficiary is once again in the situation described above.

1.3.4 The combination of legislative provisions, time-limits, lack of transparency and disincentives

When the decreases in income arising out of the transition from one situation to another are taken together, and if they are regarded as an additional form of taxation, which may be termed *marginal taxation*, a curve can be described for *marginal taxation rates* as a function of income. This curve takes the form of a flat 'U'. The marginal rates are generally higher at the two extremities of the distribution of income than for average income. But, in particular, the curve is not continuous. It has a large number of blips, which show the threshold effects.

These blips are particularly high between zero and one times the minimum wage. They are even greater than 100 percent for a single person receiving the RMI, with the result that returning to work leads to a drop in net income. Moreover, this analysis only compares the impact of social regulations in static mode, between different situations at a given time. But life is made up of a succession of non-simultaneous moments. The real benefits received by households depend on a succession of events, which in turn give rise to unexpected and perverse effects arising out of the applicable rules.

The manner in which benefits are calculated (on a quarterly basis for the RMI and on an annual basis for housing benefit, although they are immediately revised downwards for beneficiaries of the RMI who return to work), means that the profile of the benefits paid is very discontinuous. The income curve for certain standard cases shown by dynamic analyses is characterized by positive and negative movements in time (month by month), which can only be seen by those concerned as being of an arbitrary nature.

So-called *run on* measures, which are designed to leave the beneficiary with a proportion of previous benefits, do not resolve the issue, as they are well below the level at which the problem emerges.

2 In Search of Principles

2.1 What is the Role of Work, Employment and Activity?

The first question to be resolved, if it is wished to remedy the shortcomings of the social protection system, is clearly to identify the relationship that it should establish with work and employment and, to start with, the role that it is wished and possible to assign to the latter, taking into account both economic constraints and dominant ethical preferences.

If it is then concluded that the future will undoubtedly not consist either of the end of work, or the end of employment, but in the search for a new form of full employment based on new rules, and a social protection system which is not exclusively based on belonging to the world of work, but on a concept such as citizenship, most of the ideas relating to the notion of basic income would not appear to be adapted to ensuring greater liberty vis-à-vis work (at least not for everyone), nor a better response to needs or the optimization of the use of public resources.

2.1.1 What is the future of work?

One group of the authors, philosophers, economists and sociologists who propose the introduction of basic income, or a *universal or citizens allowance* base their proposals on the aspiration or diagnosis of the *end of work* (see in particular Ferry, 1995; Gorz, 1993; Steiner, 1992; Baker, 1992, Aglietta, 1998; and Caillé, 1995). But does this mean the end of society based on the exchange of labour, or the end of employment (in the sense of access to a status through the exchange of labour), the dominant form of which is wage employment? The terms of the debate are all the more ambiguous in that their context is provided by another much broader debate, concerning the relationship between work and the freedom of the citizen.

In certain quarters, the end of work is greeted as the emergence of a radiant future, in which humanity is finally freed from the chains of servitude and will be able to devote its time, not to immediate survival, but to improving lifestyles and the soul. Others, more modestly, envisage the end of Taylorized work and the emergence of a virtual society in which personal development and intellectual capacity will prevail. Finally, for others, the end of work is not the advent of a new era, but merely the absence of *suitable* jobs. This provides the justification for providing everyone, including the least efficient, with an income enabling them to survive, even without work. This is the basis for claiming a minimum social income high enough to allow people to turn down job offers which are *unworthy* in terms of working time, remuneration or conditions of work. In this third perspective, the role of work in self-development is not denied, but equal emphasis is placed on income as a guarantee of dignity and freedom.

In practice, the future is undoubtedly neither the end of work, nor the end of employment. Demographic developments could result in a decrease in the active population. Moreover, in the long term, the volume of employment and the volume of work have always in the past tended to adapt to each other. But in the perspective of a new form of *full employment* the question remains as to the forms of work and employment towards which we are heading, and their distribution.

Alain Supiot starts off from this broad approach to define four circles of social rights. The first and broadest circle marks a net rupture with the occupational basis of the French social protection system. It consists of the recognition of universal social rights guaranteed to all, irrespective of whether they work, such as the rights to health, a minimum income and training. The second circle consists of rights relating to nonoccupational work (caring for others, including domestic work, benevolent work and self-development). The third circle consists of the rights related to occupational activity (the right to security and the major collective freedoms, such as freedom of association and the right to collective bargaining). Finally, the last circle, which is the narrowest, concerns the rights generated by wage employment and arising out of the situation of subordination (Supiot, 1999).

2.1.2 Right to employment and right to income

The preamble to the French Constitution envisages a simultaneous right to employment and a right to income. *Everyone shall have the duty to work and the right to obtain employment* (fifth paragraph of the preamble to the Constitution of 1946, as retained in the Constitution of 1958). This right to employment and to income is combined with the more general right to social protection, particularly for those who could not live from their work:

> … the nation shall ensure the individual and the family the conditions necessary for their development. It shall guarantee to everyone … protection of health, material security, rest and leisure. Each human being who, by reason of her or his age, physical or mental condition or economic situation, is incapable of working shall have the right to be provided with suitable means of existence by the community.

In the post-war period, these rights were implemented through a stated policy of *full employment* and the generalization of social protection based on employment.

In the 1970s, in view of the rise in unemployment, the policy of full employment gave way to specific employment policies which endeavoured to accompany transformations in the nature of work (restructuring, in the first place, then combating long-term unemployment). However, these new measures foundered on the abstract concept of quantifiable and interchangeable jobs juxtaposed in major industrial enterprises. All employment situations come down to the norm of wage employment, with its contracts and status. When combating unemployment and exclusion, it is important to provide both income and social rights, and mechanisms have therefore been invented, such as the *employment solidarity contract* (*contrat emploi solidarité* – CES), for which the granting of a status is the purpose of the employment contract.

During the same period, based around the pre-existing right to work, employment policies developed a series of rules supplementing this right both upstream and downstream of the actual employment contract. Upstream, this consists of the right to seek work and the right of access to employment; downstream, it concerns the right to the maintenance of employment and to career progression.

In view of its incapacity to provide them with 'standard' jobs, or socially useful activities, the state finally considered itself under the obligation to guarantee an income to people in difficulties. This led to the establishment of minimum incomes for specific categories and measures designed to link the right to an income and social guarantees with the, at least, moral duty to work.

2.1.3 The ambiguities of basic income

The idea of an unconditional universal allowance, by its nature provided irrespective of any obligation to work, is in this respect fundamentally innovative and redemptive. However, even though it is generally combined with proposals for the radical simplification of the system of social transfers, based on the elimination of all or some of existing benefits and the reform of the tax system, which is not without social risks, it does not in practice make any economic sense once the question of its financing is taken into account. Indeed, an allowance cannot be uniform from this point of view, since its financing either has to be through capitation (in which case, the net effect is zero, since the necessary amount is raised from each individual to finance the uniform allowance received by that individual); or its financing is based on taxation which is proportional to income (or to consumption, if VAT is used) and the allowance in practice becomes progressive in relation to income; or it is based on taxation which is progressive in relation to income which, depending on the scale used, therefore fails to guarantee either the incentive to work or the redistribution effect. For these reasons, an allowance of this type would not appear to be appropriate to achieve the optimum use of collective resources, which is in principle sought in the use of public funds.

For a given level of budgetary resources, transfers based on differential allowances, in contrast, offer by far the best redistributional performance. Moreover, they do not undermine the level of protection enjoyed by persons in employment, or in particular the level of the minimum wage. In contrast, they can undoubtedly create *poverty traps* for their beneficiaries due to very high marginal tax rates. Provisions of this type can also contribute to widening the gap between employees who are in jobs with favourable social conditions, and a second group who have very little opportunity to gain access to employment and for whom almost the only alternative offered by society is more or less reasonably compensated inactivity.

2.2 What Form of Income Guarantee?

In the absence of a basic income, it is towards another form of income guarantee that it is necessary to turn. Such a guarantee would take into account the diversity in the attitudes of human beings to work, thereby finding a good balance between the two logics of individual rights and family rights shared by the social protection system as it is currently structured, and would be able to encompass the employment opportunities offered as an alternative to beneficiaries of guaranteed income benefits.

2.2.1 Income guarantees and attitudes to work

Do we have the right to live without working? Or, approaching the issue from the opposite direction, how far does the obligation to work go in order to be entitled to income and social guarantees?

The RMI, although abandoning any counterpart in exchange for the provision of the benefit, in practice creates a dual right to a financial benefit to tide beneficiaries over a tight situation and assistance from the community with a view to their integration, and places a duty upon beneficiaries to make the necessary efforts for such integration.

The issue of the duties of beneficiaries of solidarity benefits who are *out of work* is in practice systematically at the heart of the public debate. It lies behind the concept of the *activation of passive expenditure* and of *workfare*. The concept of workfare comes to us from the United States. *Welfare* benefits are only provided on condition that the person *works*, or manages to get sufficiently close to work, leading to the combination of *workfare*. This concept was then developed in the United Kingdom, under a slightly different form, namely *welfare to work*. The reasoning, in both cases, is as if the provision of subsistence benefits is likely to act as a disincentive to work. This is a concept which underestimates the diversity of attitudes to work, which are not only based on financial considerations, but also on a concern for dignity and self-esteem, admittedly within certain limits, particularly relating to the characteristics of the households receiving assistance and the nature of the available jobs. Jane Millar (Chapter Ten) reviews the relevant developments in this respect.

2.2.2 Individual guarantees, family guarantees

The French social protection system shares two logics, the first arising out of individual rights (such as unemployment insurance) and the second relating to family rights (for all benefits based on the recognition of a need). The often badly managed cohabitation between these two logics is not straightforward. But could a choice be made between the two?

According to the first logic, the tax and social system is focused on the individual. There is no reason to take into account the characteristics of the family. Unemployment benefits, which are solely based on the occupational history of the individual, are an example. Such a system leaves adults free to make any economies of scale which may result from their choice of lifestyle (such as living in a couple).

According to the second logic, it is the family which is the central unit. Priority is given to family solidarity, the mutual sharing of resources within the family, before calling upon national solidarity. By taking the family as an entity, measures can take into account the economies achieved within the family in determining the level of assistance.

The recognition of universal rights related to the individual tends to encourage the process of the individualization of rights, which would appear to eliminate many perverse effects. It prevents any stigmatization relating to the way of life selected by individuals (single persons, couples or any other arrangement). However, total individualization is not without dangers and constraints, particularly for the weakest, and especially in relation to the requirement to contribute and the reduction to appropriate levels of social coverage. The solution is therefore more likely to be a combination of the two logics, rather than a decisive shift towards one of them. At the very least, two issues need to be addressed: the economies of scale arising out of living in common; and the influence of minimum income benefits, whatever the form of the benefit, on the spouse's choice as to whether to work. Maria Jepsen and Danièle Meulders (Chapter Three) rightly emphasize this latter aspect.

2.2.3 A standard form of employment and level of income

Around the issue of promoting vocational integration, as well as in attitudes which tend to stigmatize beneficiaries of social transfers, and particularly beneficiaries of minimum benefits who refuse to work, there is an implicit comparison with the standard form of employment. Indeed, an implicit comparison is made between the level of resources obtained through the benefit and the level which could be attained through an available job, which in France means the half-time SMIC. This represents a surreptitious decline in the social standards which held sway during the period of full employment, namely permanent full-time wage employment paid at the level of the SMIC, towards a lower standard or, in line with certain American and British theoreticians, towards no standard at all.

If it is admitted that it is impossible to turn back, the question which arises is more that of the determination of a proper standard, which is symbolically and ethically acceptable, than of how to manage the coexistence of standards which have by the force of circumstances become pluralistic, although that it is not in itself unacceptable.

This leads to three types of questions:

1 concerning the appropriate standard: if the standard is too low, it pulls people down; if it is too high, it may also, due the effect of *poverty traps*, be a cause of exclusion. To find an issue to the debate on the standard to be adopted (replacing one standard with another), it is possible to accept the existence of differentiated standards, provided that there are counterweights, either at the collective level

(the role of the actors in negotiating) or at the financial level (the mutual coverage of risks);

2 with regard to the multiplicity of the possible uses of a same standard form of employment, around which there may or may not be a polarization. To prevent any irreversibility (from part-time to full-time work, fixed-term to permanent contracts, etc.), it is necessary to develop transitions; and

3 concerning diversified employment relations: is it necessary to develop specialized standards for each type of employment relationship, or should there be common rights for occupational activity in general?

3 Improving the Coherence of Social Protection and Labour Market Policies

3.1 Managing the Labour Market better so that a Coherent Social Protection Policy Remains Possible

The prospect of greater use being made of minimum social rights in future has its roots in the first place, as noted above, in the fragility of employment in a changing world of work, and secondly in the conditions of access to social protection. The objective to be pursued is therefore simple: improving the coherence of social protection with developments on the labour market with a view to achieving coherence once again in a system which has lost it.

From this point of view, it would not be appropriate to rely on an upturn in the employment situation to resolve the problem of precarious situations. An improvement in the management of the labour market, with emphasis on the primary distribution of income from work rather than on redistribution, is indispensable if the system of social benefits is not to exhaust itself through endeavouring in vain to correct major dysfunctions. This has a quadruple aim: the reconstruction of the employment relationship to take into account new forms of economic dependency and subordination; the clarification of the conditions under which the risks related to work are shared between employers and workers; the adaptation of systems to occupational mobility; and the renovation of collective bargaining.

3.1.1 Towards broader coverage of labour law

The employment relationship currently remains the predominant form of employment and will continue to be so. However, as noted above, employment relationships are now taking on very different forms. The prospects of a return to full employment do not spontaneously offer a remedy to this. The objective is therefore to reconstruct the employment relationship, taking into account the new forms of economic dependency and subordination which characterize contemporary contractual labour relations. In a context of the diversification of systems of production and the forms in which labour is exchanged, labour rights must not remain exclusively protective of workers in major enterprises. They will have to take into account all the contemporary forms of work, while at the same time offering identical guarantees to the workers concerned, whatever their form of employment.

The fundamental rights which form the basis of the common right to occupational activity which is applicable to all workers are undoubtedly the right to work, the right of association, the right to collective bargaining, the right to unemployment insurance, the right to training and the right to social security. But the adaptation of these fundamental rights to the various forms of work is a delicate matter. By way of illustration, the issue of the observance of safety and health standards does not arise in the same terms for an employed person as for a self-employed worker. In more precise terms, responsibility for the observance of the standards is not the same. However, it could be envisaged that the enterprise for which a self-employed worker performs a task, in its premises, should be responsible for the safety rules (which is already partly the case). Other fundamental rights, such as the right to collective bargaining, could also be organized for non-wage-earners (see, for example, the collective agreement for insurance agents, who are franchised dealers, or the collective agreements for the agricultural sector, which already exist). This is already the case in Italy.

The determination of the conditions for the transition between the situations of jobseeker, wage-earner, student or entrepreneur, and the harmonization of the rules of access to retirement benefit schemes, particularly supplementary schemes, could be pursued in the same spirit. However, in the first place, it is necessary to resolve a problem of dividing lines. The current criteria of legal subordination, particularly in relation to the hierarchical management of work, have lost part of their effectiveness. New forms of work, such as self-employment, are tending to make workers responsible for their own employment. Alain Supiot has analysed this phenomenon in precise terms (Supiot, 1999). More generally, with the development of what the Spanish call *programmed work*, which requires skills and autonomy, what is at issue is less and less who exercises authority, and increasingly who is utilizing and is appropriating the product of labour (a definition suggested by Lyon-Caen, 1993).

Experiences in France and in other countries indicate two possible orientations with a view to taking the above developments into account:

1 broadening the scope of the employment relationship, with a view to extending protection at the same time, as has been done in Germany by taking into account economic dependency; and
2 establishing an intermediary category of para-subordinated work for workers who are economically dependent on a single enterprise. In the countries which have adopted this solution, the workers remain self-employed, but benefit from certain of the types of protection deriving from the employment relationship.

Neither of these solutions appears to be totally satisfactory. By reversing the presumption of self-employment set out in the Madelin Act,[1] it could however be considered that wage employment is the normal status (which is also the case under the Act known as the second Aubry Law on working time reduction),[2] and that the creation of a self-employed activity is only recognized when assets have been assigned to it, which may take the form of either financial capital, or industrial or commercial inputs (clients, goodwill). Barthélémy has made a proposal in this respect (Barthélémy, 1997) which would also allow a distinction to be drawn between the income of the enterprise and remuneration for work, on which social entitlements could be based. Such a reform, would in effect bring into line the conditions for the creation of an individual enterprise with those governing enterprises in shared ownership (for which the rules respecting the accumulation of a contract of employment, with the related protection, and a function related to the enterprise, have been relaxed). If this proposal were to be adopted, the provision of any service by a person who has not proven the intention to establish an enterprise by the assignment of assets would have to be considered to be an employment contract.

3.1.2 A better sharing of risks

The development of new forms of self-employment is not the only way of sharing risks. In the field of wage employment, in the strict sense of the term, reforms are also needed to clarify responsibilities. The problem arises in the first place in relation to unemployment insurance. It is clear in this respect that dismissals by employers give rise to a double negative financial *externality*. On the one hand, dismissals lead to higher benefit payments, and therefore higher social contributions, for workers and enterprises as a whole. On the other hand, loss of employment gives rise to loss of income (even where workers are compensated), and a consequent decline in demand for other enterprises. The existence of these externalities confers upon employment the status of a *public good*, which provides the justification for endeavouring to inhibit the practices of enterprises in the management of employment, by means of an adjustment in their unemployment contributions, based on their record in this area.

These adjustments could, for example, be based on the rate of dismissals, or on the types of contracts used (taking into account the standards prevalent in the occupation), or even on turnover. Such adjustment of contributions is going in the right direction, namely reducing the level of unemployment and its dependence on the economic cycle, and would promote increased employment, particularly through recruitment in enterprises which are stabilizing their workforce. This latter result is particularly important: it suggests that a modulated system would promote a more efficient allocation of the workforce than a flat-rate system, such as the French system.

The adaptation of such a system to France would have to take into account the specific context of labour rights and the French institutional environment, which could act as a counterweight to the positive effects of incentive measures observed in the United States. In France, the structure of unemployment benefits (in terms of eligibility, duration and level), and the multiplicity of types of employment contract, could provide a margin of manoeuvre for enterprises, through which they could loosen the link between their policies and employers' contributions. It should also be noted that such a system could penalize enterprises in sectors which have to undertake major restructuring measures, for which redundancies may be necessary, while subsidizing enterprises in buoyant sectors, where the rate of spontaneous mobility is significant and the issue of redundancies for economic reasons hardly arises. In-depth feasibility studies are therefore required, although this does not *a priori* prevent the implementation of the system in the French context.

A modulation of contribution rates on the basis of the proportion of precarious contracts (fixed-term or temporary contracts) may appear simpler to implement than a modulation based on redundancy rates, as has sometimes been proposed. In global terms, an interesting possibility would be to envisage a bonus/malus related to the overall rotation rate within the enterprise, while at the same time taking into account the seasonal use of fixed-term contracts.

The central issue is to redefine the concept of the employer, with a view to limiting precarious situations arising out of a succession of short contracts (fixed-term or temporary contracts) and easing the situation of persons working for several employers. Two non-mutually exclusive options are possible: multiplying models of third-party employers, and endowing employment with a mutual dimension. The first option involves the development of rights arising out of the fact of making workers available to other employers, with a view to guaranteeing them equivalent rights to those of the workers employed by the entity in question. This consists of bringing together the various scattered provisions relating to such areas as equality of treatment, the observance of safety and health rules and the conditions under which disciplinary authority is exercised. The second option is to share responsibility for employment within groups of employers (see Boissonnat, 1995).

Irrespective of the manner in which employers' groupings are constituted and collaborate, it would also be necessary to take into account, as European Community law and French law endeavour to do, co-working situations resulting from the participation of several enterprises in a common operation. In the event of subcontracting, it would also be necessary to envisage:

- the inclusion of a social clause in the corresponding contracts, with a view to ensuring that the enterprises which tender for the same contract provide identical social standards (this already exists for public contracts). Within a particular pool of employment, inter-enterprise negotiation, or better still local negotiation, could determine the content of this social clause (covering, for example, observance of the same minimum wage, access to the social benefits of the entity which issues the instructions, or the mutual levelling of these benefits);

and

- the employment obligations of those issuing the instructions: for example, participation in a local placement service, or the obligation of placement in situations where an enterprise depends on a single client.

The provisions of the Labour Code respecting the sub-contracting of labour, which date from the 1940s, partly pursue these various objectives (section 125.2). However, these provisions are fragmented and now obsolete. They should therefore be revised.

3.1.3 Adapting social protection to labour mobility

It has been seen above that, due to the transformation in the characteristics of the labour market, the current rules respecting social protection are particularly penalizing in two areas: unemployment benefit and retirement benefit entitlements. In the first place, it is necessary to neutralize the effects of these rules in order to bring to an end the penalization of mobile and precarious workers. However, mobility can also gain a positive dimension through training and the development of *transitional markets* based on employment policy measures (see, on this point, Gazier and Schmid, 1998; Gazier, 1999a and 1999b; and Schmid, 1998).

If the penalization of precarious workers is to be brought to an end, it will be necessary to:

- lengthen the reference periods taken into account for the calculation of unemployment benefit; and
- apply the contributory principle less rigorously to access to unemployment assistance benefit (*allocation de solidarité spécifique – ASS*) with a view to making it into an allowance for larger numbers of people who have exhausted their entitlements (while maintaining the means-test).

This would have the effect of pushing fewer long-term unemployed persons onto the RMI. In this way, their rights to retirement benefits would be retained (also in the case of former part-time workers, who supplement their partial ASS with the RMI).

With a view to eliminating the obstacles faced by those who wish to create their own employment, it would also be necessary to:

- admit that the preparation and launching of a project for the creation of an economic activity may, within certain limits, give rise to entitlement to unemployment benefit, and particularly to the maintenance of the basic allowance during the first six months of their self-employed activity for unemployed persons who were previously entitled to unemployment benefit;
- facilitate the accumulation of personal resources by re-establishing a premium at a level to be determined for the unemployed and for beneficiaries of minimum social benefits, which could be combined, where appropriate, with a reimbursable advance, with the premium and the loan being accompanied by appropriate support measures;
- extending the reduction on social contributions for low wages (under 1.3 times the SMIC) to low earnings from self-employment; and
- extending the right to unemployment benefit in the event of the failure of the enterprise, particularly by taking into account all or part of the corresponding periods of self-employment for the purposes of assistance benefits.

It could also be envisaged that self-employed workers could contribute to the unemployment insurance scheme (ASSEDIC) to cover a period of unemployment following the closure of their enterprise, or to allow very isolated periods of self-employment by an unemployed person (micro-enterprises), as well as a reduced level of activity, to be taken into account without loss of entitlement to unemployment benefit.

Finally, certain unemployed persons whose low level of benefit is below the minimum income to which they would be entitled in view of their family situation, have to apply to a different office for the additional benefit, which is often a fairly small amount. With a view to avoiding this requirement, it is proposed that the same office should provide recipients of unemployment benefit with all their replacement benefits.

The Labour Code establishes that training (a fundamental right of all workers, whether or not they are employed) is a national obligation, even though it only implements this principle in respect of employed persons. In this regard, it would be necessary to review the right to individual educational leave to make it into a real generalized individual right based on solidarity and financed, for example, through the development of a training leave credit, the level of which would depend on the previous duration of the activity (whether wage-earning or unpaid). In the case of young persons and women who have not worked before, a credit financed by the public authorities could be established, subject to the account being replenished during subsequent periods of employment.

In addition to providing support for training strategies, it would also be necessary to:

- review retirement benefit entitlements to take into account the expansion in intermittent forms of employment, taking care not to prejudice atypical careers which provide for similar levels of accumulated earnings over the whole career. This would involve, in particular, reviewing or modifying the threshold of 200 hours per quarter so as not to penalize multiple forms of employment, particularly successive periods of multiple jobs, under the rules applicable to supplementary retirement schemes;
- improve employment assistance measures and their implementation by modifying the approach of giving priority to those who are furthest away from the labour market, or in other words, changing the order of the *waiting list*, and placing these measures within the context of a stable system designed to promote long-term partnerships;
- encourage the creation of new activities in the *tertiary sector*, with the establishment of *new services*; this raises the question of funding the corresponding needs and ensuring the quality of the proposed activities; they should not consist of low-skilled jobs without career prospects, which constitute a trap for both those who work in them and for users;
- make intermediary, or *transitional* situations, such as part-time work, reversible; a right of return to full-term work could be established on the Dutch model.

3.1.4 Renewing collective bargaining

An examination of public and private employment promotion strategies reveals, on the one hand, the duplication encouraged by, on the one hand, negative and positive competition between the decentralized services of the state and the joint unemployment insurance scheme and, on the other hand, the difficulties involved in agreeing upon the appropriate measures in a specific sector or area.

It is for this reason that it is necessary to clarify the role of each of the partners and develop truly coordinated management, at both the national and local levels. The delegation of responsibility to the traditional social partners has resulted in the protection of stable workers, to the detriment of precarious workers, and has contributed to the exclusion of the latter from the system. With regard to the state, by making the eligibility conditions for assistance benefits more stringent for unemployed persons who have exhausted their entitlement to benefit under the insurance scheme, it has contributed to raising the numbers depending on the minimum income (the *third component*, of the unemployment benefit system). Nevertheless, it is entirely evident that the measures administered by the unemployment insurance scheme (UNEDIC) and employment policy measures are broadly interdependent and that they both play the dual role of providing replacement income and assisting the unemployed to return to work.

These reflections provide grounds for advocating a reform in the operation of the unemployment scheme, so that the state becomes a real partner, and not merely a distrusted oversight authority, but with the assurance that it will intervene in the event of a grave crisis and which, in any event, has the role of covering those who are left out. The difficulty lies in making the three groups of actors into real partners and escaping from the mentality of mutual mistrust, with a view to developing a system of responsible collective administration. It is for the state, with its national representation, to define the general political objectives of what we should have the courage to call the public unemployment compensation service. Evidently, this should not be a unilateral process, but should take place after dialogue with the social partners who, in view of their historical role in the establishment of the scheme, cannot be reduced to the role of the delegated providers of a public service, but can no longer act as if their responsibilities were unrelated to the public service. Furthermore, it is the role of tripartite dialogue to agree on the means by which major objectives are to be implemented, both as regards unemployment compensation and active employment promotion measures, which are currently administered by joint bodies or by the state.

Moreover, the employment situation can only be managed on real labour markets, which only exist at the local level. To achieve this objective, it is necessary to decentralize employment funds and make local actors responsible for their distribution and use, within the context of rules set out at the national level.

If unemployment schemes are to be used as a tool for macroeconomic management, it would finally be necessary to allow the schemes to accumulate reserves, and then to use them during recessions as an instrument of counter-cyclical management. This would require a transition from an annual balance of income and expenditure to a medium-term balance, negotiated in global terms.

3.2 Towards a Social Protection System which Responds more Closely to the Diversity of Situations

Responding more effectively to the situations of precarious workers, which have not been eliminated through a more effective management of the labour market, involves in the first place an improved knowledge of the diversity of the various situations, which are currently still not well enough known. Improvements would then be conceivable, both immediately and in the long term, to strengthen the coherence of the strategies pursued, particularly with a view to equity, by eliminating threshold effects and taking into account real needs.

3.2.1 Improving knowledge

Statistical knowledge of the phenomena of poverty and precariousness has improved notably in recent years as a result of the development of new tools (surveys of specific population categories, household panels) and the increased amount of work carried out on these subjects. The establishment in France of the National Poverty and Social Exclusion Observatory in July 1999, and the recommendations contained in the March 1998 report of the National Statistical Information Council (CNIS) give grounds for hoping that there will continue to be an improvement in knowledge of the poor and those who are in precarious situations. However, specific efforts still need to be made in a number of areas.

Precariousness is a process which must be analysed over sufficiently long periods of time so that trends can be seen over a succession of unstable situations. Social and occupational integration or exclusion cannot be adequately examined without a proper analysis over time. The delayed effects of entering and exiting support measures demonstrate this need. Based on the cases of Canada, Germany, Netherlands, Sweden, United Kingdom and United States, this issue has been examined by Howard Oxley et al. (2001).

Research and analysis in the field of employment should be developed on successive or recurrent transitions from one situation to another (such as wage employment, unemployment and self-employment), or on rotations between similar types of situation (such as unemployment, fixed-term contracts, reduced working hours and subsidized employment). Are certain persons locked into precarious forms of employment and underemployment? How does this happen? Can they get out of it, and how? What is the association between employment trajectories and changes of residence, modifications in household status (precarious marriages, temporary accommodation) and changes in available resources? In general terms, this would consist of identifying ruptures in individual or family biographies, and analysing in as much depth as possible the instability of situations and the variability of resource levels.

In parallel, it would be necessary to identify the different conditions of each generation. Are the employment histories of individuals perennially subject to the conditions which prevailed at the time of their entry into the labour market? Is it possible to speak of *sacrificed generations*?

Emphasis has often been placed on the multidimensional aspects of poverty. Further analysis remains to be done on the income which is really available to low-income households, with a view to adjusting equation scales to their situations, taking greater account of the composition of the whole of the life cycle and housing constraints (the need to stay with certain people, fiscal units, etc.).

The theme of indebtedness, its consequences on household budgets and the manner in which it can be identified and addressed through assistance mechanisms should also be covered by in-depth studies.

The traditional unit of analysis is the household, namely all the occupants of a single housing unit, who are assumed to share resources and costs. This hypothesis is false in the case of a number of atypical forms of household due, for example, to the constrained accommodation with another person, or in collective housing. It would be necessary to give effect to the proposal made by the National Statistical Information Council (CNIS) to undertake a specific analysis of the living conditions of households identified as being atypical in general surveys. Specific studies are needed of the situation of young adults over 20 years of age living with their parents. The objective is to correct the concept of the household with a view to identifying the group of persons who form an income-expenditure unit.

The conditions under which rights are, or are not exercised are as important as the law itself in terms of the phenomena of poverty and precariousness. In this respect, emphasis should be placed on two areas:

- studying cases in which rights are not taken up; and
- analysing processes whereby these rights are taken up, which would also require being able to examine categories which are marginalized from these measures by threshold effects or by their status, even though their situations are very close to those of the beneficiaries of the rights.

3.2.2 Promoting equity

Although it is not being proposed either to create a universal allowance, or to combine all the social minimum benefits, a number of simplifications nevertheless appear necessary to take into account the real needs and eliminate specific legal situations which can only be justified in historical terms.

These simplifications are based on a simple principle: identical benefits for equal needs.

The Fragonard Reports (1992 and 1993) and the Join-Lambert Report (1998) have already pointed out the inadequate level of the RMI, as well as its deterioration since its creation in relation to the level of the SMIC and the average wage. Recent adjustments have merely made up the backlog in terms of purchasing power, but not in terms of its relative deterioration. To return to the level of the SMIC at which the RMI was set when it was created, it would be necessary to raise the RMI by 4.7 per cent. This measure would not be such as to give rise to perverse effects, particularly if a really dynamic policy of integration is pursued.

This adjustment could take the form of the elimination of the housing benefit, which results in a lowering of the level of the RMI for everyone except those who are homeless. However, living with third persons does not eliminate all sharing in the cost of housing. Moreover, nor does the fact of being a home-owner cancel the cost of housing, which may be unsupportable in a very small budget (unavoidable condominium and maintenance costs, etc.). The reduction of the benefit on the grounds that the beneficiary is a homeowner runs the risk in time of forcing the homeowner to sell the housing with a view to paying off debts.

3.2.3 Eliminating threshold effects

To make sense, an income guarantee measure must not only be perceived as being equitable, or in other words adapted to the various types of situation and at an identical level for identical needs, but must also not have the effect of plunging its beneficiaries into various types of unforeseen fluctuations in their situation. It therefore has to be endowed with sufficient stability and continuity, above and beyond any changes in responsibility for the financing and provision of benefits which may be justified at the institutional level by the requirement to distribute the burden between operators, so as not to aggravate the feeling of precariousness, or indeed the actual precariousness of the beneficiaries.

The provisions of the Act respecting measures to combat exclusion very clearly make assisting beneficiaries gain access to social benefits of all types an obligation for all social institutions.

In the event of uncertainty, the rule needs to be the extension of rights, and not their withdrawal, and failure to observe this rule must be penalized. To monitor the implementation of this principle, intermediaries who are sufficiently independent from the institutions responsible for providing the benefits and who have sufficient authority must be available to users experiencing difficulties. The concept of *mediators*, which was contained in one of the preliminary drafts of the Act respecting measures to combat exclusion, was finally removed from it.[3] A decision needs to be taken to set out this concept in law and implement it in practice.

The two keys to the vital issue of continuity of coverage lie in:

- the rules applicable to the award and termination of entitlements; and
- the practices of the offices responsible for receiving applications and paying entitlements.

With regard to the former, it is necessary to:

- eliminate threshold effects and exclusion from the receipt of any benefit arising out of the fact of rising above a certain level of means, or the loss of a particular *status* (unemployment, beneficiary of the RMI) and, from this perspective, introduce a progressive decrease in the benefits provided in the event of a return to an improved

situation; the problem, which has been noted in the case of *run on* benefits when returning to work, takes the same forms in other areas (RMI, universal health coverage (CMU), housing benefit); and
- exclude any waiting period and any system for determining the date of the beginning and end of the payment of a subsistence benefit which leaves the beneficiary unprotected either in terms of covering basic needs, or the costs that the specific benefit is designed to meet.

With regard to the practices of benefit offices, it would be necessary to establish the following principles, not as principles unsupported by sanctions, but as principles backed up by the sanction of the extension of the benefit which the responsible institution has failed to provide:

- that coverage by one benefit cannot be withdrawn until it has been replaced by another, except in the case of the fault or wilful negligence of the beneficiary; and
- that any institution providing benefits and called upon to interrupt their provision must take the measures that are necessary in the specific case in good time and in collaboration with the institution responsible for following on with the provision of another benefit.

Many of the problems raised above, and to which solutions are proposed on a case by case basis, either through the strengthening of the applicable rules, or the improvement of the practices followed, based on a reinforcement of the rights of users and of the obligations of practitioners, would undoubtedly be resolved in a more satisfactory manner if it were possible to develop a resolutely innovative conception of entitlement to benefits and procedures for the recognition and implementation of these entitlements. This is particularly necessary in cases that cannot be addressed equitably through legislation that is based on the approach of flat-rate benefits and resource ceilings. A term that may easily be used in this respect is *interpretable rights*. This concept, which is rarely defined with precision, could be promising if it were to be understood as being based on:

- *the recognition in law of an entitlement to benefit*, of a non-predetermined level, although possibly within predefined limits, in the event of an *objectively identifiable situation of need*, which is not in itself predetermined;

- the use of an *individual situation analysis* to determine the level of benefit;
- establishment of an *appropriate system of control*, at least in terms of oversight, of the decisions taken in this respect, which does not exclude the upstream intervention of a mediator; and
- the existence, in the budgets of the public authorities responsible for the provision of the corresponding benefit, of *discretionary budgetary lines*, which are not limitative, but may be accompanied by cost objectives.

3.2.4 Taking real needs into account

The manner in which resources are taken into account with a view to the payment of a number of benefits, such as the RMI, is based on the income received and not the resources really available after the deduction of unavoidable costs. However, when the benefits are intended, as is the case with the RMI, to provide a certain level of resources to very poor persons so that they can meet their basic needs, the desired level is not reached and the beneficiary is condemned to seek other forms of assistance from various benefit offices, which are mostly of a discretionary nature and which are not provided under conditions which guarantee the respect and dignity of the beneficiaries.

The fact of taking into account the income received, instead of the available resources, in the case of social protection measures designed to protect the poorest categories of the population, will in general have increasingly intolerable consequences for the coverage of certain contingencies as more or less automatic measures, generally based on the RMI, replace systems of assistance designed to meet needs and which take into account the resources and costs of beneficiaries. By way of illustration, the disappearance, with some exceptions, of medical assistance as a result of the establishment of universal health coverage very clearly raises the problem of persons who, due to the gap between their income and their available means, are not entitled to the new benefits established by the law and, under the terms of the law, will henceforth only be entitled to discretionary forms of assistance.

The Act respecting universal health coverage nevertheless allows the deduction of alimony payments from the means taken into account to assess entitlement to basic and supplementary coverage.[4] This is not the case in the Act respecting the RMI. This rule should therefore be extended from the universal health care coverage (CMU) to the RMI, and provision should also be made, under both Acts, that certain costs which are unavoidable for beneficiaries should be deducted from the resources that are taken into account. The moral risk, to which reference is often made, would not exist in practice if the costs to be taken into account were clearly defined.

3.3 Social Protection and Access to Work

The readjustment of the social protection system must not only lean towards taking into account the diversity of situations more effectively. It should also, to a greater extent than is currently the case, facilitate the return or access to the labour market, which raises the whole issue of the proper use of *run on* mechanisms and the manner in which individualized and family-based rights are articulated. Moreover, the situation of young persons undoubtedly requires a particular effort.

3.3.1 On the proper use of run on *mechanisms*

The rules concerning the *run on* of benefits should be adjusted to take into account the following principles:

- that the same rule respecting the *run on* of benefits is applied to all minimum social benefits and all entitlements, irrespective of the status of the beneficiary;
- that a level of income from work should be maintained which is not derisory, even if it is degressive; and
- that the duration of *run on* benefits should be long enough to be significant in the beneficiary's budget, provide better compensation for fluctuations in social benefits and prevent new ruptures in the receipt of income.

A more advantageous and durable *run on* mechanism would consist of creating a benefit (along the lines of the income compensation allowance proposed by R. Godino) for beneficiaries of the RMI who return to work, and only for them. This would consist of decreasing the RMI not by total earnings, but by a diminishing proportion of earnings up to 1.2 times the SMIC.

On the subject of a benefit of this type, which would in effect subsidize part-time work, doubts are expressed on the one hand that it would undermine the SMIC and that the resulting benefit would be *confiscated* by the employer and, on the other hand, that it would have a perverse effect on job offers for women, and particularly those providing a second wage for the household. Others fear that, by limiting the benefit to those who have received the RMI (and only to those), a *statutory bias*, the elimination of which is being advocated, would in practice once again be created.

The first category of objections fall away if a firm position is taken on the minimum wage, and if the provision of the benefit is limited to a small number of persons. Furthermore, restricting the provision of the benefit to beneficiaries of the RMI amounts to targeting expenditure towards those who are in most need, thereby achieving greater cost-effectiveness in public expenditure.

There undoubtedly remains the problem that enterprises might wish to take advantage of the existence of an income supplement to offer parts of jobs. However, there are three arguments against this objection:

- these jobs already exist and most of the persons who leave the RMI to take up employment work part-time. The measure would make the situation of these people a little more attractive and less unbearable;
- in contrast with previous forms of assistance for part-time work, which were provided directly to enterprises (a lower rate of social contributions), the type of *assistance* envisaged is for workers; and
- finally, the supply of part-time jobs, which is not infinite, could if necessary be contained through the strategies described above for the management of the labour market.

3.3.2 Individualized rights, family-based rights and work

Minimum income guarantees, by their nature and their interaction with policies respecting social transfers and the contributions paid by low-income households, do not have a neutral effect on the attitudes of individuals concerning their participation in the labour market.

In general terms, a social minimum family benefit is a strong disincentive to work for members of a couple who receive no wage from work. If one of them returns to work, the only effect is to decrease social transfers related to the right of the household as a whole to an income guarantee: the actual additional income from work after benefit reductions have been taken into account is therefore very low, and often nonexistent. In a system in which this income guarantee is individualized, the return to work of a member of a couple would only prejudice the social rights of that individual, and not those of the spouse. It would therefore have a less unfavourable impact on the income available to the household. In contrast, where a member of the household receives income from work, social measures based on the family act as a stronger incentive for the second spouse to go out to work, in view of the fact that the benefit provided before work is taken up is of a low level. In an individualized system, when a second member of the couple takes up work, the whole of the social minimum benefit is lost and the financial consequences are therefore more important.

To make returning to work *lucrative,* the rules concerning the *run on* of benefits should therefore be applied to individual income, without taking into account housing benefit or children's allowances.

3.3.3 The problem of young persons

Young persons are particularly affected by difficulties in gaining access to employment and by the instability of employment. They form the principal category of persons who are obliged to accept part-time work and fixed-term contracts, with periods of recurrent unemployment.

Under these conditions, the withdrawal of the integration allowance and exclusion from entitlement to the RMI for persons under the age of 25, when family benefits come to an end at 20 years of age, constitute a double penalty.

The only solutions to be found to this situation are in the areas of training and assistance to find a first job. The proliferation of measures to assist young persons has not resolved the recurrent unemployment from which they suffer. In contrast with the hopes expressed, some 15,000 young persons who left the school system without qualifications in 1992 never worked or attended a training course over the five years after leaving school.

Flirting with the concept of a SMIC for young persons, many assistance measures for the acquisition of skills and a first job (guidance, qualification and apprenticeship contracts, sandwich training courses, etc.) designed to respond to the needs of young persons, are in practice directed at enterprises by reducing the cost of employing young persons in exchange for the provision of hypothetical skills.

The priority is undoubtedly to enable all young persons to develop their individual and social identity through work. However, this requires a real assurance of work. What is at stake is to guarantee a social right to training and a job that is worthy of the name as an individual right, and not as a possibility offered as part of a limited package of measures. In order to identify initial inequalities, this right could be inversely proportional to the level attained in the school system. However, and in particular, it should make it possible for every young person leaving the educational system to achieve the status of worker, with the possibility, in the absence of a job, of entering remunerated training. The problem of remuneration during training would clearly need to be settled through rules which could not be circumvented, set out in law or an agreed arrangement between the state, the regions, the unemployment insurance system and enterprises.

For young persons who nevertheless remain outside the above system, it would be necessary to establish a safety net, in the form of interpretable rights and accompanied by social measures (particularly for the implementation of the individual right described above). This residual right to an *allowance for single young persons* (*allocation jeunes isolés – AJI)* would be available to single young persons not covered by any other benefit. Eligibility to this residual right would make it possible to avoid the dramatic situations that are currently to be found in the case of young persons who are not covered by any measure. It would be futile to maintain that there is an incompatibility or possibility of substitution between this residual right and the more ambitious policy of the right to training/employment described above. Entry into training in the context of a more ambitious mechanism, designed with greater rigour than is currently the case, would involve periods of friction. During such periods, young persons without family support cannot be left unprotected without running the risk of their lives running off the rails and losing their structure.

* * *

A renewal of social protection strategies commensurate with the maladjustments revealed by analysis of the current situation would involve, in the first place, a clarification of the basic principles involved. Failure to do this would undoubtedly mean that there would be no break with the tradition of *tinkering* which has resulted in the incoherence and lack of transparency criticized above. However, it is not only necessary to overcome the contradictions which too frequently taint the strategies that are adopted. It is also necessary to renew the instruments used and review the practices followed. And this needs to be done without overlooking the requirement, in certain cases, of breaking with current standards, nor the limitations of all legal measures unless they are given effect by ethically rigorous rules.

Notes

1 Act of 11 February 1994, Journal Officiel of 13 February 1994.
2 Act of 19 January 2000, Journal Officiel of 20 January 2000.
3 Act of 29 July 1998, Journal Officiel of 31 July 1998, pp. 11679 *et seq.*
4 Act of 27 July 1999, Journal Officiel of 28 July 1999.

References

Aglietta, M. (1997), *Régulation et Crise du Capitalisme*, Odile Jacob, Paris.
Baker, J. (1992), 'An Egalitarian Case for Basic Income', in Van Parijs, P. (ed.), *Arguing for Basic Income*, London, Verso.
Boissonnat, J. (1995), *Le Travail dans Vingt Ans*, Paris, La Documentation Française.
Caillé, A. (1995), 'Temps Choisi et Revenu de Citoyenneté: Au delà du salariat universel', *Revue du MAUSS*, Paris.
Ferry, J.M. (1995), *L'Allocation Universelle: Pour un revenu de citoyenneté*, Paris, Cerf.
Fragonard, B. (1992), 'Unifier les Minima Sociaux' (unpublished report), Groupe de Travail Inter-administratif, Paris.
Fragonard, B. (1993), 'Cohésion Sociale et Prévention de l'Exclusion', Commissariat Général du Plan, Rapport de la Commission du XIe Plan, Paris, La Documentation Française.
Gazier, B. (1999a), 'La Normativité des Salaires et ses Déploiements Internes et Externes à l'Entreprise', in Monnier, J.M. (ed.), *Dynamiques Économiques de l'Équité*, Paris, Economica.
Gazier, B. (1999b), 'L'Articulation Justice Globale, Justice Locale: Le cas des marches transitionnels du travail', contribution to the 1999 Congress

of the French Economic Science Association (Association Française de Science Économique).

Gazier, B. and Schmid, G. (2000), 'Financing of Transitional Labour Markets and Micro/macro Changes in Wages and Income Distribution' (second revised version), in Schmid, G. and Gazier, B (eds) (2000), *The Dynamics of Full Employment: Social integration by transitional labour markets*, Cheltenham, Edward Elgar.

Gorz, A. (1994), 'Revenu Minimum et Citoyenneté, Droit au Travail vs. Droit au Revenu', *Futuribles*, Paris, 184, February, pp. 49–60.

Join-Lambert, M.-T. (1998), *Chômage, Mesures d'Urgence et Minima Sociaux: Problèmes soulevés par les mouvements de chômeurs en France fin 1997–début 1998*, Paris, La Documentation Française.

Lyon-Caen, G. (1993), 'Rapport du Commissariat Général du Plan sur le Travail Indépendant', Paris (unpublished).

Marjolis, D. (2000), 'Etude Pour le Commissariat Général du Plan', Paris (unpublished).

OECD (1999), *Employment Outlook*, Paris.

Oxley, H., Thanh Dang, T. and Antol, P. (2001), 'Poverty Dynamics in Six OECD Countries', *OECD Economic Studies*, No. 30 (2001/1), Paris.

Schmid, G. (1998), 'Enhancing Gender Equality by Transitional Labour Markets', OECD Conference on Changing Labour Markets and Gender Equality (Oslo, 12–13 October 1998).

Steiner, H. (1992), 'Three Just Taxes', in Van Parijs, P. (ed.), *Arguing for Basic Income*, London, Verso.

Supiot, A. (1999), *Au Delà de l'Emploi: Transformations du travail et devenir du droit du travail en Europe*, Paris, Flammarion.

Van Parijs, P. (1990), 'Peut-on Justifier une Allocation Universelle? Une relecture de quelques theories de la justice économique', *Futuribles*, Paris, No. 144, June, pp. 29–42.

Feature No. 5
Taxation and Labour Market Entry

Adrian Sinfield

Make work pay has become one of the key objectives of social protection in the European Union (European Commission, 2000). The OECD has devoted a whole issue of its *Economic Studies* to *make work pay* policies (OECD, 2000a). 'The particular attraction of Make Work Pay policies is that they can promote *both* efficiency and equity by fostering employment and decent levels of *family* income' (OECD, 2000b, p. 7, emphasis in original).

In many countries, *activation* or *active line* policies have developed out of a concern, at least in part, at the alleged work disincentive of benefits (for an assessment of the positive activating role of benefits, see Sinfield, 1997). Initially, policies to tackle the *unemployment trap*, in which people may be financially better off out of work than in a job, paid more attention to levels of social protection and neglected the effect of taxes and other compulsory deductions on replacement ratios (that is, the level of net income out of work compared to net income in work). It is now more widely recognized that income tax, social insurance contributions and other bites out of gross earnings can also have an important impact in reducing the net income of low-paid workers.

The use of tax credits for low-income households has been much influenced by the remarkable expansion of the Earned Income Tax Credit (EITC) in the United States, which has been described as 'the policy equivalent of penicillin' (Howard, 1997, p. 64). It is now probably the single largest income transfer programme for low-income families in the United States, costing more than the main form of means-tested income support for poor families under the conventionally defined social security system.

In the United Kingdom, this problem is now being tackled for families on low incomes through the introduction of the Working Families Tax Credit (WFTC) (see Jane Millar, Chapter Ten). The Disabled Person's Tax Credit and the Employment Tax Credit for workers over 50 years of age have further expanded the scope of measures of this type. Proposals to introduce Employment Tax Credits by 2003 will extend their coverage to all workers on low wages (Howard, 2000).

The use of tax credits has quite deliberately shifted the issue of making work pay from social protection to the income tax system. In general, this has meant a shift from the stick to the carrot in promoting labour force participation, and therefore social inclusion, and away from the tighter policing and restriction of benefits for those who are out of work. Such measures are seen as escaping the stigma of social security benefits for the *able-bodied poor* and providing a bonus for working people.

How effective these measures have been is much debated. Employment gains have probably been modest, although still significant for groups such as single mothers, who are particularly vulnerable to poverty. In the United Kingdom, the continuing fall in overall unemployment makes it difficult to isolate the effect of these tax measures. There have been claims of *deadweight* (that beneficiaries would have found jobs anyway as unemployment fell) and of a drop in employment among the lower-paid partners of those responding to the tax carrot. However, the net resources of low-income households benefiting from tax credits have improved, which amounts to a gain in tackling poverty and social exclusion.

In contrast to the current enthusiasm for measures such as tax credits, much less attention has been paid to the actual operation of these measures (see Howard, 1997, Chapter 7; and Social Security Committee, 1998). In the United States, the EITC has not been without problems. As in the case of the means-tested programmes of the social security system, there can be high marginal tax rates as the benefit is phased out. It is also very complex to calculate and there are therefore, not surprisingly, high error rates and claims that it is very open to fraud. Almost all payments are made annually as a lump sum, limiting the scheme's value as regular support for families with low earnings. But opting for regular payments can result in demands for repayment at the end of the tax year. The same difficulties have been found in New Zealand with the Family Support and Independent Family tax credits. In the United Kingdom, these tax credits are paid fortnightly so that they are more effective in providing a regular income.

Although these and other problems in the actual administration of income tax credits for people moving into low-paid jobs have received little attention in most economic analyses, welfare and employment rights workers have drawn attention to them. Tax authorities tend to be much less experienced in dealing with the urgent needs of low-income households. For example, the initial rate of income tax to which workers may be subject for the first few weeks or months of a new job may create severe difficulties for them and their families. Without the appropriate tax document from their previous employer (a very common situation among those who have been out of work for a long time and who take up insecure and low-paid jobs), they are likely to be taxed on all their earnings at the full standard rate without any adjustment for tax allowances or other forms of relief. People with family dependants, who are expecting to pay no or only a very small amount of income tax on low earnings, can find that their pay in the early weeks or months of employment is much reduced. At the same time, families may lose entitlement to various means-tested benefits.

The total effect of these problems can give rise to significant financial disincentives for families on low incomes and with large family expenses and rent burdens. In the United Kingdom, this problem has been reduced because tax allowances for dependants have all been phased out and the standard rate of tax reduced. The WFTC may also reduce the problem, but it is still likely to take at least a month before a worker is able to gain the credit. Indeed, if any of the forms are incompletely or incorrectly filled out by the worker or the employer, the delay may be much longer, resulting in net earnings that are well below the income received from benefits while out of work.

In some countries, the reduction of payroll taxes and/or social insurance contribution holidays for employers acts as an incentive for them to take on people who have been unemployed for a long period or are over a certain age. This tax holiday, which may last for six months or longer, may apply to both employers' and employees' contributions, but is more often limited to the employer's. How far any of these measures, including tax credits, lead employers to reduce or freeze wage rates is not clear, but 'they are best combined with minimum wages at judicious levels, to limit any downward effect on wages' (OECD, 2000b, p. 8).

Australia and Canada have moved away from tax credits and other support directed only to families with an earner, towards the provision of a common family benefit or tax benefit regardless of work status. These may provide a securer and more stable system of child support, with a better impact on labour market participation (Battle et al., 2000). This may prove to be a more successful and popular approach to tackling child poverty and promoting social cohesion. The United Kingdom is also planning to introduce an Integrated Child Credit through the tax system, in addition to the universal Child Benefit.

Proposals for a full or partial basic income or citizen's income to tackle the problems of smoothing entry or re-entry into paid work have also been proposed and have given rise to much debate over whether it is necessary to make these benefits conditional on some form of activity. For example, a participation income has been proposed in the United Kingdom to 'replace the present emphasis on means-testing with a modernised social insurance scheme and a new version of basic income' (Atkinson, 1995, p. 10 and Chapter 15; see also Parker, 1989).

References

Atkinson, A. B. (1995), *Incomes and the Welfare State: Essays on Britain and Europe*, Cambridge University Press, Cambridge.

Battle, K., Millar, J., Mendelson, M., Meyer, D. and Whiteford, P. (2000), *Benefits for Children: A four-country study*, Ottawa, Caledon Institute (Australia, Canada, United Kingdom and United States): summarized in a Joseph Rowntree Finding, *Reforming Children's Benefits: International comparisons* (October 2000), www.jrf.org.uk, together with related findings, including *The Working Families Tax Credit: Options and evaluation* (March 1998).

European Commission (2000), *Social Protection in Europe 1999*, Brussels.

Howard, C. (1997), *The Hidden Welfare State: Tax expenditures and social policy in the United States* (includes two chapters on EITC), Princeton University Press, Princeton, NJ.

Howard, M. (2000), 'Designing the Employment Tax Credit', *Poverty*, 107 (Autumn), pp. 14–17.

OECD (2000a), *OECD Economic Studies*, No. 31 (2000/II), Paris.

OECD (2000b), 'Editorial: Rewarding work', *Employment Outlook 2000*, Paris, pp. 7–10.

Parker, H. (1989), *Instead of the Dole: An enquiry into integration of the tax and benefit systems*, Routledge, London.

Pearson, M. and Scarpetta, S. (2000), 'An Overview: What do we know about policies to make work pay?, in OECD, 2000b, pp. 11–24.

Sinfield, A. (1997), 'Blaming the Benefit: The costs of the distinction between active and passive programmes', in Holmer, J. and Karlsson, J. Ch. (eds), *Work: Quo Vadis? Rethinking the question of work*, Ashgate, Aldershot.

Social Security Committee (1998), *Tax and Benefits: An interim report*, House of Commons Paper 283, Parliamentary Session 1997–98, The Stationery Office, London.

Chapter Thirteen

Women and Atypical Working in the United Kingdom: the Prospects for Positive Flexibility

Peter Cressey

The Thatcher years of deregulation and the free rein of market forces continue to have a baleful influence on the labour market in the United Kingdom. For almost two decades, there was a distinct *laissez faire* attitude towards labour market exclusion, the role and position of women in the labour force and the growth of atypical labour contracts. Essentially, the labour market was dominated by an employers' agenda that sought flexibility, mainly at the expense of workers. As Bob Jessop notes:

> … neo-liberalism leads to government promotion of 'hire and fire'; flexi-time and flexi-wage labour markets; the growth of tax expenditures steeled by private initiatives and the re-orientation of state activities to the needs of the private sector (Jessop, 1994).

The issue of flexibility in working time and employment in the 1980s and 1990s was largely dominated by considerations of such negative or one-sided gain. The variation of working time arrangements was rooted primarily in the needs of employers to respond to market demands. Because of this, the concept of flexibility became associated with the removal of worker choice over working arrangements and a weakening of employment security. At that time, most interest was centred on the increasing use of part-time and temporary work arrangements, the rise of zero-hours contracts and other forms of the casualization of the working week. (For an account of earlier debates on flexibility in the United Kingdom, see Pollert, 1991; and Pillinger, 1998.)

In addition, the impact of this new labour market flexibility bore increasingly heavily on women, whose labour market participation rate was increasing and who were taking on, whether voluntarily or not, these nonstandard working time arrangements. Hence the old debate framed the issue in negative terms *and* made it gender-related, highlighting above all the domestic and childcare constraints pushing women workers into such arrangements. In this context, the response of the trade unions to working time flexibility rightly centred on its negative aspects. They were reluctant to enter into negotiations on this terrain and suspicious of any moves to further flexibilize the labour market.

Hence, by the late 1990s the labour market in the United Kingdom demonstrated significant differences from those of other leading European economies. It was characterized by higher levels of labour force participation and a high participation rate among women, who took the lion's share of atypical contracts, but benefited from little supportive infrastructure for women in work, including very poor provision of nursery care for children below the age of 5 (only 9 per cent of firms offer some kind of childcare assistance (see DfEE, 2000a and b), longer average working hours and distinctly lower employment rights and job security (European Commission, 1999). In addition to these general labour market conditions, women in the labour force faced additional barriers, such as the mantle of family carers, the double burden of paid and home work, lower levels of qualifications and training, entrenched patriarchy and informal forms of exclusion (see, among others, Brannen and Moss, 1991; Walby, 1987).

Such a context signals multiple barriers to women's equal participation in the labour market and the need for more than a single avenue of reform. There is hence a need for the simultaneous improvement of the supportive infrastructure, social and welfare provisions, labour market policies and the statutory rights of atypical contract workers. Such a package could begin to develop a *positive flexibility* orientation in the labour market, in which men and women could tailor working time and contracts to suit their circumstances, while at the same time enabling employers to meet their production and service targets.

This chapter reviews the direction of the reforms that have been introduced in the United Kingdom since the political changes of 1997 and the accession of a Labour government and endeavours to assess the prospects for positive flexibility gaining hold. This would ideally involve a critical examination of the European, national and corporate levels to see what, if any, advances have been made in this field. However, the chapter can only briefly describe the European and national contexts, with a view to concentrating on the corporate level which, as will be seen, remains the dominate field of activity in the United Kingdom. A case study is used to show both the possibilities and the problems involved in this undertaking.

Changes in the United Kingdom

The change of government in the United Kingdom in 1997 was an important landmark and signalled a shift in labour market policies and attitudes towards social exclusion. One of the key events was the publication of the White Paper *Fairness at work* in 1998 and subsequently the Employment Relations Bill in 1999. These documents pushed the idea of *family friendly policies* (FFP) at work to promote fair treatment, better procedures for collective representation and, importantly for this discussion, policies which enhance people's ability to go to work and which lessen the conflict between their responsibilities at home and at work. This has led the current government to highlight the need to combine flexibility with security. Many of the statutory reforms enacted are described in greater detail in Chapter Ten (Millar), including the working families tax credit that is beginning to address working poverty and the need for financial assistance for childcare. However, critics have been quick to point out that, without real reform of the lamentable childcare provision, many of the reforms will have little impact on employment choices by women. For instance, the Trades Union Congress (TUC) considers the EU Parental Leave Directive to be seriously deficient, as it only allows for unpaid time off. According to a poll commissioned by the TUC, one-third of parents said that they could not afford to take unpaid parental leave and one in eight indicated that they would be subject to employer pressure not to take the leave entitlement (Hall, 1999).

Non-state and Corporate Initiatives

In the absence of a concerted raft of statutory policies, it is left to government exhortation, the activities of independent agencies and corporate level agreements to tackle the unequal status of women in employment and the gender gap in terms of pay, conditions and opportunities (European Foundation, 2000). The voluntarist industrial relations system in the United Kingdom tends to encourage local agreement and corporate activity in the labour market and in industrial relations, especially in the areas of working arrangements, pay and conditions and work organization. Indeed, in the United Kingdom, at the same time as the negative aspects of flexibility were being established, incipient moves within organizations were changing the terms of the debate.

The debate had previously centred predominantly on working time and its flexibilization, with a heavy focus on part-time work and the adaptation of hours to take account of caring responsibilities. However, agencies such as New Ways to Work, the Industrial Society and the National Work-life Forum have been actively campaigning for a more extensive range of reform on this issue. Leading companies are also adapting to the changes in the social environment which have altered the focus from working time and work contracts towards a more holistic concern for balancing work and life. The demands linked to an emerging *24 hour society* are therefore continuing to alter working hours and patterns, as are moves in both private and public organizations towards greater customer responsiveness. Combined with more open-ended career patterns, flexi-organization formats and the instigation of lifelong learning, these factors are increasingly disrupting the narrow lines of the previous debate. Opportunities are arising to look at the wider notion of *flexible working lives*, rather than the narrower concepts of working time and contracts.

When the move is made from flexible working time to flexible working lives, the agenda widens considerably and involves changes not only in working time, but also in working patterns, work organization and work location. A set of options relating to working arrangements emanating from the Ministerial Advisory Committee on Work-life Balance (DfEE, 2000a) subdivides working arrangements into five areas:

- the *time* employees work;
- the *periods* worked;
- the *location* of work;
- the longer-term *pattern* of working; and
- the forms of *choice and security*.

The options emphasize the manner in which many of the choices and policies have up to now revolved around working time to the exclusion of the other elements. Such a prospective shift also underlines the fact that work life flexibility is not just a female issue, but has ramifications across the whole of the workforce and their working careers. It also illustrates the different needs for flexibility which can arise at various times in the career cycle. The working lives of both men and women involve childcare arrangements and possibly wider caring responsibilities, for instance towards spouses and elderly relations. The shift also involves issues of skill renewal, lifelong learning and periods for self-development, as well as the need to vary work locations with partial or concentrated use of teleworking, and the possibility of career breaks and longer periods away for volunteering/charitable work.

Studies of the European context and the United Kingdom show a growth in corporate policies to facilitate better caring responsibilities, training and work arrangements (Bleijenburgh et al., 1999; Spencer and Taylor, 1994). They routinely offer choice for individual workers to tailor their working week through such arrangements as flexitime, job sharing, compressed working weeks and term-time only working. For employers, this form of flexibility in working practices can allow a better targeting of resources to meet peaks and troughs in service demand. It can promote higher quality services and products and result in better staff morale (see, DfEE, 2000b; Employers Organisation for Local Government, 1998). For the trade unions, it means concluding agreements on issues that make a qualitative difference to the work lives of their members and engaging with employers and other stakeholders on proactive rather than reactive issues. For all of the parties, the outcome offers a possible win-win situation, in which all the protagonists, rather than just one, stand to gain (TUC, 1998). One sector where pressure is mounting to enact such forms of positive flexibility is in local government. It is to this area, and to the Bristol City Council case in particular, that I now wish to turn.

The Public Sector Context

Much of the turbulence affecting the private manufacturing and service sectors is having an impact on the public sector. Indeed, additional demands by the government are hastening profound organizational and cultural changes in this sector. It has been necessary for the sector to achieve cost reductions, emulate private commercial practice and adopt a customer service orientation and an entrepreneurial culture, while at the same time being the subject of constant monitoring and review. The response from the Employers Organisation for Local Government (previously the Local Government Management Board) has been a root and branch reassessment of what this means for the future of work and flexibility in local authorities. This process first started in 1997 with the Single Status National Agreement which included, alongside the harmonization of terms and conditions, specific provisions for the development of a flexible approach to providing community services, reductions in working hours and the removal of inequalities originating from old gendered working patterns. It was left to the local level to agree on the introduction of flexible working practices, such as annualized hours, extended hours and other arrangements.

This employers' initiative is a clear illustration of the widening flexibility agenda, which needs to extend the scope of the issues covered, bring in new aims and objectives related to users and forge new partnerships with staff and trade unions to achieve all-round improvements. For the public sector, such a move towards partnership faces particular problems rooted in the institutions, traditions and organizational context of the sector. The legacy of Thatcherism, with its years of attacks on direct labour, the emphasis placed on subcontracting ploys and the weakening of collective agreements, has left a high level of trade union distrust. Local authorities face perennial problems of low staff morale as a result of having to deal with successive upheavals, while being provided with fewer resources to meet the new demands. Staff increasingly see themselves as being forced to work harder and more flexibly in order to meet externally set targets. This context is not helpful in strengthening the relationship between the major social actors and those seeking agreement and conflict resolution. The structure of local authorities, with their divisional composition and compartmentalized services, also breeds sectionalism and problems of inter-organizational cooperation. This makes it difficult to introduce enterprise-wide changes. The public sector may be fertile ground for experimentation, but it also has to overcome long-standing problems if innovative and positive flexibility policies are to be introduced (Bach et al., 1999).

However, the very scale and continual nature of change have brought the parties together in many organizations to consider how best to respond to the new environment. There is a growing body of cases in local authorities where the pressures for change are bringing about different forms of agreement, experimentation and partnership in the area of working life.

Bristol City Council: the *Time of our Working Lives* project

The *Time of our Working Lives* project in Bristol City Council was animated in large part by the social partners at the national level, in this case the TUC and the former Local Government Management Board (LGMB). (For a detailed account of the project, see Mortimer, 1999.) The TUC had a long-standing interest in developing examples of positive flexibility and had undertaken a number of studies with other European trade union federations. The former LGMB had, as noted above, committed itself to developing models of flexibility and was looking for examples that widened the meaning of flexibility to bring in the crucial element of the balance between work and life. The project sat alongside a set of existing and entrenched policy commitments to tackle the gender gap. For example, the Bristol City Council has an active equalities unit, an equalities action plan and a mentoring system to facilitate the promotion of women. It also has a woman's management network and a contact scheme that allows women who have taken maternity leave but not returned to their job to maintain employment contact with the Bristol City Council until the child reaches school age. As a public sector organization, it has the formal and political will to facilitate changes for disadvantaged workers. Furthermore, it proved to be open to dealing with the issue of flexibility in terms of a widened agenda that went beyond working time and equal opportunities into questions of working arrangements, work location, service enhancement and employee and community development. An examination of the process therefore gives a good indication of the spread of family friendly policies within a voluntaristic system.

The project commenced in 1998 and aimed to explore the inter-relationship between flexibility and the organization of social and working time. It was intended to study how *positive* flexibility could be achieved across the whole of the workforce, while at the same time enhancing equal opportunities. The project set itself the following aims:

- improvements in the quality of working time use and greater choice and control by employees over their working lives;
- the enhancement and improvement of access to work for women and men;
- the development of equal opportunities and family friendly policies, the key to which is an improved balance between work and life for both women and men;
- the creation of forms of partnership between the social partners which can lead to better and more sustainable forms of working relationships;
- an indication of how better, more inclusive and responsive forms of service can be achieved through such a reorganization; and
- the development of transnational exchanges for the documentation and transfer of good practice across Europe.

The project set out to identify areas in which new flexible working time initiatives could be introduced, as well as to benchmark the organization in terms of the existing working arrangements and their adequacy in relation to the caring responsibilities of the staff.

Developments in Flexibility

The project steering group oversaw the creation of subgroups in the two areas of leisure services and health and environmental services. Pilot projects were agreed upon in each of these areas. These have been followed by other divisional pilot sites where the actors have developed a plan based on the wishes of the managers and staff in those sectors. After running a number of open seminars, which drew on international and other local authority speakers, one concrete proposal for a *rolling* leave year is under serious consideration. Such a scheme would end the annual practice of a single cut-off date by which accrued leave and time off in lieu has to be taken. This would end the annual scramble to take leave which denudes many service departments and would give a degree of discretion and control back to the workforce as to when leave is taken. The outcomes of the first nine months of operation are described below.

Libraries

The library service has been running two projects from the beginning. One concerns the opening of the libraries on Sundays using volunteer staff. The six-month pilot project, which started in May 1999, has been running for over a year and looks like becoming a permanent addition to the central library opening hours.

The loan figures for Sundays in the central library demonstrate the success of the pilot scheme. These increased from 305 on the opening Sunday to a peak of 1,062 at the end of February 2000. The staffing of the central library has been provided by a combination of existing staff and temporary contract library assistants. Some weekday library assistants have been given extra experience by fulfilling supervisory roles on a Sunday. Additional opportunities have also been created for security staff.

A second initiative in the libraries service is the self-rostering project. This was agreed upon as a result of focus group meetings with the staff, who identified the disproportionate amount of time that managers spent working on rotas. One local group of five libraries was chosen as a pilot area after its staff expressed 100 per cent interest in participating in the pilot project. One senior library assistant and three library assistants now meet to timetable 23 staff in the libraries in the group. The team prepared over 10 weeks of time sheets and the process was being monitored, with a review due at the end of April 2000. In essence, the staff are taking more responsibility for their rotas. In doing so, they gain more control over their future work pattern, experience less friction with management, improve services to the public and enable time savings.

Health and Environmental Services

These services cover waste disposal, highway maintenance and cemeteries, as well as technical, scientific and trading services. The result is an heterogeneous workforce with very different work patterns and demands. As a result, six different service areas were identified as possible pilot areas. Of these, three were chosen with a view to experimenting with new forms of working patterns, including partial home-working for senior managerial staff. Home-working for one group was proposed in order to reduce traffic congestion and dead commuting time. The women members of the services are working on proposals for more extensive school term only working.

The pilot project achieved a number of its first targets during its initial period, including the establishment of teams and projects, the identification of definable outcomes and the improvement of services. Nevertheless, the improvements so far have been modest and have not been directly linked to women staff. The steering group believes that one of the key barriers to positive flexibility is the lack of commitment of male workers to the process. Two reviews of the process have been undertaken, one in August 1999, and most recently in April 2000. Both reviews emphasize the positive results, while the second review also sets out a plan for the future. In short, the proposals are to mainstream this work within the Bristol City Council and extend the working group which is leading the process. It is also planned to embed the principles and standards in a new three-year strategy to underpin future work on flexibility. In addition, a tool kit is being developed to assist departments and staff groups in the development of a flexible working approach building on the experience acquired to date.

Benchmarking

This part of the project has provided extensive data, some of which are shown below. A research questionnaire was sent by the author to every staff member in the Council asking them about their current working time arrangements, what was available to them and the particular arrangements they would in fact prefer. The survey asked for details about the working time, work location and other working arrangements of the staff and their preferences. A total of 2,173 responses were received, from 668 men and 1,475 women staff members. The main findings indicate that current flexible working is concentrated in two main areas: flexitime, where employees can vary the length of the working day within certain limits (53 per cent of staff reported using this system) and part-time work (reported by a little over 20 per cent of the staff).

When considered in gender terms, women appear to be more likely to take up options that give them greater flexibility in work than men, especially in relation to part-time work, term-time only working and job-share arrangements. However, men clearly seem to prefer flexitime, which has been taken up by 71 per cent of men, compared with 45 per cent of women.

Figure 13.1 Current working patterns

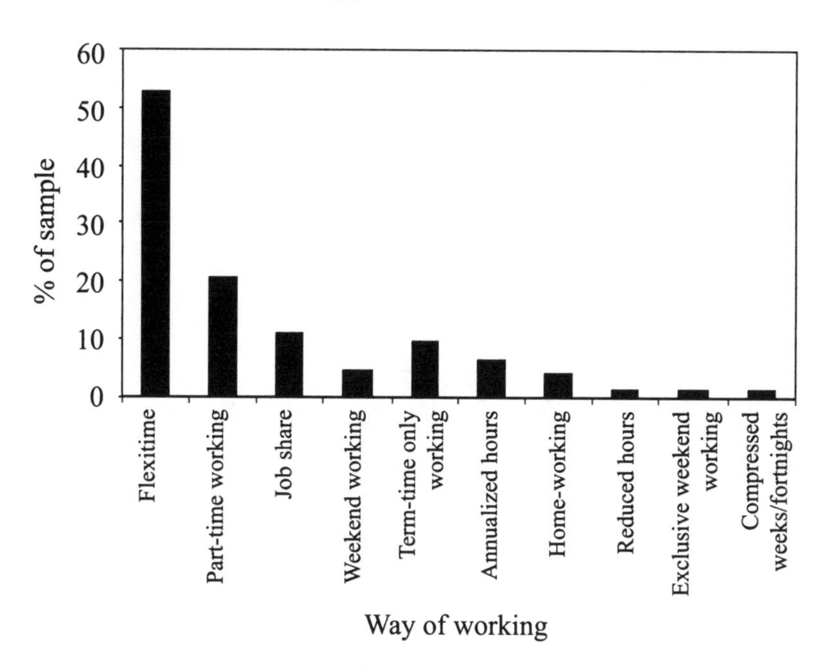

However, a substantial pool of workers would like to change their working patterns and work locations. In addition to the current popularity of flexitime, a high number of preferences were expressed for: home-working – 27 per cent of all those responding; compressed weeks or fortnights – 18 per cent; flexitime – 17 per cent; and flexible weekend working – 11 per cent. On the other hand, there was much less enthusiasm for exclusive weekend working, job sharing and for more part-time working (1, 3 and 5 per cent of those responding, respectively).

The overall pattern of working practices and preferences can be seen in Table 13.1. The important findings are that many women with caring responsibilities are already utilizing part-time work, job sharing and term-time only working much more frequently than their male colleagues. Of the staff already availing themselves of these three arrangements, some 91 per cent of part-time workers were found to be women and 88 per cent of all job-shares were occupied by women, who also accounted for 87 per cent of the staff members working term-time only arrangements. Male respondents showed little interest in part-time work, term-time only working and job sharing, and very few of them are currently making use of these arrangements. This pattern illustrates

Table 13.1 Preferences for flexible working practices

Working practice	Number preferring the option	Men No. (%)	Women No. (%)	Already working	Available
Home-working	573	221 (33%)	350 (24%)	91	475
Compressed week	387	176 (27%)	209 (14%)	30	47
Flexitime	371	103 (16%)	264 (18%)	1,148	266
Flexi weekend working	248	111 (17%)	137 (9%)	99	96
Annualized hours	225	93 (14%)	132 (9%)	135	25
Term-time working	219	39 (6%)	178 (12%)	213	63
Voluntary reduced hours	161	55 (8%)	105 (7%)	23	69
Part-time	110	28 (4%)	81 (6%)	442	206
Job sharing	96	22 (3%)	73 (5%)	231	475
Exclusive weekend working	24	13 (2%)	11 (1%)	24	13

Note: A total of 2173 responses received, 668 from men and 1475 from women.

the potential danger of women falling into the *mommy trap,* with their working arrangements putting them at a disadvantage vis-à-vis other workers. The result of a subsequent survey of women workers in these situations in Bristol City Council shows that many women on nonstandard contracts feel that they are not taken as seriously as full-time workers. They often miss out on information and decision-making opportunities. They find it difficult to attend vital meetings and engage in training. On the other hand, they consider that some practices, such as job sharing, constitute positive arrangements offering much needed support when taking on greater responsibilities at work. These practices are also seen as an essential bridging arrangement through which they can keep in touch with work prior to returning to full-time employment once their caring responsibilities diminish.

When examining preferences, they have to be judged against the background of these different working patterns. In this case, it appears that proportionately more men are looking for home-working (33 per cent) and compressed working time (27 per cent) than their women colleagues, with a substantial number of men indicating an interest in flexible weekend working, flexitime and annualized hours. In addition to their current arrangements, a further one-quarter of women also want some form of home-working, followed by more flexitime (18 per cent), compressed week working (14 per cent) and term-time only working (12 per cent).

Summary of Outcomes

The relative success of the flexibility project has still to be properly addressed, even though it has been awarded a silver medal in the British Diversity Awards. Analysis of the outcomes shows a number of important results. As indicated above, one of the key outcomes is that the process of social partnership has resulted in a constructive union-management problem-solving format. The two selected project areas, namely leisure services and health and environmental services, have created their own partnership groups in which trade unions and manage participate, and which have also benefited from assistance from the national social partners, as well as from external analytical support. In each case, they are developing concrete initiatives that are having a real impact and which already include:

- the development of a joint protocol on home-working for interested staff;
- the promotion and development of a scheme for Sunday opening in libraries, which is now in operation and uses staff who have volunteered to work on certain Sundays;
- the development of a system for self-managed shift rotas in a pilot library site; and
- an agreement on the introduction of a system for the more flexible use of annual leave.

The project has also developed a joint management and union training course, in collaboration with the TUC education service, to further define, increase awareness and develop knowledge of flexible working and its possibilities. The outcomes in this respect have been early drafts of a joint protocol on home-working and self-managed rostering for certain areas in the Council. A further outcome has been the development of a Council-wide newsletter and a series of seminars that have spread awareness of the benefits of positive flexibility throughout the Council. The project has provided opportunities to compare and discuss experience of national best practice and positive European ways of working. Staff have also been kept abreast of the project though information in their pay notifications. Finally, a database of actual and preferred working practices has been created and a subsequent survey has been undertaken in the Bristol City Council of the working time, caring responsibilities and preferred outcomes of all staff.

This demonstrates both the potential for and the obstacles to change in certain areas. The potential for partnership that builds upon and extends the formal joint consultative structure is very evident. However, the space and formats created are new and have given rise to suspicion by both management and trade unions concerning their sustainability. Similarly, the need for greater flexibility is constantly asserted, so that the workforce can gain substantive improvements in their situation and so that management can have the opportunity to achieve better service provision and delivery. Much work still needs to be done for the pilot projects to take root and flower. Nevertheless, in view of the mutual benefits that are on offer, the chances are that the pilot projects will be extended to other sections, even though the degree of dissonance to which they give rise means that progress will inevitably be slow.

Reflections

The context of any discussion of work life flexibility has changed significantly. Any such discussion now has to take into account the national and corporate drivers of change described above. This means that the issue of flexibility in working life is not simply about women taking on part-time work, or specific equal opportunities policies to redress elements of unfairness at the margin, but rather is an important mainstream area for social partner agreement that cuts across a range of issues at the company, industry, national and European levels.

As noted above, flexibility issues in enterprises have expanded beyond part-time working to encompass a wide range of topics, such as flexitime, compressed weeks and term-time working. These have in turn been further expanded in view of the opportunities to change working patterns and locations offered by new information technology, including teleworking, virtual organization formats and internet connection. A description has been provided of the manner in which one particular organization has dealt with partnership and work life flexibility. However, the case cited should not be allowed to obscure the fact that the scope for agreement at the level of the enterprise/organization is both enabled and constrained by external regulation, the economic context and the forms and traditions of social partnership. This emphasizes the crucial role of European directives, national reforms of laws and regulations and broader sectoral agreements.

While the prime issues of working time and work contracts remain and are subject to both general European regulation and specific enterprise agreement, it is increasingly being recognized that the achievement of a positively flexible labour market means looking seriously at supportive measures for workers to enable them to perform wider caring duties, including the provision of reliable childcare facilities which go beyond the current ad hoc arrangements, with a view to kick starting and sustaining training and learning for real adaptability, employability and mobility.

To take the issue of childcare as an example, there are startling differences between countries in the provision of state/municipal childcare facilities. In the United Kingdom, such services are patchy or nonexistent, while in some areas of Italy, for example, responsibilities and choices regarding childcare services are the result of political and social action beyond individual agencies and the enterprise. National social agreements, supplemented by tailored municipal arrangements, mean that in Modena, for instance, 100 per cent of families are assured of free preschool facilities for children aged three years and above and that, when two parents work, they can arrange for care over an extended period of the working day. The facilities are also good for younger children and it is claimed that one-third of children below the age of three are provided with places in kindergartens and crèches. The impact of these provisions on the labour market and its flexibility is enormous. At a stroke, they change the work-related opportunities, possibilities and decisions of *all* family members. They also have an important impact on employers and their working time strategies. As a direct result of the universal provision of childcare, twilight shifts and extended part-time hours are used much less in Italy than in the United Kingdom. When married couples with children benefit from extended childcare cover during the working day, their availability for work within those hours is guaranteed, thereby making special arrangements redundant. The other consequence is that a large number of the persons who opt for part-time work do so from choice, rather than being constrained to do so by a lack of ancillary facilities.

One statutory development in the Netherlands has also sought to tackle this issue. The recently enacted Working Time Act gives employees a right, in reasonable situations, to vary their working hours to accommodate personal circumstances. This offers men a chance to escape the long hours culture from which many suffer and to increase their involvement in family caring. It offers women the opportunity to tailor the working time of the whole household, and not merely their own, and therefore to include training, development and personal needs. The universal and statutory nature of this initiative makes non-standard hours a mainstream rather than a single gender issue, with the potential to counter the *mommy trap* mentioned above.

Experience from the TUC project *Time of our Working Lives* also suggests that supportive needs in areas beyond childcare are located at the level of the municipality. Both Italy and the Netherlands provide examples of the necessity for city-based dialogue and agreements on working time, care arrangements and working patterns. As Pillinger states, a number of these experiments aim to: 'create citizen-friendly cities by finding a balance between peoples' working hours, and their need for extended and citizen-friendly services' (Pillinger, 1999, p. 21).

This involves the traditional social partners engaging in discussions about working arrangements and multiple timetables in a city context, covering such issues as how and when public services are to be provided, how and when transport is available, the synchronization of shopping hours and the provision of care and education. It also presupposes an extended dialogue with actors in areas such as the municipality, transport providers, commerce and education with a view to tailoring timetables and allowing popular participation in their determination.

In a system such as the one in the United Kingdom, which is rooted in voluntarism, such a prospective change moves the debate beyond the enterprise as the sole focus for agreement through its recognition of the key role of supportive services and contexts. Furthermore, it widens the concept of social partnership, with dialogue being extended beyond the enterprise and into the wider community, where many working life and working time issues are in practice decided. Finally, it underlines the fact that the inequalities surrounding working time and working practices can only be dealt with seriously when deeper issues are addressed, thereby allowing a shift in male patterns of work, and when choices can be made uncluttered by sexual stereotyping.

Experience from other European countries indicates that *joined-up policies* are needed, based on new types of partnerships that are not confined to the enterprise-by-enterprise approach to collective bargaining. This means that a more strategic approach has to be adopted by the social partners which recognizes the wider context, the interconnections between actors and issues and the need for common solutions. Such a context would provide greater opportunities to pursue new and innovative agreements about working practices. While the United Kingdom may traditionally have pursued a voluntaristic approach and left it largely to the parties within organizations to conclude agreements, there are increasing signs that partnership agreements and joint approaches to positive working life flexibility are now being pursued.

References

Bach, S., Winchester, D., Bordogna, L. and Della Rocca, G. (1999), *Public Service Employment Relations in Europe: Transformations, modernization or inertia?*, Routledge, London.

Bleijenburgh, I., de Bruin, J. and Dickens, L. (1999), *Strengthening and Mainstreaming Equal Opportunities through Collective Bargaining*,

European Foundation for the Improvement of Living and Working Conditions, Dublin.
Brannen, J. and Moss, P. (1991), *Managing Mothers: Dual earner households after maternity leave*, Unwin-Hyman, London.
Department for Education and Employment (DfEE) (2000a), *Work-life Balance: Changing patterns in a changing world*, London.
DfEE (2000b), *Work-life Balance: The key facts*, http://www.dfee.gov.uk/work-lifebalance/kf.htm.
Department of Trade and Industry (DTI) (1998), *Fairness at Work* (White Paper), London.
DTI (2000), *Employment Relations Bill*, London.
Dex, S. and Scheibl, F. (1999), 'Business Performance and Family-friendly Policies', *Journal of General Management*, 24 (4).
Employers Organization for Local Government (1998), *Flexible Working: Working patterns in local authorities and the wider economy*, London.
European Commission (1998a), *Modernising the Organisation of Work: A positive approach to change*, Communication from the Commission (COM(98) 592), Brussels.
European Commission (1998b), *Employment Guidelines*, Brussels.
European Commission (1999), *Employment in Europe 1999*, Brussels.
European Foundation (2000), *Equal Opportunities, Collective Bargaining and the European Employment Strategy*, European Foundation for the Improvement of Living and Working Conditions, Dublin.
Forth, J., Lissenburgh, S., Callender, C. and Millward, N. (1996), *Family-friendly Working Arrangements in Britain*, DfEE Research Report No. 16, London.
Hall, M. (1999), *Labour's 'Family-friendly' Employment Agenda*, EIRO, http://www.eiro.eurofound.ie/1999/05/features/uk9905103f.html.
Jessop, B. (1994), 'Post Fordism and the State', in Amin, A. (ed.), *Post-Fordism*, Blackwell, Oxford.
Mortimer, J. (1997), *Managing the Flexible Workforce*, The Local Government Management Board, London.
Mortimer, J. (1999), *The Time of our Lives in Bristol: Developing positive flexibility for employees and services*, TUC, London.
Pillinger, J. (1998), *Working Time in Europe: A European working time policy in the public services*, European Federation of Public Service Unions, Brussels.
Pollert, A. (1991), *Farewell to Flexibility*, Blackwell, Oxford.

Spencer, L. and Taylor, S. (1994), *Participation and Progress in the Labour Market*, Department for Education and Employment, London.
Trades Union Congress (1998), *The Time of our Lives: A TUC report on working hours and flexibility*, London.
Walby, S. (1987), *Patriarchy at Work*, University of Minnesota Press.

Feature No. 6
Early and Later Retirement Simultaneously: the Trend of the Future?

Gerry J.B. Dietvorst

It would seem that the tendency of the Dutch government to encourage early retirement has come to an end. The government has been compelled to change its policy. The reasons for this change are the cost of early retirement and, most importantly, the fact that the pension burden will become too heavy in view of the rapid ageing of the population. All the Member States of the European Union will be facing this problem in the near future. The so-called baby boomers will reach the age of 65 around the year 2015 while, at the same time, the number of younger people will be declining.

Because supplementary occupational pension schemes in the Netherlands (the *second pillar*) are funded, in contrast with most other countries in the European Union, the problem of pensions becoming unpayable because of the rapid ageing of the population will cause less unrest in the Netherlands than, for instance, in France, Germany or Italy. In the latter countries, not only basic state pensions (the *first pillar*), but also supple-mentary occupational pensions (the *second pillar*) are financed on the pay-as-you-go system. Demographic development is the time-bomb under the European Union. Member States that finance *second pillar* occupational pensions on the basis of the pay-as-you-go system will have to take action in the short term. They will have to turn to a system in which supplementary occupational pensions are funded. This will require a long transition period. It is therefore right that emerging pension problems should be taken up by the European Commission.

To clear the way for younger workers on the labour market in the Netherlands, the so-called VUT schemes were introduced about 30 years ago. VUT schemes are intended to encourage early retirement by employees on a voluntary basis (see also Pennings, Chapter Eleven). They were created to promote employment. In recent years, VUT schemes have been transformed into early retirement schemes. It is noteworthy that the Dutch legislator is phasing out fiscal incentives for early retirement over the next few years. Employees who wish to retire before the regular retirement age will have to take action on their own account. They could, for instance, buy a life annuity. In this way, the cost of pensions is transferred to the employee. This is in line with the policy of the Dutch Government that the pension burden borne by employers has to decrease and pension schemes have to become increasingly prudent or, in other words, cheaper for employers.

On the other hand, many employers will need a sound age distribution among their staff. It is not wise for a company to employ only ambitious and angry young workers, or only older workers. Most companies would prefer to have a workforce composed of all age categories. Older workers have more experience than their younger colleagues, and are familiar with the company and the corporate culture. They can also guide and train younger staff members.

It is important for employers' policies to be focused on organizing the jobs of older employees as well as possible. Clearly, this has everything to do with stress at work, the length of the working day and the need to slow down work for older employees. I believe that it is in the interests of employers, as well as employees, for workers to stay in the labour force as long as possible.

Part-time old-age pensions combined with part-time jobs will be a key issue over the coming decades. Pension schemes will have to support this trend and facilitate partial early retirement. In the case of a part-time pension combined with a part-time job, workers will receive an old-age pension for one, two or three days a week. For the other days, they will receive their salary. A compulsory retirement age is no longer suited to the needs of society. Workers should retire on the basis of a sliding scale and should no longer be confronted with an abrupt and sudden transition to retirement and doing nothing. In this way, they will work both longer and shorter at the same time. The European Commission, as well as Member States, will have to take legal measures to stimulate and facilitate this development, of which an integral feature will be the possibility to opt for early or later retirement under the state pension.

Chapter Fourteen

Older Workers and Active Labour Market Policy in a Full Employment Economy: the Case of the United States

Peter B. Doeringer, Andrew Sum and David G. Terkla

The United States economy has been marked by low unemployment since the mid-1990s, with unemployment rates recently falling to about 4 per cent nationally and to 3 per cent or less in New England and the Midwest farm belt. Almost all prime age males between 25 and 44 years of age are at work or in school and traditional labour reserves, such as married women, are nearly exhausted. Immigration quotas, despite recent and projected increases, are also insufficient to meet the demand for new workers. These tight labour markets are leading to rising real wages and reports by employers of labour scarcities are growing.

The only labour reserve of sufficient size to meet this growing labour scarcity over the coming decade is older workers. The older population (between the ages of 45 and 69) has been increasing rapidly since the early 1990s and will do so at an accelerated pace over the coming decade. Its overall share of the working age population will rise from 30 per cent in 1995 to 39 per cent by 2010 as the baby boom generation enters its 50s and 60s. Improved health has increased the expected life span of the older population by 25 per cent since 1950, which means that older persons can have both longer working lives and more years for their retirement.

Even this rapid growth in the older population, however, will be inadequate to meet the full growth potential of the economy because of changes in the labour supply and the retirement behaviour of older males. While the labour force participation rate of older women (between the ages of 45 and 69) increased from 43 per cent in 1970 to 61 per cent in 1999, that of older men has been declining (from 81 per cent in 1970 to

74 per cent in 1999). The retirement ages of men are dropping, with only two-thirds of men still active in the labour force at the age of 60, while older workers are also switching from full-time to part-time employment at a higher rate than ever before.

Whether and how the labour reserve of older workers can best be tapped is a matter of some debate. The convention among economists is to explain trends in labour supply through the interaction of *income* and *substitution* effects. Rising real wages provide an incentive for older persons to participate more actively in the labour market (substitution effects), while rising earnings, pension incomes and disability payments induce workers to leave the labour force (income effects).

There is a vast literature demonstrating the effects of social security benefits on the rate and timing of withdrawal from the labour market, and on the annual hours worked by older workers (Burtless and Moffitt, 1984; Fields and Mitchell, 1984; Friedberg, 1999). A similar conclusion has been reached for European countries, such as Belgium, France, Italy and the Netherlands, where the social security systems tax continued work heavily (Gruber and Wise, 1999).

The labour supply effects of pensions provided by private employers are stressed in another strand of retirement literature (Burkhauser, Couch and Phillips, 1996; Brown, 1996; Turner and Watanabe, 1995; James, 1997; Fields and Mitchell, 1984; Lumsdaine and Mitchell, 1999). Because workers can become eligible for private pension benefits as early as 50 years of age, and more typically by the age of 55, private pensions can have an earlier influence on labour supply than social security retirement benefits, for which workers are not eligible until the age of 62 (Burkhauser, Couch and Phillips, 1996). These traditional retirement incentives are often reinforced by the addition of early retirement incentives, particularly in companies that are downsizing (Brown, 1996). Moreover, the amount of an individual's private pension benefit is often far larger than the social security benefit, which has lead some studies to conclude that private pension provision has a much stronger overall influence on retirement decisions than social security benefits.

Similarly, there are studies showing that the combination of high marginal tax rates and the diminished income needs of workers nearing retirement can encourage workers under 70 years of age who are receiving social security benefits to favour part-time over full-time employment (Quinn, 1999). The attractiveness of retirement, with or without part-time employment, is also confirmed by a recent Harris poll showing that 44 per cent of persons aged 65 and older regard their retirement 'as the best years of their lives', compared to only 32 per cent in 1974 (National Council on Aging, 2000).

One factor offsetting the income effects of pensions arises from the improvements in real wages among some groups of older workers, which can cause workers to substitute work for retirement. Real weekly earnings have risen substantially over the past two decades for older women workers, but much more modestly for men aged between 55 and 64. However, older workers with labour market disadvantages have experienced a decline in real wages and the overall pattern for older men has been of stagnant real weekly earnings.

The rising real wages of women are providing a net incentive for more older women to work for more hours per year than ever before. Conversely, the net effect of pension incomes and retirement incentives, coupled with smaller gains and even some losses in real wages, is to encourage older men to retire earlier. These same net income effects may also account for the increasing shift from full-time to part-time jobs.

The policies that typically flow from these analyses are that retirement can be deferred and the labour supply increased by reducing or postponing pension benefits and reducing the implicit taxes on the income earned by recipients of social security benefits. This emphasis on the *income effect* of pensions and the adverse substitution effects of taxes on labour supply tends, however, to neglect the possibility of other types of work disincentives which may affect older workers. For example, obsolete skills, corporate downsizing or age discrimination may limit the wages and employment opportunities of older workers, causing an adverse net substitution effect and leading workers to reduce their hours or retire prematurely from the labour force.[1]

Despite this emphasis on pensions and retirement, recent research suggests that factors other than pensions may have a far greater impact on the labour market and retirement behaviour of older workers (Anderson, Gustman and Steinmeier, 1999). Moreover, the importance of the income effects of pension benefits is also likely to diminish in the future as the benefit tax on continued work by persons aged between 65 and 70 is eliminated and the age of eligibility for social security benefits is gradually raised. In addition, there has been a recent movement away from traditional private pensions, which provide defined benefits that are not adjusted for delayed retirement, towards *defined contribution* (‘*401K*’) plans that are actuarially more neutral with respect to retirement.

This chapter seeks to shift the focus of policy discussions about older workers from issues of the adverse income effects of pensions and taxes towards the positive contribution of the substitution effects of high wages and attractive employment opportunities. Strengthening work incentives in the job market for older workers can simultaneously extend their working lives, help to alleviate labour scarcities and decrease economic hardship for older workers. Tapping reserves of older workers can also promote national economic growth and contribute to reducing the financial problems of underfunded social security systems.

While these are national issues, for which national evidence is reviewed, the active labour market policies needed to expand the supply of older workers and reduce labour scarcities have to be implemented at the state and local levels. The example of older workers and labour market policies in Massachusetts is therefore used to illustrate the more general policy issues surrounding the role of older workers in a full employment economy.

1 National Trends in the Labour Market for Older Workers

The movement of the baby boom generation into their late 40s and 50s is substantially altering the size of the national population of older workers (between the ages of 45 and 69) and will continue to do so throughout the current decade.[2] Between 1995 and 2010, the nation’s population of working age (16 years and older) is projected to increase from 201.2 million to 233.8 million, a rise of 32.6 million or 16 per cent. Over the same period, however, the number of 45–69 year olds is projected to rise by 28.8 million or 46 per cent, a growth rate nearly three times faster than the growth of the entire working age population. As a result, the population of older workers will increase its share of the working age population from slightly under 31 per cent in 1995 to nearly 39 per cent in 2010, the highest such proportion in the history of the United States.[3]

The population of older workers will account for nearly all (almost 90 per cent) of the net growth in the nation’s working age population over the period 1995–2010, thereby radically reversing trends in earlier decades.[4] Whether or not the ageing baby boomer generation actually transforms the United States into a new *gerontocracy*, in which economic and political power is held by the older population (Dychtwald, 1999), it is clear that there will be a radical transformation in the demographic structure of the population and the workforce in the coming decade.

1.1 The Older Workforce

The impact of the growing population of older workers on the size and age structure of the nation's civilian labour force in the coming decade will depend critically on the labour force participation behaviour of older men and women. Over the past 30 years, there has been a decline in the labour force participation rates of most subgroups of older men in the United States, although there has been a stabilization in the labour force participation rate of men aged between 55 and 64 years and a modest increase in those aged 65–69 over the past decade (Table 14.1). In 1999, the labour force participation rate of men aged 45–54 was nearly four percentage points below its 1970 level, while the participation rate of men aged 55–69 was 10–13 per cent below the level in 1970. A growing proportion of the older male population has been withdrawing from labour market well before the *normal* retirement age of 65. Over the past two years, only 83 out of every 100 men were in the labour force at the age of 55 (Table 14.2). This figure falls to 68 by the age of 60, and to 41 by the age of 64.

The decline in the labour force attachment of older men (aged 45–64) in the United States over the past two decades has disproportionately affected those with the lowest educational levels. Generally, older men who lack a high school diploma and those who only graduated from high school have exhibited the greatest declines in their labour force participation rates as their real wages and work incentives have declined (Welch, 1997).

The overall impact of this decline in the labour force attachment of older men on the size of the older male labour force is considerable. If the 1999 labour force participation rates for older men had remained at their 1970 levels, there would have been 2.46 million more older men in the civilian labour force in 1999. This is equivalent to an increase of 10 per cent in the older male labour force and to 3.3 per cent in the entire male labour force.[5] Similarly, if the same proportion of older men were employed in full-time jobs as in 1970, the total hours worked by older men would rise by at least 3 per cent.

In contrast to the labour force behaviour of older men, over the past 30 years older women have substantially increased their attachment to the labour force, with gains accelerating during the 1990s (Table 14.1). By 1999, nearly 77 out of every 100 women aged 45–54 were active in the labour force, compared with only 52 in 1970. Among women aged 55–64, nearly 52 out of every 100 were working or looking for work in 1999, a gain of nearly 10 percentage points since 1970. However, the differences in the labour force participation rates of older women with different levels of educational attainment are slightly more pronounced than for older men. Depending on age, there is a difference of 27–31 percentage points in the labour force participation rates of women high school drop-outs compared to women with college degrees (1998–99).

Table 14.1 Trends in civilian labour force participation rates of 45–54, 55–64 and 65–69 year old men and women, US: selected years, 1970 to 1999 (per cent)

	Age group					
	(A) 45–54		(B) 55–64		(C) 65–69	
Year	**Men**	**Women**	**Men**	**Women**	**Men**	**Women**
1970	92.4	52.5	80.5	42.0	38.9	17.2
1979	91.4	58.4	73.0	41.9	29.6	15.3
1989	91.1	70.5	67.2	45.0	26.1	16.4
1992	90.8	72.7	67.0	46.6	25.9	16.2
1997	89.5	76.0	67.6	50.9	28.4	17.6
1999	88.8	76.7	67.9	51.5	28.5	18.4
Change 1970–99	-3.6	+24.2	-12.6	+9.5	-10.4	+1.2
Change 1989–99	-2.3	+6.2	+.7	+6.5	+2.4	+2.0

Sources: 1970 Census of Population and Housing, United States Bureau of Labor Statistics, *Employment and Earnings*, January 1980, January 1990, January 1993, January 1998 and January 2000.

These increases in labour force participation rates are consistent with the strong gains observed in the real earnings of older women. Between 1979 and 1999, the median real weekly earnings of women in full-time employment aged 45–54 and 55–64 increased by 24 and 16 per cent respectively, in contrast to the declines in real weekly earnings

Table 14.2 Percentage of the older worker population in the civilian labour force at various ages, total and by gender and educational attainment: 1998–99, US averages

Age	(A) All	(B) Men	(C) Women	(D) <12 years	(E) 12 years	(F) 13–15 years	(G) 16 or over
45	85.3	92.0	79.0	70.2	82.9	87.7	91.5
50	82.4	88.9	76.2	62.8	78.3	85.5	90.7
55	74.7	82.7	67.0	56.2	73.0	77.7	84.5
60	58.1	68.3	49.0	44.2	56.3	62.2	71.0
62	45.8	53.5	38.7	30.2	44.3	50.5	61.3
64	34.7	41.2	29.0	25.4	32.4	38.7	46.7
65	29.2	35.8	23.4	20.9	26.4	32.3	42.6
70	16.1	21.0	12.2	12.3	14.5	18.3	24.6

Sources: January 1998 to December 1999, Current Population Survey (CPS) public use tapes, tabulations by Center for Labor Market Studies, Northeastern University.

experienced by their male counterparts (US Bureau of Labor Statistics, 1979 and 1999). Similar trends in earnings and labour force participation rates can also be seen for younger age groups.

1.2 The Projected Size of the Labour Force of Older Workers

Over the decade 1998–2008, the US Bureau of Labor Statistics estimates that the labour force participation rate of men aged 45–54 will be basically unchanged (a decline of 0.4 per cent), while there will be a modest increase for men in the 55–64 and 65–74 age groups (Table 14.3). The recent adoption by Congress of legislation eliminating the social security earnings penalty tax on persons age 65–69, combined with very strong labour market conditions, may further increase the labour force participation rates of men in their late 60s. Much larger increases in labour force participation rates are projected for older women, with particularly strong gains for women in the 45–54 and 55–64 age groups. By 2008, some 80 per cent of women aged 45–54 are expected to be active in the labour force, a participation rate that is within 9 per cent of that of older men. The combined effects of the very

Table 14.3 Projected trends in the civilian labour force participation rates of older men and women in selected age groups: US, 1998 to 2008 (%)

Gender/ age group	(A) 1998	(B) 2008	(C) Percentage change 1998–2008
Men			
45–54	89.2	88.8	-0.4
55–64	68.1	69.4	+1.3
65–74	22.6	25.5	+2.9
Women			
45–54	76.2	80.0	+3.8
55–64	51.2	57.7	+6.5
65–74	13.7	14.8	+1.1

Source: Fullerton, 1999.

high growth rates in the population of older workers and the projected increases in labour force participation rates mean that workers aged 45–74 will account for nearly all the growth in the civilian labour force between 1998 and 2008.

2 Labour Market Problems of Older Workers

Many older workers have fared well in the labour market over the past decade in comparison with their younger counterparts. On average, older workers have higher earnings, greater job security and lower unemployment rates than younger workers.[6] Nevertheless, older workers with relatively little education, those who are displaced from their jobs and those facing race or gender discrimination routinely experience a variety of labour market problems, including long spells of unemployment, chronic underemployment, hidden unemployment and low earnings.[7]

Despite seven years of strong job growth, unemployed older workers in 1999 averaged 17 to 20 weeks of unemployment, compared with 9 to 11 weeks for younger unemployed workers. Similarly, two decades of special studies of dislocated workers by the Bureau of Labor Statistics have consistently confirmed the greater difficulties faced by older workers in regaining employment. The most recent survey conducted in February 2000 found that only 56 per cent of older workers displaced from their jobs over the previous three years (1997–99) had been able to obtain replacement jobs, compared with an 80 per cent re-employment rate for younger displaced workers in the 25–54 age category (Table 14.4).

Table 14.4 Percentage distribution of dislocated workers by their labour force status at the time of the February 1996 and February 2000 dislocated worker surveys, by age group

Year of survey/age group	(A) Employed	(B) Unemployed	(C) Not active in labour force
February 1996			
20–24	71.3	17.9	10.7
25–54	78.5	12.0	9.5
55–64	52.1	16.6	31.3
65+	31.6	4.1	64.3
February 2000			
20–24	87.7	3.7	8.7
25–54	79.5	10.3	10.2
55–64	56.0	13.6	30.4
65+	26.3	5.2	68.6

Sources: US Bureau of Labor Statistics, press releases on findings from the February 1996 and February 2000 dislocated worker surveys.

A second labour market problem faced by older workers is that of hidden unemployment among persons who wish to be employed, but are not actively looking for work.[8] The estimated average number of older persons (aged 45 and over) who are among the hidden unemployed each month is 1.281 million, or 3 per cent of all older persons (aged 45 and over) who were not actively participating in the civilian labour force in 1998 and 1999 (Table 14.5).[9] Such hidden unemployment is a particular problem among displaced workers. The latest dislocated worker survey shows that 30 per cent of displaced older workers had withdrawn from the labour force, a rate that is three times higher than for persons aged 25–54 years.

Table 14.5 Older persons (aged 45 and over) not active in the labour force but who wanted a job, by age group, US

Age group	(A) Number wanting a job now	(B) % of not active persons
45+	1,280,834	2.9
45–54	485,108	7.9
55–64	375,554	4.1
65+	420,172	1.5

Sources: January 1998 to December 1999, CPS surveys, tabulations by Center for Labor Market Studies, Northeastern University.

A third problem is involuntary part-time employment. Approximately 16 per cent of employed men between the ages of 45 and 69, and 31 per cent of employed older women work part time, a proportion that has increased steadily since the early 1970s.[10] While a substantial majority of older part-time workers report that they are working part-time out of personal choice, between 6 and 8 per cent of the part-time workers aged 55 and above have been classified as working part-time over the past four years because they cannot find full-time work, or because of cutbacks in their customary hours (Table 14.6).[11] The proportion of older part-time employed persons who involuntarily work part-time tends to be higher among those aged under 55, among men and among those with a lower educational level.[12]

Table 14.6 Percentage of part-time employed older workers (aged 55+) who were working part-time for economic reasons, total and by gender: US, 1996, 1998, 1999 (annual averages)

Gender groups	(A) 1996	(B) 1998	(C) 1999
Both sexes	8.1	6.6	6.2
Men	9.1	7.3	7.0
Women	7.4	6.1	5.6

Sources: US Bureau of Labor Statistics, *Employment and Earnings*, January 1997, January 1999 and January 2000.

A fourth labour market problem encountered by older workers is that of low weekly earnings, even when they are employed full time. Between March 1998 and March 1999, the estimated number of full-time employed older persons (aged 45–69) with weekly earnings below the four-person poverty line was equal to 4.144 million, or nearly 13 per cent of all older full-time employed persons.[13] The incidence of low wage problems among older full-time employed persons tends to vary quite widely by educational attainment, as well as by age, with older full-time employed persons being more likely to occupy low wage jobs.

The incidence of these four labour market problems, namely unemployment, hidden unemployment, involuntary part-time employment and full-time employment at weekly wages below the four-person poverty line, can be used to define a universe of older workers in need of employment and training services.[14] On average, some 7.6 million persons between the ages of 45 and 69 experienced one or more of these labour market problems in 1998–99 (Table 14.7). These include 1.35 million unemployed, 1.03 million hidden unemployed, 1.07 million underemployed[15] and 4.14 million full-time employed persons earning less than $320 a week.

This group of older adults with labour market problems is equal to one-sixth of the labour force aged between 45 and 69 years. The combined incidence of such problems is higher among those aged 55 and older than in the 45–54 age group, higher among women then men (21 per cent, compared with 13 per cent) and substantially higher among the poor and near poor (47 per cent), compared with labour force participants with family incomes two or more times above the poverty line. Even in the full employment economy of the late 1990s, there remains a considerable pool of unutilized and underutilized older workers who represent both a potential labour reserve and a serious social concern.

3 Lessons from Massachusetts

The preceding description of the labour market of older worker demonstrates both the growing importance of older workers to the economy and the magnitude of their employment difficulties, even in a full employment economy. However, the considerable regional variations in labour markets makes it easier to review the issues surrounding older

Table 14.7 Estimated numbers of older persons (aged 45–69) experiencing labour market problems (average March 1998–March 1999) (millions)

Age group	(A) Adjusted civilian labour force	(B) Unemployed	(C) Employed part-time for economic reasons	(D) Labour force reserve	(E) Work full-time at poverty wages	(F) Total B to E	(G) Total as % of adjusted labour force*
45–69	45.250	1.348	1.068	1.031	4.143	7.591	16.8
45–54	29.067	0.840	0.679	0.495	2.573	4.588	15.8
55–69	16.183	0.508	0.389	0.536	1.570	3.003	18.6

Note

* Official labour force statistics exclude members of the labour force reserve. The adjusted labour force includes the employed, the unemployed and members of the labour force reserve.

Sources: March 1998 and March 1999 CPS surveys, tabulations by Center for Labor Market Studies, Northeastern University.

workers in a full employment economy by examining specific regional labour markets in the United States.

Massachusetts is in many respects an ideal state for the exploration of these issues. It has a diversified economy, a workforce that is on average well educated and a substantial number of disadvantaged workers and recent immigrants who face employment problems, while its active labour market policies are ranked among the best in the nation. Massachusetts is also at the leading edge of the full employment economy in the United States, with its unemployment rate having fallen from a high of nearly 9 per cent during the severe regional recession in the early 1990s to below 3 per cent today. Its population is also ageing at a faster rate than most states, and it will therefore be a bell-wether for at least eight other states in the Northeast and Midwest which will experience even more rapid ageing in the coming decade.

3.1 Full Employment and Older Workers in Massachusetts

Even though the Massachusetts economy has reached the level of full employment and is experiencing labour scarcities, employment projections show that further job growth of over 1.1 per cent a year could be achieved if there were no labour supply constraints. However, even the most optimistic workforce projections show that only one-third to one half of that job growth can be realized under reasonable assumptions about future population growth and labour supply behaviour. Massachusetts will need at least 217,000 more workers by 2006, or about 7 per cent of its current workforce, if it is to achieve its full growth potential. This labour supply gap could rise to as high as 268,000 if labour force participation rates do not increase over their 1995 levels (Doeringer, Sum and Terkla, 2000).[16] Furthermore, these projections understate the shrinkage in the labour supply of older males because they do not reflect the decline in the hours worked or the doubling of the proportion of older males who have been in part-time employment since 1970. If the share of the older population in full-time jobs in 1970 had not fallen, Massachusetts would currently have over 120,000 additional older men working in full-time jobs, or almost 30 per cent more than were actually employed full time in 1996–97. If left uncorrected, this shortfall in labour supply is likely to choke off growth, either by creating bottlenecks of critical skills or by raising the costs of doing business in Massachusetts as employers compete for scarce labour.

3.2 Options for Closing the Labour Supply Gap

Massachusetts has few alternatives, other than its ageing workforce, to close the projected gap in the labour supply. Its pool of younger workers (aged 25–39), and especially those with college degrees, is nearly fully employed, with unemployment rates in this age group of between 1 and 2 per cent for holders of bachelors' degrees. Massachusetts already ranks among the top 12 states in terms of the participation of women in the labour force, leaving only a small margin for further growth. Attracting more young workers to the state or expanding the supply of younger married women workers is likely to be quite difficult and would raise the costs of doing business in Massachusetts (Sum et al., 1998). A substantial increase in the supply of foreign immigrants is also unlikely. Massachusetts already ranks fifth highest in the nation in its reliance on immigrants for its labour force growth (Center for Labor Market Studies, 1999), and annual immigration quotas for skilled workers are considerably oversubscribed.

As is the case nationally, the older worker population represents Massachusetts' largest known labour reserve. The number of older persons between the ages of 45 and 69 in the state's population began rising in the 1990s, after remaining stable for two decades. This trend will accelerate over the current decade. Barring unforeseen events, all of the net growth in the Massachusetts labour supply up to 2006 will come from persons aged 45 and older, with these older workers expected to account for an all-time high of at least two out of five workers by 2010.

Enhanced employment prospects and rising wages have helped to tap the labour reserve of older women, whose labour force participation rates have risen from 51 per cent in 1970 to 61 per cent in 1996–97. In contrast, the older male workforce has experienced only modest gains in real earnings (20 per cent) over the past two decades. The older male labour force participation rate in Massachusetts, which was once among the highest in the nation, has fallen from 84 per cent in 1970 to 74 per cent in 1996–97, with Massachusetts now ranking about 22nd among the states in this respect. This means that there are 74,000 fewer older male workers in the state than there would have been if their labour force participation rates had not fallen.

If the projected labour supply gap in Massachusetts is to be reduced through better utilization of the older workforce, a substantial increase of 6 or 7 per cent will be required in the projected labour force participation rates of the older population. A much higher proportion of older persons will have to remain at work in Massachusetts than has been the case in recent years, more and better jobs will have to be found for those who are unemployed and underemployed, while some of those currently outside the labour force will need to return to work.

There are three relatively distinct groups within the labour reserve of older workers, each of which offers somewhat different prospects as a source of additional labour. One fits the conventional economic stereotype of retired workers whose real wage incentives are not strong enough to offset the income effects of pensions, particularly in the case of those who combine social security benefits with income from private pensions and from assets. People in this group are relatively well educated and have marketable skills, but they also have less need of earned income and are more likely to be highly satisfied with retirement. Encouraging this comfortably retired group of older workers to return to the labour market will require sufficient training and other employment services to raise their wages to a level which can offset the income effects of pensions and their satisfaction with the quality of their lives as retirees.

A second reserve of older workers consists of those who have been displaced from their career jobs. Most of these workers have considerable recent work experience, were strongly attached to the labour market until they lost their jobs and are likely to remain in the labour market full time if they can become re-employed at their previous levels of wages and earnings.

The main labour market problem for these older dislocated workers is the mismatch between their existing education and skills and those required for the available job opportunities. Although full employment in Massachusetts is improving their re-employment and replacement wage prospects, one continuing result of labour market mismatches is that they would earn lower wages and would have weaker incentives to return to work.[17] These displaced older workers represent a high potential labour reserve, provided that they receive sufficient training to prepare them for jobs that are comparable to those they have lost.

The most important challenge for workforce development policies, however, is to improve the employability of the third group, namely those older workers who only have a low level of education, low earnings and little or no private pension income. With the exception of their human capital disadvantages, the members of this group constitute an excellent source of labour because the work incentives to be derived from reversing the substantial declines in real wages that they have experienced since the 1970s are likely to be relatively strong, while the income effects of pensions and assets are relatively weak. In view of the lengthening of potential working lives, substantial investments in improving the education and training of these disadvantaged older workers can be expected to have a greater pay-off than in the past.

3.3 Labour Market Mismatches

Tapping the potential of older workers to close the labour supply gap in Massachusetts is not only a matter of increasing the number of older workers in the labour force. There are also a number of major mismatches between the educational levels and skills of older unemployed and underemployed persons and those required in emerging higher wage jobs. This mismatch is most severe among poor older workers.

One set of mismatches involves education. Almost half of all new jobs in Massachusetts will require a bachelor's degree or higher (Massachusetts DET, 1999). Although older workers have more education and skills than ever before, on average they fall short of the educational requirements of most high growth occupations. For example, only 30 per cent of workers aged 55–65 in Massachusetts have a bachelor's or higher degree, and over one quarter of all unemployed older workers lack a high school degree. Many older workers have also acquired skills and experience in manufacturing occupations and other industries that are expected to be shedding labour. These out-of-date skills are a significant barrier to employment (Wagner and Bonham, 1998).

3.4 The Special Problems of those Left Behind

One-in-five unemployed, underemployed and discouraged older workers in Massachusetts during the mid- to late-1990s were members of low-income families (defined as having incomes below 125 per cent of the US poverty line). Typically, these workers have a limited education, few skills and other labour market disadvantages, such as poor fluency in English, patchy work experience and physical disabilities. Moreover, they may be subject to various forms of discrimination. The unemployment rates of older workers with less than a high school degree are double the average for all older workers, and their rates of labour force participation have declined since 1970 (Doeringer, Sum and Terkla, 2000, Research Brief No. 21). Older male workers lacking high school diplomas have experienced a near 30 per cent decline in their real annual earnings since 1979, while older women without high school diplomas earned less in real terms in the mid-1990s than they did in 1979 (Doeringer, Sum and Terkla, 2000, Research Report No. 13). The failure of educationally disadvantaged and displaced older workers to benefit from the booming economy has widened inequality and increased rates of poverty and income inadequacy among older persons in Massachusetts (Doeringer, Sum and Terkla, 2000, Research Report No. 11).

4 Labour Market Policy in Massachusetts

Massachusetts offers a diverse array of employment and training programmes to address labour market skill mismatches and the employment and training needs of older workers, which are typical of those available nationally. Most of the short-term occupational training programmes have been operated under the Job Training Partnership Act (JTPA), which is being replaced by the new Workforce Investment Act (WIA). There are also basic education programmes for adults, which provide instruction in literacy and basic skills up to the high school level, as well as a community college system that offers both basic education and advanced skills training. Subsidized part-time work experience opportunities are available for low-income persons aged 55 and over through the Senior Community Service Employment Program (SCSEP).

4.1 Policy Limitations

Through a combination of short-term training programmes, training for displaced workers and supported community work, Massachusetts has only had the resources to serve approximately one in 100 of the total number of older persons who are eligible for assistance under such programmes (Doeringer, Sum and Terkla, 2000, Research Report No. 12). Most federal job training programmes that were reserved specifically for older workers are being phased out and older workers are under-represented in many of the programmes that remain. This is especially true of JTPA Title IIA programmes for economically disadvantaged adults.

Because of inadequate resources, these programmes have emphasized job placement and short-term training over upgrading skills or raising wages. There has been too little investment in long-term education and training, which are the only kinds of programmes that have consistently resulted in meaningful economic improvement for workers. Programme linkages with employers and unions have been weak, and too little attention has been paid to using labour market policy to reduce labour scarcities and assist economic growth.

In addition to resource problems and the lack of bridges to the workplace, active labour market policy in Massachusetts (and nationally) has been hampered by a patchwork of federal and state programmes, funded under many different statutory authorizations. These programmes operate with a large measure of independence from one another, often suffer from inconsistent eligibility requirements that make it difficult to assemble sensible training sequences, and their performance accountability is inadequate. Although the needs of the participants in these different programmes overlap considerably, there is no single entity responsible for coordinating all of the programmes.

With the exception of JTPA programmes, no systematic evaluations have been carried out of post-programme outcomes. Moreover, most JTPA performance data cover only the first 90 days of post-training labour market experience. It is therefore impossible to compare the short-term performance of many of the components of the employment and training system, while there is no information on the long-term effectiveness of any of the programmes.

However, the limited data available concerning JTPA programmes show that the short-term outcomes for older participants in Massachusetts compare very favourably with those of older workers nationally (Table 14.8). For example, approximately 70 per cent (compared with 62 per cent nationally) of all older persons completing Massachusetts JTPA Title IIA programmes in 1996 were able to obtain employment upon leaving the programme. The employment rate for older Title III participants was also higher in Massachusetts than nationally (72 per cent compared with 68 per cent). Similarly, the wages received by older workers following training programmes have consistently and substantially exceeded those recorded at the national level.

Some of the most detailed data on programme impact are available

Table 14.8 Selected employment and wage outcomes for older persons (aged 45-69) completing JTPA Title IIA, Title III and section 204(d) programmes (1996)

Programme	(A) US	(B) Massachusetts
Employment rate		
JTPA IIA	62.3	70.3
JTPA III	67.9	71.7
Section 204 (d)	62.5	69.7
Median hourly wage		
JTPA IIA	$7.00	$8.25
JTPA III	$9.37	$11.20
Section 204 (d)	$6.00	$8.00
Mean hourly wage		
JTPA IIA	$7.73	$8.75
JTPA III	$11.47	$15.36
Section 204 (d)	$6.87	$8.75

Sources: Program year 1996, Standardized Program Information Reporting System, tabulations by the Center for Labor Market Studies.

for JTPA Title III programmes, which are among the best training programmes for older workers in Massachusetts. One key outcome for displaced workers is the replacement wage, or the percentage of their previous hourly wage that programme graduates receive upon re-employment. Over the past few years, the median wage replacement rate for older workers in Massachusetts has been relatively high, ranging from 84 per cent in 1993 to 91 per cent in 1996, and is 6 per cent or more above the national average for Title III programmes (Doeringer, Sum and Terkla, 2000, Research Brief No. 20).

However, the relatively strong performance of the various programmes conceals more serious employment and earnings problems. This is best illustrated by displaced older workers, who as a group are among the most likely to remain attached to the labour market. Only about three quarters of all displaced workers aged 45 and above who concluded their training in 1998 obtained employment. While the median wage replacement rate for older workers who were re-employed was relatively high, one-third of those placed in jobs experienced wage losses of 20 per cent or more, while 21 per cent suffered wage losses of 30 per cent or more.

Data for New England during the mid-1990s show that these re-employment and wage replacement rates are substantially below the rates for younger dislocated workers under the age of 45, and are lowest for older workers without a high school diploma (separate data are not available for Massachusetts). Older displaced workers in New England also work fewer hours when they are re-employed than in their previous jobs. The combined effect of lower wages and fewer hours worked meant that dislocated older workers in New England experienced on average a drop of 30 per cent in their weekly earnings when they were re-employed in the mid-1990s (Doeringer, Sum and Terkla, 2000, Research Brief No. 9). Rates of withdrawal from the labour force have been high for those who are not re-employed (Doeringer, Sum and Terkla, 2000, Research Brief No. 1).

In the same way as at the national level, a rising proportion of older disadvantaged persons in Massachusetts have come to rely on some form of public assistance income to support themselves and their families, including social security disability and supplemental security income payments, emergency aid to the elderly and dependent children, Medicaid and food stamps. Because there are few substantive links between these income support programmes and the employment and training system in Massachusetts, many of these older workers become permanently lost to the workforce (Doeringer, Sum and Terkla, 2000, Research Report No. 5).

4.2. Policy Reform

Despite these shortcomings in current programme performance, neither new policies nor radically different programmes are needed to address the key problems of labour scarcities, skill mismatches and low wages of older workers in Massachusetts. Existing programmes represent a more than adequate set of building blocks from which an effective labour market policy for older workers can be fashioned. Focus groups of older workers who have participated in JTPA training programmes show that they would have appreciated a more comprehensive evaluation of their individual skills and training needs and referral to programmes that could do a better job of building on these skills (Doeringer, Sum and Terkla, 2000). They also stressed the importance of computer training, but felt that it should be targeted at specific areas, such as word processing, working with spreadsheets, graphic design and manufacturing-related computer capacities, rather than short-term computer literacy. The overall conclusion from these groups is that training should be more comprehensive, directly transferable to jobs and more individualized, but not that new types of programmatic intervention are needed.

What is more important is a political commitment to fund and implement a coherent workforce development system of sufficient scope and accountability to achieve a substantial improvement in the wages and work incentives of older workers. By focusing on job quality and higher wage incentives, it is possible for employment and training policy to address both the growth and business competitiveness problems related to labour scarcities and the social problems of poverty and income inadequacy. The new Workforce Investment Act takes important steps in this direction, but these reforms need to be extended to the entire workforce development system.

A major study of older workers in the Massachusetts economy recently proposed a comprehensive blueprint for reforming employment and training policy in Massachusetts (Doeringer, Sum and Terkla, 2000). The major steps to build an active and effective labour market policy include:

- focusing all elements of workforce development on achieving high quality job placements and the long-term upgrading of the workforce in order to raise earnings and strengthen work incentives;
- harmonizing programme eligibility and training content between the different programmes so that older workers can accumulate higher levels of education and skills during their extended work careers more easily;
- targeting programme resources at alleviating skill scarcities and mismatches in the Massachusetts economy;
- strengthening workforce development through public-private partnerships with employers and unions;
- establishing an evaluation process that ensures both long-term monitoring and continuous improvement in the performance of workforce development programmes; and
- providing the additional financial resources needed to close the labour supply gap under conditions of full employment.

5 Reducing Obstacles to the Employment of Older Workers

These labour market policy reforms must, however, also be accompanied by equally active policies to reduce barriers to the employment of older workers. One such obstacle is the stereotype that older workers are more costly to hire than younger workers because they are less adaptable to workplace changes and less able to master new technologies. Second, is the common perception among older workers that age discrimination is a major obstacle to employment. Finally, there are the well-documented employment obstacles embodied in the work disincentives of pension plans and the eligibility criteria for Medicare.

5.1 Employers' Internal Labour Market Policies

Employers will inevitably have to make major changes in their internal labour market policies in order to increase recruitment rates of older workers (AARP, 1998). Hiring and selection practices will have to be adapted to a workforce that has more experience, but less up-to-date education. Training and promotion practices will need to be attuned to differences in the manner in which recent school graduates and experienced older workers learn new job skills. Wage and fringe benefit structures will need to accommodate differences in the compensation preferences of younger and older workers, and more flexible working hours will be needed for older workers, whose family and caring responsibilities are different from those of younger workers. Pension and retirement plans will also need to emphasize retention incentives for older workers, with a view to reducing the need to for firms to recruit replacement workers.

These adjustments may not come easily. One problem is that some employers have been reluctant to hire or train older workers, partly because they believe that older workers are not interested in training and are often *afraid* of modern technologies. Managers often regard older workers as excellent assets to the firm, believing them to be more hard-working, reliable and motivated than their younger counterparts (Sterns and McDaniel, 1994), and they give older workers very high marks for their use of good judgement, quality control, attendance and low turnover (AARP, 1995). However, they are also concerned that older workers are less willing to adapt to changing workforce practices and technologies. But the older workers in the focus groups routinely challenged this conventional wisdom by asserting a strong commitment to obtaining training in up-to-date skills.

Unfortunately, these negative perceptions by employers are also reflected in actual workplace training practices. Older workers are less likely than their younger counterparts to be trained by their employers. In a nationwide survey of almost 1500 establishments, 78 per cent of employees aged 25–34 had received some training during the previous year, while only about half of employees aged 55 and over had received such training, most of which was short-term and often not occupationally related (Frazis et al., 1998).[18]

A further problem is that a disproportionate burden of the adjustment process will fall on small employers (with fewer than 50 employees), which tend to employ more than their share of older workers. Such employers often lack the human resources development capacity of larger companies.

5.2 Age Discrimination

These concerns of employers about training and learning contribute to a widespread perception among older workers that they encounter discriminatory stereotypes when looking for new jobs (Doeringer, Sum and Terkla, 2000). Many older workers interviewed for the Commonwealth of Massachusetts Blue Ribbon Commission on Older Workers described situations in which they were told 'You are overqualified' or 'The job has already been filled' (despite clear evidence that it was still open), or that the company was 'not looking for senior people'. Little is known about the quantitative extent to which age discrimination compounds the effects of the other labour market disadvantages of older workers. Nevertheless, age discrimination now accounts for roughly one-in-five of all employment discrimination complaints filed at the national level with the Equal Employment Opportunity Commission (Bureau of National Affairs, 1999).

5.3 Pensions and Health Care

A final set of obstacles consists of the work disincentives that are built into many pension plans, disability income programmes and health care benefit schemes for retirees. By taxing benefits at high rates, the social security programme continues to penalize full-time year round employment for older workers under the age of 65, the group which might otherwise be most likely to defer retirement. Benefits for those with incomes in excess of $9,600 are reduced at a 33 per cent rate for each additional dollar of earnings in excess of this threshold (that is a reduction of $1 in benefits for every $3 of earned income). This high marginal tax rate on earnings is both a financial and a psychological impediment to working.

Medicare is another important work and employment disincentive. Because persons aged 65 and above are eligible for Medicare only if they are not employed, taking a job comes at the cost of foregoing subsidized health insurance, unless their employers provide alternative health insurance. Employers who met with the Commonwealth of Massachusetts Blue Ribbon Commission on Older Workers frequently expressed concern about the higher health-care costs of older workers. It would therefore seem likely that these costs deter firms which offer health insurance plans from hiring older workers. Allowing a Medicare option for employed older workers would reduce these work disincentives.[19]

Summary

Labour scarcities and skill mismatches could cost the United States a substantial amount of future economic growth. Older workers (aged 45 and above), whose numbers are growing rapidly both at the national level and in Massachusetts, provide the largest known labour reserve to avoid these labour scarcities and labour supply deficits. Utilizing this reserve, however, means deferring retirement, increasing full-time employment rates and raising the labour force participation rates of the older population. To accomplish these goals, the education and skills of older workers will have to be improved substantially in order to increase their wages and work incentives. It is therefore timely for employers, unions and public policy-makers to recognize the central contribution that the older workforce can make to the economy in the next decade by adapting labour market policies to the changing demographics of the labour force.

What also is needed is a seamless public-private workforce development system that allows adults to combine training and working more easily, so that they can upgrade their skills and education throughout their working lives. Such an all-inclusive workforce development system will have to be backed by increased financial resources and by a strong and uniform programme of oversight based on comparable performance criteria for the different programmes.

Better workforce development programmes and stronger work incentives can go a long way towards reducing labour scarcities and skill mismatches. However, ensuring that the potential contribution of older workers is fully realized and that older workers receive a fair share of the benefits of growth also requires equality of labour market opportunities. Older workers report encountering widespread prejudice in the job market, with older women experiencing the double jeopardy of age and gender discrimination. Whether the cause is intentional age discrimination or uninformed stereotypes, the attitudes of employers towards older workers must change if these barriers to employment and training are to come down.

The remaining financial and psychological disincentives to the continuation of work that are built into pension and other income support programmes will also have to be reduced. Prime among these disincentives are the early retirement incentives contained in some private pension plans, the high marginal tax rates on earned income applied to certain retirees under the age of 65 in the social security system and the loss of Medicare coverage for persons aged 65 and over who return to work.

Acknowledgement

This chapter draws upon the authors' work as staff members for the Commonwealth of Massachusetts Blue Ribbon Commission on Older Workers. The research assistance of Alison Gottlieb, Neal Fogg, Sheila Palma and Mykhaylo Trubs'kyy is gratefully acknowledged.

Notes

1 Evidence of such adverse employment effects is found in the long duration of unemployment among older workers, the relatively large earnings losses and high rates of labour market discouragement among older workers who are displaced from their career jobs and the earnings losses experienced by

older workers who take part-time or full-time *bridge jobs* prior to retirement (Ruhm, 1990; Sum and Fogg, 1991; Doeringer, Sum and Terkla, 2000).

2 The baby boom generation is frequently defined as those persons born between 1946 and 1964. The earliest members of the baby boom generation reached the age of 45 in 1991, while the tail end of the baby boom generation will not reach 45 until 2009.

3 While the number of 16–24 year olds in the civilian noninstitutional population will increase by nearly 4.9 million between 1998 and 2008, the 25–44 year old population will shrink by nearly an identical amount (-4.7 million), due to the movement of the *baby bust* generation into these age groups.

4 These findings are based on the civilian noninstitutional population, which excludes members of the armed forces and inmates of institutions, such as jails, prisons and nursing homes.

5 Doeringer, Sum and Terkla (2000) give a similar set of simulations for older men in Massachusetts in the late 1990s.

6 Tabulations by the Center for Labor Market Studies based on the January 1998–December 1999 CPS surveys. The unemployment rates of 45–64 year olds were below 3 per cent at the end of the 1990s, the lowest of all age groups. Over the period 1998–99, the average monthly unemployment rate for 45–54 year olds ranged from a high of 6.2 per cent for those older workers with only a primary education to a low of 1.7 per cent for those who had obtained a bachelor's or higher degree. Similar, although somewhat less extreme unemployment differentials, prevailed for workers in the 55–64 and 65 and older subgroups.

7 For earlier reviews of the labour market problems of older workers in the United States and Massachusetts, see (Sum and Fogg, 1991 and 1998a).

8 These *hidden unemployed*, who are not working and not looking for work, but want a job, should not be confused with the BLS concept of *discouraged workers*, who must also meet certain job search and workforce availability tests. Such discouraged workers are only a small subset of the labour force reserve (sometimes referred to as the hidden unemployed). Fewer than one in ten members of the labour force reserve were classified as discouraged, and among older workers (55+) only 7 per cent were classified as discouraged in 1998 and 1999.

9 The share of the economically inactive population desiring immediate employment tends to decline uniformly with age. In 1998, some 16 per cent of the members of the economically inactive population aged between

16 and 24 were members of the labour force reserve, compared with 11 per cent of those aged 25–54 and fewer than 2 per cent of those aged 65 and over.

10 The tendency for employed persons aged 65–69 to work part-time was undoubtedly influenced by the social security earnings penalty test, which reduced social security benefits by one-third for all earnings above a specific threshold. This penalty was eliminated for 65–69 year olds in 2000.

11 The Bureau of Labor Statistics classifies people as part-time for economic reasons only if they cite a desire for full-time work and report that they were available for full-time work during the reference week of the survey. Table 14.6 shows all persons working part-time for economic reasons, regardless of their availability for full-time work. Men were somewhat more likely than women to be working part-time for economic reasons in each year.

12 On average, over the 1998–99 period, approximately 13 per cent of 45–54 year old part-time workers were employed part-time for economic reasons, compared with only 9 per cent of those aged 55–69. These estimates are based solely on the reasons cited by the older workers for working part-time and do not take into account their current availability for full-time work.

13 In 1998, the average poverty threshold for a four-person family in the United States was slightly above $16,600. To avoid being poor, a full-time year-round employed family head would have needed gross weekly earnings of approximately $320. These estimates are somewhat conservative due to the fact that the CPS survey only collects weekly earnings data from wage and salary workers. Some self-employed persons also experience low wage problems during the year, but are not identified in CPS weekly earnings data.

14 The findings of the March 1998 and March 1999 national CPS household surveys were combined to estimate the number of 45-69 year olds experiencing one of these four mutually exclusive types of labour market problems.

15 The underemployed consist of persons involuntarily working part-time. While they are employed, they typically work only half as many hours as their full-time employed counterparts (23 compared with 45 hours).

16 The 217,000 figure reflects the difference between the projected growth in state employment (12 per cent) and the most optimistic projected growth (5.9 per cent) of the labour force, which leaves a 6.1 per cent gap (approximately 3.2 million persons).

17 Studies show that these workers often experience earnings reductions prior to job loss, followed by even sharper declines in their replacement jobs (Jacobson, Lalonde and Sullivan, 1993; Mangum, Mangum and Sum, 1998).
18 The survey also suggests that training rates are about 50 per cent higher for college graduates than for employees with high school education or less, and that a disproportionate share of employer training goes to managerial and professional occupations.
19 The recently enacted Ticket to Work and Work Incentives Act represents one step in this direction by allowing persons receiving federal disability benefits to return to work without losing their health insurance benefits.

References

AARP (1995), *Valuing Older Workers: A study of costs and productivity*, American Association of Retired Persons, Washington, DC.

AARP (1998), *Preparing for an Ageing Workforce: A practical guide for employers*, Washington, DC.

Anderson, P.M., Gustman, A.L. and Steinmeier, T.L. (1999), 'Trends in Male Labor Force Participation and Retirement: Some evidence on the role of pensions and social security in the 1970s and 1980s', *Journal of Labor Economics*, 17 (4), Part 1, pp. 757–83.

Brown, C. (1996), *Early Retirement Windows: Evidence from the health and retirement study*, NBER Working Paper.

Bureau of National Affairs (1999), 'EEOC Charge and Resolution Statistics through 1998', *Daily Labor Report*, February 9.

Burkhauser, R., Couch, K. and Phillips, J. (1996), 'Who Takes Early Social Security Benefits: The economic and health characteristics of early beneficiaries', *The Gerontologist*, 36 (6), pp. 789–99.

Burtless, G. and Moffitt, R. (1984), 'The Effect of Social Security Benefits on the Labor Supply of the Aged', in Aaron, H. and Burtless, G. (eds), *Retirement and Economic Behavior*, Brookings Institution, Washington, DC, pp. 135–75.

Center for Labor Market Studies (1999), *Foreign Immigration in New England: Its recent contributions to regional population and labor force growth and composition*, Northeastern University (mimeo).

Doeringer, P.B., Sum, A. and Terkla, D. (2000), *Older Workers: An essential resource for Massachusetts*, The Massachusetts Blue Ribbon Commission on Older Workers, Boston.

Dychtwald, K. (1999), *Age Power: How the 21st century will be ruled by the new old*, Tarcher, J.P./Putnam, New York.

Fields, G.S. and Mitchell, O. (1984), 'Economic Determinants of the Optimal Retirement Age: An empirical investigation', *Journal of Human Resources*, 19 (2), pp. 245–62.

Frazis, H., Gittleman, M., Horrigan, M. and Joyce, M. (1998), 'Results from the 1995 Survey of Employer-provided Training', *Monthly Labor Review* (June), pp. 3–13.

Friedberg, L.K. (1999), 'The Impact of Technological Change on Older Workers', NBER Working Paper, University of San Diego and NBER.

Fullerton, H. Jr (1999), 'Labor Force Projections to 2008', *Monthly Labor Review* (November).

Gruber, J. and Wise, D. (eds) (1999), *Social Security Programs and Retirement around the World*, University of Chicago Press.

Jacobson, L., Lalonde, R. and Sullivan D. (1993), *The Cost of Worker Dislocation*, The W.E. Upjohn Institute for Employment Research, Kalamazoo.

James, E. (1997), 'Public Pension Plans in International Perspective: Problems, reforms, and research issues', in Valdes-Prieto, S. (ed.), *The Economics of Pensions*, Cambridge University Press, Cambridge and New York, pp. 350–70.

Lumsdaine, R.L. and Mitchell, O. (1999), 'New Developments in the Economic Analysis of Retirement', in Card, D. and Ashenfelter, O. (eds), *Handbook of Labor Economics*, Elsevier Science Publishing Co., New York, pp. 3261–307.

Mangum, G., Mangum, S. and Sum, A. (1998), *A Fourth Chance for Second Chance Programs: Lessons from the old for the new*, Sar Levitan Center for Social Policy Studies, Johns Hopkins University, Baltimore.

Massachusetts Division of Employment and Training (DET) (1999), *The Massachusetts Job Outlook through 2006*, Boston.

National Council on Aging (2000), *Myths and Realities of Aging: Comparison of 1974 survey to 2000 survey results*, Washington, DC.

Quinn, J.F. (1999), 'New Paths to Retirement', in Brett Hammond, P. et al. (eds), *Forecasting Retirement Needs and Retirement Wealth*, University of Pennsylvania Press, Philadelphia, pp. 13–32.

Ruhm, C.R. (1990), 'Career Jobs, Bridge Employment, and Retirement', in Doeringer, P.B. (ed.), *Bridges to Retirement: Older workers in a changing labor market*, ILR Press, Cornell University, pp. 92–107.

Sterns, H.L. and McDaniel, M.A. (1994), 'Job Performance and the Older Worker', in Rix, S.E. (ed.), *Older Workers: How do they Measure up? An Overview of Age Differences in Employee Costs and Performance*, American Association of Retired Persons, Washington, DC.

Sum, A. et al. (1998), *The Road Ahead: Emerging threats to workers, families, and the Massachusetts economy*, Teresa and H. John Heinz Foundation and Mass. Inc., Boston.

Sum, A. and Fogg, N. (1991), 'Labor Market Turbulence and the Older Worker', in Doeringer, P.B. (ed.), *Turbulence in the American Workplace*, Oxford University Press, New York.

Sum, A. and Fogg, N. (1998a), 'The Older Worker Population of Massachusetts and its Labor Force Behavior and Labor Market Problems in the 1990s', Research paper prepared for the Massachusetts Blue Ribbon Commission on Older Workers, Boston.

Sum, A. and Fogg, N. (1998b), *Trends in the Level and Distribution of the Annual Earnings of Workers in Massachusetts, 1979–1997*, Report 13 for the Commonwealth of Massachusetts Blue Ribbon Commission on Older Workers, Boston.

Turner, J. and Watanabe, N. (1995), *Private Pension Policies in Industrialized Countries*, W.E. Upjohn Institute for Employment Research, Kalamazoo, Michigan.

US Bureau of Labor Statistics, *Employment and Earnings, 1979 and 1999*, Washington, DC.

Wagner, D.L. and Bonham, G.S. (1998), 'Factors Influencing the Use of Older Workers: A survey of U.S. employers', paper delivered at Gerontological Society of America, Annual Scientific Conference, Philadelphia, November 1998.

Welch, F. (1997), 'Wages and Participation', *Journal of Labor Economics*, 15 (1), pp. S77–S103.

Feature No. 7
Pensions at Risk? The Ageing of the Population, the Labour Market and the Cost of Pensions

Roland Sigg

We are always hearing about the threat posed to pensions by the ageing of the population, and particularly pensions in the *first pillar* (public pension schemes) financed by the working age population (pay-as-you-go systems). Over the next half century, it is predicted that the proportion of people over 60 years of age in industrialized countries will double, rising from 20 to 40 per cent of the total population. As these people will essentially depend on old-age insurance schemes for their well-being, how can the viability of such schemes be ensured insofar as they are principally financed through the wages earned by a diminishing labour force? According to current projections, the ratio between the retired population and the working age population will fall from between four and five working age persons for every retiree today, to two working age persons for each retiree in 2050 (United Nations, 2000).

Based on linear projections of the population and social expenditure, the World Bank concluded that 'if trends continue public spending on pensions will soar over the next fifty years in all regions' of the world (World Bank, 1994). Indeed, in OECD countries, which currently spend some 10 per cent of their GDP on pensions, these projections predict that the level of spending on pensions will stabilize at around 17 per cent of GDP in 30 years time. A rise of 70 per cent in the cost of pensions would be difficult to bear! More recently, a report by the United Nations Population Division calculated that, to maintain the current ratio between the numbers of working and retired members of the population (around 4/5 working age persons for each retired person) by 2050, it would be necessary either to bring in a massive number of immigrants (for example, for the European Union, around 12.7 million a year, or over

30 times the net migratory flow in 1998!), or to increase the retirement age in 2050 to over 75! These solutions are clearly not viable. Is rapid action therefore imperative to reform, or even dismantle old-age insurance schemes with a view, paradoxically, to safeguarding the future income of the elderly and, according to the advice of the World Bank, thereby preserving future economic growth imperilled by the ageing crisis?

The hard reality of the figures appears to be unquestionable! The ageing of the population and its corollary, the crisis of social security systems, would today seem inevitable. Moreover, politicians, the media and other influential groups appear to doubt the capacity of governments to resolve this problem effectively.

In contrast with this doomsday scenario, other experts are suggesting that the ageing of the population is not the principal threat currently facing social security systems, and therefore pension schemes, despite the worrying deterioration in the *dependency rate* (see Concialdi, 1999; Gillion, 1999; and Mullian, 2000). In particular, these authors are suggesting that what has been true for the past 50 years (a period that has seen the establishment of effective old-age protection schemes which have achieved a major reduction in poverty among the elderly, without imperilling economic growth) is also true today: or in other words, that society and the economy have the capacity to provide the whole of the population, irrespective of age, with a decent standard of living. What matters in the end is the level of production. In other terms, the ageing crisis is only a cause for concern if the life force of society, and particularly its economy, fails to develop.

Prejudices are persistent: it would therefore seem useful to demonstrate, using examples, that in the final analysis, it is the economic dependency rate (the ratio between the wage mass generated by workers and the volume of retirement benefits) which is the determining factor, and not the demographic dependency rate. Indeed, it is possible to demonstrate, based on the hypothesis of a dynamic economy, which has been the case in industrialized countries for the past 20 years, that the cost of retirement benefits will only increase slightly over the next 50 years, in relation to both GDP and the total wages and salaries of workers, and that the overall level of retirement benefits could be maintained at the same time.

Can the Level of Pension Benefits be Maintained without their Cost Rising? A Demonstration based on Examples

The wealth of statistical resources available, particularly from the United Nations (2000), the ILO (1999) and the OECD (1998), make it possible to measure the combined effect of the ageing of the population and of labour market developments. The examples of three countries (France, Germany and Switzerland) are presented below to illustrate the conditions that have to be met if retirement benefits are to be financed more easily in 50 years time. These tables are taken from a study carried out within the framework of the International Social Security Association's research programme, the full results of which will be published subsequently.

In the two projections described below, a constant replacement rate is assumed for retirement benefits, which means in general terms that the level of pensions as a proportion of wages will be the same in 2050 as today. In this scenario, the retirement age would therefore be maintained and the level of benefits would keep pace with wages. Moreover, an annual economic growth rate of 2 per cent is assumed (the average rate in OECD countries since 1980 has been 2.3 per cent), together with the maintenance of the level of productivity growth experienced over the past 20 years. Finally, the most recent United Nations figures are used for population projections (United Nations, 2000).

First Hypothesis: a Static Labour Market

According to this hypothesis, it is assumed that the structure of the employment market will not change (with the proportion of persons in work or looking for work - the labour force - therefore remaining stable as a percentage of the population aged 15 years and over), and that old-age pensions (the *first pillar*) will continue to represent the same proportion of wages (an identical replacement rate). The results in terms of costs are presented in Table F7.1.

The projections for the proportion of GDP devoted to the cost of retirement benefits in this hypothesis are similar to those of the World Bank. With regard to the level of these costs as a proportion of the wage mass (all wages and salaries), it is predicted that contributions will be more or less at the level required to finance the old-age insurance system (minus the direct contributions made by the state). In the improbable hypothesis of a static labour market, it can therefore be seen that the deterioration in the dependency rate has a direct effect on the cost of pensions: the doubling of the proportion of GDP required to finance a level of pension benefits similar to today's, and a financing need representing between 14 and 21 additional contribution points for the countries concerned. However, this hypothesis has the major failing of not taking into account the fact that economic growth requires a rise in production levels, and therefore employment. In practice, it is an economic impossibility.

Second Hypothesis: a Labour Market Designed to Optimize the Labour Force

Three types of trends are envisaged:

- An increase in the labour force. The participation rate shown in the above table can be improved in two ways in particular: by increasing the participation of women in the labour market, and by more actively encouraging older workers, before and after the formal retirement age, to remain in employment. In this hypothesis, it is envisaged that between now and 2050 the participation rate of women in the labour market will progressively reach that of men in 1997, with a participation rate of older workers equivalent to the existing level of 1980.
- In its projections of the net immigration rate, the United Nations has been very conservative. In our second hypothesis, in contrast, a slight increase is envisaged over the immigration rate in the 1980s and 1990s. Table F7.2 shows the (fairly minor) increase assumed in the projections.

Employment experts predict a reduction in the numbers of persons available for work over the next few years due to the employment needs of the economy and the decline in the 25 to 65 age group. This should greatly diminish unemployment and the related expenditure. Furthermore, the number of children will also fall, leading to a decline in overall social expenditure on families. In this second hypothesis, the savings which can be envisaged in the areas of unemployment and family assistance are transferred to pensions. For the countries taken into

Table F7.1 Labour force, pension replacement rate and cost of pensions, 1995–2050, 'static' hypothesis

	Labour force in 1997 (% of persons aged 15+)	Replacement rate of pensions in 1995 (%)	Cost of pensions: % of GDP/% of wage mass		
			1995	2020*	2050*
Germany	57.4	58.6	10.2/18.9	14.6/27.1	21.5/39.8
France	54.4	43.9	10.4/19.9	14.3/27.5	18.3/35.2
Switz.	67.4	39.5	6.3/10.1	9.0/14.6	14.9/24.1

Source: * Based on United Nations (2000) population projections.

Table F7.2 Immigration, 1995–2050

	Annual average net immigration 1980–95 (% of total population in 1995)	Net annual immigration, 2000–50, based on United Nations projections	Net annual immigration, 2000–50, assumed in this hypothesis*	Total population in 2050 in millions according to this hypothesis (population in 1995)
Germany	240,000 (0.29)	204,000	385,000	82.3 (81.7)
France	40,000 (0.07)	6,500	50,000	63.0 (58.0)
Switz.	31,000 (0.43)	4,100	37,000	8.6 (7.1)

Source: * Based on an annual increase of 1 per cent in the figure in column 1.

consideration, these transfers represent a rate of between 8 and 11 per cent of total social expenditure.

The trends shown above considerably improve the ratio between persons in employment and retired persons in our projections.

Taking the example of Germany, the evolution would be as indicated in Table F7.3.

What is significant is the ratio between the employed population and recipients of retirement benefits. In the table above, it may be noted that the deterioration in this ratio (bottom line) is much lower than the level usually predicted and that, in any case, the deterioration is significantly less than for the other ratios (first and second lines) which are normally cited.

The impact on the cost of retirement benefits is as indicated in Table F7.4.

In general terms, a moderate increase may be noted in this hypothesis between 2020 and 2030, followed by a decrease over the following 20 years. The contrast with the first table is dramatic.

These results, obtained on the basis of aggregates of publicly available data, are corroborated by an important report (published after the projections shown here had been calculated) by the ECOFIN Council of the European Commission (Economic Policy Committee, 2000). Using a rigorous methodology, this report evaluates the impact of the ageing of the population on public pension systems in the countries of the European Union. Based on various hypotheses, particularly for fertility, migration, economic growth and the labour market, it evaluates the impact of demographic ageing on the cost of retirement benefits in relation to GDP. The report develops a dynamic scenario, known as the *Lisbon scenario*, in which the following hypotheses are assumed: economic growth at 3 per cent; an increase in the employment rate from 60 to 70 per cent by 2010 (and particularly, an increase in the employment rate of women from 51 to 60 per cent) and to 80 per cent by the year 2050; and a slight rise in the fertility rate, as well as in the net migration rate, which is higher than the figure usually cited.

By way of comparison, in the case of *Germany*, the rise envisaged by this report in the cost of pension benefits between the year 2000 and the highest point (reached in 2030) is 2.3 per cent, resulting in an increase from 10.3 to 12.6 per cent of GDP. According to our calculations (see the table above), this increase is slightly higher, around 3.7 per cent, although our predictions for 2050 are lower (12.1 compared with 12.3

Table F7.3 Ratio between persons in employment and retired persons, 1995–2050

	1995	2020	2050
Ratio of population aged 15–64 to population aged 65+	4.4	3.0	2.1
Ratio of active population[1] to population aged 65+	3.1	2.2	1.5
Ratio of population in employment[2] to population aged 65+	2.9	2.2	1.9

Notes

1 For 2020 and 2050, calculated according to the first hypothesis. The unemployed are included in the labour force.
2 For 2020 and 2050, the calculation is based on the second hypothesis.

Table F7.4 Cost of pension, 1995–2050, 'labour market optimization' hypothesis

	Cost of pensions: % of GDP/% of wage mass			
	1995	2020*	2030*	2050*
Germany	10.2/18.9	12.2/22.6	13.9/25.8	12.1/22.4
France	10.4/19.9	11.9/23.0	12.5/24.0	11.0/21.1
Switzerland	6.3/10.1	6.8/11.0	7.8/12.5	6.6/10.6

Source: * Based on United Nations population projections (United Nations, 2000).

per cent). In the case of *France*, the difference between the two sets of predictions is inverted, with the increase forecast in the ECOFIN report being 2.7 per cent (a rise from 12.1 to 14.8 per cent of GDP in 2040), while our calculations foresee an increase of around 2.1 per cent between 1995 and 2030. These variations can be explained by a difference in the methodologies used. But the conclusions are similar, namely that an increase is to be expected in the cost of pensions as a proportion of GDP, particularly between the years 2030 and 2040, of the order of 2 to 3 per cent in most industrialized countries. It may be concluded, without great risk of error, that these increases will be significantly lower than those usually cited, both in many expert reports and in the media.

An Imaginary Ageing Crisis?

This analysis of the situation of these three countries suggests the following:

- the ageing of the population, as well as the deterioration in the ratio between working and retired persons, will only constitute a problem if no measures are taken to improve the employment rate of the population;
- the working age population in the industrialized countries still offers a potential which should not be neglected, since many countries are experiencing high rates of unemployment and underemployment in certain categories of the population, and particularly among women and older workers;
- it would seem evident that the economy will not grow at the same rates as over the past 20 years without a certain increase in employment, even taking into account a continued improvement in productivity. The *optimization* of the working population will, however, have to be accompanied by a rise in the immigration rate in order to guarantee the necessary labour supply. This will also make it possible for many European countries to avoid the sharp decrease in their populations forecast by United Nations projections;
- finally, it would appear that, provided sufficient attention is paid to labour market issues, no *ageing crisis* is to be feared, nor indeed any inability by the public authorities to continue providing old-age pensions at their current level. The risks associated with the ageing

of the population have been widely exaggerated in terms of predicting the cost of pensions over the coming years.

Care needs to be taken to identify the right target. Measures are required to dynamize the labour market in order to guarantee lasting economic growth and, in so doing, preserve old-age pension schemes. These, in turn, will help maintain growth by guaranteeing continued consumption levels.

These reflections should also be taken into account in current reforms of pension schemes. In particular, they point to the need to eliminate any negative incentives for employment, at all ages, with a view to encouraging the employment of workers who are approaching, or have passed the retirement age. Several studies have shown that older persons are ready to increase their economic activity, and are often prevented from doing so by age discrimination or a saturated employment market.

Knowing that the worst case scenario is not a foregone conclusion should confer a certain serenity upon the debate which has to be held on the reform of old-age insurance schemes. It is also necessary to set a number of priorities for employment policies, namely: facilitating the participation of women in the labour market; reducing age discrimination; and introducing measures to facilitate the integration of immigrant workers.

References

Concialdi, P. (1999), 'Demography, Employment and the Future of Social Protection Financing', *Financing Social Protection in Europe*, Ministry of Social Affairs and Health, Helsinki.

Economic Policy Committee (2000), *Progress Report to the Ecofin Council on the Impact of Ageing Populations on Public Pension systems* (EPC/ECFIN/581/00) European Commission, Brussels.

Gillion, C. (1999), 'Current Situation and Trends in Social Protection Financing in Europe in 2035: The financing of pensions and other social protection programmes', *A European way to combine sustainable economic growth, high employment and social protection*, Ministry of Social Affairs and Health, Helsinki.

ILO (1999), *Key Indicators of the Labour Market*, CD-ROM.

Mullan, P. (2000), *The Imaginary Time Bomb: Why an ageing population is not a social problem*, I.B. Tauris, London.

OECD (1998), *OECD Social Expenditure Database*, CD-ROM.

United Nations Population Division (2000), *Replacement Migration: Is it a solution to declining and ageing populations?* (ESA/P/WP.160), New York (March 2000).

World Bank (1994), *Averting the Old Age Crisis: Policies to protect the old and promote growth*, Oxford University Press, New York.

Chapter Fifteen

The Future Role of Trade Union Organizations in Social Protection

Henri Lourdelle

The role that the social partners, and more specifically trade union organizations, could play in future in the field of social protection, both in the management of schemes and the implementation of reforms, raises very broad questions.

In endeavouring to answer them, the lessons to be learned from the example of Europe are taken as a starting point. Europe is of particular interest in view of the fact that European social protection systems are both the product of their history and are, in a certain manner, based on a social contract. They are therefore specific to each of the Member States of the European Union. For this reason, they are varied in their structures, which include systems of the *social insurance* type, also known as *Bismarckian* systems, which prevail in continental Europe (Belgium, France, Germany, etc.), *universal* systems, based on the model developed by *Beveridge* (United Kingdom, Ireland and Northern Europe), and mixed systems in Mediterranean Europe. These variations are reflected in their financing systems (mainly through contributions for social insurance systems, principally from taxation for universal systems, and both in mixed systems).

This variety is a source of strength. But it does not exclude a common characteristic, which is unique in the world, namely the ambition to achieve both economic and social cohesion and to give effect to what is currently known as the *European Social Model*, which consists of:

- reconciling social needs (such as combating poverty and building effective public social protection systems) with economic needs (implementation of the Single Market and the efficient economic development of the European Union);
- while at the same time endeavouring to ensure that European citizens are not too marginalized.

This is a vast challenge in which varying degrees of success have been achieved. On the positive side, reference may be made to the fact that the European Social Model has made it possible to double the living standards of citizens since the creation of the European Union. Moreover, as shown by all the indicators, the health of European citizens has never been better. It has also made it possible for several million Europeans to escape from poverty. If the European Union had only followed market rules, some 40 per cent of households, or 150 million European citizens, would be living below the poverty line, whereas with social protection systems and their redistribution effects, some 100 million people in Europe have risen above the poverty line, even if 17 per cent of European households have not yet done so!

Yet, alongside these undeniable achievements, there remain serious problems to be addressed and resolved. As noted above, economic and social progress is not shared by all European citizens and their families, and poverty coexists with prosperity (50 million people are affected by poverty in Europe). It should also be noted that, although the numbers of marginalized persons remain relatively stable, the gap is widening between the rich (who are growing richer) and the poor (who are becoming poorer). Long-term unemployment is persistent and there are major forms of discrimination in such areas as access to the labour market, career development and training. Almost 9 per cent of the workforce in the European Union (14 million people) are unemployed, of whom half are in long-term unemployment. A significant number of young persons leave school without obtaining the skills that they need for the labour market. In all Member States, between 25 and 30 per cent of workers experience difficulty in understanding simple instructions and in basic skills (reading and mathematics).

These are significant challenges which need to be addressed, not only to preserve, but also to improve the European Social Model and the various social protection systems of which it is composed. In this context, the social partners have an essential role to play. Although their role was uncontested in the past, will it be as important and necessary in the future?

The response given below to this question is based on the impact that the presence and role of the social partners has had in recent years in the areas of the management and reform of European social protection systems. Then, adopting a more forward-looking approach, the new challenges confronting them are reviewed and the possible responses outlined.

But before proceeding, a rapid clarification is needed to specify the sense in which the term *social protection* is used. It encompasses both *social security*, which is composed of public systems, and schemes which *supplement the statutory schemes* in such fields as health care and retirement pensions.

1 The Role of Trade Union Organizations in Social Security: Management Responsibilities and Catalysts for Reform

1.1 Their Involvement in the Management of Schemes

The involvement of the social partners, and particularly trade union organizations, in social security schemes may take various forms depending on whether the system is of the *social insurance* or the *universal* type, although, as will be seen below, this distinction is not totally hermetic. It may vary, for example, according to the nature of the contingency covered by the schemes.

In *social insurance* systems, for example, which are financed mainly through contributions paid by employees and enterprises, the social partners are often associated with the management of the system:

- either directly, through their representative organizations, which are either designated or elected, as is the case in France, Germany and Luxembourg;
- or less directly, through *mutual organizations*, as is the case in Belgium, or through *Chambers* (of workers and employees, agriculture or professional workers, such as in Austria).

However, the term *management* conceals different realities. It may consist of a presence in administrative bodies as representatives of users (presence on the boards of the various funds), such as in the cases of Austria and Luxembourg, or the real delegation of responsibility for management, with the responsibility of ensuring the financial balance of the system and with the power, in certain cases, to modify benefits and contributions, such as in Belgium and Germany. In such instances, it consists of a type of *co-management*.

In historical terms, the involvement of the social partners (or in certain countries, more broadly, of civil society) in the management of social protection has its roots, among other factors, in the manner in which such protection was administered before the systems were established (for example, by the churches in Germany and by the mutual societies movement in France). Although the establishment of social insurance schemes marked a break with previous practices, traces of the past were nevertheless retained including, for example, not expecting the State to do everything and giving users *responsibility* by associating them with the management of the schemes. It is not therefore surprising that in his celebrated *Imperial Message* of November 1881, Bismarck established the principle of *social insurance,* according to which financing and management should be under the responsibility of insured persons and employers, or in other words of the interested parties. The inclusion of employed persons (and not trade unions, which were prohibited at the time) in the management of social protection was first introduced in 1883 with the establishment of local health funds.

This principle was taken up in France in the 1945 Decrees, which created the social security system, even though at the time the representation of trade unions and employers' organizations on the boards of funds was not on an equal footing. Indeed, the Decree of 4 October 1945 conferred upon the representatives of employed persons, appointed in this case by the most representative trade union organizations, 75 per cent of the seats on such boards, except for family allowance funds, where they were only accorded half of the seats, with the others going to representatives of employers and of self-employed workers. It was not until the Decrees of 1967 that parity was established in the representation of the two social partners. More recently, the Decrees of 1995 brought other partners onto the boards (such as the mutual societies movement in the case of health funds and representatives of retired persons in pension funds). Why entrust insured persons with managerial responsibilities in this manner? In the first place, this option corresponds to the French tradition of the mutual societies movement, which originally managed the systems. But, in particular, it conforms to the logic of a system which is essentially occupational in its basis: funds have to be administered by those who finance the system. This approach is also based on the concept of *social democracy*, on which social relations in the country are based and which also encompasses the management of social institutions.

Nevertheless, and in accordance with the provisions of the ILO Social Security (Minimum Standards) Convention, 1952 (No. 102), the involvement of the social partners in the management of social security systems cannot exempt the State from its responsibilities in this respect. In the last resort, the State retains responsibility for the sustainability and financial solvency of the system.

In systems based on the Beveridge model, which tend to be financed through taxation, the social partners are involved in a different manner. In general, they do not participate in the strict sense of the term in the management of these systems, but are *consulted* through ad hoc institutions. By way of illustration, in the United Kingdom, the Social Security Advisory Committee (SSAC), whose members include a representative of the employers' organization (the Confederation of British Industry – CBI) the trade union organization (the Trades Union Congress – TUC), has the role, as its name indicates, of advising the Secretary of State for Social Security on practically all issues related to social security. It therefore plays a purely advisory role.

In Sweden, the National Social Security Council (Riksförsäkringsverket – RFV), which includes representatives of the principal trade unions, is the authority responsible for supervising the administration of social security and interpreting the relevant legislation.

Spain has developed another formula for the participation of the social partners in the management of social security, through general councils or executive commissions in the National Social Security Institute, the National Health Institute and the National Employment Institute, within which the representatives of the social partners participate in monitoring and supervising the management of social security.

Furthermore, in the Nordic countries (Denmark, Finland and Sweden, as well as Iceland), the trade unions administer the system of unemployment insurance, which is voluntary. This system is known as the Ghent system, as it was applied for the first time at the beginning of the last century in the city of Ghent in Belgium.

In Switzerland, the unemployment insurance system is administered by the Secretariat of State for Economic Affairs. Trade unions and employers' organizations only play an advisory role in the management of unemployment funds. However, the agencies which provide unemployment benefit are established at the cantonal level, with some of them being administered by the local government and others by trade unions. The latter also have their own funds for the provision of unemployment allowances, although they are all managed on the same basis (with identical levels of contributions and benefits). Individuals therefore have a choice between the various systems, based on the services that they provide for the unemployed.

1.2 Their Often Decisive Role in Social Security Reforms

The involvement of trade union organizations is not limited to the management of social security systems. In many cases, they also play a major role in developing reforms of the systems. This concerted action with the social partners, and more particularly with trade union organizations, has often been at the basis of the reform process or even, in the majority of cases, a prerequisite for its implementation. A good illustration is the reform of pension systems which is currently being carried out in all the Member States of the European Union.

In France, the process was set in motion by the *White Paper on pensions* issued by the Prime Minister, Michel Rocard, in 1990. However, it has suffered reverses on occasions, particularly in the case of the reform of pensions of private sector employees carried out in 1993 by Edouard Balladur, which was undertaken without any social dialogue. Nevertheless, dialogue was included once again in the mission conferred on 29 May 1998 on a senior member of the Planning Commission (*Commissaire au Plan)*, Jean-Michel Charpin, by the Prime Minister, Lionel Jospin, as well as when he established the Pensions Guidance Council on 29 May 2000.

Germany has experienced a similar process, with the same vicissitudes. Indeed, the last measures advocated by Chancellor Helmut Kohl were outside the framework of any dialogue, which has since been renewed by the Socialist Chancellor, Gerhard Schröder. At a meeting held in Berlin on 4 September 2000, the Chancellor and the President of the German Confederation of Trade Unions (DGB) brought their positions closer together on pension reform: in exchange for a return to the indexation of pensions on net wages, and no longer on prices, the two parties agreed (one year in advance of the initially planned schedule) on the principle of a reduction in the level of pensions based on the pay-as-you-go system, offset by the introduction of a dose of *funding*. There remains a single point of disagreement: the trade unions consider that the proportion of funding proposed (the possibility of investing up to 4 per cent of wages) is too high. A joint working group has been set up to resolve this disagreement.

Another subject which is being debated in both France and Germany consists of enterprise savings plans, which allow employees to become shareholders in their enterprise. At the moment, these plans have met with limited success on both sides of the Rhine.

The social partners were also involved, at least in the beginning (from 1984 to 1990) in pension reform in Sweden, with which they were associated as experts. However, the process of dialogue has subsequently been confined to the political parties, although this does not mean that the trade union organizations no longer have any influence, or indeed that they are not exerting pressure.

Trade unions are also associated, sometimes not without difficulties, in reforms of unemployment insurance schemes. In countries such as France, Germany, Sweden and Switzerland, to name but a few, *active policies* have been introduced to combat unemployment, consisting of the development of training programmes for the unemployed to improve their employability and the provision of financial incentives to seek and accept a job.

While the social partners are unanimous in recognizing the need for such measures, there are very real differences in their views as to the extent to which they should be compulsory. This was demonstrated by the debate in France during the summer of 2000 on the reform of the unemployment insurance system. In the *workfare* systems in the Netherlands and the United Kingdom, jobseekers are obliged to take a specific job or participate in training, or they may lose their benefit in part or in whole. In Switzerland, these active labour market policies are closely linked to unemployment allowances. If an unemployed person is officially invited to participate in measures of this type and refuses, the benefit may be lost. Penalties of this type also exist in Sweden, although it would appear that they are almost never applied.

But the best examples of the involvement of the social partners in the reform process are provided by Italy and Spain. In Spain, the process has been covered by a double agreement:

- first, by what is known as the *Toledo Pact* of February 1995, through which all the political parties in the country reaffirmed their support for a pay-as-you-go retirement system and laid down the principles for a reform; and

- then the agreement of 9 October 1996, concluded between the government of José Maria Aznar and the two majority central trade union organizations, the General Union of Workers (UGT) and the Workers' Commissions (CC.OO.), which marked an important stage in the pension reform process.

In Italy, after the failure of the attempt to *force through* pension reform by the government of Silvio Berlusconi, negotiations were conducted directly between the trade unions and the new government of technicians directed by Lamberto Dini. They resulted in an agreement concluded on 8 May 1995 by the government and the Italian trade union organizations (CGIL, UIL and CISL) modifying the overall Italian pensions system (see also Bacasso, Feature No. 8).

There are, however, two 'blemishes' on this picture. The first concerns the United Kingdom where, in contrast with the other Member States of the European Union, decisions in the field of social security, including the reforms to be undertaken, are essentially determined by *policies* set out in the electoral programme. The Social Security Advisory Committee, referred to above, only plays a formal role in the process. By way of illustration, the programme of the Conservative Party, defended in 1997 by the Prime Minister, John Major, envisaged completing the process of the privatization of British pensions initiated by Mrs Thatcher, with a view eventually to the development of a system inspired by the Chilean model. The victory of New Labour and Tony Blair put a stop to that process.

The second 'blemish' concerns the social partners involved. For example, in both Italy and Spain it has already been indicated that the trade union organizations, or at least the most important of them (CGIL, CISL and UIL in Italy, and UGT and CC.OO. in Spain) fully assumed their responsibilities and were involved in discussing the reforms. However, it has to be noted that in these two countries employers remained very distant from the negotiations, either because they considered that they did not go far enough (Italy), or because they entertained doubts as to the financial feasibility of the measures adopted (Spain). In view of this attitude by employers' organizations, it is legitimate to wonder whether, when faced with reforms which require a responsible attitude by all the parties, it is legitimate for some of them to flee such responsibility by refusing to be committed to the process, leaving others to assume responsibility for the reforms that are adopted.

Finally, as shown in France by the debate on social reconfiguration (*refondation sociale)*, the dividing line between the responsibilities of the social partners and the state in the management of social security systems is sometimes extremely flexible. Irrespective of any other consideration, the recent decision by the Minister of the Economy and Finance, Laurent Fabius, to make use of the *generalized social contribution* (*contribution sociale généralisée – CSG*) to reduce social contributions for the low-paid, a decision taken without any prior dialogue, cannot fail to raise questions concerning the manner in which governments sometimes understand the concept of concerted action and the role of the social partners. In this particular case, the government has shown that it does what it likes with the income of social security funds (a proportion of the health contribution had in practice been transferred to the CSG). In some cases, therefore, little is needed to undermine the responsibilities assumed by the social partners.

2 Developments in Social Protection: a New Area of Responsibility for the Social Partners

2.1 The European Dimension of Social Protection Involves the Social Partners

Social protection, or to be more precise *social security*, is not in theory a *Community* competence in the European Union. Even though the Treaty of Rome envisaged in Article 117 the 'harmonization of social systems', and in Article 118 established as the objective of the European Commission '... promoting close co-operation between Member States in the social field, particularly in matters related to ... social security', it has to be said that, notwithstanding these statements of principle, social security remains the competence of individual states (see also Salais, Chapter Sixteen), in the same way as tax matters. Moreover, any modification in this respect requires unanimity, as provided in Article 51 of the Treaty, which states that the European Council of Ministers shall, 'acting unanimously on a proposal from the Commission, adopt ... measures in the field of social security ...'.

Nevertheless, a closer examination of the texts and guidance proposed by the Council and/or the Commission shows a clear hardening of their positions in favour of a more European perspective for social protection, however indirectly and *informally*. A number of recent examples serve as an illustration.

In the first place, it may be noted that the Commission is addressing issues of social security and social protection increasingly frequently in its publications, either with a view to initiating a debate, or even making proposals. Admittedly, on each occasion it takes care to recall that 'each Member State remains responsible for the organisation and financing of its own particular social protection system'. However, this does not prevent it from recalling in its Communication of 31 October 1995 on the future of social protection, a framework for a European debate, that however different social protection systems may be, they are confronted with problems which are broadly similar. The Commission therefore proposed a convergence strategy in the field of social protection, which was approved by the European Parliament and the Economic and Social Committee (European Commission, 1995).

But it also goes further in another text issued on 12 March 1997, entitled *Modernising and improving social protection in the European Union* (European Commission, 1997a), in which it sets a:

> dual purpose:
> – to indicate the routes along which modernisation can be pursued;
> – to present some specific proposals for European level support.

Finally, in a very recent Communication on this subject, dated 14 July 1999 and entitled *A Concerted Strategy for Modernising Social Protection*, the Commission proposes to take a further step forward in the debate, namely to establish 'a concerted approach to the modernisation of social protection', and adds its intention to seek, in particular, 'the involvement of the social partners' (European Commission, 1999b).

Following this Communication, the main lines of which it approved, the Council decided on 29 June 2000 to establish a Social Protection Committee at the European level. As a result, not only has the debate on social security, and even more broadly on social protection, been launched at the European level, but structures are starting to emerge and the social partners are invited to be associated with them.

In view of these developments, it is important for trade union organizations not only to be vigilant, but also to demonstrate their capacity for innovation, particularly to ensure that social systems do not bear the brunt of competition between Member States now that the single currency has been adopted and the Member States of the European Union have decided to develop a code of good practice on tax matters.

The social partners are playing their full role in the coordination of social security institutions or, in other words, in the implementation of Regulations 1408/71 and 574/72 (European Council, 1971 and 1972). The European Trade Union Confederation (ETUC) is represented on the two committees which are responsible for addressing matters relating to migrant workers, particularly with regard to the problems encountered and improvements to be made, namely the Advisory Committee on Social Security for Migrant Workers and the Advisory Committee on Freedom of Movement for Workers.

With other *experts*, the ETUC also represents *users* on the working group that the Commission entrusted with examining the simplification and reform of rules for the coordination of social security schemes in Member States (the SLIM group).

Instead of being narrowed down, a vast field with multiple entry points is therefore opening up for action by the social partners, and in particular by trade union organizations, which is resulting in them being involved at the national and European levels.

2.2 Supplementary Schemes: a New Area of Responsibility for the Social Partners

Another common trend is emerging in relation to social protection systems in most industrialized countries, namely the development of *supplementary* social security schemes in both the pensions and health care branches. In these fields, as in others, the social partners, and in particular trade union organizations, also have a role to play.

2.2.1 Supplementary pension schemes

It is in the field of supplementary pension schemes, and particularly in the establishment of such schemes, that the intervention of trade union organizations is most noticeable.

In the Netherlands, which has already acquired long experience in the field, the establishment of *pension funds* is the outcome of negotiations between employers and trade unions at the enterprise or sectoral level. In the latter case, as recently confirmed by the Court of

Justice of the European Union (see section 2.2.2 below), adherence to the funds is compulsory for all enterprises in the sector.

However, the involvement of the social partners can go even further. For example, in Spain, the two trade union confederations (UGT and CC.OO.) have agreed to offer employees supplementary trade union retirement schemes (which are administered by the above confederations).

In most countries in which occupational schemes have been established, the social partners are associated with their management through various supervisory bodies. Nevertheless, the exceptions include the United Kingdom, where their management is conferred upon *trustees*, and Germany in the case of enterprise schemes, where the funds are managed internally by the enterprises.

This approach is in accordance with the aspirations of the ETUC, as expressed by its Secretary General, Emilio Gabaglio, in a letter addressed to the Commission on 27 May 1999, following the publication of its latest communication on occupational schemes, which explained that, as recognized by the Court of Justice of the European Union, contributions paid to supplementary schemes are a supplement to remuneration, and therefore a real deferred wage. The ETUC therefore considers that the social partners, and particularly trade union organizations, should be associated in supervising the management of supplementary retirement funds.

Moreover, the ETUC fully intends to use supplementary schemes as instruments for the promotion of employment, and not as elements going against the European employment strategy (ETUC, 1999). The point at issue is in practice the reconciliation in investment strategies of both financial performance (to guarantee the best possible level of pensions) and the concern to promote employment by investing in wealth-creating enterprises through *socially responsible* or *ethical* investments.

This dual objective implies that, alongside traditional financial criteria, such as liquidity, diversity, security and profitability, the selection of enterprises in which investments are made should be in accordance with other criteria of a social and/or environmental nature. For this purpose, enterprises have to be *assessed* by bodies which are specialized and competent in the field. One of the first such bodies to have emerged in Europe is Swiss. It is a non-profit-making *investment foundation* (ETHOS) established in 1997 at the initiative of two pension funds: the Pension Fund of the Canton of Geneva (CIA) and the Joint Insurance Fund for the Construction Industry in Geneva. This foundation, which is supported by Swiss trade unions, covers 78 pension funds in the country, for which it manages investment funds in accordance with criteria that are not only financial, but also environmental and social. At the same time, a similar bureau was created in France for social analysis and research concerning enterprises (ArèSE).

Is it not a *natural* objective of trade union action to control the use made of employees' contributions, even where they are paid by enterprises, with a view to ensuring the rights of retired persons and future retirees, while at the same time defending and promoting employment?

2.2.2 Supplementary health schemes

The debate on pension funds and supplementary retirement schemes also concerns supplementary health schemes.

In the view of the ETUC, which initiated reflection on this subject, it is clear that *supplementary health schemes* cannot be left to the laws of the market, which are a factor of social exclusion and patient selection. In this field, trade union organizations also have a role to play:

- in ensuring 'high quality and sustainable health care' (European Commission, 1999b);
- but also in preventing any questioning of the basic principles underlying the European Social Model, to which the ETUC is committed and in which social protection systems participate, namely the principles of solidarity and collective responsibility (*social insurance*), as well as social cohesion.

For all these basic reasons, not only should trade union organizations not remain indifferent to these subjects, but they must intervene in them.

3 The Treaty of Amsterdam and New Forms of Work: New Prerogatives for the European Social Partners

With the signature of the Treaty of Amsterdam on 2 October 1997, the social partners saw their role and prerogatives increase sharply: social issues in Europe have become their priority responsibility. Admittedly, this does not (yet) directly concern social security, but two examples can be used to illustrate the opening which has been offered to the social partners and the benefits which they can draw from it, including in the field of social security.

A Social Protocol (Protocol No. 14) had already been annexed to the Maastricht Treaty, on the basis of which the Council issued a Directive (94/45/EC) on 22 September 1994, on the establishment of European Works Councils (European Council, 1994). Up to now, over 600 European works councils have been established. In addition to matters relating to remuneration and conditions of work, several of them are investigating ways of *harmonizing* social protection, while at the same time envisaging the possibility of establishing *European pension funds*.

Another example is the third framework agreement concluded on 18 March 1999 on fixed-term work. In the preamble to this agreement, the European social partners which are signatories thereto recognize that

> innovations in occupational social protection systems are necessary in order to adapt them to current conditions, and in particular to provide for the transferability of rights …

and add in the twelfth consideration that

> the social partners are best placed to find solutions that correspond to the needs of the employers and workers and shall therefore be given a special role in the implementation and application of this agreement (European Council, 1999).

Admittedly, these are only the first *murmurings*. But they demonstrate a far-reaching ambition to be actors in the European social protection of tomorrow.

Moreover, the Court of Justice, in the ruling Albany et al., issued on 21 September 1999 (C-67/96), on the issue of supplementary pensions, has recently given real judicial recognition to collective bargaining in relation to pension funds. It recognizes in particular in the field of supplementary social protection the capacity and role of the social partners in the *conclusion and implementation* of joint agreements. And it reaffirms the primacy of social agreements, including those relating to matters of free competition: 'the social objectives pursued by such agreements would be seriously undermined if management and labour were subject to Article 85 (1) of the Treaty', that is the Article which prohibits all agreements:

> which have as their objective the prevention, restriction or distortion of competition within the common market … it therefore follows from an interpretation of the provisions of the Treaty as a whole which is both effective and consistent that agreements concluded in the context of collective negotiations between management and labour in pursuit of such objectives must, by virtue of their nature and purpose, be regarded as falling outside the scope of Article 85 (1) of the Treaty.

Out of the law comes forth legitimacy …

Conclusion for Trade Union Action: Combine a High Level of Social Protection with Economic Performance

In the view of the ETUC, the *adaptation* of social protection goes hand in hand with its *improvement*, so as to be able to respond to the new challenges which are currently arising (such as new forms of employment and the evolution of family structures). Based on the European experience that the countries with the best systems of social protection (such as the Nordic countries, France and Germany) are also those which have achieved the best economic performance, the ETUC considers that there is no contradiction between a high level of social protection and an efficient economy. Furthermore, allowing trade union organizations to exercise influence over the development of social protection systems amounts to refusing social protection which is totally *administered* or *state controlled* and refusing a society in which the citizens are either dependent on assistance or are left to the law of the market jungle.

For this reason, in the resolution adopted in July 1999 at its Helsinki Congress, the ETUC advocates that:

> following the example of the European employment policy guidelines, a similar initiative should be launched with the setting of guidelines for social convergence, with a timetable and a monitoring system in which

> the social partners are represented. This would leave to national governments and the social partners the method of implementation.

In other words, it intends to promote the active participation of all citizens in tomorrow's society.

References

Communication from the Commission (1997c), *Consolidated Versions of the Treaty on European Union and the Treaty establishing the European Community incorporating the changes made by the Treaty of Amsterdam*, http://europa.eu.int/eur-lex/en/treaties.

Communication from the Commission (1998), *Social Protection in Europe Report 1997*, Brussels.

Communication from the Commission (1999a), *Commission Communication: Towards a single market for supplementary pensions: Results of the consultations on the Green Paper on supplementary pensions in the single market* (COM(99) 134 final), Brussels.

Communication from the Commission (1999b), *A Concerted Strategy for Modernising Social Protection*, Communication from the Commission (COM(99) 347 final), Brussels.

Communication from the Commission (2000), *Surveillance des Institutions de Retraite Professionnelle*, Markt/2076/99 compl.-FR, Commission working paper (March 2000).

Court of Justice of the European Communities (1999), *Albany International BV v Stichting Bedrijfspensioenfonds Textiel-industrie* (Case C-67/96).

European Commission (1995), *The Future of Social Protection: A framework for a European debate*, Communication from the Commission (COM(95)466 final), Brussels.

European Commission (1997a), *Modernising and Improving Social Protection in the European Union*, Communication from the Commission (COM(97)102), Brussels.

European Commission (1997b), *Supplementary Pensions in the Single Market: A Green Paper*, Communication from the Commission (COM(97)283 final), Brussels.

European Council (1971), *Regulation (EEC) No.1408/71 of the Council on the Application of Social Security Schemes to Employed Persons and their Families moving within the Community.*

European Council (1972), *Regulation (EEC) No. 574/72 of the Council of 21 March 1972 fixing the Procedure for Implementing Regulation (EEC) No.1408/71 on the Application of Social Security Schemes to Employed Persons and their Families moving within the Community.*

European Council (1994), *Council Directive 1994/45/EC of 22 September 1994 on the Establishment of a European Works Council or a Procedure in Community-scale Undertakings and Community-scale groups of Undertakings for the Purposes of Informing and Consulting Employees.*

European Council (1999), *Council Directive 1999/70/EC of 28 June 1999 concerning the Framework Agreement on Fixed-term Work concluded by ETUC, UNICE and CEEP.*

European Trade Union Confederation (1999), *General Trade Union Policy Resolution*, adopted by the IXth Statutory Congress, Helsinki, June 1999.

ILO (1952), *Social Security (Minimum Standards) Convention (No. 102).*

Reynaud, E. (ed.) (1999), *Social Dialogue and Pension Reform: United Kingdom, United States, Germany, Japan, Sweden, Italy, Spain*, ILO, Geneva.

Université des Sciences Sociales de Toulouse and UNEDIC (2000), *Indemnisation du Chômage: Expériences et approches internationales.*

Feature No. 8
Negotiating Pension Reform with the Unions: the Italian Experience in European Perspective

Lucio Baccaro

Politicians throughout continental Europe are quickly learning, sometimes to their own cost, that implementing what is arguably one of Europe's most urgent policy priorities, namely pension reform (Boldrin et al., 1999), requires either reaching some form of deal with the trade unions, or constructing broad parliamentary coalitions, or both at the same time (Myles and Pierson, 2000; Reynaud, 2000).

The one case in which pension reform was introduced by governmental fiat was the 1986 privatization of SERPS (the State Earnings-Related Supplementary Pension Scheme) in the United Kingdom. Other attempts at unilaterally imposing pension cuts by the government of the day, most notably in Italy (1994), France (1995) and Germany (1997), met with staunch opposition, particularly from the trade union movement, and failed. In contrast with these continental schemes, SERPS was in its early stages of maturity (the first payments to the scheme had been made in 1978). The total amount of accumulated pension credits was therefore still relatively marginal. Moreover, the government agreed to take over this debit and repay it through tax revenues. Even so, the privatization of SERPS was not without problems (Pierson, 1994).

In Germany (1989) and Spain (1997), pension reform was the result of political agreements involving both the ruling and opposition parties. These deals were also followed (and strengthened) by peak agreements with the social partners, and particularly, in the case of Spain, the labour movement (Schmähl, 1993; Guillén, 1999). The Swedish pension reform (1994–98) dispensed with explicit union consensus. However, it was supported by both the conservative parties and the Social Democratic Party (Anderson, 1998). This not only effectively depoliticized the issue of reform, in the sense that no party could claim political credit for defending the status quo, but also contributed to spreading the blame.

In this context, the 1995 Italian pension reform stands out for a variety of reasons. First, it was implemented by an extremely weak executive, a *technocratic* government without a clear parliamentary majority. Nevertheless, it turned out, alongside the Swedish pension reform, to be one of the most ambitious in Europe (Myles and Pierson, 2000; Reynaud, 2000). Secondly, the involvement of unions in the reform was perhaps the most extensive in comparative terms. In other cases of negotiated reform, such as in Germany and Spain, the unions were one of the actors involved in the process, alongside others, including the respective governments, political parties, business associations and social security experts. In contrast, in Italy, the unions not only negotiated the details of the new pension system, but in practice designed it.

Thirdly, and perhaps most importantly, this level of extensive involvement by the Italian labour movement would appear to be surprising. In view of its fragmented and highly conflictual industrial relations structure, Italy has long been regarded as one of the most unlikely cases for a concerted, or *neo-corporatist* approach to policy-making. Analysis of the Italian pension reform therefore offers the opportunity for a critical re-examination of neo-corporatist theory with a view to understanding the aspects which need to be amended in the light of the recent re-emergence of concerted policy-making in Europe.

In short, while neo-corporatist theory can persuasively explain why the Italian government may have had good reasons to involve the union movement, as well as why Italian unions were willing to participate in the design and implementation of a policy that brought (short-term) losses rather than benefits to their members, the manner in which it accounts for the appropriate internal mechanisms through which consensus is secured within unions is, at best, incomplete.

Governments which are faced with the need to implement unpopular reforms may find it expedient to include broadly representative social groups in the policy-making process (Lehmbruch, 1979). Politicians seek, insofar as possible, to avoid taking direct responsibility for policies that take things away from people, particularly when the structure of party competition is such that the opposition parties can credibly present themselves as the defenders of pensioners' rights. Viewed from this angle, reform of pay-as-you-go pension systems would appear to be especially difficult, since the real beneficiaries of such reforms are future generations who, as a result of the reform, will be less burdened by the repayment of the pension debt. By definition, however, these beneficiaries do not vote and cannot reward their political sponsors.

In other similar circumstances, labour unions may be valuable allies for governments, since their participation is likely to both increase the legitimacy of policies and activate alternative, non party-based, mechanisms for the mobilization of consensus. In Italy, the presence of quarrelsome governmental coalitions, based on a multiplicity of parties in constant competition with one another, and relying on slim parliamentary majorities, has made interest-group participation in all major policy reforms, and not just in pension reform, almost a functional necessity.

With regard to the issue of why the unions participate in the development of these policies, the most common explanations emphasize the organizational characteristics of specific unions, and especially the notion of their *encompassing* nature or, in other words, the fact that because some unions represent a large cross section of the economy as a whole, rather than purely sectional groups, they may experience the negative consequences of the status quo directly and therefore be more willing than, for example, craft-based or industry-specific organizations, to do something about it (Olson, 1982). Another line of argument focuses on the credibility of government threats of unilateral action if unions refuse to cooperate. Yet another argument emphasizes the strength of external constraints (Katzenstein, 1985).

The presence of all three conditions (encompassing organizations, a credible threat of government action and external constraints) neatly accounts for, and virtually *over-determines* the choice of the Italian unions to cooperate. Italian unions are, in practice, of the *encompassing* kind. They are organized on the basis of confederations representing both blue- and white-collar workers in all sectors of the economy at the same time. Moreover, because the concerted pension reform of 1995 had been preceded by attempted unilateral action by the government in 1994, the unions legitimately believed that, had they failed to reform the pension system on terms with which they were comfortable, a future government might try again, and perhaps be more successful in marginalizing them. Finally, the Maastricht parameters were clearly important in mobilizing consensus in support of fiscal consolidation.

The process by which Italian union leaders mobilized consensus for pension reform within their own ranks stands in stark contrast with the diagnoses (and prescriptions) of neo-corporatist theory, which implicitly assumes and sometimes explicitly argues that to ensure rank and file acquiescence to *austerity* policies, union leaders need to possess a series of institutional resources (such as compulsory membership, public or semi-public recognition and/or financing) enabling them to *impose* upon workers a series of outcomes to which they might not otherwise subscribe. This would also mean that an *undemocratic* internal process is required within trade unions (see Baccaro, 2000). The possibility that leaders could retain (and perhaps even expand) their control over members through persuasion and rational argument through a formal *democratic* decision-making process is not even taken into consideration by standard neo-corporatist theory.

In contrast with these views, the Italian pension reform shows that the systematic consultation of workers *and* a binding union referendum were key factors in generating rank and file support for the reform. Rather than following the prescriptions of neo-corporatist theory, and seeking to insulate themselves from their base, the Italian unions took the opposite route. While they were still negotiating the proposed reform, they involved the workers in a first round of plant-level assemblies. After reaching an agreement with the government, they organized a new wave of thousands of assemblies, followed by a referendum by secret ballot, in which 64 per cent of the workers consulted (58 per cent of active workers) voted in favour of the reform.

This *democratic* decision-making process served the cause of reform well. The perceived fairness of the decision-making process increased the legitimacy of the collective decision (see Lind and Tyler, 1988). Pension reform met with the fierce opposition of industrial workers, particularly metalworkers in the north of the country. Previous episodes of grassroots mobilization (for example, in 1984 and 1992) had suggested that similar levels of internal opposition could have very well led to the demise of the reform. However, in contrast with previous occasions, none of the groups which contested the proposed policy change mobilized against it. This is likely to be due to the perceived fairness of the process by which pension reform was discussed and voted upon. In other words, because the results of the referendum unambiguously showed that reform was supported by a majority of the workers involved, even dissenting groups accepted the *will of the majority* and did not engage in collective action to contest the proposed change.

Moreover, the decision-making process gave union leaders an opportunity to shape the process of preference formation by workers.

Union leaders explained clearly to the rank and file why pension reform was both necessary (because the state pension system was on the verge of financial collapse) and equitable (because the previous system was too onerous for the younger generations). It is interesting to note in this respect that workers in very similar structural conditions sometimes voted in favour of, and sometimes against the proposed reform on the basis of the way in which the reform was presented to them, particularly by union representatives at the plant level.

References

Anderson, K.M. (1998), *Organized Labor, Policy Feedback, and Retrenchment in Swedish Pension and Unemployment Insurance*, paper presented at the 11th International Conference of Europeanists, Baltimore (26–28 February 1998).

Baccaro, L. (2000), 'Centralized Collective Bargaining and the Problem of "compliance": Lessons from the Italian experience', *Industrial and Labor Relations Review*, 53(4), pp. 579–601.

Boldrin, M., Dolado, J.J., Jimeno, J.F. and Peracchi, F. (1999), 'The Future of Pension in Europe', *Economic Policy*, 14 (29), October, pp. 287–320.

Guillén, A.M. (1999), *Pension Reform in Spain (1975–1997): The role of organized labour*, EUI Working Papers No. 99/6, European University Institute.

Katzenstein, P.J. (1985), *Small States in World Markets: Industrial policy in Europe*, Cornell University Press, Ithaca, NY.

Lehmbruch, G. (1979), 'Liberal Corporatism and Party Government', in Schmitter, P.C. and Lehmbruch, G. (eds), *Trends toward Corporatist Intermediation,* Sage, London, pp. 147–83 (first published in *Comparative Political Studies* (10), 1977).

Lind, E.A. and Tyler, T.R. (1988), *The Social Psychology of Procedural Justice*, Plenum, New York.

Myles, J. and Pierson, P. (2001), 'The Comparative Political Economy of Pension Reform', in Pierson, P. (ed.), *The New Politics of the Welfare State*, Oxford University Press, Oxford.

Olson, M. (1982), *The Rise and Decline of Nations: Economic growth, stagflation and social rigidities*, Yale University Press, New Haven.

Pierson P. (1994), *Dismantling the Welfare State? Reagan, Thatcher and the Politics of Retrenchment*, Cambridge University Press, New York.

Reynaud, E. (ed.) (2000), *Social Dialogue and Pension Reform: United Kingdom, United States, Germany, Japan, Sweden, Italy, Spain*, ILO, Geneva.

Schmähl, W. (1993), 'The "1992 Reform" of Public Pensions in Germany: Main elements and some effects', *Journal of European Social Policy*, 3(1), pp. 39–51.

Chapter Sixteen

Security in a Flexible Economy: Towards a Third Age in Relations between Work and Social Protection?

Robert Salais

Current transformations of work are throwing up two contradictory trends, especially from the viewpoint of the knowledge-based economy. The first is the growth of models of employment based on higher levels of responsibility and autonomy, and the second is the expansion of phenomena of selectivity on the labour market. The first require a social approach to the issue of security, with emphasis on the development of capabilities; in contrast, the second, centred around the narrow concept of individual adaptation, generates social exclusion. The concept of capacities will be defined below. At this juncture it may be said that, for particular individuals, it refers to their power to act and succeed in what they are undertaking, based on various types of resources, particularly of a legal nature. This will be the subject of the first section of this chapter. In the second section, an attempt will be made to draw out a number of implications for the future of employment and social protection policies in Europe. The basic argument is that we are at the threshold of a third age of work and social protection, which is giving rise to major tensions and is accompanied by a resurgence of old and socially regressive models. What is important is not whether we should deplore or rejoice in these transformations, but how to predict their implications for the future of Europe from the standpoint of work and social protection. It is on this point that the chapter will conclude by raising the question of whether Europe has not missed its chance to victoriously anticipate these developments.

1 Transformations of Work

Much has been written about the end, or indeed the future of work (Gorz, 1998; Méda, 1995; Supiot, 1998 and 1999). The unease that this denotes relates to the contradictory nature of current transformations of work. In basic terms, there is a contradiction between two trends.

The first is the development of new models of employment, based on greater responsibility, initiative, independence and relational skills. This means that those who work, or who wish to do so, require a combination of general and specialized knowledge and personal qualities. The capacity to work together with others is increasingly widely sought, since it cannot automatically be ensured by technical means. These models, which have their origins in new sectors, such as services, communications and, more broadly, new information technologies, are also spreading to traditional industries and the more standard jobs of manual and office workers. There are several contributory factors, such as: the flattening of hierarchical command structures and the indirect reduction in staffing levels that this entails; requirements relating to security and the optimal operation in real time of costly and sophisticated installations (such as supervising traffic movements in the Metro, automated chemical plants and power stations). Similarly, in contacts with clients in office work, the concern to adapt responses to the diversity of demand is resulting in the requirements of autonomy and individual initiative. Another contributory factor is the new aspiration of at least a part of the workforce, and perhaps more among young persons and women than adult men or older employees (although the trend is not systematic) to be able to lead their working lives with a certain freedom of choice, including the choice of the enterprise in which they wish to work, the choice of their working time arrangements and conditions of work. In exchange for the greater responsibilities that they are being asked to take on in their work (and which they are not rejecting), they aspire to share in these choices, or in other words, that their opinion should be sought and taken into account. Without exaggerating them, these demands and this power to influence choices must not be overlooked in the most sought after occupational categories (who have many openings on the labour market). This takes nothing away from the fact that, below a certain wage level, the pressure to attain a reasonable standard of living and the need for security prevail over all else, as illustrated (if proof were needed) by the development of involuntary part-time work and the persistence of inequalities between men and women workers.

The second trend is the parallel transformation of the labour market towards greater selectivity in recruitment. The principal indication of this is the individualization of evaluation processes. The usual general references are becoming inadequate to evaluate the unique qualities of individuals, namely their individual capacities. Over and above university degrees, for example, these individual capacities consist of the qualities that are needed to work effectively and independently (in the sense of knowing when and where it is necessary to take the appropriate action, all of which are factors which cannot be foreseen with precision in advance).

The emphasis placed on employability reflects these trends on the labour market, as does the slogan *lifelong learning*. This is a way of expressing, from the point of view of needs, the insight that the labour market is a *space in which individuals are judged*. During their lives, individuals enter and return to this space at different junctures, depending on factors such as their mobility, periods of unemployment and their level of integration. Individuals are then evaluated or re-evaluated according to the specific requirements of the jobs for which they are applying. They have to have the capacity to succeed in these tests. The problem lies in the fact that these processes of rotation and selection could mark the beginning of the slippery slope towards precarious jobs and exclusion from *good* jobs. Failure in these tests (as well as the fear of failure) is the anti-chamber of social exclusion. The accompanying train of poverty and indignity are deplorable, and clash with the feeling that they should no longer be possible in wealthy countries.

Contrary to a simplistic and too widely held fatalism, exclusion from work is not an unavoidable phenomenon written into the genes and trajectories of individuals or their social categories. Indeed, such simplistic fatalism is contradicted by the experience of those working in the field of vocational integration. It is impossible to say that any particular individual is definitively and completely unemployable. Integration is related more to the adequacy of the vocational integration methods, resources and measures adopted by the community (on this point, see the works gathered in Paugam, 1996). The significance of this remark is heightened by the probability that we are entering a period of rising employment levels. What are needed are exchanges of good practices in which, it should be said right from the start, Europe should be much more involved than it now is.

There is a contradiction between these two sets of trends (Figure 16.1) in terms of their implications for employment and social policies. Selectivity on the labour market is accentuating a narrow definition of skills, based on a type of individual competence that is closely adapted to the needs of a specific enterprise. And, in particular, it is leaving individuals on their own faced with the market and having to manage the situation with the inadequate and insufficient resources at their disposal. Models of employment based on autonomy and responsibility, on the other hand, leave the way open to a broad definition of the capabilities of individuals to control their working lives, and indeed their lives in general, and to manage them effectively and successfully through changes on the market and in the economy, all with a view to their own personal progress.

From the point of view of collective objectives, this second definition is by far the most satisfactory. It is related to free and equal access of all individuals to the management of their work and lives. Effective forms of access, including access to knowledge, skills, work and economic and social rights which, are legitimate claims in a knowledge-based society. This involves adequate collective investments and a new approach by the public authorities, namely the continuous adaptation in practice of the conditions under which such access is attained. A great attention must be paid to the diversity and heterogeneous nature of individual situations, by listening to needs as they are expressed at the individual level. These new dimensions can be perceived in employment policy measures such as, in France, local employment missions for young people and assistance to unemployed persons to create their own enterprises (Aucoutourier, 1998).

This contradiction between immediate individual competence and the capacity to control one's working life (a capacity which has a strong collective dimension) has implications for a whole series of factors. Two of them will be photographed. Although the comparison is forced, situations in enterprises and on the labour market can, to varying degrees, be covered by both at once.

First Highlight: Negative Restructuring

European firms, workers and citizens are increasingly aware of the fact that European countries have already gone beyond the stage of experimentation and are advancing rapidly, at least at the grassroots

Figure 16.1 Contradiction between two sets of facts

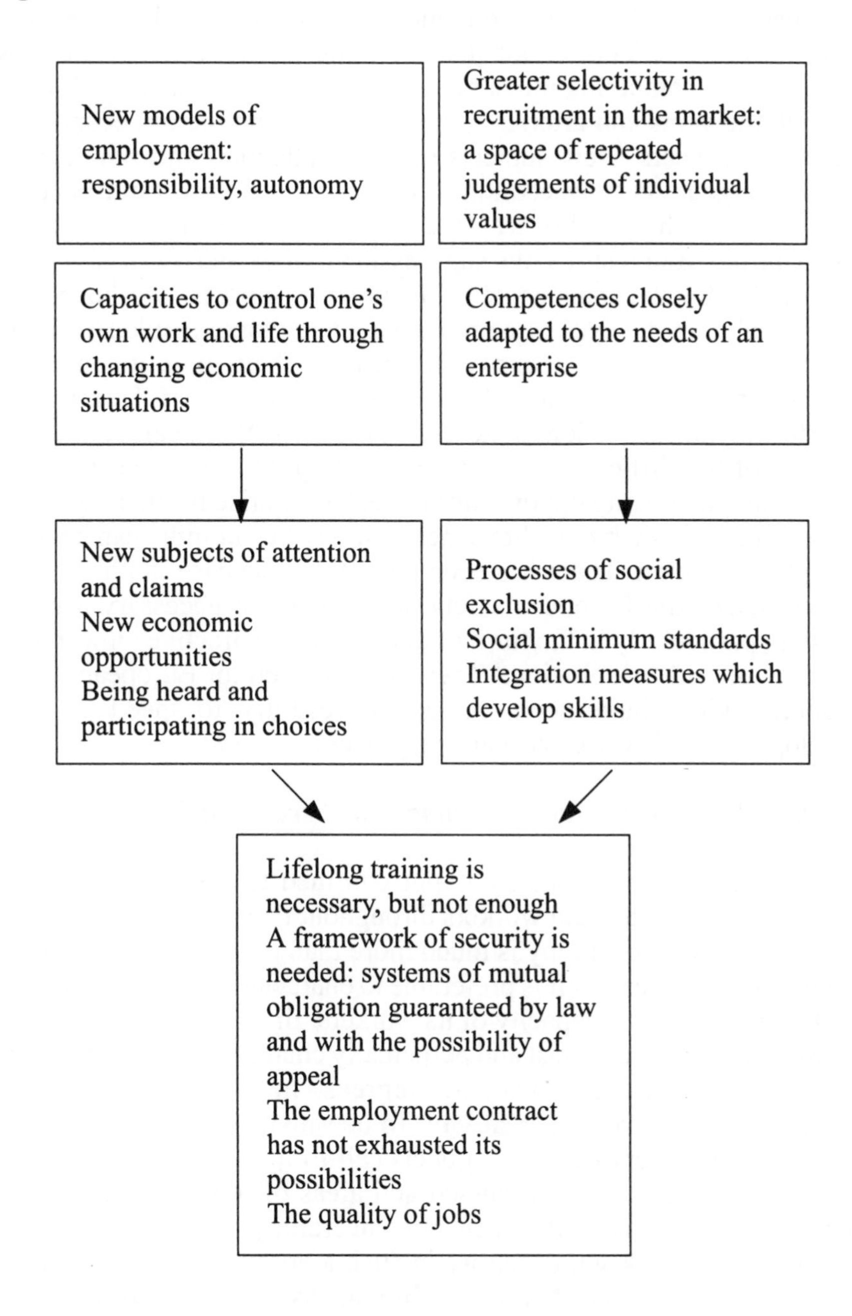

level, towards a new type of economic development based on information technologies and continuous innovation in products, services and occupations. This is not just the icing on the cake of the new economy, but something much more profound which has been flowing through the veins and arteries of both the new and the old economies for over ten years. New subjects of social attention and new claims have emerged. As new economic opportunities arise (and become accessible to those who are able to identify them), the negative restructuring of industries, the suppression of jobs and *downsizing* as a philosophy for the management of human resources, are becoming unacceptable in the eyes of entrepreneurs and workers alike. Workers are calling for greater security in terms of their jobs, income and prospects to compensate for the requirements of flexibility, transformations of work and the risk of mobility. Work can be created. In view of the difficulties of foreseeing, in particular reverses in the market and interesting opportunities which may arise for those who are open to them, it is very insidious merely to say that nothing can be done except close down. There has been more than one case in point. And, unfortunately, the European safety nets which are necessary are still missing, particularly in the form of the European Directive on workers' information and consultation.[1] There is great need for European works councils, which have been created too recently, to speed up their development and collective learning process.

Second Highlight: Lifelong Learning and Freedom of Choice

A knowledge-based economy is not confined to the need, however evident it may be, to train workers throughout their working lives. The knowledge-based economy is much more than a slogan or a marching order: it is also a reality. It is preferable to characterize this economy, in the first place, by the capacity of its workers, firms and public policies to create and produce a vast and perpetually changing array of products and services which, to varying degrees, incorporate aspects of innovation, initiative and creativity. To be satisfactory and effectively produced, these services and products call for participatory structures in which options can be discussed and areas of initiative developed. But, by the same token, they generate uncertainty.

Endowing work with security in such a context requires rigorous and reliable systems of mutual obligations (particularly between employers and those they employ, in such areas as the level and progression of wages and the balancing of responsibilities in working time arrangements), which means that they have to be guaranteed in law and that recourse procedures must be envisaged in the event of abuse. Over the longer-term, it can be seen in France, for example, that certain rights have emerged, such as the right of expression, the right of whistle-blowing and the right of works councils to go to court over *social* plans. All the legal consequences of the traditional model of the employment contract are far from having been exhausted in the field of labour. However, envisaging an individual right to lifelong learning as a solution to insecurity might well turn out to be an exclusion trap for many workers, by making them responsible for managing the risks of the market. Making transitions on the labour market more secure through social drawing rights, as suggested in the Supiot Report (Supiot, 1999), or through formulae which create broader mutual responsibility for employment (such as groups of employers) are therefore welcome innovations (see also Belorgey, Chapter Twelve).

However, the development of capabilities (within the meaning described above) starts with employment and the actual process of work. The definition of employment has to facilitate the acquisition of capacities. The development of capabilities and real freedom of choice are two facets of job quality. An individual's job must be able to give access to real freedom of choice, in such areas as changing jobs within the enterprise or moving to another job, as well as choosing whether or not to work. The quality of employment is one of the new objectives which should be covered by the traditional model of the employment contract (and not only by labour market measures). This concept of quality of employment has, moreover, recently made its appearance in the European Social Agenda, as decided upon at the Nice Summit (7–9 December 2000).

These new objectives still have to be attained, through an examination of real situations at work and through the development of qualitative indicators adapted to the follow-up of policies. This should provide a basis for the further development of employment guidelines. The renewal of social dialogue, supported by a firm legislative framework, is essential to overcoming these problems.

But are all these issues given their true importance and are they properly understood in European reflection on work and social protection? There are many signs that give grounds for doubting, despite certain reactions, that the real significance of these issues has been really taken on board in public, national and European reflection and policy-making. The traditional terms of employment, work, social protection and poverty have been supplemented above by three other terms: exclusion, security and participation. These seven terms have to be remodelled. What might be expected to emerge to revitalize our reflection processes in the areas of work and social protection?

2 The Three Ages of Work and Social Protection

In the end, we never get away from *the social problem* in the broad sense of the term (this historian's term is used intentionally), nor in the manner in which they are treated. These issues encompass both work and its protection (or security). The hypothesis will be advanced that to the two formative ages of poverty (the original, but still topical age) and unemployment (or, in other words, access to employment, which is also still topical), transformations in the world of work are adding a third age, revolving around the reformulation of social issues in terms of participation (or inclusion). The debate is complicated by the fact that the range of possible options is broad. It would be simplistic to believe, or to pretend that the arrival of a new age legitimises the disappearance of the guarantees and rights offered by previous ages (as claimed, for example, by French employers, in their attempts at social reconfiguration – *refondation sociale*). Or to believe that it merely supplements previous ages. Established attitudes and practices do not just disappear. Paradoxically, emerging phenomena give them a new lease of life. They offer their solutions to the new problems, leading to greater tension and divergences between the proposals that are made.

Figure 16.2 proposes an analytical framework focusing on the relations between work and social protection:

- in the first age of poverty, the categories of the population who are protected exchange subsistence for social dependency, with the responsibility of the State being confined to guaranteeing a minimum level of subsistence. The basis of protection is charity. This first age has not totally disappeared;
- in the second age (of which our current labour and social protection institutions bear the massive imprint), access to employment and

social protection, whether in the form of a right or through the structure of the labour market, has the counterparts of subordination and the obligation to work. Economic employment policy is committed to optimizing the overall level of employment. It is the beginning of *freedom from want,* which is principally a negative freedom (this was the focus of the New Deal – the real one – in the 1930s, advocated by Roosevelt and given a theoretical basis by Beveridge). It gave rise to *rights to* social and legal protection, benefit, etc. This is a major gain, and not just a 'social acquired right' or an *acquis social* (to use the modern European term), but also an economic and political gain. Economic, because the fact of receiving a replacement income and being assisted against the various risks sustains global demand and, at the micro level, allows time to make the necessary adjustments more effectively and to attain a better match between supply and demand. As a result, unemployed people who are adequately compensated for an appropriate period can find a job which is more suited to their capacities. A good match between supply and demand improves overall productivity. It is also a political gain, because it frees people from dependency and offers effective conditions for the exercise of political rights (this must not be underestimated);

- the third age arising out of transformations in the world of work, of which we are seeing many manifestations, links higher levels of responsibility with the right to inclusion and to effective participation in economic and social life, and particularly in decision-making. In this case, public action is aimed at the quality of employment in terms of social justice and of its conditions, in the sense of not just working conditions, but also living conditions in work. At a stroke, the concept of work is extended beyond the narrow notion of immediate work under constraint. The requirement to broaden the concept of work, without at the same time weakening it, then becomes necessary for the conservation of social guarantees, through their adaptation to transformations in the world of work, for all those who experience difficult employment trajectories (Supiot, 1999). The framework of social and legal security is intended to provide effective means (in terms of resources and rights to take action) of positive freedom (to act, to be and to choose). It is aimed at a transition from *freedom from want* to *freedom to act* (an issue examined by an economist such as Amartya Sen, 1989 and 1992). It offers *rights of,* with the status of rights of action.

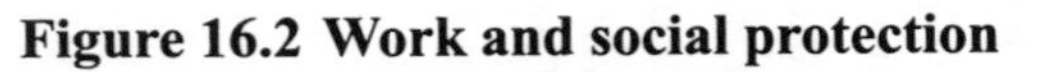

Figure 16.2 Work and social protection

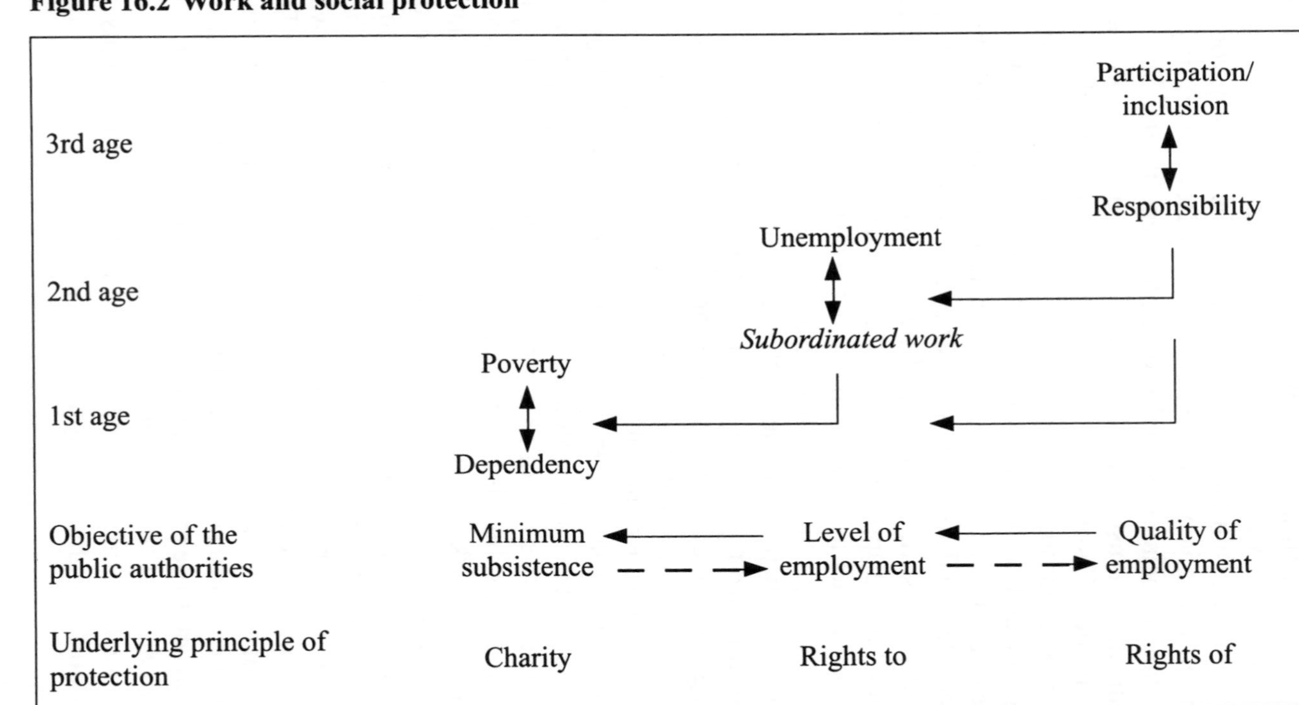

There are three readings of this figure, two spontaneous, and the third considered. The two spontaneous readings lead on to slippery slopes in terms of the future of work and social protection. They sharpen fears. If the future on offer is a transition towards the third age, the risk can be understood of letting go of the bird in the hand and of vainly overturning institutions and a right which, whatever its value, offers advantages. Requiring unemployed people who have no real capabilities to adapt to new models of employment is surely a means of excluding them or marginalizing as *working poor*. Although they no longer swell the unemployment statistics (which is excellent for political purposes), is their situation improved (this appears to be one of the consequences of *workfare* policies in the United States)? Moreover, is there not a parallel danger in refusing to see the danger and to innovate? There is also a third reading, which is the result of deeper reflection. In my view, if it can do so politically, Europe should become the advocate of this reading. The three readings are as follows:

Reading A: the succession of models in time;
Reading B: social segmentation;
Reading C: positive retroaction.

According to reading A, the ages (or regimes) follow on from each other, with the latest replacing the earlier ones. All new institutions should be designed according to the new model. This would lead to the abandonment, through the allocation of fewer material and financial resources, of the policies and institutions of previous regimes and would result in those who previously benefited from them being called upon to demonstrate attitudes which are appropriate to the new regime. This involves, for example, urging the unemployed to demonstrate an appropriate level of responsibility for their own situation if they wish to continue to receive benefit. It also involves requiring those who are dependent on the former regime to accept any work that is offered (the logic of *workfare*). Historians have adequately demonstrated that historical processes are more complex than a succession of regimes. Nevertheless, old solutions, repainted in the colours of the age, retain their attraction in the political debate. For example, are good old-fashioned Victorian values really absent from the *Third Way*?

Reading B is more pernicious. It involves finding in this figure a principle of segmentation and social stratification and setting it out rigidly in law. At the top end, the new categories of employed workers have access to the maximum level of rights (particularly *freedom to*); in the middle are the renewed (and possibly more flexible) Fordist workers who only benefit from traditional social rights; and at the lower end are precarious workers and those who are marginalized, who only have access to an incompressible minimum level of rights. This social stratification is contrary to the principle of equality before the law and foreign to the spirit of European integration. It endorses a miserly interpretation of fundamental rights. In contrast with this interpretation, European social policy intends to use fundamental rights to make access to basic guarantees universal throughout Europe. The labour movement can then improve on these basic guarantees (for example, through collective agreements), precisely through the application of these rights. Unfortunately, even among writers who are undoubtedly well intentioned, and in a more sophisticated manner, there is a drift towards Reading B (reference may be made in this respect to a recent publication – the last before its disappearance – of the Saint-Simon Foundation – Beffa, Boyer and Touffut, 1999).

Reading C consists of adding the effect of retroaction. This third reading is the only one which, in social and economic terms, is adapted to current transformations in the world of work, both in support of the transformations and anticipating their costs. New forms of security and concepts of work, rights to, the quality of the supply of employment, access to the capacity to control one's life, must be available right away to all workers, both new and traditional, whether they are covered by the *unemployment* or the *poverty* model. This is a truly historical task which the European Social Agenda should set as an objective. This perspective will be examined briefly below, taking the example of measures to combat exclusion. This reading has to be adapted to the diversity of situations. History of the second age of social protection and employment, shows how long and conflictual such a process can be (Salais, Bavarez and Reynaud, 1999). There are no beds of roses. Whatever our views, progress will go on. Responsibilities have to be assumed and choices explained publicly if they are to be the best possible.

The Example of Measures to Combat Exclusion

The Council of Europe at its Lisbon Summit on 23 and 24 March 2000 turned its attention to both the knowledge-based society and exclusion.

As has been pointed out in discussing the transformation of work, the link is justified. Exclusion from work in the first place (but also from housing, health care and fundamental rights) is a qualitatively new phenomenon. It is new in the sense that a marginalized person is, by definition, someone who has fallen through the gaps, small as they are, in the safety net of the current social protection systems in our developed countries. The marginalized are a living demonstration of a crisis at the very roots of these systems (especially systems which are basically products of the first two ages) and their failure to adapt to the new situation of work (on these points, see Raveaud and Salais, 2001 (forthcoming)).

What is the spectrum of available proposals? Based on a poverty approach (the first age), the main response is a means-tested minimum income. From an unemployment approach (the second age), the requirement to work prevails over access to assistance. Between the two, various compromises have been advocated. The minimum insertion income (RMI), on the French model, is based on a concept of *rights to* (see Belorgey, Chapter Twelve). It involves resource conditions, but without the stigmatization of the English model of the *means test*. Anglo-Saxon *workfare* hardens the issue of poverty by adding the requirement to work (see Millar, Chapter Ten). It adds to the constraints weighing upon benefit recipients, without offering them any long-term issue from their situation.

Nevertheless, these compromises persist in the approaches adopted by the first two ages. The participation approach seeks solutions which are both just and effective and which are based on the *effective* restoration of the capabilities of individuals to attain integration into society and economic activity. Earlier solutions do not disappear, but are modified from within. In the case, for example, of access to work, emphasis should be placed on the progressive development of freedom of choice based on real social and occupational capacities. Support is provided, on a case by case basis, in such forms as the minimum income guarantee, the multifarious types of subsidized contracts or jobs, public measures and associative initiatives to assist in occupational integration, the creation of appropriate jobs by enterprises and the improvement in the conditions under which they are performed. What matters is the development of an ascending trajectory for the individual. The aim is that, ultimately, individuals can be responsible for themselves, without losing the protective safety net if they fall.

Incorporating an objective of participation into the fight against poverty implies creating the social and economic conditions for effective respect of the basic rights of the person – dignity, self respect. In so doing, dependence and stigmatization could be avoided. It must be acknowledged that many existing measures do not meet these requirements.

The third age of social protection (the age of participation) therefore requires important transformations in the measures adopted, in institutions (including enterprises) and in their day-to-day operation. Fundamental rights are indivisible. Without access to housing, how can the right to privacy be respected? Without the right to be informed and consulted about choices, how can workers be expected to commit themselves on a long-term basis to effective and motivated work? A somewhat cynical view might be that, as full employment comes closer, the threat of unemployment will be less important in obliging workers to provide a quality service and that it is therefore all the more urgent to achieve progress in the field of rights. Anticipation may therefore be welcome.

3 And Social Europe?

There are therefore grounds for hoping that a Europe is emerging which will take responsibility, at its own level of competence, for the development of this third age of security in accordance with Reading C, namely positive retroaction. A few arguments plead in favour of this perspective. Transformations in the world of work immediately take on a European dimension. The growing interdependence of economies makes this natural. Have employment policies, rights and national social protection systems not remained to a very great extent locked in the first two ages? Is it not for Europe to act as a catalyst? Taking responsibility for the overall development of this third age at all levels would offer a unique opportunity to achieve progress through and as a result of European construction (and, in particular, would stimulate the interest of European citizens).

What is ultimately at stake for Europe is not a technical or instrumental issue, but a political one. When, in 1991, the Maastricht Treaty was being prepared, the European Commission was very aware of what was at stake, as shown by its initial draft of the 'social dimension'

(European Commission, 1991). In this draft text, Article 118 (which subsequently became Article 137) envisaged that the European Union would complement and support the action of Member States in fields which dropped by the wayside as the process evolved. However, these fields, which have up to now disappeared from the Treaty, in retrospect appear to take on strategic value from the point of view of the transformation of work and the development of social protection. They include, for example, *living and working conditions, with a view to guaranteeing the protection of fundamental workers' rights, initial and continuing vocational training* and *skill levels* (Salais, 2001).

A European strategy to promote the implementation of a third age of work and security could have been based on the Treaty. The link which was initially made between living and working conditions is essential if the quality of employment is to be improved. Occupational flexibility would have had a greater chance of being addressed at the European level in the joint interests of freedom of choice and basic security, on the one hand, and the needs of enterprises, on the other. This link disappeared in the final version of the Treaty, only leaving, in isolation from life, the field of working conditions.

The Luxembourg employment process can contribute to putting it back on the agenda. However, its chances are weakened by the absence from the Treaty of an ambitious social dimension incorporating the new objectives arising out of transformations in the world of work. The door is half open for the participation of European social actors in the development and implementation of national action plans for employment. Similarly, the social partners can conclude, and have already done so, agreements which become European Directives that are binding on Member States (parental leave, temporary work, fixed-term work and sectoral agreements on working time in the maritime and air transport sectors). However, governments continue to consider social issues as their own backyard. European economic integration and its trail of restructuring measures have not hitherto been accompanied by any commensurate European safety net. However, nothing is ever definitive in Europe. A reminder of what was overlooked in terms of the need, which is clearer now than it was ten years ago, for European action to promote inclusion and participation may create greater awareness of the urgency of such action.

Note

1 Which was still in draft form when this chapter was written.

References

Aucouturier, A.-L. (1998), *Evaluation des Politiques d'Emploi et Action Publique: L'exemple de l'aide aux chômeurs créateurs d'entreprise*, Thèse d'Économie, Université de Paris X.

Beffa, J.-L., Boyer, R. and Touffut, J. Ph. (1999), 'Le Droit du Travail face à l'Hétérogénéité des Relations Salariales', *Droit Social*, 12 (December), pp. 1039–51.

European Commission (1991), *Initial Contribution by the Commission to the IGC on Political Union* (SEC(91)500), Brussels.

Gorz, A. (1988), *Métamorphoses du travail: Quête du Sens*, Galilée, Paris.

Méda, D. (1995), *Le Travail: Une valeur en voie de disparition*, Flammarion, Paris.

Morel, S. (1996), 'Le *Workfare* aux Etats-Unis', in Paugam, S. (ed.), *L'Exclusion: L'État des savoirs*, La Découverte, Paris, pp. 472–83.

Paugam, S. (ed.) (1996), *L'Exclusion: L'État des savoirs*, La Découverte, Paris.

Raveaud, G. and Salais, R. (2001), 'Fighting against Social Exclusion in a European Knowledge-based Society: What principles of action?', in Mayes, D., Salais, R. and Berghman, J. (eds) (2001), *Social Exclusion and European Policy*, Edward Elgar, Aldershot.

Salais R. (2001), 'Filling the Gap between Macroeconomic Policy and Situated Approaches to Employment: A hidden agenda for Europe?', in Strath, B. and Magnusson, L. (eds) (2001), *From Werner Plan to the EMU: A European political economy in historical light*, Peter Lange, Brussels.

Salais, R., Baverez, N. and Reynaud, B. (1999), *L'Invention du Chômage*, PUF, Paris ('Quadrige') (1st edn 1986).

Sen, A. (1989), *On Ethics and Economics*, Blackwell, Oxford.

Sen, A. (1992), *Inequality Reexamined*, Oxford University Press, Oxford.

Supiot, A. (ed.) (1998), *Le Travail en Perspectives*, Librairie Générale de Droit et de Jurisprudence, Paris.

Supiot, A. (ed.) (1999), *Au-delà de l'Emploi: Transformations du travail et devenir du droit du travail en Europe*, Flammarion, Paris.

Chapter Seventeen

Conclusions: the Policy Implications of a Changing Labour Market – Social Protection Relationship

Giuliano Bonoli and Hedva Sarfati

The studies presented in this volume show that the relationship between social protection and labour markets is evolving rapidly. Labour markets are changing and, since the golden age of industrial economies (1945–75), they have already been transformed beyond recognition. At the same time, social protection systems, because their interaction with work is so close, need to adapt and have already done so to a significant extent. The directions of change are multiple, and the adaptation of social protection systems is an ongoing process, characterized by a good deal of trial and error. This makes it difficult to understand the shape that will be taken by the emerging labour market – social protection relationship, particularly in view of the existence of important exogenous variables, such as changes in family structures and the ageing of the population.

In addition, some of the underlying labour market trends reviewed in Chapters One and Two may be reversible, with implications for the way in which the relationship between the labour market and social protection will be structured in welfare states. Unemployment, which had been on the increase throughout the OECD area from the mid-1970s, is now declining in many European countries and in North America. Similarly, the quality of the new jobs that are created may improve over the years, as demand for semiskilled and skilled workers may exceed supply. The analysis by Auer and Cazes illustrates that, contrary to widespread perceptions, the overall duration of job tenure is not diminishing, although there are important differences across groups, with young workers, women and older workers being less likely to have long-term jobs (Auer and Cazes, Feature No. 1). However, over the past decade, the proportion of women with long tenure has increased in a number of European countries, and particularly in the United Kingdom (Doogan, 2001).

Against this background, an attempt will be made in this chapter, based on the comparison of the national labour market and social protection trajectories contained in the present volume, to identify the various combinations of labour market trends found in different countries, as well as cases of success and failure of the adaptation strategies used in different national contexts. The methodological starting point used is the labour market-social protection relationship as it was during the golden age of the welfare state, that is the three post-war decades of fast and steady economic growth, as a basis for highlighting the new features. The goal is to identify the new shape of the relationship, as well as to point to examples of adaptation that we regard as being particularly successful.

This chapter begins by reviewing policy changes in the labour market – social policy relationship over the past 25 years or so. Some of the issues raised by such changes are addressed and the range of policy options available to policy-makers to deal with them is considered. The conclusion is that the adaptation process of social protection and labour market systems is most successful when it is based on carefully balanced policy mixes, which are generally associated with important efforts of coordination by the relevant actors (such as governments and the social partners).

1 Key Policy Trends in the Labour Market – Social Policy Relationship

The welfare states which developed during the post-war years were designed above all to protect citizens against labour market failure, in reaction to the social, political and economic costs of the inter-war depressions. In the event that a person, generally a male breadwinner, was unable to obtain an income sufficient to ensure a decent living for himself and his family, social protection schemes were there to provide a replacement income. In many countries, the protection of the income of male breadwinners went beyond simply providing income security through social transfers, and included measures intended to secure their position in the labour market by means of legislation offering varying levels of employment protection. The combined overall objective of social protection and labour market regulation were economic security for breadwinners and their dependants, whether they were inside or outside the labour market. This objective was achieved through a relatively simple mix of income replacement schemes and employment protection laws.

Over the past two decades, social protection systems have become considerably more employment oriented, although they have not lost their original compensatory function. In the event of unemployment, government intervention is not confined to income replacement through cash benefits, but may include a whole range of activation policies, ranging from the workfare programmes in the style of the United States to the Nordic active labour market policies. Policy-makers can draw on a much wider policy mix than was the case during the post-war period. In old age, retirement income is increasingly being provided by pension systems that combine pay-as-you-go and funded schemes and that mix compulsory with voluntary forms of provision. Broader recognition of women's need for an independent income has contributed to adaptations in social insurance systems to protect their entitlements during periods of family caring. Moreover, the 1980s and the 1990s have seen the development of totally new forms of social intervention, such as negative income tax measures, parental leave schemes and child and tax credits. The relationship of social protection to employment would appear to be more than the simple compensation of market failure.

1.1 Promoting Youth Employment

In countries facing serious youth unemployment problems (particularly Italy and Greece, where 30 per cent of young persons below 25 are unemployed, but also Belgium, Finland, France and the United Kingdom), governments have developed policy initiatives targeting this jobless group, such as the new deal for unemployed people aged between 18 and 25 in the UK (Millar, Chapter Ten). The success of such initiatives depends very much on the overall demand for labour and the economic situation. The economic upturn in the European Union since 1994 has resulted in a sharp reduction of unemployment among the under 25s, which has been three times stronger than for adults (a 4 per cent decline for young persons compared with 1 per cent for adults). However, youth unemployment in the European Union still stands at about 25 per cent, or 2.5 times the average unemployment rate for adults (Sarfati, Chapter

One; European Commission 2000, p. 21). The quality of training and education systems is also of paramount importance in preventing youth unemployment. Indeed, the emphasis on the quality of education and training has contributed to low rates of youth unemployment in Austria, Denmark, Germany, Netherlands, Norway and Switzerland. Germany, in particular, with its world-renowned apprenticeship system, has fared much better than many other European Union countries in this respect over the past few years. The best cure for youth unemployment seems to consist of macroeconomic policies to stimulate growth and measures to provide young people with the skills and competencies required in rapidly developing sectors.

The importance of education and training in combating youth unemployment is emphasized by Belorgey, who advocates a system of vocational training for school-leavers based on individual rights, as opposed to the prevailing approach, which entails a limited number of places for training and apprentice-ship. He argues that school-leavers should be entitled to spend a substantial period of time in vocational training programmes, to improve their labour market opportunities (Belorgey, Chapter Twelve). The European Union employment strategy adopts this approach, although still in more of a remedial than a preventative manner (prescribing that youth should be offered a job or training after six months of being unemployed).

1.2 Increasing the Employment Rates of Women

Women's employment rates have been rising more or less constantly throughout the OECD since the early 1970s, but with substantial cross-national differences in the rate of increase. In the late 1990s, there were still substantial variations in the degree of women's involvement in paid work across OECD countries. In 1998, women's employment rates ranged from a high of 73.3 per cent in Sweden to a low of 35.2 per cent in Spain, a much broader variation than is found in male employment rates (Sarfati, Chapter One; European Commission, 2000). This suggests that there is still some potential for growth in women's employment rates, particularly in countries where they are below the European Union average, such as Belgium, Greece, Ireland, Italy, Luxembourg and Spain, but also in Germany and France where they are just above the average.

Women's involvement in the labour market depends on a range of factors, many of which are determined by government policies. In a comparative study of women's employment, Daly finds that government policies can affect both the supply and demand for women's labour (Daly, 2000). To increase women's labour supply, the degree of state support for caring, both for children and dependent persons, is crucial. Tax systems, and the degree to which they recognize the existence of dual earner couples, also have an impact, albeit a smaller one. On the demand side, the availability of part-time work, the magnitude of employment in the services sector and of public employment are all strongly correlated with women's employment rates.

These factors may be combined in different ways in the various countries. Generally speaking, the policy mix found in the Nordic countries is the most favourable to women's employment, while that in Southern Europe is least favourable. Between these two extremes, policy mixes are to be found which combine obstacles and bridges to the increased labour market participation of women. This is the case in Continental European countries and in most English-speaking countries. The fact that the latter manage to achieve near Nordic women's employment rates suggests that a large private service sector may compensate for minor or nonexistent state support for care (Daly, 2000, p. 506).

The importance of state support is confirmed by Esping-Andersen's econometric analyses, which find that the availability of affordable childcare is the stronger predictor of women's employment rates (Esping-Andersen, 2000b, p. 104). He suggests that the high cost of child care may in fact be one of the main sources of labour market rigidity in Continental European countries, and a more potent obstacle to women's employment than employment protection legislation or high minimum wages. The availability of child care is also an important factor in the ability of women to maintain their occupational status and avoid downgrading. In the Nordic countries, where high quality subsidized child care is widely available, women are abandoning part-time employment and an increasingly large proportion of them are now working full time. This trend contrasts with the situation in the United Kingdom, where the younger cohorts of women were no more likely than their predecessors to be engaged in full-time employment (Hakim, 2000). The kind of employment that women obtain influences not only their career opportunities, but also the private pension entitlements that they are able to build up (Ginn, Feature No. 1).

Obstacles to increased women's employment also include the unattractive jobs and wages often available to them, and particularly to those who are educated and skilled and who all too often cannot attain higher managerial jobs as a result of a *glass ceiling*. Jobs, career paths and pay in the private sector have been tailored to the needs of male breadwinners, with promotion and career development depending on the performance of people in their 20s or early 30s, or precisely the age of childbearing. The prevalence of women in *atypical jobs*, among single-parent households and among the poor make it all the more urgent to rethink the manner in which labour market re-entry could provide career opportunities, income security and adequate social protection coverage, with due account being taken of discontinuous careers. To some extent, welfare states have already been adapted to take account of the larger number of women in the workforce. This has been the case, in particular, in the Nordic countries, where schemes for breadwinners, such as sick pay, have been turned into schemes for *working parents*, for example by also providing for paid leave in the event that children are ill and need care (Overbye, 1998).

There are important policy implications in Esping-Andersen's conclusion that the major determinants of European unemployment levels are restrictive macroeconomic policies (which reduce real private consumption expenditures) and low women's activity rates (which depress job growth through a reduced demand for services) (see also Ughetto, Feature No. 3). While acknowledging that an excess supply of low-skilled labour aggravates unemployment in Europe, he argues that this effect can be cancelled out by increasing women's employment. He therefore advocates a reduction in obstacles to labour market entry by housewives as the best strategy to reduce unemployment (Esping-Andersen, 2000b, pp. 102, 103, 107–8).

1.3 Increasing the Activity Rates of Older Workers

Since the 1970s, the employment rate of older workers, generally defined as persons aged between 55 and 64, has declined throughout the OECD countries. To a large extent, this has been the result of the increased use of pre-retirement and disability insurance as a means of facilitating the adjustment of employment in declining industries or in economic activities undergoing profound restructuring. The extent to which this has happened has varied significantly between countries, with the result that by 1998 the labour force participation rates of men aged 55 to 64 were lowest in Continental Europe, Australia and Canada (33.9 per cent in Belgium, 41.3 per cent in France, 42.5 per cent in Austria, 44.5 per cent in Finland, 55.6 per cent in Germany, 59.6 per cent in Canada and 60.5 per cent in Australia), but much higher in some other countries (Japan 85.2 per cent, Switzerland 81.7 per cent, Norway 75.8 per cent, Sweden 71.4 per cent, New Zealand 70.6 per cent, United States 68.1 per cent and United Kingdom 62.6 per cent) (OECD, 1999b, pp. 231 *et seq.*). In some countries, the decade-long trend towards lower labour market participation by older people may have come to an end. This is clearly the case (in decreasing order) in Portugal, New Zealand, Netherlands, Norway, Spain, United States, Japan, Germany, Sweden and United Kingdom, where labour force participation rates for the 55–65 age group started increasing, although slightly, in 1999 (OECD, 2000, pp. 209–11).

The reduction in the labour force participation rates of older workers has proved to be an extremely costly means of facilitating industrial restructuring and economic adjustment, both for the public budget and in terms of human capital. Today's older people are in better health than a generation ago and can continue to work much longer in activities which do not require physical effort. That is why the reversal of the trend towards early labour market withdrawal has increasingly become a policy objective in OECD countries. In terms of policy measures, governments can increase the activity rates of older people by raising the retirement age or the years of contributions required to be eligible for a full pension, introducing flexible and partial pensions which enable people to receive pension benefits while remaining partly in a gainful activity and removing incentives for early retirement. However, the success of these measures depends on the broader economic context. If industries are going through labour-shedding restructuring, then an increase in the retirement age may prompt employers to use other instruments, such as disability or long-term unemployment benefits, to adjust their labour force (Ebbinghaus, 2000, p. 531). According to Rein and Friedman, this is precisely what has happened in a number of European countries, where attempts in the 1990s to reduce withdrawals from the labour market through one programme generated increases in reliance on other programmes, often not specifically designed for older people (Rein and Friedman, 1998, pp. 77–80).

Despite the adoption of measures to increase the age of leaving the labour market in many European countries, there has not been a clear reversal in the secular trend towards early retirement (European

Commission, 2000, p. 126; on the Dutch case, see Dietvorst, Feature No. 6). This may require a change of attitudes among individuals, who have come to consider early retirement as an acquired right, and even more so, among employers and unions, who have found it a more acceptable mode of leaving work than unemployment. For the middle classes, the opportunity of early retirement on an enhanced private pension encourages early exit in some countries, and particularly in the United Kingdom. Later retirement also implies the availability of jobs that are suitable for older workers. But cut-throat competition and rapid technological change are resulting in hiring and termination practices which focus on high performance, productivity, creativity and rapid adaptability. Because of the relatively low educational levels of older workers and age prejudice among employers, this is tending to exclude people at an increasingly young age. With the extension of contributory requirements for pensions in many European countries, exclusion from the workforce at an early age may result in a permanent penalty in terms of lower pensions (Belorgey, Chapter Twelve). A strategy of combating ageism and legislating against age discrimination (as in the United States) may help to increase the availability of jobs for older workers. The United States has recently taken an important step towards facilitating employment after the retirement age by abolishing a tax which was levied on social security benefits if recipients received income from work (the retirement earnings test).

There is a structural aspect to the question, as many older workers are employed in low growth or declining sectors (European Commission, 2000, pp. 95–108). Institutional rigidities also play a role, including the lack of training opportunities for middle-aged people, age-related pay increments and career paths. Compared with young people aged 25–29, higher skilled people aged 55 and over tend to earn twice as much, while those aged 45–54 earn 50 per cent more. This is hampering the capacity of European societies to adjust to the ageing process. There is a need to rethink the role that older experienced and healthy people could play in societies in which unsatisfied skill needs abound.

A proactive effort to increase the employment rates of older workers is already under way in some states of the United States. Doeringer et al. show how active labour market policies targeted on this group can increase their earnings potential and facilitate their re-entry and retention in the labour market. Such programmes are targeted mostly at older workers who have become unemployed, and consist mainly of job placements and short-term training. In the future, active labour market policies for older people may have to take a longer-term view, by providing training linked to the skill needs of the local economy (Doeringer et al., Chapter Fourteen).

1.4 Reducing the Cost of Unemployment and Providing Incentives to Return to Work

The 1980s and 1990s have seen the reform of unemployment insurance and compensation systems throughout OECD countries. Generally, such reforms have reduced the level and/or duration of unemployment benefits, tightened eligibility conditions and broadened the definition of what is considered to be a suitable job offer. At the same time, measures have been introduced to make work more attractive to the unemployed by increasing take-home pay from work in relation to the income received from social transfers, with benefit levels being reduced gradually as income rises, rather than being withdrawn abruptly (for an overview, see Kalisch et al., 1998). The objective of these initiatives has generally been twofold: on the one hand, to contain rising expenditure and, on the other, to strengthen incentives to work.

An example of such policies is the 1992 French unemployment insurance reform, which introduced a new benefit structure. The scheme now provides generous benefits for the first four months of unemployment, which are gradually decreased if the beneficiary fails to re-enter the labour market. The incentive dimension of the new benefit structure is clear: the longer a person remains in unemployment, the stronger the financial incentive to re-enter the labour market (Join-Lambert, 1998; Bonoli and Palier, 2000). This policy trend has gone furthest in the United Kingdom, where the social insurance aspect of unemployment benefit has been gradually dismantled since the early 1980s, by removing the earnings-related component, reducing the duration of insurance benefits and lowering the amount of the benefit to the same level as means-tested social assistance (Atkinson and Micklewright, 1989; Erskine, 1997). In addition, limiting the indexation of benefits to inflation has widened the gap between benefit levels and wages. Again, the result has been to strengthen work incentives, while at the same time making the living conditions of the unemployed harsher. In the United Kingdom, unemployment has been more strongly associated with poverty than in any other European Union country, at least in the 1980s and early 1990s (Atkinson, 1998; Andersen, Chapter Two). The shift in the United Kingdom towards means-testing the unemployed can also be counterproductive for employment, since it creates a disincentive for the partners of unemployed persons to go out to work, as their earnings reduce the amount of social assistance received by the couple pound for pound.

In assessing the importance of the disincentive to work faced by benefit recipients, it should be recalled that a significant proportion of the unemployed do not in practice receive unemployment benefits. In the European Union as a whole, between one quarter and one-third of all the unemployed do not receive unemployment benefits. Moreover, in eight out of ten European Union countries for which comparable data are available, only about one-fifth of the unemployed receive benefits amounting to 80 per cent or more of their previous earnings (European Commission, 1998). Finally, it should also be borne in mind that that the decisions of the unemployed on whether or not to take up employment are not based solely on financial considerations. Sociologists have shown that the desire to work is generally strong among the unemployed, and that the obstacles to employment are often of a very practical nature, such as the lack of transportation or child care. In such situations, a stronger financial incentive, simply based on the reduction of benefit levels, will have little impact on decisions to go out to work.

In overall terms, a strategy that aims to increase employment simply by cutting unemployment benefit is unlikely to be successful. While the potential for improvement would seem to be limited, there appears to be a strong risk of inflicting unnecessary suffering on the unemployed. Such a strategy may also be unfavourable to employment in the long term, as poor unemployed people are less ready to take up jobs when they become available. Moreover, cutting unemployment benefits also reduces the capacity to search for jobs.

1.5 Active Labour Market Policies

Changes in unemployment benefit schemes have usually been accompanied by measures to improve employability, including training, job counselling and placement assistance. A shift in emphasis from passive income support for the unemployed to active labour market programmes has achieved success in some countries, particularly in

Scandinavia, Austria and the Netherlands, and was strongly recommended in the OECD Jobs Study and Job Strategy reports in 1994. Madsen shows that in Denmark active labour market policies have been a key feature of Government policy since the 1970s. They were strengthened in the mid-1990s, with overall positive results in terms of reductions in both the level and duration of unemployment. As regards the rather small group of long-term unemployed (estimated at 6 per cent of the total unemployed), the highly developed active labour market programmes in Denmark have been found to have only a limited impact on low-skilled unemployed immigrants and on people aged over 50 who have been laid off (Madsen, Chapter Nine).

In the Netherlands, as pointed out by Pennings, active labour market policies have also been expanded in the past few years to include groups such as the disabled. Moreover, the unemployment benefits legislation was amended in 1999 to allow the Minister of Social Affairs and Employment to adopt experimental measures in this policy area. The overall evaluation of the Dutch experience of activation policies highlights the higher level of effectiveness of policies which include a strong component of individual case management (Pennings, Chapter Fourteen).

In the United Kingdom, as emphasized by Millar, activation was not a key aspect of Government policy until the late 1990s. Various *New Deals*, which are activation policies targeted at specific groups of non-working people, such as the young unemployed, unemployed single parents and non-employed partners of the unemployed, were introduced in 1997 and 1998. The variant of activation developed in the United Kingdom seems to be a strategy against *worklessness* (the lack of paid employment), and not simply against unemployment. Compared with past initiatives, more women are involved in these programmes, which raises the issue of compatibility between work obligations and caring responsibilities. How far work requirements should be extended is currently a contentious issue in the debate on active labour market policy measures in the United Kingdom.

Finally, Australia has also developed a substantial set of activation policies over the past few years. Harbridge and Bagley describe the key features of the Australian approach to activation, namely improved fiscal work incentives for non-working spouses and the introduction of an activity obligation for some recipients of unemployment benefits (unpaid or paid work, training or education). The overall evaluation of these measures by the government has been positive (Harbridge and Bagley, Chapter Six).

These assessments of active labour market policies are confirmed by international comparative studies. However, despite the overall positive appreciation, analysis shows that active labour market policies have not come to grips with the core problem of the long-term unemployed. The OECD acknowledges this limitation, stating that 'the track record of many active programmes is patchy in terms of achieving their stated objectives' (Martin 2000, p. 88). Moreover, if their purpose is to reduce the burden of income support measures, this cannot be achieved in the short run (European Commission, 1998, p. 44).

1.6 Tax Credits

The United Kingdom and United States have developed tax credits as an instrument to help the working poor without at the same time diminishing work incentives. The principle underpinning these measures is that work should pay. In practical terms, this is achieved through two types of measures. First, tax credits are paid only to individuals who work a minimum number of hours a week. Second, if the earnings of persons benefiting from the tax credits increase, for example because they start to work more hours, the extra income is not entirely deducted from the credit. The objective is to avoid the 100 per cent effective marginal tax rates which occur in traditional social assistance programmes.

The longer established American version of the tax credit (the Earned Income Tax Credit, or EITC) is widely seen as a successful social measure that has improved the living standards of many working poor, thereby partly offsetting widening wage gaps, and has lifted many families above the poverty line (Myles and Pierson, 1998; Greenstein and Shapiro, 1998; Hotz and Scholz, 2000). The British *Family Credit*, a similar scheme which supplements the wages of low-income workers with children, which operated for several years before being converted into a standard tax credit programme (the Working Families Tax Credit), has also received generally favourable evaluations (Evans, 1996).

However, policies designed to *make work pay*, such as tax credits, have some drawbacks. According to a recent OECD study (Pearson and Scarpetta, 2000; see also Millar, Chapter Ten; Sinfield, Feature No. 5), policies that *make work pay* often generate considerable administrative problems, since there are high error rates and the schemes are open to fraud. In addition, like all means-tested programmes, tax credits imply high effective marginal tax rates for increases in earnings by beneficiaries of the credit. Finally, in the long term, the fact that the state is *de facto* subsidizing low wage employment may discourage employers from investing in human capital. Overall, however, the experiences of several OECD countries have been positively evaluated even though, as Sinfield argues, social policy objectives such as tackling child poverty or promoting social cohesion may be better achieved through benefits that are not limited to working families or individuals (Sinfield, Feature No. 5).

1.7 Subsidies Covering Social Contributions

Social contributions are widely believed to discourage recruitment. A number of governments (in France, Belgium and to a lesser extent Germany) have introduced subsidies to reduce employers' contributions with a view to encouraging recruitment, particularly of the low-skilled unemployed. The objective of these programmes is to reduce the size of the tax wedge, or the difference between gross and net earnings, which is detrimental to job creation, particularly in low-skilled services (Scharpf, 2000, pp. 75–85).

In France, since the mid-1990s, low-wage workers (earning up to 1.3 times the minimum wage) have benefited from a lower rate of contributions to compulsory social insurance schemes. The result has been a reduction in labour costs of approximately 12 per cent at the level of the minimum wage. Other forms of exemptions and reductions in contributions exist for specific groups of workers, such as those who have experienced long-term unemployment. More recently, exemptions and reductions in contributions have also been used to encourage employers to reduce working hours and take on additional employees (Levy, 2000). It is difficult to assess the real impact of these policy measures on employment creation, partly because most of them have been operating over too a short period of time. The expansion of employment in services in France since 1994, however, may be linked to these policies (Pearson and Scarpetta 2000, p. 13). *Ex ante* evaluations of generalized reductions for low wage-earners in France estimated that they would lead to the creation of 350,000 additional jobs (Fitoussi, 2000).

Whether reduced contribution rates will lead to the creation of lasting jobs and re-entry into the labour market remains to be seen, as such schemes seem predominantly to favour *insiders* who already have jobs. Moreover, there is no evidence that the companies which benefit from these subsidies would not have recruited anyway, nor, for time-limited subsidies, that they will keep people in the jobs once the subsidy comes to an end. Schemes of this type may also discourage the payment of wages above the threshold at which the tax wedge rises, thereby resulting in the depression of already low wage levels.

1.8 Reducing Social Exclusion by Developing Community and Other Services

Active measures to involve people who are not in the labour market or are difficult to place have been adopted by various countries. Such measures are part and parcel of anti-poverty programmes and can be instrumental in the provision of community, social, cultural and personal services that are in demand, but which are not provided due to budgetary constraints. They are an important source of job creation in local economies. They therefore deserve particular attention in view of the very broad and persistent disparities in employment and economic performance between regions in European Union countries and the growing demands of ageing and isolated households throughout OECD countries.

1.9 From Income Security to Employment Promotion

This brief review of key policy trends in OECD countries suggests that perhaps the biggest change in the labour market – social policy relationship between the three post-war decades of growth and today is a shift in the goals of government intervention from income security to employment promotion (Salais, Chapter Sixteen). Indeed, since the mid-1990s and early 2000s the main policy objective of intervention in the labour market – social policy relationship seems to be to facilitate and encourage labour market entry and retention. The population targeted by these policy measures consists mainly of able-bodied individuals of working age. However, increasingly, they are being expanded to encompass social groups for whom in the past it was more acceptable not to work, such as mothers, older people, single mothers and persons with disabilities (Millar, Chapter Ten; Doeringer et al., Chapter Fourteen). This reflects a view that seems to be gaining ground rapidly on both sides of the Atlantic, as expressed by Tony Blair, that 'the best form of welfare is work'.

This shift can be explained in various ways and has serious implications for individual welfare. These trends probably reflect changing societal values, particularly insofar as the labour market role of women is concerned. Over the past two decades, the presence of women in the labour market has been acknowledged increasingly widely in public discourse and policy, although policy is probably lagging behind discourse in this area. The shift, however, has also been made possible by structural changes in the economy and the age structure of the population, which are resulting in more employment becoming available than was the case in the 1970s and 1980s.

This trend is arguably general across OECD countries, and possibly beyond, as testified by a recent World Bank report on social protection (World Bank, 2001). There are, however, national variations in the extent to which a shift is occurring from economic security to employment promotion as a policy objective. Broadly speaking, it has gone furthest in English-speaking and Nordic countries. However, in this latter group of countries, the focus on activating the unemployed and on facilitating the access of women to employment is not new, as these policy trends have been present for a few decades. Progress in this direction is probably slowest in other Continental European countries, where a larger proportion of the unemployed are covered by social insurance. The benefits that they deliver tend to be considered as acquired rights and these systems are therefore more resistant to the shift in policy objectives towards employment promotion (Clasen, 2000). In addition, ideological resistance to schemes of the workfare type appears to be stronger in Continental Europe than in the English-speaking world.

2 New Policies, New Issues

The shift towards employment promotion as the principal objective of social protection systems can be seen as a response to the changing economic and demographic conditions that make such a shift both desirable and possible, as well as a possible change in societal values. However, this shift in policy orientation generates a new set of issues and problems, which have started emerging after the schemes have been in operation for a few years and which, in general terms, have not been adequately addressed. These issues raise economic and social questions, as well as more fundamental ethical questions, some of which are discussed below.

2.1 What Kind of Work?

The contrast between the United States and Continental Europe in terms of employment creation in the services sector is often interpreted as proof of the existence of a trade-off between the number of jobs that are created and their quality.[1] The inability of some of the larger European economies to match the creation of jobs in the services sector in the United States is often attributed to the higher degree of labour market regulation, lower wage dispersion and higher taxes on labour in Europe (see, for example, OECD, 1994; Esping-Andersen, 1999; Scharpf, 2000; for a critical review of this literature, see Andersen, Chapter Two). The implication of this view is that European policy-makers are facing a dilemma: in order to increase job creation, they need to deregulate their labour markets, which will result in the expansion of low quality low-paid jobs. Jobs of this type are widely regarded as socially unacceptable in many European countries, and are incompatible with public expectations in terms of social cohesion and perceptions of social justice, or in other terms, *social quality* (Beck et al., 1997).

It is evident that, as far as employment creation is concerned, other macroeconomic factors are also involved, such as stringent monetary or fiscal policy, which may play a more important role in labour market outcomes than the level of employment protection. For example, in Germany, the obsession with inflation led to the adoption of deflationary policies, which probably explains a large part of the high unemployment levels experienced, at least in the Western Länder. In contrast, job creation in the United States may have been a result of factors other than labour market flexibility, such as: macroeconomic policies under which interest rates were raised or lowered in support of exchange rate objectives (first for a low dollar, and then for a strong one); economic deregulation (of airlines, telecommunications, road transport and banking); very active and highly developed capital markets and venture capital; and fewer administrative burdens for enterprise creation and a well developed entrepreneurship culture. All of these provide a favourable environment for business creation and hence for employment generation. These factors were supplemented by the wealth creation effect of the equity held by consumers, which stimulated demand when the stock market became exuberant, encouraging a rise in consumption levels that has been twice as rapid as in Europe over the past decade; the rapid and early shift of the economy to the services sector, which is labour intensive; the massive investments in new information and communication technologies, which contributed to the strong increase in demand for highly-skilled jobs, enhancing productivity since the mid-1990s; and, not least, demographic factors, and particularly immigration, especially of skilled people, and the massive entry of women into the labour force, as result of which civil employment increased in the United States by more than 50 per cent, from 80 to 130 million, between 1970 and 1996, at a time when it almost stagnated in Europe (Sarfati, 1999, pp. 197–201). Differences in consumer preferences may also help to explain the different rates of job creation in services in Europe and the United States (see Ughetto, Feature No. 3).

The existence of multiple trade-offs in the field of job creation is widely accepted by political economists, and confirmed by sophisticated analyses. Iversen and Wren show that governments faced a *trilemma* in the early 1990s, namely of reconciling earnings equality, full employment and a balanced budget. Essentially, they argue, only two of these three goals could be attained in the economic context of the period. A government could decide to regulate the labour market in order to protect the incomes of low-skilled workers. As a result, it had to accept high unemployment (Germany), or expand public sector employment (Sweden), and hence generate budget deficits. Alternatively, it could decide to give priority to full employment and a balanced budget, but would be forced to accept high wage inequality (United States) (Iversen and Wren, 1998). In the late 1990s, during a period of expansion, the trilemma may have lost some of its force, with countries such as Sweden and Denmark managing to achieve budget surpluses. But outside Scandinavia, where high employment rates are achieved through a large public sector, the trade-off between jobs and equality appears to persist.[2] A similar conclusion is reached by Esping-Andersen, who uses the employment ratio as the dependent variable and finds that employment protection legislation is a more important obstacle to job creation than earnings equality (Esping-Andersen, 1999, pp. 132–4).

Analyses that use unemployment rates, rather than job creation, as the dependent variable, have generally concluded that neither wage inequality nor employment protection legislation have an impact on overall unemployment levels, but that employment protection does influence the composition of the unemployed population: the youth and low skill bias is stronger in countries where employment contracts are more protected (Esping-Andersen, 2000a).

Overall, the evidence for the impact of employment protection legislation and wage equality on job creation is mixed. However, for some specific groups of the population, there is strong evidence of a trade-off between the quality and the number of the jobs available. These groups essentially consist of persons who, in the past few decades, have either not been employed or who have been marginalized from the labour market because of structural economic changes, and particularly women and young unemployed people (Esping-Andersen, 1999 and 2000). This view is also accepted by the OECD, according to which:

> Employment Protection Legislation (EPL) strictness has little or no effect on overall unemployment. [... although it] may affect the demographic composition of unemployment, with lower unemployment for prime-age men being offset by higher unemployment for other groups, particularly younger workers (OECD, 1999, p. 88).

The groups whose access to the labour market is most impaired by the existence of employment protection legislation are also precisely those who are supposed to be helped into jobs by the new social protection systems. In this respect, policy-makers, especially in Europe, face a dilemma between the quality and quantity of the jobs that their political choices may generate. If labour markets are deregulated, jobs may be created, but the quality of these jobs, and the quality of the life of the workers who accept them, may be lower than the level that is commonly regarded as being socially acceptable.

Some countries, and particularly the United Kingdom and the United States, have chosen what might be termed an *ex-post compensatory strategy* to this dilemma. It is an approach which accepts high wage inequality and job precariousness, but tries to redress some of the worst consequences by intervening downstream with instruments to improve the living standards of those who take up these jobs, such as tax credits. As noted above, this strategy has generally been positively evaluated insofar as its impact on the living standards of the working poor is concerned. However, it creates new problems in relation to the administration of the measures adopted and the exclusion of the non-workers.

Alternatively, governments can opt for selective re-regulation, based on the assumption that not all forms of regulation are harmful to employment creation. Reviewing evidence from a large comparative study on the impact of deregulation on unemployment, Esping-Andersen and Regini argue that while '... there are some regulatory practices that do seem to systematically bias the chances of being unemployed towards youth, women, or low skill workers, ... there are other regulatory practices that apparently have little bearing in this bias' (Esping-Andersen and Regini, 2000, p. 3). Deakin and Wilkinson go even further and argue that intelligent forms of labour market regulation are not only beneficial in terms of the quality of employment, but that they can also be conducive to more efficient labour markets. Their reading of the persistence of long-term unemployment and social exclusion in the United Kingdom, despite 15 years of labour market deregulation, is that deregulation alone is not a sufficient condition for an efficiently functioning labour market (Deakin and Wilkinson, 2000).

In this respect, carefully chosen interventions in the labour market can dramatically improve the situation of the most disadvantaged workers, without impairing too greatly the ability of the economy to create the kind of jobs that are suitable for such workers. For instance, minimum wages, if set at economically acceptable levels, can protect the incomes of the most vulnerable workers, without necessarily pricing them out of the labour market (Gregg, 2000). Even a low minimum wage can have a positive impact for some disadvantaged workers, as shown by the experience in the United Kingdom. As a result of the introduction of a minimum wage of £3.60 an hour in 1999, over two million workers benefited from wage increases of up to 40 per cent (Rhodes 2000, p.60; Millar, Chapter Ten).

Somewhat ironically, labour market re-regulation appears to be a strategy adopted by countries, such as New Zealand and the United Kingdom, which in the 1980s were at the forefront of deregulating labour markets. The government in the United Kingdom, in addition to a national minimum wage, has taken steps to implement European Union labour legislation in relation to working time and works councils. In New Zealand, the legislation adopted in 1991 that strictly limited the ability of trade unions to collectively negotiate wage settlements was reversed in October 2000 (Harbridge and Walsh, Chapter Seven; De

Bruin, Feature No. 4). In the same way, the extension of social protection rights for atypical workers can significantly improve their employment conditions, without impairing job creation. In the Netherlands, following the dramatic increase in the employment rate as a result of the expansion of part-time work,[3] a key issue is now to include part-time workers in good quality social protection arrangements, such as occupational pensions (van Oorschot and Boos, 1999).

These experiences suggest that there are limits to the extent to which the deregulation of rigid labour markets has a positive effect on overall welfare in terms of delivering a decent standard of living for everyone. Belorgey makes this point very strongly. Employment regulation has a crucial role to play in his vision of a new model of the effective integration of labour markets and social protection systems. Such regulation should discourage the use of precarious forms of work, such as fixed-term contracts, which have expanded significantly in France over the past few years. On the other hand, social protection should be re-oriented to take into account the needs of the large and growing number of workers who do not correspond to the traditional full-time permanent model of employment (Belorgey, Chapter Twelve).

More generally, it can be argued that some form of labour market regulation that goes beyond basic aspects, such as health and safety, is needed to safeguard welfare standards. Overall, the case studies in this volume suggest that there are alternatives to the trade-off between equality and jobs, based on carefully balanced policy mixes of flexibility, regulation and *ex-post* intervention, a concept that is captured well by the term *flexicurity* (Madsen, Chapter Nine; Keller and Seifert, 2000; Visser and Hemerijck, 1997). In the same way, Andersen suggests that while deregulation may be conducive to more job creation in some specific sectors of the services economy, this is by no means the only route to employment expansion, as shown by the experience of small European countries in the 1990s (Andersen, Chapter Two).

2.2 The Shifting Line between Employment and Non-employment

During the post-war period, the model of the male breadwinner and the ternary division of the life cycle between education, employment and retirement, underpinned a very clear division in society between those who were expected to work and those who were not. Essentially, participation in the labour market was expected of able-bodied men of working age. While women sometimes engaged in paid work, this was generally only out of economic necessity (Lewis, 1995). Over the past few decades, the dividing line between employment and *legitimate* non-employment, as defined by policies respecting the provision of income substitution benefits, has shifted in various directions. First, with the expansion of early retirement programmes as a strategy to cope with mass unemployment, it came to encompass older workers. More recently, however, this line has been moved in back again with a view to expanding the size of the potential workforce.

Women have been one of the main sources of the expansion of the workforce over the past two decades in most OECD countries. This development has generally not been the result of deliberate policies, which have tended to follow rather than precede social change. However, throughout OECD countries, tax systems have been adapted to remove the bias in favour of one-earner families, which constituted an important *de facto* obstacle to women's entry into the labour market (Sainsbury, 1999).[4] Policies that help women reconcile employment and family life are also expanding rapidly in most European Union countries (Lemière and Silvera, 1999).

Improved access to employment is a prerequisite for women's economic independence, and in this respect constitutes an instance of social progress. However, as noted by Millar, the strong emphasis in current policy on employment for all may increase the pressure on women who are expected to participate in the labour market, while at the same time continuing to fulfil caring responsibilities. This is a particularly important issue for single parents, most of whom are women and who, if forced to take up work, may not have the opportunity to care for their children and dependent relatives (Millar, Chapter Ten). This is the case in the United States, where single parents in schemes of the workfare type are allowed increasingly short periods outside the labour market when they have a child. In such cases, they may be denied the *right to care* (Knijn and Kremer, 1997).

If current trends continue, the dividing line between employment and *legitimate* non-employment may start to encompass other social groups which have not traditionally been expected to participate in the labour market. In the United Kingdom, for instance, persons with disabilities are being invited to an interview where their job prospects are evaluated. This may be the prelude to a more decisive policy in relation to this group of benefit recipients. In the United States, in view of current and expected labour shortages, attention is turning increasingly towards older people (Doeringer et al., Chapter Fourteen). This employment-centred approach to social protection appears to have fallen on the most fertile ground in the English-speaking world. In contrast, in Continental Europe, the prevailing social norms and welfare institutions are less conducive to an *employment-at-all-costs* approach.

These developments raise a number of fundamental issues which have not hitherto been properly addressed in policy debates. Perhaps the most crucial of these is where to draw the line between employment and *legitimate* non-employment. Decisions in this respect will be made by governments and legislatures and will probably reflect dominant national perceptions of what is most appropriate, as well as the national institutional context. The risk is that marginal groups will be forced against their will into low quality employment in order to comply with the values of an anti-welfarist and employment-oriented majority.

2.3 What Coverage for those who Cannot Work?

In the view of the Labour government in the United Kingdom, employment is the best form of welfare, but those who cannot participate in the labour market should be guaranteed access to a decent income. This apparently sensible statement hides some crucial problems, mostly related to the trade-off between work incentives and the prevention of poverty. In order to provide economic security to the *legitimate* non-employed, they must be provided with benefits of a decent level. In the context of a deregulated labour market, where low-skilled workers can only command low wages, this may generate a serious work incentive deficit. If benefits are generous and wages low, the incentives available to those with low skills may not encourage them to take up employment. Once again, policy-makers face a dilemma: either they offer decent benefits and accept that some potential workers will decide not to take up a job or, alternatively, they reduce benefit levels to lower than the minimum wage, thereby keeping work incentives intact. As seen above, this strategy has been followed over the past two decades in the United Kingdom, with the result that there is a higher incidence of poverty among the unemployed in that country than in any other European country.

Developing the appropriate level of coverage for the non-employed also gives rise to problems in relation to the shifting nature of the dividing line between employment and what is regarded as legitimate non-employment. Doeringer et al. show that previous pension policy is a key obstacle to increasing the activity rate of older workers. The availability of adequate pensions before the age of 65 constitutes a powerful disincentive to older people remaining in the labour market (Doeringer et al., Chapter Fourteen). However, while other commentators also recognize the influence that financial incentives may have on the decision to retire, they consider that this outcome is not unexpected, since the incentives in question were originally designed precisely to encourage older workers to leave the labour market. In a different environment, they maintain that a reversal of the trend towards early retirement is possible, even if the level of retirement income is not reduced. Indeed, they note that the participation rates of older workers have increased over the past few years in the United States and that this has not only been due to the strong economy but, more importantly, to the emergence of new attitudes towards working late in life (Quinn, 1999; Quinn and Quadrano, 1997). This expansion in the employment rates of older workers has not, however, been equally strong across social groups, since the most disadvantaged have found fewer opportunities to increase their participation in the labour market. In addition, the expansion has taken place through a rise in flexible forms of employment, which are often part-time and of low quality. The fine-tuning of benefit levels for non-workers is a difficult but crucial exercise. What is at stake is the quality of life of individuals who are regarded by society as legitimate non-workers. Once again, the solution probably lies in carefully balanced policy mixes. A combination of minimum wages, tax credits and workfare can ensure that work pays in most cases, and that work incentives therefore remain intact, even if non-work is compensated with decent benefits. This policy option, however, is only available in countries where political institutions concentrate power in the central government, such as the United Kingdom. In a country like Germany, this sort of policy would require a very problematic coordination exercise between the federal government, the social partners (who are responsible for setting wage levels) and the governments of the *Länder*, which have responsibility for social assistance (Bonoli, 2001).

The strategy that Nordic countries have adopted to deal with the trade-off between benefit levels and work incentives is also interesting. Benefit levels have been maintained at a high level, but are accompanied by a series of work-oriented measures, such as rehabilitation, medical examinations, therapeutic interventions and individual work plans. The objective of this policy mix is to make sure that benefit recipients, wherever possible, are put back on an employment path. In this case, the potential negative incentive of generous benefits is counteracted by a set of accompanying measures, with the overall result that any significant disincentive effect is virtually eliminated, as testified by the high employment rates in these countries. The absence of benefit-induced negative work incentives in the Nordic countries is also helped by the comprehensive system of wage regulation, which ensures that minimum wage levels are among the highest in the OECD countries.

2.4 What Social Protection for New Workers?

The broadening of the categories of people who are expected to work has introduced into the labour market a whole new range of life-cycle profiles, which are not generally well covered by current social protection arrangements. This is particularly the case for women, whose careers are often interrupted by several years of non-employment due to motherhood and caring. In most social security systems, such profiles result in lower social protection rights, especially in relation to pensions. The existence of derived rights is of little comfort to those who divorce (even though, increasingly, pension rights are split in the event of divorce), and does not reflect the current reality of gender roles (Jepsen and Meulders, Chapter Three).

In the case of public pay-as-you-go pension schemes, most European countries have introduced contribution credits that protect pension entitlement during years spent performing caring tasks. But these are generally limited in time, and may not always compensate for the loss of entitlements due to career interruptions. This is obviously a more serious problem in those countries, mainly in Continental Europe, where the pension systems are based on the contributory social insurance model. Improvements could, however, still be made. Switzerland, for instance, has introduced a contribution-sharing system between spouses. Contributions paid by the members of a couple are added together, then divided by two and counted separately and individually for each of the two spouses (Bonoli, 2000, pp. 112–13). More generally, keeping paid employment as the only basis for social protection entitlements is becoming anachronistic. Other activities, including caring, participation in education and training and the performance of benevolent activities for the community, should all generate social protection rights (Freyssinet, Chapter Four; Boissonnat, 1995; Supiot, 1999).

The problem seems more intractable insofar as private pension schemes are concerned, since the scope for redistributive solutions is considerably more limited (Ginn, Feature No. 2). Women are less likely to be covered by a private (individual or occupational) pension arrangement than men. Some countries, such as Switzerland and Australia (Harbridge and Bagley, Chapter Six), have made coverage by occupational pension schemes compulsory. However, because the requirement to be affiliated to a pension fund generally only starts above a certain earnings threshold, the coverage rates of women are still significantly lower than those of men. The trend towards defined-contribution pension schemes, which is very strong in the United States, as well as in some European countries such as Switzerland, will give rise to additional disadvantages for workers whose careers are interrupted by spells of non-employment, who are mostly women.

There is the possibility that women's employment patterns may change over the next few years towards a stronger reliance on full-time uninterrupted employment, which would reduce the need to adapt social protection systems to the current career patterns of women. However, as noted above, a shift towards more full-time employment among women is currently only found in the Nordic countries, where support for working mothers is particularly strong. In other countries, women's employment continues to be characterized by a higher incidence of part-time contracts.

The increased participation of women in the labour market also generates new needs and expectations that can be grouped under the heading of *reconciling work and family life*. Generally, the social protection systems inherited from the post-war period are not particularly well developed in this area, as their main objective has traditionally been to protect the income of the male breadwinner. Today, however, with both parents increasingly being expected to perform caring tasks and participate in the labour market, policies to help them combine these two activities are of particular importance. This is all the more urgent for single-parent households, whose numbers have increased significantly over the past two decades (Sarfati, Chapter One). These elements are steadily being developed and included in the standard policy repertoires of OECD countries. Examples include the provision of child care facilities at an affordable price, parental leave schemes and the right to return to the same job on a part-time basis following childbirth (Hantrais and Letablier, 1996).

Reconciling work and family life will require adaptation in the welfare state, as well as in the realm of work. Standardized working time arrangements, which have been predominant during much of the post-war period, are evidently not well-suited to workers who perform caring tasks, who need flexible arrangements. In this respect, many employers are experimenting with new forms of flexibility in working time, which are explicitly designed to facilitate the combination of work and caring. These include measures such as annualized working time, or even more creative proposals, including the calculation of working time over the whole working life, with *drawing rights* for early retirement (Boulin and Hoffmann, 1999). Greater flexibility in working time does not necessarily constitute an additional cost for employers if it can be adapted to fluctuations in labour demand within the company. For once, rather than a trade-off, there is the possibility of a win-win situation, in which the needs of both employees and employers for flexibility in working time can be addressed through the same arrangements (Cressey, Chapter Thirteen).

3 The Winding Road to Adaptation

The studies collected in this volume show the persistence of national and regional diversity in the approaches adopted to the adjustment of social protection and labour market systems to a changing socioeconomic context. Although it is true that the stronger emphasis on employment promotion and the assignment of a secondary role to income maintenance are common trends, closer analysis shows that there are substantial differences in the extent to which employment promotion has replaced income maintenance as the key objective of social protection systems, and in the instruments used to achieve this new objective.

As noted above, emphasis on the requirement to work is considerably stronger in English-speaking countries, where workfare schemes can actually force benefit recipients into employment. It is weakest in some continental European countries, perhaps most notably in Germany, where the contributory social insurance system tends to limit the capacity of the government to impose conditions (other than the payment of contributions) on the provision of unemployment benefits. In the Nordic countries, social protection for the working age population remains strongly work-oriented, although this is not a new feature in the region. In addition, the Nordic approach to increasing employment rates is not simply based on reinforcing work incentives, but entails a proactive effort to facilitate the labour market entry of specific groups, such as mothers, single mothers and recipients of disability and sickness benefit.

In Central and Eastern Europe, after the collapse of the communist regimes, new social protection systems are being developed. The overall orientation of these systems is partly influenced by the mostly Bismarckian tradition which was interrupted after 1945, and partly by the recommendations of international agencies, such as the World Bank. The latter has been very influential in establishing *multi-pillar* pension systems, which include a sizeable private component. Policies for the unemployed have included a combination of benefit targeting and activation, based on the strengthening of employment incentives. These countries are still going through a transition phase and it is not yet clear precisely what forms will be taken by the emerging welfare arrangements. What is at stake is their capacity to develop welfare states that are capable of providing the levels of economic and social security that are common in Western Europe (Lourdelle, Chapter Eight).

There is also considerable variation in the policy instruments used. In the English-speaking countries, social protection for the working age population consists basically of developing a set of financial incentives that push individuals into employment in a largely unregulated labour market. This system is principally based on meagre unemployment benefits, work requirements for benefit recipients and, on the positive side, tax credits for the working poor. In contrast, in Continental Europe and the Nordic countries, labour market measures play a much more important role in maintaining acceptable living standards, especially for low-skilled workers. The high coverage rates of collectively negotiated wage agreements guarantee relatively high minimum wages for the vast majority of the working population. At the same time, this coordination capacity has been used successfully to further job creation, on the one hand through wage restraint, for example in the Netherlands, Italy and the Nordic countries, and on the other hand, through the expansion of part-time employment (particularly in the Netherlands). In the Nordic countries, in addition to a regulated labour market that prevents the emergence of problems such as the working poor, policy has been geared towards improving the labour market opportunities of women, resulting in some of the highest employment rates among OECD countries.

These findings suggest that, in contrast with the views that were widely held at the beginning of the 1990s, there is probably more than one route to successful labour market and social protection adjustment (Andersen, Chapter Two). What is interesting in this respect is that the new strategies seem to lead to high employment rates and low unemployment, without the unequal distribution that has characterized experiences in the United States and the United Kingdom. The *deregulation plus ex post compensation strategy* chosen by the United States and the United Kingdom, although successful in terms of net job creation, has been accompanied by growing inequalities in wages and lifetime opportunities. In contrast, the expansion in employment in several small European countries has occurred in the context of broadly stable and small wage differentials (OECD, 1996, pp. 61–2).

In this respect, the analyses presented in this volume share a seemingly optimistic view of the capacity of social protection and labour market systems to adapt to changing social and economic contexts. The descriptions of some *success stories*, such as Denmark and the Netherlands, show that there are effective ways of approaching the many trade-offs identified in the literature and discussed above. Generally, these solutions entail carefully balanced policy mixes and coordination between policy domains, two objectives that are notoriously hard to achieve in democratic systems.

What would appear to be essential in this respect is the capacity of governments to involve the other relevant actors, and particularly the social partners, in the policy-making process. As already seen in the field of pension reform, the involvement of the social partners in the formulation and acceptance of the objectives of reform measures would appear to be a prerequisite for successful policy-making (Baccaro, Feature No. 8; Lourdelle, Chapter Fifteen). Governments which endeavoured to reform pension systems without sufficient consultation during the 1990s have faced huge political problems. In the view of many commentators, the electoral losses of centre-right coalitions in Austria, France, Germany and Italy were more or less directly related to attempts to impose pension reforms. The involvement of the social partners in welfare reforms is also a safeguard against over-reaction. Countries such as the United Kingdom and New Zealand reformed their welfare states despite resistance from the trade unions in the 1980s and 1990s, yet New Zealand is now reverting to more traditional policies. Moreover, in the United Kingdom a whole range of measures have been taken since 1997 to provide incentives to make work pay, to help low wage earners return and remain at work and to help workers reconcile work with family responsibilities, including initiatives shared by business, trade unions and local authorities (Millar, Chapter Ten; Cressey, Chapter Thirteen).

Cooperation in policy-making can be expected to become even more important in the years to come. Most of the problems and challenges discussed in this chapter span traditional divisions between such areas as social protection and fiscal and labour market policies. Coherent responses in these different fields would seem to be an essential prerequisite for successful adaptation. In general, the success stories of the 1990s, in such cases as Austria, Denmark, Ireland, Netherlands, Norway and Sweden, are in countries which have developed complex policy responses to socioeconomic challenges, involving the active participation of governments, trade unions and employers. Difficult reforms in the fields of employment, training and social protection have also been made possible through social dialogue in Italy, Spain and Portugal (Sarfati, 1999).

The adaptation of social protection and labour market systems to the emerging socioeconomic context, which is characterized by increased competition in a rapidly globalizing economy, the ageing of the population and a greater range of individual choices of lifestyle, is arguably one of the key challenges that policy-makers will have to face over the next few decades. An efficiently functioning labour market, with high participation rates and easier two-way mobility between activity and inactivity, as well as between part-time and full-time work, may be even more important than the age structure of the population in guaranteeing the long-term sustainability of today's welfare states (Sigg, Feature No. 7; European Commission, 2000).

Notes

1 Not all the jobs in services created in the United States are at the bottom end of the earnings distribution. In fact, probably as many highly-paid as low-paid jobs were generated by the employment boom in the past decade

in the United States. But when it comes to the reintegration of persons who are not in work, the sort of jobs that are relevant are generally those which require low skills, and are therefore low-paid.

2 Bonoli and Mach have shown that, while it is true that the correlation between earnings inequality and employment ratios for 11 OECD countries is very weak, if Denmark, Sweden and Switzerland are excluded from the analysis, the correlation is considerably stronger. If the analysis focuses only on English-speaking countries and the main continental European countries, or in other words, if the *size of public sector employment* variable is controlled, then the negative correlation between employment ratios and wage equality is clearer (Bonoli and Mach, 2001).

3 Between 1985 and 1998, the Dutch employment/population ratio increased by 11 per cent to 62 per cent (for the population aged 15–65). Over the same period, part-time employment doubled, accounting for 22 per cent of the population of working age (OECD, 1999a).

4 In this respect, there are important differences between OECD countries. In general, the Nordic and English-speaking countries have moved towards individual taxation, whereas Continental European countries tend to tax dual-earner couples jointly.

References

Atkinson, A.B. (1998), 'Social Exclusion, Poverty and Unemployment', in Atkinson A.B. and Hills, J. (eds), *Exclusion, Employment and Opportunity*, CASE Paper No. 4, Centre for Analysis of Social Exclusion, London School of Economics.

Atkinson, A.B. and Micklewright, J. (1989), 'Turning the Screw: Benefits for the unemployed 1979–1988', in Dilnot, A. and Walker, I. (eds), *The Economics of Social Security*, Oxford University Press.

Beck, W., van der Maesen, L., Tomèse, F. and Walker, A. (eds) (1997), *The Social Quality of Europe*, Kluwer Law International, The Hague.

Boissonnat, J. (1995), *Le Travail dans Vingt Ans*, Odile Jacob, Paris.

Bonoli, G. (2000), *The Politics of Pension Reform: Institutions and policy change in Western Europe*, Cambridge University Press.

Bonoli, G. (2001), 'Political Institutions, Veto Points and the Process of Welfare State Adaptation', in Pierson, P. (ed.), *The New Politics of the Welfare State*, Oxford University Press.

Bonoli, G. and Mach, A. (2001), 'The New Swiss Employment Puzzle: Research note', *Swiss Political Science Review*, forthcoming.

Bonoli, G. and Palier, B. (2000), 'How do Welfare States Change?', in Leibfried, S. (ed.), *Welfare State Futures*, Cambridge University Press.

Boulin, J.-Y. and Hoffmann R. (eds) (1999), *New Paths in Working Time Policy*, European Trade Union Institute, Brussels.

Clasen, J. (2000), 'Motives, Means and Opportunities: Reforming unemployment compensation in the 1990s', *West European Politics*, 23 (2), pp. 89–112.

Daly, M. (2000), 'A Fine Balance: Women's labour market participation in international comparison', in Scharpf, F.W. and Schmidt, V.A. (eds), *Welfare and Work in the Open Economy: Volume II: Diverse responses to common challenges*, Oxford University Press.

Deakin, S. and Wilkinson, F. (2000), *Capabilities, Spontaneous Order and Social Rights*, paper presented at the 12th Annual Meeting on Socio-Economics (7–10 July 2000), London School of Economics.

Doogan, K. (2001), 'Insecurity and Long-term Employment', *Work, Employment and Society*, Vol. 15, No. 3, pp. 1–23.

Ebbinghaus, B. (2000), 'Any Way out of Exit from Work? Reversing the Entrenched Pathways of Early Retirement', in Scharpf, F.W. and Schmidt, V.A. (eds), *Welfare and Work in the Open Economy: Volume II: Diverse responses to common challenges*, Oxford University Press.

Erskine, A. (1997), 'The Withering of Social Insurance in Britain', in J. Clasen (ed.), *Social Insurance in Europe*, Policy Press, Bristol.

Esping-Andersen, G. (1999), *The Social Foundations of Post-industrial Economies*, Oxford University Press.

Esping-Andersen, G. (2000a), 'Who is Harmed by Labour Market Regulation? Quantitative Evidence', in Esping-Andersen, G. and Regini, M. (eds), *Why Deregulate Labour Markets?*, Oxford University Press.

Esping-Andersen, G. (2000b), 'Regulation and Context: Reconsidering the correlates of unemployment', in Esping-Andersen, G. and Regini, M. (eds), *Why Deregulate Labour Markets?*, Oxford University Press.

Esping-Andersen, G. and Regini, M. (2000), 'Introduction', in Esping-Andersen, G. and Regini, M. (eds), *Why Deregulate Labour Markets?*, Oxford University Press.

European Commission (1998), *Social Protection in Europe, 1997*, Luxembourg.

European Commission (2000), *Employment in Europe 1999*, Luxembourg.

Evans, M. (1996), *Giving Credit where it's Due? The Success of Family Credit Reassessed*, WSP 121, London School of Economics/STICERD Welfare State Programme, London.

Fitoussi, J.-P. (2000), 'Payroll Tax Reductions for the Low Paid', *OECD Economic Studies No. 31*, 2000/II, pp. 115–32.

Greenstein, R. and Shapiro, I. (1998), *New Research Findings on the Effects of the Earned Income Tax Credit*, Center on Budget and Policy Priorities, 11 March, Washington, DC.

Gregg, P. (2000), 'The Use of Wage Floors as Policy Tools', *OECD Economic Studies No. 31*, 2000/II, pp. 133–46.

Hakim, C. (2000), *Work-lifestyle Choices in the 21st Century: Preference theory*, Oxford University Press.

Hantrais, L. and Letablier M.-T. (1996), *Families and Family Policies in Europe*, Longman, London.

Hotz, J. and Scholz, J.K. (2000), 'Not Perfect, but still Pretty Good: The EITC and other policies to support the US low-wage labour market', *OECD Economic Studies No. 31*, 2000/I, pp. 25–42.

Iversen, T. , and Wren, A. (1998), 'Equality, Employment and Budgetary Restraint: The trilemma of the service economy', *World Politics*, 49 (July), pp. 507–46.

Join-Lambert, M.-T., Bolot-Gittler, A., Daniel, Ch., Lenoir, D. and Méda, D. (1997), *Politiques Sociales*, Dalloz, Paris.

Kalisch, D., Aman, T. and Buchele, L. (1998), *Social and Health Policies in OECD Countries: A survey of current programmes and recent developments*, Labour Market and Social Policy Occasional Paper No. 33, OECD, Paris.

Keller, B. and Seifert, H. (2000), 'Flexicurity: Das Konzept für mehr soziale Sicherheit flexibler Beschäftigung' ('Flexicurity: The concept for more social security in flexible employment models'), *WSI-Mitteilungen* (53), pp. 291–300.

Knijn, T. and Kremer, M. (1997), 'Gender and the Caring Dimension of Welfare States: Towards inclusive citizenship', *Social Politics. International Studies in Gender, State and Society*, 4 (3), pp. 328–61.

Lemière, S. and Silvera, R. (1999), 'Equal Opportunity Policies for Women and Men: A critical analysis of the 1998–1999 employment action plans', *TRANSFER: European Review of Labour and Research*, 4/99, pp. 502–21.

Levy, J. (2000), 'France: Directing adjustment?', in Scharpf, F.W. and Schmidt,V.A. (eds), *Welfare and Work in the Open Economy: Volume II: Diverse responses to common challenges*, Oxford University Press.

Lewis, J. (1995), 'Egalité, Différence et Rapports Sociaux des Sexes dans les Etats-Providence du XXème siècle', in Ephesia (ed.), *La Place des Femmes: Les enjeux de l'identité et de l'Égalité au regard des sciences sociales*, La Découverte, Paris.

Martin, J. (2000), 'What Works among Active Labour Market Policies: Evidence from OECD countries' experiences', *OECD Economic Studies No. 30*, 2000/I, pp. 79–114.

Myles, J. and Pierson, P. (1997), 'Freedman's Revenge: The reform of liberal welfare states in Canada and the United States', *Politics and Society*, 25, pp. 443–72.

OECD (1994), *The OECD Jobs Study: Evidence and explanations*, Paris.

OECD (1996), *Employment Outlook*, Paris.

OECD (1999a), *Statistical Compendium*, Paris.

OECD (1999b), *Employment Outlook*, Paris.

OECD (2000), *Labour Force Statistics*, Paris.

Oorschot, W. van, and Boos, C. (1999), 'Dutch Pension Policy and the Ageing of the Population', *European Journal of Social Security*, 1 (3), pp. 295–311.

Overbye, E. (1998), 'Policy Responses to Household Vulnerability: The Norwegian case in an international context', in Flora, P. , De Jong, P. , Le Grand, J. and Kim, J. (eds), *The State of Social Welfare 1997*, Ashgate, Aldershot, pp. 191–216.

Pearson, M. and Scarpetta, S. (2000), 'An Overview: What do we know about policies to make work pay?', *OECD Economic Studies No. 31*, 2000/II, pp. 11–24.

Quadrano, J. and Quinn, J.F. (1997), 'Does Social Security Discourage Work?', in Kingson, E. and Schultz, J. (eds.), *Social Security in the 21st Century*, Oxford University Press, New York.

Quinn, J.F. (1999), *Retirement Patterns and Bridge Jobs in the 1990s*, Employment Benefit Research Institute, Issue Brief No. 206, Washington, DC (February).

Rein, M. and Friedman, B.L. (1998), 'Employment and Retirement: Conflicting aims within the welfare society', in Flora, P. , De Jong, P. , Le Grand, J. and Kim, J. (eds), *The State of Social Welfare, 1997*, Ashgate, Aldershot, pp. 57–82.

Rhodes, M. (2000), 'Restructuring the British Welfare State: Between domestic constraints and global imperatives', in Scharpf, F.W. and Schmidt, V.A. (eds), *Welfare and Work in the Open Economy: Volume II: Diverse responses to common challenges*, Oxford University Press.

Sainsbury, D. (1999), 'Taxation, Family Responsibility and Employment', in Sainsbury, D. (ed.), *Gender and Welfare state Regimes*, Oxford University Press.

Sarfati, H. (1999), *Flexibilité et Création d'Emplois: Un défi pour le dialogue social en Europe*, L'Harmattan, Paris.

Scharpf, F.W. (2000), 'Economic Changes: Vulnerabilities and institutional capabilities', in Scharpf, F.W. and Schmidt, V.A. (eds), *Welfare and Work in the Open Economy: Volume I: From vulnerability to competitiveness in comparative perspective*, Oxford University Press.

Supiot, A. (ed.) (1999), *Au-delà de l'Emploi: Transformations du travail et devenir du droit du travail en Europe*, Flammarion, Paris.

Visser, J. and Hemerijck, A. (1997), *A Dutch Miracle? Job Growth, Welfare Reform and Corporatism in the Netherlands*, University of Amsterdam Press, Amsterdam.

World Bank (2001), *Social Protection Sector Strategy: From safety net to springboard*, Washington, DC.

Index